HEROIC MISADVENTURES

Australia: Four Decades - Full Circle 1970 - 2009

by

RON MANNERS

Mannwest Group Pty Ltd
Hayek House
25 Richardson Street
West Perth
Western Australia 6005
Australia
Telephone: +61 8 9322 6777
Facsimile: +61 8 9322 6788
Email: mannwest@mannkal.org
Web: www.mannwest.com
The website for this book is – **www.heroicmisadventures.com**
where additional appendix information is available.

National Library of Australia Cataloguing-in-Publication data
24722.49418 RF:1

Heroic Misadventures
Australia: Four Decades - Full Circle

Bibliography.
Includes Index.
ISBN 978-0-646-52212-8

1. Prospecting and mining. 2. Gold mines, nickel mines and mining - Western Australia - Kalgoorlie Region - History. 3. Personal narratives - Australian. 4. Kalgoorlie (W.A.) - History. Manners, Ron (Ronald B.). 5. Banking, investment, economic aspects - Australia. 6. Political parties.

Printed by: Quality Press –Western Australia

Dedication

The detours in this journey have often led to "portals of discovery".

This journey has been made worthwhile by a great collection of fellow travellers and I thank them for their patience, understanding and, most of all, their friendship This book is dedicated to each of them.

Many of these friends have become leaders in their fields and have managed to fully integrate their ethics throughout their business, personal and family lives.

I hope they don't mind me giving them a mention as I skip through so many *Heroic Misadventures*.

Transferring one's thoughts to paper
is like standing naked and alone.

Not a comfortable feeling
allowing others to enter your zone.

I've been asked to commit them to paper
including my failures and sins.

I'd rather they fill this slim volume
than top-up some local trash bins.

So here we go my friends and I
with prejudices cast aside.

Open up these private doors
Welcome—to you—come inside ...

Also from Ron Manners:

So I Headed West—W.G. Manners. Ballarat to Broken Hill, to Kanowna, to Kalgoorlie. "When miners were heroes" 1863–1924.

Kanowna's Barrowman—James Balzano. The early history of Kalgoorlie Goldrushes—(with George Compton).

Never A Dull Moment. Kalgoorlie's golden years through to the seventies, including life in the World War I trenches—(with Charles & Nancy Manners).

All available through:
www.mannwest.com

No pessimist ever discovered the secret of the stars or sailed an uncharted land, or opened a new doorway for the human spirit.

Helen Keller (1880–1968)

Success is the ability to go from one failure to another with no loss of enthusiasm.

Sir Winston Churchill (1874–1965)

Many of life's failures are people who did not realize how close they were to success when they gave up.

Thomas A. Edison (1847–1892)

Contents

Part 3 Cont'd...

Foreword

Entertaining all the way ....

In his book, economist William Easterly contrasts "planners" with "searchers." Each planner has Big Plans — a detailed blueprint for achieving in one fell swoop fundamental, large-scale, magnificent change through top-down direction. In contrast, each searcher wisely realizes that Big Plans are hopeless (and fraught with danger). A searcher might desire fundamental, large-scale change as sincerely as any planner does, but the searcher is practical; he judges courses of action not by how fine they sound to romantic ears but rather by their *practicability.*

Ron Manners is a searcher. He aims to achieve that which is within his reach.

Having been exposed to what he sees as the obvious benefits of individual liberty and personal responsibility, he is keen to share these ideas with others, on a non-intrusive basis. He has had some good economic teachers, some of the best, but he knows that no Grand Plan will overcome the present inertia so that he achieves his goal step by step, by talking to friends and acquaintances and writing lots of stuff that pops out all over the place.

Ron also possesses two other qualities of the searcher.

First, the searcher understands how to formulate achievable goals so that, once achieved, each one serves as a stepping stone toward the ultimate goal. We might call this "the searcher's vision". Anyone can easily envision his own version of the good society. But many people let their vision of the ultimate goal turn them into planners longing for a Powerful Authority to implement and enforce the vision.

Superimposed over these qualities, Ron has lived, and is still living, a remarkable life and to many of us who meet him at economic conferences around the world, this book will come as something of a surprise, but consistent with his application of principles, and equally important to all of the above, this book is entertaining all the way.

Donald J Boudreaux

Prof. of Economics at George Mason University in Fairfax, Virginia, USA

President of the Foundation for Economic Education (Inc.), 1997-2001

Author of *Globalization* (Greenwood Press, 2007)

The Cover Photo

Photo taken of the author by Gavin L. Bunning on July 11 2000 during a visit to Lake Eyre, inland South Australia.

Lake Eyre National Park covers an area of 8,430 square kilometres. It has filled, or had water in it, a number of times in the twentieth century, including 1956, 1971, 1974, 1976, 1989 and 1997. The most extensive flooding occurred in 1974 when the lake filled to capacity with up to 34 cubic kilometres of water.

The main river systems which feed Lake Eyre include the inland river systems of the Diamantina/Warburton, the Thomson/Barcoo and Cooper, the Georgina/Eyre Creek, the Peake, Neales, Macumba and Hamilton Rivers.

It is a remarkable river system that runs inland, rather than discharging to an ocean.

Widespread rains had fallen across the outback during February and April 2000. These rains brought about a prolific resurgence of activity and breeding of bird, animal, aquatic and plant life in the South Australian outback. These rains covered extensive areas of outback Australia and flooded a number of inland rivers. Lake Eyre had increased to approximately 75 per cent coverage at the time the photo was taken. Water from the Warburton River was still flowing into the lake.

For more information on Lake Eyre and its access from Australia's Outback Highway, click on the 11.2MB file at .....

http://www.mannkal.org/downloads/submissions/sub20000701.pdf

Acknowledgements

My wife, Jenny, has patiently lived with this manuscript and many drafts strewn around our home and welcomes its completion. Sincere thanks to Ross Louthean, Dr Chris Ulyatt and Nan "Nanushka" Witcomb for their editorial assistance, Ian Manners for his scanning expertise and to Reynolds Graphics for the cover design. My Personal Assistant, Judy Carroll, also deserves another gold medal for retaining her composure as we worked toward our self-imposed deadlines. Responsibility for the content remains with the author.

Introduction

This book, *Heroic Misadventures*, after a very brief step backwards in time, moves quickly into the era covering 1970 through to 2009, an era in which I am an enthusiastic participant.

I'm not sure if I took this journey or the journey took me. It's all about change and the response to change.

Life is all about choices and discovery, and discovery is often about making mistakes.

'Change is the essence of life. Be willing to surrender what you are for what you could become.' —Anon

Samuel Crothers put it well when he said:

> Try as hard as we may for perfection, the net result of our labours is an amazing variety of imperfectness. We are surprised at our own versatility in being able to fail in so many different ways.

On reflection, having a few failures under the belt is never terminal; it simply prepares us for subsequent successes.

Throughout this book, I mention from time to time what I should have learnt from each experience.

Sometimes I feel that I've attended so many of "life's lessons" that I wonder what significant future challenges I've now prepared myself for.

Feeling fortunate to have been a participant in the past 40 tumultuous years, I'm now optimistic about the future.

Meanwhile, please enjoy these *Heroic Misadventures*. This book is simply a collection of self contained adventures (sample them in whichever order you choose, some you will enjoy more than others, depending on your interests), as we skip through the changing attitudes, politics and culture of the past 40 years, with our eyes firmly fixed on the future.

Ron Manners
November 2009

Heroic Misadventures is the fourth book in this "series".

The first, *So I Headed West*[1] covered the Manners' 1853 transition from Scotland to the Eureka stockade, and then the Ballarat, Broken Hill, Kanowna and Kalgoorlie sequence which gave the book its title. It concluded with the death of my grandfather, W.G. Manners, in 1924.

The second book, *Kanowna's Barrowman—James Balzano*[2] brought to life the wheelbarrow travels of this old friend of my father, Chas Manners. My colleague George Compton and I felt that Balzano's original chronicles of the early Goldfields "diggings" were worth sharing with subsequent generations of Australians.

The third, *Never A Dull Moment*[3], combined my mother's "Life on the Leases" stories of outback hardships, and my father's meticulous diary of his World War I experiences in the trenches of the Western Front, with the book concluding with my own collection of word pictures, events and characters through to the late 1960s, just before the significant iron ore, nickel and alumina discoveries dramatically changed the dynamics, the people, the politics and our way of life in Western Australia.

ENDNOTES:

1. Book details on page 391
2. Book details on page 389
3. Book details on page 388

Australia: Four Decades – Full Circle

Travelling along with me on the journey outlined in this book, was this great country we call Australia.

As this book developed, it became clear to me that human action by Australians, in response to good and bad political policies, has created an interesting case study.

Australia entered the 1970s with a sense of adventure, fresh from a resource boom, nickel and iron ore, with a sense of exuberance. Our spirits were completely flattened in the 70s as we were firstly Whitlamized[(1)] and subsequently Fraserized,[(2)] so looking back on the 70s I regard it as a lost decade.[(3)]

Surprisingly we were rescued by the Hawke[(4)] / Keating[(4)] / Howard[(4)] eras when policies meticulously devised by a small and ignored group within the Fraser Government, called the 'Dries'[(5)] were picked up by the newly elected Hawke Government. We then saw a remarkable resurgence of the nation as a result of deregulatory reforms being enacted.

These gains are possibly being squandered as we reach the end of the first decade of Century 21. (This theme covered in later chapters.)

Australia may change, for better or for worse, from time to time, we understand this, but many Australians are now looking on with alarm as future generations are being plundered and burdened with debt.

The 'Dries' were inspired by a remarkable individual called C.R. "Bert" Kelly.[(6)]

Where is the modern day group of 'Dries' who are developing policies that may be found useful by future governments? Politicians will again grasp the concept that a productive population with incentives to produce, can really stimulate the economy in a far more sustainable fashion than loading more layers of debt and tax onto an increasingly cynical band of Australian voters and taxpayers.

Who can they look to for leadership?

ENDNOTES:

1. Gough Whitlam, Prime Minister, December 5, 1972–November 11, 1975.
2. Malcolm Fraser, Prime Minister, November 11, 1975–March 11, 1983.
3. The ASX All Ordinaries Index was 408 in June, 1970 and at 410, virtually the same, in 1979.
4. Bob Hawke, PM, March 11, 1983–December 20, 1991; Paul Keating, PM, December 20, 1991–March 11, 1996; John Howard, PM, March 11, 1996–December 3, 2007.
5. John Hyde's book 'Dry': In Defence of Economic Freedom http://www.mannkal.org/bookshop.php
6. Refer Bert Kelly, Appendix www.heroicmisadventures.com

The Author, 2004 - photo, courtesy of W.A. Business News, when they invited me to speak to an audience of 570 at Perth's Hyatt Regency on October 6, 2004. The following chapter is based on those comments.

The Adventure Begins

Although I have been chairman of several very public companies, my private corporate entitites—Mannwest Group and the Mannkal Economic Education Foundation — are very private, so talking about myself at any length is a little uncomfortable for me.

Any modest success that I've been fortunate to enjoy has come about through my contacts with a remarkable bunch of people who have travelled with me on so many journeys.

Even more important have been the ideas that have influenced me, and I hope I can illustrate how highly I value the input and support of those people and their ideas.

Let's start at the very beginning!

My first business venture was as a ten-year-old paper boy, selling the *Daily News*, after school each day.

Like so many Kalgoorlie kids, I was desperate to gain my financial independence and have a bit of fun too.

I shall offer only three memories of this career:

The first was, going home late one bleak winter's night, some little old lady, feeling sorry for me, invited me in and fed me.

She probably picked me as a homeless orphan. Easy to do, as nobody in Kalgoorlie had any money in those days and we all looked like orphans.

Unremarkable, but I can still remember having difficulty eating my second meal when I eventually got home.

The second, on another occasion, was when some guy approached me and asked me where the brothels were.

I had no idea of what a brothel was (remember I was only ten), so he started gesticulating with his hands and fingers, making like a puppet show.

“Oh”, I said, “you mean the ‘knockers’—first turn to your left and four blocks down, you can’t miss them.”

The third incident was when I was again approached by a seedy looking guy in front of the Mount Lyall Hotel.

He asked me if I would come down the back lane with him for a while.

“Well,” I said, “You’ll have to buy all my newspapers.” (I had a great armful of *Daily News*.)

To my surprise he said, “yes”. Then he gave me all this money and he took all my newspapers.

Well, I looked at him and he looked at me and that’s when I started running. (Down the back lane of course, because that was “the deal”.)

About one block later, I could still hear him huffing and puffing behind me, so I took a look over my shoulder and you know what? He still had all those newspapers in his arms so I knew that I would eventually out-run him!

I’ve often wondered what he ever did with all those newspapers.

My next venture was selling “crystal sets”.

For those of you who don’t know what a crystal set is, back in those (pre-transistor) days kids used to make a very rudimentary radio consisting of a germanium crystal with a fine steel wire, that we called a ‘cat’s whisker’, connected by copper wires to a variable condenser, which enabled you to tune into the various radio stations.

There was no battery in these things, but you could listen to the radio through a set of headphones.

They didn’t cost much to make but you could mount all the bits and pieces on a nice polished aluminium base and sell them for £5.

So without my parents’ knowledge, I stuck a sign up beside the front gate saying “chrystal sets for sale”. (Spelt C-H-R-Y-S-T-A-L.) Ten minutes later my first customer knocked on the door. A lady asked my mother if she could speak to the person selling crystal sets. I went to receive my first order and she said to me, “Young man, you don’t know how to spell crystal, that should be C-R-Y-S-T-A-L.”

I soon graduated to ‘one valve’ radio sets. These were complete with a battery and a small speaker. Again, that market didn’t take long to fill.

I had a go at playing the trumpet and used to practise vigorously.

One day, a guy knocked on the door with a £5 note in his hand. He explained that he was trying to sell his house next door and that if I promised not to play for a month, he'd give me the £5.

That was much better than making crystal sets!

Perhaps it was all this musical inspiration that led me, several years later, to bring to Kalgoorlie the City's very first juke box.

This great mechanical monster played 80 of those 45 rpm discs with the big hole in the centre. The Everly Brothers were at their peak in 1959, and the young teens only wanted to hear the Everly Brothers and, in particular, their song "All I Have to Do is Dream".

That's when I stumbled across what I can now identify as the Bill Gates Business Model.

I couldn't understand what was going on for a while because I was clearing more money out of that juke box than there were hours in the day to play that number of records.

Then it clicked. When you walk into the Peter Pan Milk Bar and put your shilling in to play that particular Everly Brothers' track, you go over and have yourself a drink in the corner, then somebody else comes along and sticks their shilling in (they might choose the same record as you). Then somebody else comes in .... Same again, and they go for the Everly Brothers again. Eventually, when the track comes up, everybody in the room is happy because they've had their shilling's worth. But irrespective of how many people have put their shilling in, it only plays once.

I call that the Bill Gates model because, when he sells software over the Internet, he starts with one in stock, sells a lot through the day and ends up with one in stock, after thousands of stock turns per day. It beats the hell out of the old conventional model where you only turn your stock over four or five times a year.

The Long Business Journey

Life's business journey is all about pointers and deciding on those you absorb for future use.

In this way my life has been delightfully messy because although I may not have always gone where I intended to go, I'm certainly ending up where I intended to be.

In telling this story it's important that I nominate the person who influenced me the most, so I'll tell you about a fellow called Leonard E. Read.

Then we can follow on with several incidents from some very unstructured business training, leading into the Australian Nickel boom of the late '60s and early '70s and how that changed so much, so quickly.

If this coverage is too brief to do full justice to these interesting years, there are more details in later chapters.

There, we deal with how things got really messy, and then how they are now getting back on track.

Take me to your leader

In my personal view, "leaders" are people who influence others to the point of making a change in their life or behaviour patterns.

It's a useful experiment, sorting through the people for inclusion in that category. There are literally hundreds of people from whom I have learnt something, but very few who have actually modified or shaped my behaviour or thinking.

So few in fact, that I could count them on my fingers. It goes beyond the natural influence of one's parents, to whom I'm eternally grateful, or one's environment or events.

Perhaps the one person who influenced me the most was Leonard E. Read.(1)

Through my involvement with Read, many years later, I became a representative for the Foundation for Economic Education in Australia which, in turn, led to the establishment of my own Mannkal Economic Education Foundation (www.mannkal.org).

One day, in 1982, Leonard "sprang it on me" to give a lunchtime talk to a group of his associates in New York, to explain how I first became involved with his Foundation in 1952.

To me it seemed simple enough, but they were fascinated to hear how a 16-year-old, working after school in his father's mining engineering supply business, used to open big pine cases of Timken roller-bearings that we imported from Canton, Ohio, USA.

The packing in the boxes included coloured comic-strips (our Australian comic-strips in the '50s were all black-and-white) together with

Leonard E. Read in his Foundation for Economic Education (FEE) office, explains some of the finer points of the free market to his Australian colleague, Ron Manners, New York, 1982.

A Publication of the Foundation for Economic Education

THE FREEMAN

Ideas On Liberty

Freedom's Magazine for Over 50 Years

- Borders and Liberty
- Herbert Spencer: Libertarian Prophet
- The Lasting Legacy of the Reagan Revolution

JULY/AUGUST 2004

FEE's monthly magazine 'The Freeman' has always had a wide circle of readers crumpled literature from the Foundation for Economic Education. Timken had been a supporter of the Foundation and I can still remember the circulation list affixed to the front of the papers bearing all their senior staff's initials and then directing its way down to the packing department.

This crumpled wisdom covered topics such as business ethics, the moral foundations for capitalism, the concepts of limited government and increased individual responsibility.

(As an aside I should say that I enjoyed the message so much that I used some of it several years later when I was the Editor of the Kalgoorlie School of Mines magazine, and did that bring the house down! Kalgoorlie was pretty much a union-based town in those days and wasn't quite ready for this kind of wisdom.)

But back to my teenage education: I felt this Foundation was on the right track, but I needed a little more information so that I could defend myself and these views. So I wrote to them explaining I was having a bit of trouble. They responded with helpful material and a regular copy of their monthly magazine *The Freeman*.

Several times over the following years I wrote material and submitted it for publication in their *Freeman* magazine.

They never published anything of mine, but one day I received a letter from their President, Leonard E. Read, explaining why.

He politely explained that I might have been a little too pushy and, in his own quiet words, "You only have a licence to change yourself, not others. All you can do is to bring an idea to the threshold of someone's consciousness, and then it is up to them to accept it or reject that idea after due consideration. If they then accept that idea, it will be with them for life".

On another occasion he explained, again in his own words:
"As one acquires an awareness of how little one knows, humility replaces arrogance; this tends to improve a person's nature and sense of humor."

Not earth-shattering stuff, but I got the message. I have never forgotten his quiet reasoning and it has certainly modified my own approach.

It has also helped my strike rate for having articles published all over the globe, even at Buckingham Palace.[2]

So what did Leonard do to make him a "leader" for me?

He simply took the time to write me a letter.

As it has been said, the great dividing line between success and failure can be expressed in five words: "I did not have time". But in Read's case he did take the time, and this is probably why I now reply to far more letters than I really need to.

Read's colleagues enjoyed my story of "opening up old boxes" and they were encouraged that their material, after doing the rounds of all the executives at that great manufacturing enterprise, then being reduced to "packing", could later be recycled on the other side of the world. It proved to them that their 'ideas had consequences'. More consequences for me I suspect, than for them.

In this investigation of what type of leaders I admire, high on the list are those who have managed to fully integrate their ethics throughout their business, personal and family lives.

Living by a double standard only brings people undone, as we have witnessed with the crop of failed politicians and businessmen of recent times.

Becoming an Electrical Engineer

I was actually keen to do geology at the Kalgoorlie School of Mines as my mother had studied geology there (I found out later that she was the school's first female geology student). Like most Kalgoorlie homes, ours was littered with rocks. People were always bringing in samples and explaining how they had discovered the next Golden Mile.

However, the Director of the School of Mines talked me out of geology because the view at that time was there was not much of a future for mining.

He was nearly correct for the next decade.

You need to realise that in the late '50s, in our part of the world, there was no iron-ore or nickel mining and gold mining was stuck with a government-fixed price of US$35 per ounce which was throttling the industry to death. So I became an electrical engineer.[4]

At least that was useful, as our family business, W.G. Manners & Co., was busy converting all the steam driven winders to electricity. Same headframe and mechanical drums, but replacing the steam components with electric, complete with some quite sophisticated (for the time), over-speed and over-wind protective controls.

By the time we converted all these, the mine operators started closing them down, one by one, and many were shipped off overseas, as Kalgoorlie was then suffering advanced "death-rattles".

That was about the time my father had a serious heart attack which put him out of action for many years.

Formal Business Training

The State Manager of Noyes Brothers-Crompton Parkinson (electrical engineers) was in Kalgoorlie on the day my father had this heart attack and, alongside Dad's hospital bed, Syd Webster said, "Charlie, you have no-one to run your business, your boy hasn't got a clue, so if you hire a professional manager, we will take Ron off your hands for a year and give him back to you with at least a fighting chance".

That was to prove an interesting year in Perth, Melbourne and Sydney. Their idea of formal business training was for me to do all the senior departmental heads' jobs while they took turns having holidays.

What a year! I became an instant expert on Industrial Lighting, Master-Key Systems, Commercial Cooking Equipment, electric motors, conrols and switchgear, non-ferrous metals and bulk material handling equipment. Looking back, now 50 years later, I feel that this was one of the luckiest breaks I ever had in my life, to have a whole year doing the jobs of all those Department Heads.

All was going smoothly until, one day, I was called into Mr Webster's office where he announced that he was sending me on a diplomatic mission for the company, and that it was important I present myself positively and overcome my natural tendency to be shy. So that I would look the part and not disgrace the firm, he insisted I take a trip into the city and "get a hat".

At age 18 I had never been a "hat person" but, feeling a great deal was expected of me, I made the purchase and received instructions from the "gentlemen's outfitters" on just how to wear a hat and when to take it off, and importantly the part it plays in making a statement that you are, in fact, on a very important mission[3].

With hat in hand I presented myself back at Mr Webster's office, where he briefed me on this new challenge.

He said that the firm had been fortunate in being appointed State Distributors for a new product made by Lee-Acme, and there was a great need for this item in every one of Perth's important buildings.

This was to bring me in contact with every big company in Perth's Central Business District. He explained that, in years to come, I would remember how I played a major part in solving their problems.

I could see he had a technical file which he was about to present to me. He certainly had a wonderful way of preparing my appetite for the challenge.

He then outlined the plan of attack. I was to go to the Head Office of each of the companies he had listed and ask to see the head girl.

For the first time I "smelt a rat".

"What is the product we are selling?" I asked.

He replied, "They are Lee-Acme Sanitary Incinerators". (Later I found out that in the "trade" they were given a far more colourful name, which in print must remain unmentioned).

Now, please bear in mind this was in the days before disposable plastic bags and that, without proper disposal facilities, ladies were prone to dispose of their unmentionables by flushing them down the toilet, which in turn created huge plumbing problems, huge plumbing bills and general pandemonium.

Well, on receiving this news, I just about shrank through the floor, but I did have the presence of mind to ask him, "Why the hat?".

He explained that if I got too embarrassed, I could just pull the hat down over my face.

Well, the best bit of advice I could give anyone who is shy, with a tendency to stutter and totally lacking in self-confidence, would be to get a job selling Lee-Acme Sanitary Incinerators.

I ended up in more ladies toilets in Perth than I care to remember.

I measured up for and supervised the installation of more of these units than the company ever thought possible.

There was a huge demand for them, and most of them managed to pay for themselves, through reduced plumbing costs, within the first week.[4]

I later learned that the firm had been sitting on this agency for three years and no-one would get involved with it. In that sense I was set up, albeit in a rather good-natured way.

Strangely enough, Syd Webster and I remained very good friends, and some 35 years later he again visited Kalgoorlie as a shareholder of a public mining company of which I was Chairman. So in a way he was still my employer. Again, another lasting friendship.

Booms & Busts

Now, let's cover the fifty years between my year of "formal business training" and today, with a series of word pictures.

- We skip through some dismal years of business survival in Western Australia from about 1960, including some monumental political bungling called the "credit squeeze"[5] that closed down thousands of Australian companies. That's when I started my hobby of collecting examples of "perverse consequences" or "how government always achieves the opposite of their stated intent".
- During these years, our family company survived and then responded enthusiastically to the new opportunities that flowed to the region when Western Mining Corporation's (WMC's) nickel discovery at Kambalda marked the end of what you could call "a long bleak drought".
- The nickel boom started slowly at first, but WMC were able to get the Kambalda mine operating from drilling to mining in nine months. More specifically, Sir Arvi Parbo[6] told me recently that the first drill hole was sunk on January 28, 1966 and about 19 months later they had the grand opening on September 15, 1967 when they had completed the milling concentrating facilities. Not only had they built the township by then, but they had already been producing nickel concentrates for three months.

This is a tribute not only to the company, but to the lack of beauracratic impediments at that time.

Today, with the acceptance of the bizarre notion that everyone else has more control over a mining property than the mining title owner, it could take up to five years to get the operation up and running, if it ever got up at all.

By 1969 the Nickel boom[7] was in full swing. The intense exploration around the Kalgoorlie region involved over 350 Australian and international companies.

There were more geologists in Kalgoorlie than in any other city in the world (strangely enough, the second highest concentration of geologists was in New York City).

Our own family company's staff increased from four to 48, and of course we moved into much larger, brand new premises—as everyone did—thinking that this "boom" would go on forever.

I was flying around the world, signing up new agencies for the latest and greatest mining equipment. We were sending mechanics to be trained in Sweden, etc—and that's about when everything stopped dead.

WMC had got up and running, mainly because they had moved quickly and, more importantly, because they raised the money through share issues.

Poseidon, the second-largest nickel mining company, failed mainly because although they got up and running, they did so on borrowed money.

Of the 350 companies that were actually seeking nickel around Kalgoorlie, quite a few actually found nickel, but how many actually made a profit from mining nickel?

Two! WMC and Metals Exploration.

Retrenchments were common-place around Kalgoorlie as companies departed almost on a weekly basis.

Our family company was over-staffed and was similarly affected. Eventually we moved out of our brand new building and then operated from our home for quite a few years—but we did survive through all this.

The Tax Man Cometh

During all this activity I was also an active prospector, and a problem emerged when many such *bona fide* prospectors[8] received income tax assessments that seemed like a bad dream.

The lovely lads at the tax department assessed me on some vendor shares in a company called Westralian Nickel, assessed at the price of $8.50 per share, which they were on June 30, the previous year. The only problem was I couldn't sell them as they were escrowed Vendor Shares (which I subsequently sold for 15 cents each).

A fat file of correspondence developed between me and the Tax Department. They were actually charging me 10 per cent interest on this fictitious "big number" which they debited against my account.

I busied myself by writing them poems and letters,(9) ridiculing their calculations.

All I got back was a letter saying they had decided to increase the interest rate from 10 per cent to 20 per cent.

Of course, I told them that this was irrelevant because 20 per cent of nothing is still zero.

But when you can't reason with people, it's best to just walk away. So that's what I did.

Our business was actually running well, with good people that I could communicate with from a distance, and our Esperance farm had good management.(10) So, for the next seven years or so, I was pretty much on the run, involved in a series of what I'd call Heroic Misadventures such as:

• *Looking for nickel in Indonesia.*

• *Running a hotel in Bali.*(11)

• *The South Pacific RockCruise*(12)—organizing a "Rock Cruise", a 1,600-berth ocean liner to tour the South Pacific with a bunch of Australian rock bands (Renée Geyer, Skyhooks, AC/DC, etc.). This venture may have succeeded had it not been for the combination of a Postal Union strike, an Airline Union strike and the NSW Coal Mining Union strike.

• *Working through the Chambers of Commerce.* Through this work, many of Western Australia's archaic and oppressive transport laws were repealed.(13)

• Joining a start-up group of 10 individuals to form *our own political party* in Australia. We may not have been politically successful, but we influenced a lot of important outcomes.(14)

• *A Merchant Banking Career.*(15) Working for a rapidly expanding merchant bank by the name of Nugan Hand. This was an exciting adventure. It was like a huge "laundry". Please understand that Australia was in such a political mess in the 1970s and Prime Minister Gough Whitlam's policies were driving businessmen out of Australia. It was common to see a sign on office walls saying:

"Will the last businessman leaving Australia, please turn off the lights."

As these business people were leaving, they needed to take some of their own money with them, so these draconian government policies gave birth to a flourishing "money laundering" business. This worked well for a time until the boss, Frank Nugan, was murdered on Australia Day in1980.[16]

Time to Come Home

Well, after a few years of this high adventure, it was time to come home. So, I wrote a polite letter to the Taxation Department explaining that their "big squeeze" had extracted no blood and suggested that if they tore up my tax file I would re-join the persecuted and oppressed band of Aussie taxpayers.

They quickly agreed, and I've been a very reluctant tax-slave ever since.

ODE (OWED?) TO THOSE LOVELY
FELLOWS OF THE TAX DEPARTMENT
Their little souls wish you to be unhappy.
It aggravates them to have you,
Vigorous, efficient and free!
They like to feel that fate,
Is disciplining you.
It gives their egos wings,
If yours are clipped.
You can ruin your life in an hour,
By listening to their puerile opinions.

Rehabilitating Ron

There were two reasons why I decided to rejoin conventional society. The first was my four children said that they were embarrassed at school when all the other children were able to answer the question of what their father did. (The Rotary Club allocated me the profession/classification of "wandering minstrel".)

The second was that there were signs of a stirring in the gold industry after so many years of paralysis, and I felt I should be part of this stirring.

Our family company had soldiered on bravely during all my "misadventures".

Since we had Volvo (trained in Sweden) mechanics for the big Kiruna underground diesel trucks, we were approached by Volvo Truck and Volvo Car to see if we would handle their products. So for seven years we were also Volvo distributors, until the Liberal State Government put us out of that business. Why? Because we wouldn't join the "protection racket" they were operating, called the Motor Vehicle Dealers Licensing Board.(17)

The Minister for so-called Consumer Protection, Ray O'Connor, took us to court for being the State's leading independent unlicensed car dealer.

We asked the well-known Labor lawyer, Julian Grill, to defend us, and he had me explain to the magistrate how proud I was of not requiring government protection against competition and how we were successful because of continuing support from our clients. The magistrate asked if there were any victims, i.e., disadvantaged clients.

When it was clear that the answer was 'no', he threw the case out.

Interestingly enough, a few years later, our persecutor and subsequent State Premier, Ray O'Connor, had a few problems of his own.

Having cleared the deck of this minor irritation, we expanded our family companies into the gold prospecting business. This led to a series of joint-ventures with major companies, where they earned interests in our mining properties by following up our first-pass prospecting work and continuing with exploration.

This also led to a series of public company board appointments for me.

WEEKEND NEWS, SATURDAY, JULY 26, 1980

I was bugged —car dealer

By Michael Parry

The Kalgoorlie Chamber of Commerce has called for an investigation into claims that Bureau of Consumer Affairs officers used a hidden tape recorder when questioning one of its members.

The matter also is to be raised in Parliament next week by the Labor MLA for Yilgarn-Dundas, Mr Julian Grill.

The Commissioner for Consumer Affairs, Mr N. R. Fletcher, said that if a tape had been used—and he stressed that he was not admitting that such a device had been used—then there was nothing illegal about that activity.

The alleged incident took place on June 24 in the offices of Kalgoorlie businessman Ron Manners, the chamber's immediate past president.

Mr Manners said he was being "interrogated" by two bureau officers over his unwillingness to fill in government forms.

Ron Manners

After 15 minutes of questioning, he heard a clicking noise come from the senior officer's inside coat pocket.

"I immediately called in a witness from an adjacent office and we stood over the officer while he sheepishly withdrew a mini tape recorder which he had concealed on his person," said Mr Manners.

The matter was reported to the Kalgoorlie Chamber of Commerce.

Chamber president Chris Fyson said his members believed the practice of government officers resorting to "this subterfuge" to obtain information had to be condemned.

"The practice is abhorrent to members of this chamber," he said.

"We feel it is a matter which does require more investigation."

Mr Fletcher was not willing to comment and referred me to the Minister for Consumer Affairs.

"We are partly an enforcement agency here and if you tried to get comment from the RTA or the police about their enforcement you would strike as much of a brick wall as you're striking with me now," Mr Fletcher said.

"I don't see why the hell I should disclose what methods we use to gain information which may lead to prosecutions.

"Why should I discuss these things? If they are illegal we will be pulled up on them."

Mr Fletcher made it clear, however, that he did not consider the use of tape recorders to be illegal.

"There's an act called the Listening Devices Act. You want to check that if you're unsure of the situation," he said.

The chairman of the NSW Privacy Committee, Mr Bill Orme—told of the incident by Mr Manners in a letter—said in a reply that in NSW only duly authorised police officers may use tape recorders.

"And while a tape recording could be taken in such an instance, substantially it would be an offence under the NSW Listening Devices Act to use it," Mr Orme said.

The Minister for Consumer Affairs, Mr O'Connor, said through his Press secretary: "In view of legal proceedings against Mr Manners, I make no comment other than to deny it."

Mr Manners admitted that he faced prosecution.

He said his offences were against an Act of Parliament and not against a person.

cribes himself as an independent car dealer said: "No one has been a victim of my actions. My argument is against licensing.

O'Connor goes on record

By Michael Parry

When is a tape recorder not a tape recorder?

When it is a "small dictating appliance," according to the Minister for Consumer Affairs, Mr O'Connor.

The minister, in his capacity as acting Premier and the man in charge of the Bureau of Consumer Affairs, was replying to complaints by a Kalgoorlie businessman, Ron Manners.

Mr Manners wrote to the government alleging that a hidden tape recorder was used by one of two bureau officers who questioned him in his office on June 24.

Mr Manners, an independent car dealer who is the subject of legal action instituted by the Bureau, wrote to the Premier asking whether the use of tape recorders was government practice.

Mr O'Connor has replied: "It is not State government or departmental practice at any time to record interviews such as those to which you refer.

"In the case you mention I am advised that the department's officer did not have a tape recorder.

"He did, however, have a small dictating appliance which he uses to record brief notes after a meeting or a discussion."

Mr O'Connor ended his brief reply: "I think you will agree that this is not an uncommon practice in many areas of commerce and industry."

Mr Manners said he could not understand the difference between a tape recorder and a dictating appliance. Both recorded the spoken word.

"I agree it is common practice in commerce and industry," he said.

"But it is uncommon practice to have it switched on in your inside pocket."

WEEKEND NEWS, SATURDAY, AUGUST 2, 1980

Reflective Notes @ Oct. 2009

Further harassment continued in the State Government's attempts to have me pay their "protection money" (to protect me from competition).

Shortly after ultimately being "put out of this business" I received a phone call from the same State Government inviting me to become a director of their "Small Business Advisory Service Limited. ..... See Appendix .....

WEEKEND NEWS, SATURDAY, SEPTEMBER 27, 1980

Bugging bid confirmed

By Michael Parry

Bugging did take place in a Kalgoorlie business man's office in June—despite denials by the government that investigators tried to tape an interview.

An investigation by the Ombudsman, Mr I. M. Evans, has established that an officer of the Consumer Affairs Bureau tried to secretly record an interview.

As a result of this investigation, the Commissioner for Consumer Affairs, Mr N. R. Fletcher, has censured the officer responsible. He also has ordered his investigators not to secretly use recording devices in future.

The incident took place on June 24 in the offices of Mr Ron Manners, immediate past president of the Kalgoorlie Chamber of Commerce.

Mr Manners said he was being "interrogated" by two Bureau officers over his unwillingness to fill in government forms.

After 15 minutes of questioning, he heard a clicking noise come from the senior officer's inside coat pocket.

Mr Manners said: "I immediately called in a witness from an adjacent office and we stood over the officer while he sheepishly withdrew a mini tape recorder which he had concealed on his person."

He complained to the Premier's office and to the Minister for Consumer Affairs, Mr O'Connor.

Mr O'Connor, who was acting Premier at the time of his reply, told Mr Manners that it was not State government or department practice to record interviews.

He repeated an earlier verbal denial that a tape recorder had been used. But he did say that the officer was carrying "a small dictating appliance which he uses to record brief notes after a meeting or discussion."

Mr Manners then complained to the Parliamentary Commissioner for Administrative Investigations, Mr Evans.

Mr Evans has told Mr Manners that his investigations included an interview with the Bureau office who "frankly admitted to me that he did attempt secretly to record his interview with you."

PARLIAMENTARY COMMI

Our ref: 7069-E

14th August 1980

Mr R Manners
W G Manners & Co Pty Limited
PO Box 33
KALGOORLIE WA 6430

Dear Mr Manners

I refer to my letter of the 28th of July. I have now investigated your complaint. My investigations included corresponding with the Commissioner for Consumer Affairs and interviewing Mr Coughlin, the Bureau's Acting Senior Investigating Officer.

Mr Coughlin frankly admitted to me that he did attempt secretly to record his interview with you. Whilst his action was not, as I understand it, unlawful, I am firmly of the opinion that it was morally wrong. The Commissioner shares my opinion and has censured Mr Coughlin and has instructed his investigating staff not secretly to use recording devices.

Accordingly, and to the extent that the secret use of the recorder was wrong, I find your complaint to be sustained, and I have so informed the Commissioner, and I now close my file.

Yours sincerely

I M EVANS
PARLIAMENTARY COMMISSIONER FOR
ADMINISTRATIVE INVESTIGATIONS

DATE RECD ... 8.80

Well, I was thoroughly enjoying this renewed interest in gold and building up a few mining assets when, one day in 1982, Keith Parry[18] (a former School of Mines student with me who later became a Director of Western Mining Corp (WMC) and Chairman of Central Norseman Gold Corp.) walked into my office in Brookman Street, Kalgoorlie, with a book in his hand and said, "Ron, I owe you a book, so please have this one. Do you mind me telling you why I am giving you this book?"

Naturally I was curious, so I let Keith continue to explain how he had been worrying about the way I had been developing exploration properties over the years and joint-venturing them out to the larger companies.

In the long-run, he explained, that approach was not good value as larger companies were very inefficient with any early-stage exploration. He said to me, "You will get more 'bang for your buck' if you do the exploration yourself."

"This book," he continued, "will hopefully stimulate you to gather a key team of people around you and float a company to take care of the exploration yourselves."

"The mining equipment supply company that you have been running for so long has got something that some of the larger companies lack—you guys will go beyond the call of normal duty to keep our WMC operations going. I have watched the way you 'borrow' components off some of your new drill jumbos and other mining equipment to keep our equipment running, because you are aware that downtime costs us around $250,000 per hour. The larger companies we deal with often spend all their time seeking permission from head office before they make any move at all."

"If you can apply that sort of fast decision-making to your exploration, then you will succeed. WMC used to be like that, but we are 'losing the plot' the larger we get."

The book Keith gave me, *The Hunters* by John Masters, is described on the cover as "the intimate personal record of the building of a uniquely successful Canadian oil exploration company … by the President of Canadian Hunter Exploration."

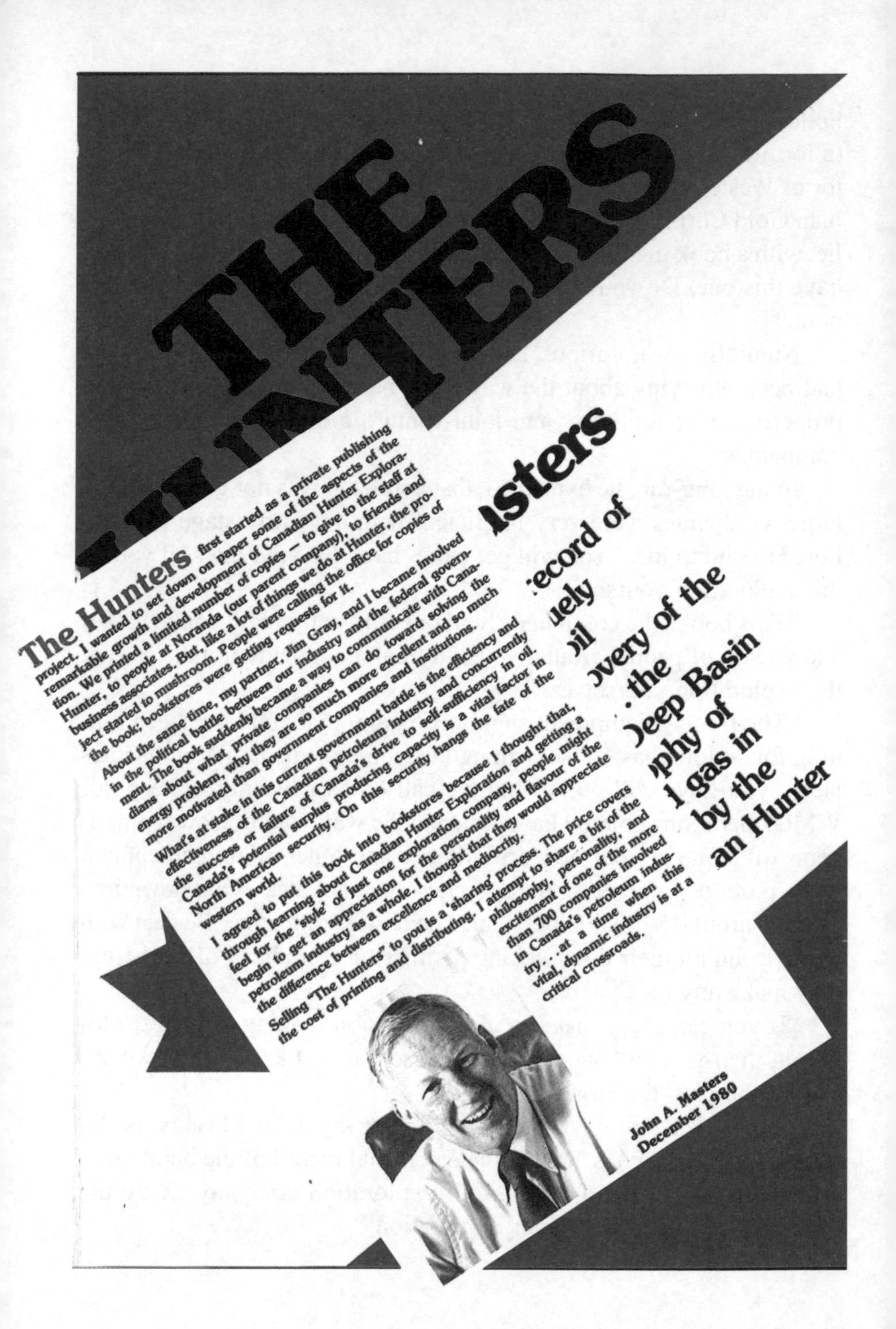

THE HUNTERS

…asters

…ecord of
…uely
…il
…overy of the
… the
…Deep Basin
…phy of
…l gas in
by the
…an Hunter

The Hunters first started as a private publishing project. I wanted to set down on paper some of the aspects of the remarkable growth and development of Canadian Hunter Exploration. We printed a limited number of copies — to give to the staff at Hunter, to people at Noranda (our parent company), to friends and business associates. But, like a lot of things we do at Hunter, the project started to mushroom. People were calling the office for copies of the book; bookstores were getting requests for it.

About the same time, my partner, Jim Gray, and I became involved in the political battle between our industry and the federal government. The book suddenly became a way to communicate with Canadians about what private companies can do toward solving the energy problem, why they are so much more excellent and so much more motivated than government companies and institutions.

What's at stake in this current government battle is the efficiency and effectiveness of the Canadian petroleum industry and concurrently the success or failure of Canada's drive to self-sufficiency in oil. Canada's potential surplus producing capacity is a vital factor in North American security. On this security hangs the fate of the western world.

I agreed to put this book into bookstores because I thought that, through learning about Canadian Hunter Exploration and getting a feel for the 'style' of just one exploration company, people might begin to get an appreciation for the personality and flavour of the petroleum industry as a whole. I thought that they would appreciate the difference between excellence and mediocrity.

Selling "The Hunters" to you is a 'sharing' process. The price covers the cost of printing and distributing. I attempt to share a bit of the philosophy, personality, and excitement of one of the more than 700 companies involved in Canada's petroleum industry. . .at a time when this vital, dynamic industry is at a critical crossroads.

John A. Masters
December 1980

The book was a real "ball grabber" of how Masters, his colleague Jim Gray, and two geologists left the safety and expertise of a large company to enter the realm of exploration. They became a company without assets, but with lots of ideas.

Their ideas were good and they had a great bunch of friends to help them over the corporate hurdles.

Keith Parry knew I would be sucked into the challenge and about a month later, when he next saw me, he said, "Have you got that company together yet?"

I had "Croesus Mining" registered as a company early the following year.

There were many good reasons why we didn't actually list for another three years, but at least the wheels were set in motion.

I later thanked Keith for the book and explained how it had brought a few threads together for me, and I clearly remember his answer, "Ron, I would have to give you a whole library of books to repay you for giving me that copy of Ayn Rand's *Atlas Shrugged.*[19]

He continued, "Until I read that book, I could never really understood why mining and other productive industries got such a hard time from the very people who benefited most from them."

"I used to think it was ignorance, but now I understand exactly what is going through their minds."

Now for those who have not read *Atlas Shrugged*, I would urge you to put it as number one on your reading list.

It is like no other book you have ever read. It is a dramatic explanation of the changing pattern of today's society and events. Events, for example, where we currently see the Australian Taxation Office and unions taking priority over secured creditors, and dubious Native Title Claimants taking priority over legally granted exploration rights, and so on.

Atlas Shrugged also explains the heroic dimension of the creators of this world, as opposed to the parasitical class, or those who simply wish to re-distribute that which others create. This book has been on the best-seller list since 1947.

My sincerest regret was that Keith Parry could not attend the listing party for Croesus on July 24, 1986, having died suddenly and unexpectedly just two months earlier. Nonetheless, Croesus Mining contains a lot of the spirit generated by Keith Parry.

In the lead-up to listing Croesus Mining as a public company,[20] I ended up back at the Kalgoorlie School of Mines to study a couple of geology subjects which I thought might be useful. They said "not you again", and I'm always threatening to go back for what will be the fourth time because the older I get, the more interested I become in knowledge.

Fast Forward to "Now"

Some of these personal experiences from the past, or "misadventures", are covered in greater detail in the following chapters.

They may appear somewhat surreal when viewed from Australia's current climate of stability and prosperity.

If I have any sense of apprehension about Australia, as we gallop into the 21st century, it is that there are so few who are asking questions, who simply accept what is dealt out to us by our political masters (who are in fact our servants).

We, as reflective individuals, have at least two courses of action: we can retire from this political, economic social world into our private occupations and private lives, or we can set out to try and change the world for the better (or at least spend time on formulating some views with this hope in mind). Anyone who fights for the future certainly enhances their perceptiveness of today's texture.

We can remain engaged in this world, enjoying ourselves immensely, as we observe the daily servings of human folly that are served to us from the political capitals of the world.

To remain an individualist on this path we need an unquenchable sense of self-confidence to avoid disillusionment and the fear of swimming against the tide.

Having chosen to lead a fully engaged life, it puts me under considerable pressure to operate our business profitably and thus afford to indulge my "hobby" of "fighting for and investing in the future" and "observing the human folly" flowing from governments when they step beyond their few legitimate functions.

The Private Occupation

Fortunately I enjoy running the private family company, Mannwest Group Pty Ltd, which was initiated by my grandfather, W.G. Manners, in 1895.

W.G. was the son of a Scottish ship's carpenter who jumped ship after falling in love with a passenger. Following her to Ballarat, he became a prospector and later confronted the brutal bureaucrats at the Eureka stockade Rebellion.

Subsequently, the family was somewhat ashamed of this event (concerned at his brush with the authorities), but I'm rather proud of him because the Eureka stockade Rebellion was Australia's first tax revolt. Many of the prospectors were actually killed by the over zealous "troopers" or were subsequently jailed.

Because of this family connection, I was invited to particpate in the 150th celebration ceremonies of the Eureka stockade in December 2004.(21)

Our family business, inspired by this early Eureka involvement, celebrated its own 110th anniversary in 2005.

What were we celebrating? Three things: over those 110 years we "fed, clothed and educated" four generations of our family.

We employed and trained over 1,000 people and we always paid our bills, so there were never any victims.

After so many years of riding booms and bust cycles(22) we have managed to survive and be ready for the next round of excitement.

Investing in the Future

Compared with public companies, one of the great things about private companies is that they are just that—private.

However, over the years we have "spawned" or "hived off" many entities and organisations, one being the Mannkal Economic Education Foundation.(23) The Mannkal Foundation is an emerging Free-Market Think-Tank operating in Perth, Western Australia.

The Free-Market, Free-Enterprise, Capitalism sector is that phenomenon which has brought to mankind unprecedented longevity, good health, prosperity, liberty, opportunity and philanthropy.

Individuals around the world benefit from this phenomenon in proportion to the willingness of their nations to embrace it.

The poor and under-privileged will continue to suffer so long as they are denied access to capitalism.

So? Nothing new in all that you say.

So why are Australians generally inadequate in defending our Western Civilization which is "under attack" from so many quarters?

The self-evident is usually the hardest thing to communicate, and the Mannkal Foundation encourages more questions and more debate by organizing events and sponsoring students for seminars and essay contests.

Expansion is underway for these activities.

Observing Follies

Part of enjoying life and observing its follies, is "writing".

Why should this be the case?

Albert Einstein once said, 'You don't solve problems with the same kind of thinking that created them.'

Perhaps by writing about such problems we can formulate rules that can be used later to solve other problems?

One of my favourite writers, Robert Heinlein, described writing in another way:

'Writing is not necessarily something to be ashamed of, but do it in private and wash your hands afterwards.'

Writing is a rather lonely occupation as you sit into the early hours of the morning staring at a blank piece of paper watching the beads of creative blood as they are squeezed from your brain to become words.

The Separation

It is not easy to separate and balance these activities and conflicting deadlines. Business tasks (where everyone else thinks they own you) threaten to take over, especially if your colleagues have little interest in any of your other "segments".

Scoring a victory for one of your own segments often means getting in early each day to seize that little goal for yourself.

Perhaps that is what Henry David Thoreau had in mind when he said, "Seize the day!"

Endnotes

1. Further comment on Leonard E. Read—see Appendix www.heroicmisadventures.com
2. Further comment on"H.R.H. Prince Philip"—see Appendix www.heroicmisadventures.com
3. Of course this convention of dressing the part is really a load of rubbish. One of my favourite philosophers, Henry David Thoreau once reflected on:

   "How far men would retain their relative rank if they were divested of their clothes". He even distrusted any enterprise that required new clothes. But as long as it remains a convention, we are stuck with it.).
4. With a developing interest in efficiency, hence the thesis "Vertical Burial" page 99.
5. More on that credit squeeze, refer page 121.
6. Further comment on Sir Arvi Parbo — refer page 333.
7. See later chapter.
8. Philosophy of prospecting—Truth, like gold, is to be obtained not by growth, but by washing away from it all that is not gold.—*Leo Tolstoy*–1828–1910).
9. More details at www.heroicmisadventures.com
10. "Forty Years of Farming" (The bureaucrats got me in the end) page 109.
11. Refer page 31.
12. Refer page 45.
13. Refer page 163.
14. Refer page 121.
15. Refer page 57.
16. Refer page 70.
17. Motor Vehicle Dealers Licensing Board
18. Further comment on Keith Parry—see Appendix www.heroicmisadventures.com
19. Atlas Shrugged - go to 'Google'
20. For an overview of my 20 years with Croesus Mining see Mining with King Croesus on page 197.
21. Refer to page 265.
22. Refer page 281 'Do Booms Always End in Tears?'
23. Mannkal Economic Education Foundation, go to—www.mannkal.org

The Rotary Club Gold Medallion 1977

(Ron's rule for dealing with the bureaucracy)

Even the mention of Rotary Clubs (see page18) brings back many memories of my seven years' involvement.

One of the projects for the Kalgoorlie Rotary Club in 1977 was to produce a pure gold medallion to commemorate Paddy Hannan (one of the three prospectors credited with the discovery in 1893).

So what's difficult about producing a commemorative medallion?

Well, after completing the initial artwork for both sides of the quarter ounce medallion (approximately the size of a gold Sovereign), we came upon the news that such medallions would attract a 27.5 percent sales tax (which was the ruling rate of sales tax for medallions at that time).

Everyone in the community knew the price of gold and there was no way that anyone was about to pay a 27.5 per cent penalty over that price.

Our project was 'stalled' until we discovered that sales tax was only 2.5 per cent on spoons (tableware). So without further ado, each medallion was lightly glued to a cheap spoon and sold with an instruction sheet — 'To remove the gold medallion from the spoon, hold briefly over a flame and they will easily separate.'

Ron's rule: 'Ingenuity will beat the bureaucrats every time.'

"With spoon and without."

Have You Ever Been Shot,
Right Out of the Sky?

Skimming the sea,
lifting for land,
soaring the hills.

The wind is just right,
weather's your slave,
work is a breeze.

Years of hard work
at last it seems
about to pay off.

Self Esteem,
ends joining together,
building up steam

Then BANG!
Shot out of the sky
crashing below.

Uncomfortable landing.
No broken bones.
Time will heal all.

What to do next?
I need a rethink.
Remain hidden right here.

Or fly higher next year?

RBM–1982

BALI HOTEL
INVESTMENT PROJECT

Expressions of Interest sought for participation in a BALI (Sanur Beach) Hotel project

Due to the recent financial crisis in Indonesia, a number of attractive property investment opportunities in BALI have become available. Amongst these is a beachside hotel development consisting of sixteen rooms, lobby, offices, restaurant and pool built on 3,500 meters of land along the strategic SANUR beach.

The property is available through a 30 year lease, with an option to extend a further 20 years; and building permits will be granted to construct additional rooms on the property. It is proposed that an additional 46 rooms be built, the bulk of these on three levels, directly above existing rooms and other structures. Upon completion, there will be 62 rooms. There will be, therefore, 62 shares at $50,000 per share, shareholding to be offered through an offshore corporate entity.

The shareholders will enjoy profits generated from the hotel operation, Two weeks free accommodation in each calendar year and 50% discount on F & B during any stay. The shareholders will also enjoy any capital gain derived from the project, in the event a majority of shareholders agree to sell the development.

Interested parties are invited to contact the project developers by email for further information at: merdeka@bigpond.net.au

ISBN 0 85905 174 9

Only A$39
including GST
and postage

NEVER A DULL MOMENT

Author, Ron Manners, says in the introduction "I hope you enjoy this quick skip through these selected events from Kalgoorlie's formative century", but there is far more behind this modest invitation.

One suspects that the multi-faceted Manners may have initially set out to commemorate his illustrious family's involvement on the Western Australian Goldfields, but the final result is a grand sweep of Australiana and life in Australia's outback.

How these generations lived, worked, played and developed that persevering streak that climbs over all obstacles, is a timeless story for us today."

Buy a copy of "Never a Dull Moment" for each person you care about who likes history and applauds liberty. And please buy one for your local school library. For each copy, simply send $39 each (including GST, and delivery within Australia) to **Mannwest, 25** Richardson Street, West Perth, Western Australia, 6005.

Ron Manners and Trevor "Pierpont" Sykes launched "Never a Dull Moment" at 12.30pm on Monday 12 May 2003 at the Sydney Tattersalls Club 181 Elizabeth St, Sydney.

Page reproduced from "Michael Darby's Newsletter", May 2003

Nickel and Hotels In Indonesia

(The Bali tourism adventure)

In May 2003, an invitation arrived in the mail to speak at an investment conference on the topic "Entrepreneurial Opportunities for Australians".

The very next piece of mail to arrive was "Michael Darby's Newsletter" from Sydney, featuring a book review of my *Never A Dull Moment*.

However, the thing that caught my eye was the same-page article — "Bali Hotel – Investment Project" (*see facing page*).

This snapped my memory back to 1975, during a time when I was precluded from working in Australia due to the heavy-handed Tax Department, which at the time believed that it owned me. I didn't believe in slavery, so I left, and during my wanderings in Indonesia looking for nickel, I sat next to an accountant on a plane and he mentioned an exciting business opportunity of running a hotel in Bali; almost a dead-ringer for the opportunity offered in this current advertisement.

Not bad, I thought! A great lifestyle and close to Western Australia, so I could still spend a lot of time back home and use what contacts I had to promote the hotel to Australian travel agents.

They say that wisdom comes from learning from your own mistakes, and I only wish we could make things better by talking about them.

It didn't take me long to slip into the due-diligence process. I arrived at the hotel in Bali with a Sydney solicitor to check out the title and security while I looked at the figures and the suggested strategy for expanding the hotel from 12 thatched units to 48.

I must say that, in 1975, Bali had a lot going for it and this made the financial projections ooze with excitement.

The island was still enjoying the long-running publicity from the old Bing Crosby/Bob Hope movie "The Road to Bali".

Coconut Grove - tropical paradise

Evening Paradise

There were direct flights to Bali from airlines such as KLM in Europe and PanAm in USA. This guaranteed full houses for most of the Balinese tourist destinations.

The existing 12 cottages at the Coconut Grove Hotel were always full and we thought that the existing restaurant, bar and staff could easily handle the additional 36 units. It's not often that you have an opportunity to quadruple your cash flow from existing infrastructure.

Building was cheap in Bali, using local builders and material, so this also helped the feasibility study.

All this was without much Australian input, as there were then no direct Australian flights to Bali, but they were planned and this would certainly be a bonus.

The UK born proprietor, Mr Tony, was sclling out and offered a smooth transition before he left. He was well-connected in Bali and had developed a close relationship with the famous Australian artist, Donald Friend (see page 34), who lived just up the road in another thatched cottage. Mr Tony introduced us to the local bank manager, and he eagerly verified the trading figures that we had been given. He offered us every assistance in getting off to a good start. Mr Tony's Sydney accountant (whom I had sat next to on the plane) was able to supply us with all the figures we required and it didn't take me long to form a syndicate, set a takeover date and fill the role of new manager.

Mr Tony & Mr Ron (standing) with landowners Anom & Soerodjo.

Australian artist Donald Friend had a long relationship with Bali and, in particular, Sanur Beach.
First reading about Bali, when living in London in 1937, he finally took up Balinese residency in 1966.

He then wrote of Sanur Beach ....

"On awakening I felt light and free and careless, as though at last I had thrown off that skin which so chaffed me in Australia. It was a delight to sit in amongst the beautiful warm brown people."

Donald Friend's book *"The Cosmic Turtle"* contained many anecdotes about Coconut Grove Hotel, and following his death in 1989 his ashes were scattered nearby, "back among the people he loved, in the place where he came nearest to finding happiness".

Chef Ho. The food was nothing short of scrumptious

A brand new career — and a great beginning to a five-year nightmare!

We had a few hiccups along the way. Not long after we launched into the extensive building project for the additional units, it was pointed out that we had not paid the officials enough "pocket money" to continue with our building programme. This involved protracted, seemingly never-ending negotiations that bear a striking resemblance to Australian mineral explorers' experience with our Native Title Act.

PanAm and KLM were both suddenly banned from landing direct flights into Bali as the central Indonesian government in Jakarta felt that all tourist entry should be via Jakarta, with tourists then transferring to regional Garuda (Indonesian Government-owned) airline flights to destinations such as Bali. This is exactly what US and European tourists did not want to do.

The bank manager then arrived, armed with his own solicitor, and casually mentioned that the bank had a first mortgage over the property and that interest was accruing at the rate of 48 per cent per annum. It appeared my Sydney solicitor had been incompetent in not having asked the right questions and conducting the proper title searches.

After two loss-making seasons, we were rescued, just in time, by Qantas running direct flights from Perth to Bali. This enabled us to participate in the packaged tour market and it became very much an Aussie style destination with "one mob" flying out on Friday afternoon and "another mob" moving in, having arrived on the same plane.

Much later, when the units were completed to the point of being operational, we had the delightful experience, from time to time, of an occasional Indonesian General arriving to announce that "he had a group of friends arriving and he would like six units set aside for him and his friends, completely outfitted with appropriate female companions". They had no consideration whatsoever for the firm bookings we already held from Qantas. However, we always managed to relocate the firm bookings at other hotels, often with very mixed results.

Probably the worst feature was that Mr Tony decided not to leave, despite his having sold out. His quaint behavioural traits were becoming a problem. He had developed a partiality to small Balinese boys. The Balinese boys were often brutalized and, unfortunately, were in such fear of Mr Tony that they declined my invitation to be interviewed by the local police.

After about a year of exploring conventional methods of removing Mr Tony, all to no avail, I decided to use a little "self-help", often useful when conventional methods fail.

This "self-help" was in the form of a large thug imported from Sydney (we shall call him "Mr Marty") who promised to explore all manner of verbal threats before embarking on a "leg-breaking" exercise.

Mr Marty came with excellent credentials. He was a prominent Balmain Gangland figure who, for an agreed figure, guaranteed complete satisfaction.

In my wisdom I decided not to be in Bali at that time, and you can imagine my surprise when my deputy-manager relayed, by phone, the astonishing news that Marty shared some of the strange characteristics of Mr Tony, and that they had struck up a deep and affectionate physical relationship and were seen by the pool-side holding hands.

Ever since that time I have always doubted my ability to judge people, and now I always ask twice as many questions during interviews.

The "management team" Budi, Ketut, Prapto, Kraemer, Ho (chef), Kadek

Anyway, despite all this, we still managed to keep the hotel operating at a high level of occupancy. It was always difficult to calculate profitability, as I suspected that, on many occasions, we were actually feeding the whole village.[(1)]

Interestingly, we managed to halve the hotel's food consumption, simply by abandoning bulk purchasing and buying only on a daily basis.

The hotel generated its own electricity and we were mystified at our power generation costs, until we found a buried power cable running off in the direction of the neighbouring village.

Although we only had 18 staff, we had to have more than 100 uniforms as they had a complex system of job-sharing. We only paid the 18 who were actually on the payroll. They then shared jobs with others who were currently unemployed, sometimes four or five people sharing the one job. This system worked reasonably well. Although we only paid one a salary, we still appeared to be feeding all the other stand-ins and their direct and indirect families.

Perhaps My Darkest Day?

I can clearly remember what probably developed into being my worst day on the job up there.

It was a 4 am start, on a day to promote the hotel to Jakarta travel agents (approximately a 1.5 hour flight from Bali to Jakarta). The early start saw me leaving at dark on the back of a motor cycle (of course the pre-booked taxi didn't arrive), briefcase held firmly in my left hand and an eight millimetre movie projector held firmly in my right (please remember we didn't have video projectors at that time). Somehow we managed to negotiate all the potholes and stray dogs to arrive at the airport on time. I saw several travel agents in Jakarta and found there to be little interest in Bali, as there were many better and more accessible resorts closer to Jakarta, on the main island of Java.

By the end of the day I'd had enough and one of the travel agents, Bali International Travel, suggested I should stay at their hotel called Bali International Hotel. The proprietor assured me it was "almost completed".

I'm always good for these half-price offers, especially as it was already starting to rain that warm, humid Javanese rain. So as the sun was setting, I headed off for the Bali International Hotel. There I left my bags in the foyer and rushed off to meet a geological colleague by the name of Colin Bryant, as we were involved in several nickel exploration joint ventures together.

Colin had told me that he was expected back in Jakarta from an exploration trip and I was to meet him at a certain bar, some distance from the Jakarta business district. If he couldn't make it, he promised to leave a message with the bartender and give me some idea of where I should go for an entertaining night, before flying back to Bali the next morning.

It's never easy finding a taxi in Jakarta when it's raining, but one managed to get me to the bar and, to my disappointment, Colin had left a message with the barman.

A fairly cryptic message, all it said was that in his absence I should make my way to the local cemetery and just have a good walk around there. His words were, "good fortune would come my way".

The taxi driver had a bit of a chuckle as he dropped me off. He assured me that everything would be okay.

I was certainly not alone, as there was a lot of activity around the headstones. In the dim light it didn't take me long to realize that they weren't quite normal people. There seemed to be a bizarre collection of females and semi-females. Some with far too much makeup on, but all intent on transacting some type of arrangement.

In short, I had been dropped off into a demi-world of transvestites and specialists in odd behaviour and I apparently looked so startled that I could have just about been one of them. Anyway, as they started chasing me, I started running as fast as I could. As luck would have it, no sign of any taxi and it was raining even heavier than before. I seemed to be running for about 45 minutes before I managed to get a taxi back to the Bali International Hotel.

I can remember stepping out of the taxi and seeing a cigar vendor on the footpath selling large wooden boxes of oversized Indonesian cigars. Seeing as I hadn't spent any money that night, I thought at least I should buy a box of cigars before collecting my bags and making my way up the half-finished staircase to the room on the second floor.

In Australia, I'm sure that building regulations would prevent occupancy of any hotel without handrails on external stairways, but not so in the mid–1970s Jakarta. Halfway up the stairway, down came the heavy rain and as I walked through a few puddles to the door of the hotel room I was fascinated to see that the wooden louvres on the door had been fitted on the wrong angle and were collecting rain instead of deflecting it.

This explained the wet floor in the hotel room. The wet floor did not worry me too much for at least I was inside and out of the rain. The room had two narrow beds, each covered with a single white sheet. To my horror, crawling across one bed was the largest cockroach you can imagine. Quick as a flash I removed my boot and flattened the cockroach.

Lifting the boot I found a large technicolor bulls-eye impressed on the sheet. I must have stood on a fresh dog-turd coming up the steps.

I decided to sleep on the other bed; but not before taking a shower.

Surprisingly, no plumbing had yet been completed to the shower recess, but within reach there was a hand-basin and a plastic bowl. It was obvious that the only way to complete the ablution project was to stand in the shower recess and repeatedly reach out for the refilled plastic bowl. Amazing what you can do when you have to.

Anyway, I then managed to happily climb into the one remaining bed, even though I was perturbed that it only had a single sheet, and I was lying on a raw, exposed mattress.

It took only a minute to realize that I wasn't alone in the bed. There were thousands of "creepy-crawlies" all over me. Well, this was about the last straw. I had put up with so much that day, I felt I should start fighting back.

The last thing I can remember of that night was lighting up one of those giant Indonesian cigars and blowing smoke under the sheet before holding it tightly around my neck and repeating this with relentless determination to exterminate every single remaining creepy-crawly.

My closing thought for the day was "tomorrow has just got to be better than this".

So where does all that get us?

How did that bad investment end up?

Remembering something that John F. Kennedy once said, "An error does not become a mistake until you refuse to correct it", we struggled on for a few years and through continued promotional efforts, a restructured bank debt and direct flights from several Australian capital cities, we achieved profitable performance. This enabled an Australian-based syndicate, of which I was a member, to take over the hotel until, through a different set of circumstances, the enterprise eventually collapsed. Our investment was completely written off.

Entrance to hotel - new temple gates

Many years later, when I revisited in 1999 in an attempt to analyze the outcome, I found the hotel completely without guests, the pool empty as they couldn't even afford chlorine, and my hoped-for discussion with the famous Mr Tony was not possible as he had recently died of a "big disease with a little name".

Did I learn anything from this fatiguing and disastrous investment?

I personally felt that despite the lessons learned (about all the things that can go wrong with a perfectly sound project) the five years wasted were simply a disruption to my overall progress. So I was ready when, shortly after that, I was again seated next to an accountant on a flight and he explained how he had "an exciting South Pacific adventure that could not fail because of these following reasons .... etc. ....."

He was right, but only in that it was an exciting adventure, and I call that "My Career in Tourism Part 2", but that's for the next chapter.

Be very wary of an investment proposal being offered by an accountant or a solicitor. Ask first what is in it for them!

Much later, I spent a considerable sum of money seeking legal advice on action I might take against the solicitor for not checking the existence of the mortgage over the Coconut Grove Hotel. After spending this money it was explained to me that solicitors don't like acting against each other any more than doctors like testifying against each other.

The question I ask now is, "what sort of fool rushes from one bad investment into another?"

What sort of fool writes off five years of his life on one investment and then follows it up with a further couple of years in another?

I don't quite know the answer — but you've now met him, and if I can prevent you from writing off seven-or-so years of your own lives, your time reading this has been well spent.

It was only later that I did any in-depth analysis, and then managed to learn something from that sobering nightmare.

We are never deceived, we deceive ourselves.

The real trouble with this world of ours is not that it is an unreasonable world, not even that it is a reasonable one. Most of our investment failures come from the fact that it is nearly reasonable, but not quite.

The philosopher G.K. Chesterton has said that life " is not an illogicality; yet it is a trap for logicians. It looks just a little bit more mathematical and regular than it is; its exactitude is obvious, but its inexactitude is hidden; its wildness lies in wait".

In seeking reasonable investments we often follow "leaders".

Ever since Plato, humankind has been seeking to determine the qualities that leaders must possess. None of us yet has a satisfactory answer, but, as in love, it is the search that matters.

Leadership is not just hitting a ball further than someone else, or running faster than the next guy. It includes an intellectual component that enables us to stand apart from the popularity polls, and work for an ideal, a code of ethics or a new idea, no matter how small the prospect of its early realization.

Learning Versus Influence

Looking back at our own lives at some point in the future, we will realize that while we *learn* from many, perhaps thousands of people, we are only permanently *influenced* by very few. Perhaps you can count them on the fingers of one hand.

We, ourselves, when working amongst our own people, are constantly mentoring them even if we don't realize this. We should think more about our influence on others and let it develop our own character to new heights. If we do, we will be even more successful than the goals we have set for ourselves.

Life is more than simply being a good citizen or a good boss, or a good husband or simply being a person who never says or does, or thinks, anything that is unusual.

Most of our schools are, unfortunately, run with a view to bringing uniformity to the forefront.

H.L. Menken, wise writer, once described schools as:

> A hopper into which children are heaved while they are still young and tender, therein they are pressed into certain standard shapes and covered from head to heel with official rubber stamps.

These people won't do any harm, but nor will they achieve anything great.

We have to get this leadership concept right, if we want to get where we visualize ourselves and our future.

What is our own leadership style?

What are the leadership qualities that we need in our personal fields?

Strong moral character? Passion for a point of view? If that's it, we will have to fully research this point of view, otherwise we will get blown out of the water.

Is it a vision that we believe in?

Later, as our careers advance, we will all look back on who and what made the difference for us.

Was it a major challenge, something that became a "stretch assignment" like my Bali Hotel experience? Something you get into easily and have to fight like hell to get out of?

Or will it be a mentor, a single person who made a difference in our lives?

Endnote

1. I had a similar feeling 30 years later when mining gold at Norseman, Western Australia.

A pessimist sees the difficulty in every opportunity;
an optimist sees the opportunity in every opportunity.

Winston Churchill

However beautiful the strategy,
you should occasionally look at the results.

Winston Churchill

He who learns but does not think, is lost!
He who thinks but does not learn is in great danger.

Confucius

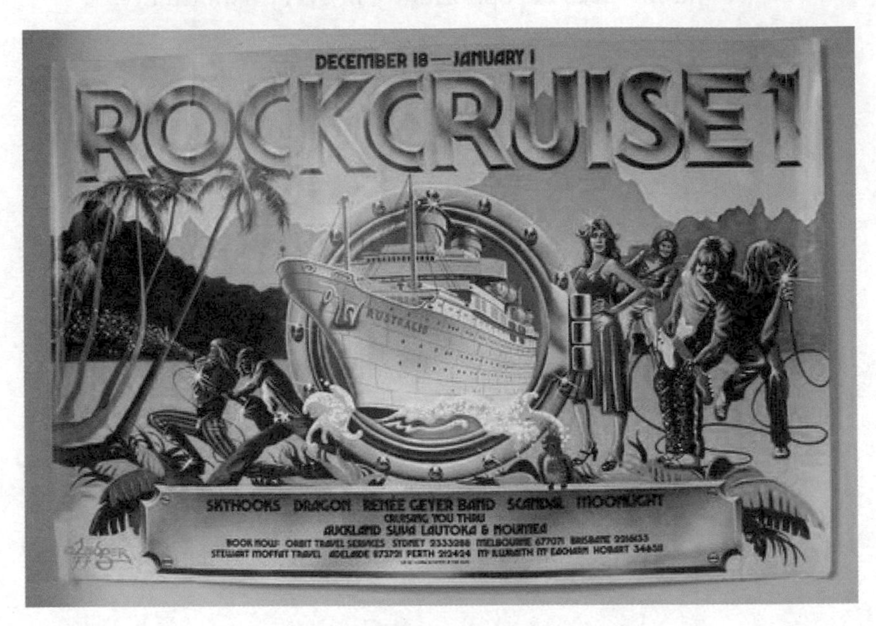

The Fabulous RockCruise

South Seas - Rock'n'Roll

(An offer too good to refuse)

There I was, in September 1977, sitting on yet another plane. The accountant, seated alongside, mentioned to his colleague, just loud enough so I could hear, "The RockCruise project is going really well, all arrangements are well in hand and it can't miss being a huge success. There is still room for another investor, but they will have to be quick, because there is so much interest."

Of course I spoke up ..... "What is this big deal that sounds so good?"

He then explained. "It's a cruise ship promotion called RockCruise that I'm involved in back in Sydney. The investors will get all their capital back before the end of November, with the split-up of the very substantial profits early next year."

He offered to sit down with me when we arrived at our destination and outline the whole venture, which he did.

He said that the group had chartered the *SS Australis* and would be filling 1,200 berths from Sydney, and 400 from Auckland for the RockCruise. In total, there were to be 2,200 berths but 30 or 40 of these would be given away for promotional purposes.

The total amount of ticket funds would be released on November 13, and the investors would get all of their capital back before the end of November.

At that stage, there would already be a profit of $100,000. On top of all this, there would be additional areas of profit, and he listed items such as alcohol sales, sponsorships from Levi Jeans and many others.

Profits were also promised from rock concerts arranged in each South Pacific port, and in addition there would be the "banking exchange" (currency conversion of travellers' cheques on board and when passengers get onshore).

Again, he stressed there would be a full capital refund to each investor on November 30, 1977 with the only thing beyond that point being their profits. These profits were to be calculated no later than March 30, 1978.

Many other assurances were given about the guaranteed profitability, such as the fact that all Christmas cruises out of Sydney were fully booked with long waiting lists, "and we can pick up all of these people from the waiting lists".

He also used wonderful, comforting phrases such as, "the venture is already under way and can't go wrong", and, "the involvement of the Chandris Shipping Line and Orbit Travel virtually guarantee this".

Well friends, how could one resist an offer like this?

Of course a more detailed document that you could call a Prospectus was subsequently supplied. It even improved on these initial assurances, together with the Investor Agreement, and included details of the top-flight industry experts they had signed up to attend to all the logistical arrangements.

The calculations now included the spectacular concert profits, indicating a total return to the investors of 137.5 per cent over the five–month period. Not bad!

Now we were under way, the reports started flowing in and the project just got better every week.

By November 14 we were advised, "Ticket sales are going really well now, over 600, nearly 700, and we still have another month to top up the ship."

With ticket sales going like this they were already planning a RockCruise II, to cater for the overflow with another cruise a month later.

All these arrangements gave us comfort to release our funds.

By now additional sponsorship had come "on board", in particular, Coca Cola and Fabergé Babe. The latter was to be the major sponsor, with the cruise now being officially titled The Fabergé "Babe" RockCruise.

The experts had also visited all the exotic South Sea destinations and made arrangements for the concerts, with these ticket sales also progressing well.

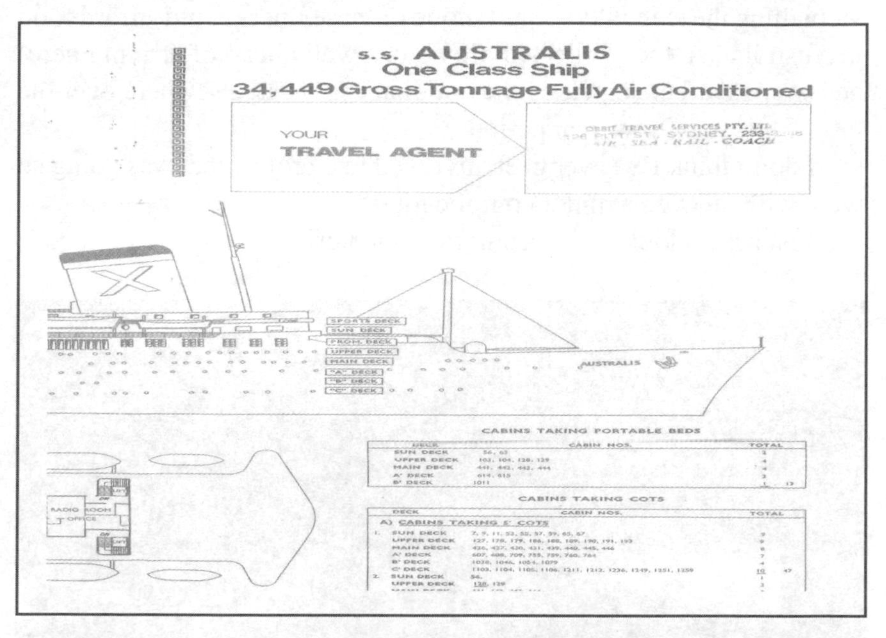

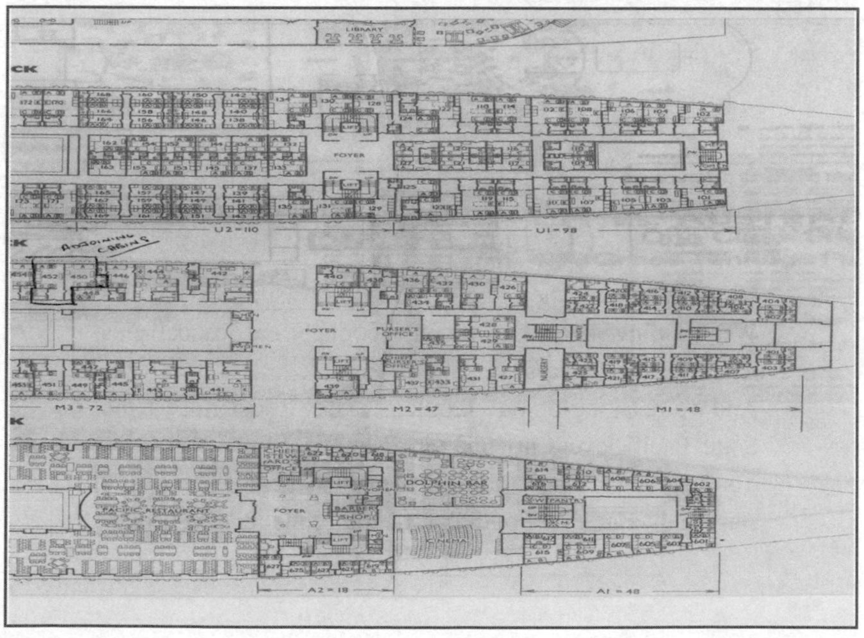

Ship Cabin Plan

In fact, everything looked so good that we had no hesitation in fully victualling the ship in Port Said (none of these liners could afford food in Australia, so they collected provisions well ahead of arriving here) and we paid all the bands so they couldn't perform elsewhere over the busy Christmas/New Year period.

I don't think I've ever been involved in a project that was going so well, without even a minor complication.

Just have a look at the promotional material.

"We've chartered the Chandris Liner SS Australis.
We're putting Skyhooks, Dragon, Moonlight and Scandal! plus special guest Renée Geyer Band on board.
And we're taking-off on a fabulous 15 day RockCruise in the South Pacific over Christmas and New Year.
You're going to visit Auckland, then on to Suva where we are staging the first ever South Pacific rock concert, next beauti-

ful Lautoka and then Noumea for two days, a second concert, then back to Sydney.
Bands will be playing for you on board every night and it's not going to cost you a cent.
And you'll be buying yourself the most fantastic experience you have ever had.
Live concerts every night.

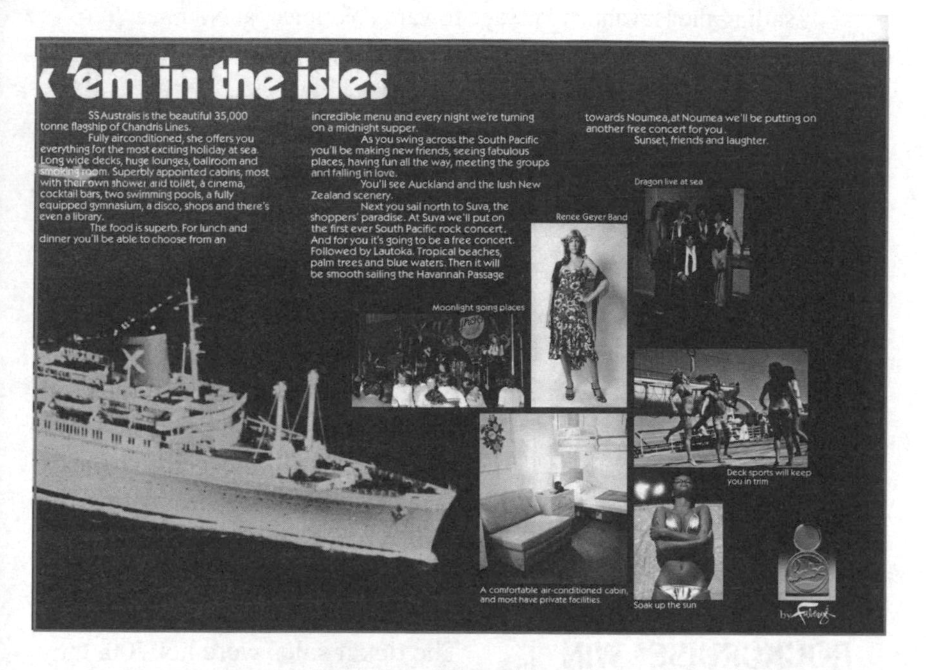

- Breakfast, lunch and dinner, morning and afternoon tea, and a lavish midnight supper.
- Cruising around the romantic South Pacific.
- Tropical rock concerts in Fiji and New Caledonia.
- Live disco featuring top television personalities and radio DJ's.
- Some of the world's best duty-free shopping in Suva.
- A non-stop film festival on board ship.
- Get a healthy tan."

"As you swing across the South Pacific you'll be making new friends, seeing fabulous places, having fun all the way, meeting the groups and falling in love.
You'll see Auckland and the lush New Zealand scenery.
Next you sail north to Suva, the shoppers' paradise. At Suva we'll put on the first ever South Pacific rock concert. And for you it's going to be a free concert. Followed by Lautoka. Tropical beaches, palm trees and blue waters. Then it will be smooth sailing the Havannah Passage towards Noumea, at Noumea we'll be putting on another free concert for you.
Sunset, friends and laughter.
Soak up the sun."

ROCKCRUISE WIN FOR LUCKY DEBBIE

THIS is Debbie Knight, the lucky winner of our Fabulous Babe Rockcruise competition.

Eighteen-year-old Debbie from Parramatta was stunned when SUNDAY broke the good news to her this week.

"I just can't believe it!" she kept on repeating. "I've never won anything like this before. I'm sure I must be dreaming."

Debbie will join top rock groups Skyhooks, Dragon, The Renee Geyer Band, Scandal and Moonlight, who will perform on the 15-day Pacific cruise.

All passengers will be agrd between 18 and 35 years.

The Fabulous Babe Rockcruise on board the luxurious liner SS Australis sets sail on December 18 and returns on January 1.

A special bonus will be open air concerts performed by the rock stars at the ports of call.

SUNDAY, NOVEMBER 20, 1977

"Lucky Debbie", from Parramatta, then became the famous face of the Fabulous Fabergé Babe RockCruise competition and won a free cruise.

She was on all of Sydney's talk-back programmes for 24 hours.

All good news until just three days later, on November 17, when just a glimmer of a problem emerged. Chandris Lines requested an urgent meeting the next day, where they insisted on us finding a guarantor for $300,000, otherwise they would cancel the cruise.

The ticket sales were not 700, they were actually 450, and under further questioning we discovered they were not even fully paid, they were in fact "deposit paid".

The next day, the gravity of the situation struck home and I was on the train from Kalgoorlie to Perth and then the flight from Perth to Sydney. We then stalled Chandris until we could get some answers.

Rockers may get Xmas cruise

DAILY MIRROR, TUESDAY, DECEMBER 6, 1977

A South Pacific rock-cruise which almost foundered through lack of sales may be salvaged.

The promoters said today the shipping line involved had given them 24 hours to get the necessary finance.

"If we can sell 150 more tickets or get someone to guarantee for them the cruise will be on," said Mr John Williams, of Rocktravel.

"Everyone in the rock business wants the cruise to go on.

"And the bands and sponsors have said they will hang in with us."

Skyhooks

The cruise aboard the Australis, scheduled to leave Sydney on December 18, will feature Skyhooks, Renee Geyer, Dragon, Moonlight and Scandal.

Mr Williams said his company had sold more than 600 tickets in the limited time available.

"If we had more time we would have easily filled the ship," he said.

'Most of these cruises take at least six months to fill, and we tried to do it in half that time."

Mr Williams said that if the cruise had to be cancelled tickets would be refunded.

We needed our own expert, and a mate of mine, John Singleton, lined up his personal advisor to sit through our interrogation of the promoter and his assembled team of experts.

It was becoming obvious that the promoter and his assembled experts knew less about the project than even the two non-executive investors (of which I was one).

They were still parroting all their marketing clichés but there was very little substance to them. So the two investors took on the task of selling tickets on Sydney's street corners, with Chandris giving us a couple of weeks as the *SS Australis*, fully provisioned, made its way towards Sydney.

My whole family joined me in Sydney right through until mid–December, where we spent all daylight hours proudly wearing our RockCruise T-shirts and selling tickets like there was no tomorrow.

During the evenings we meticulously planned the next day and phoned many metropolitan Sydney and Melbourne travel agents seeking their support (most of whom had not previously been offered tickets for sale).

These were four challenging weeks for us in Sydney, which were made even harder because of:

- A Postal Union strike (preventing us getting our brochures into the hands of travel agents).
- An Airline Union strike, preventing interstate flights from joining the cruise in Sydney.
- The NSW Coal Mining Union strike which plunged Sydney into darkness on the day the *SS Australis* berthed.

During this time, while working into the night, we assembled a checklist to confirm all the other promises which had been made by the promoter and his assembled experts.

We found that very little had actually been finalised by them.

There was no sponsorship money forthcoming, as all such agreements were still in draft form. The sponsors were willing but had not been followed up.

The media started to pick up the smell of death and articles of doubt appeared in the press.

Faint hope held for Rockcruise

There is a "very slight possibility" the Pacific island Rockcruise might still be on, one of the promoters said yesterday.

By CLIFF NEVILLE

Mr John Williams, a director of Rocktravel, said the cruise might go on if a guarantee of $50,000 were raised by midday today.

"We have spent all day looking for someone willing to guarantee this amount against ticket sales," he said.

"But I don't want to raise people's hopes. It is only a very slight possibility."

Alternative

The cruise, aboard the Australis, was due to leave on December 18 but was cancelled on Monday after ticket sales did not reach the anticipated level.

A spokesman for Chandris Lines said as far as the company was concerned the contract was still cancelled.

"But if the promoters come up with something new, we will certainly put their proposal to the ship's owners," he said.

"We didn't want this cruise cancelled. We thought it was a good idea."

Passengers booked on the Rockcruise have been offered their money back, or passage on alternative cruises aboard the Ellinis early next year.

DAILY TELEGRAPH, Wednesday, December 7, 1977

Probably the greatest disappointment was for us to find that, despite detailed descriptions, no venues whatsoever had actually been booked at any of the exotic South Pacific ports.

When we phoned people on-site it was explained that when "our experts" visited, they realised that suitable fenced venues simply did not exist, so they converted their investigation into a holiday at our expense.

We had no alternative other than to cancel the cruise and refund all the ticket money.

On the night the ship was due to sail out of Sydney, it remained berthed in a blackened-out Sydney, fully laden with provisions (there was a lot of food on board, as you can see (refer to ship cabin plan on page 47), this was a serious ship, but nowhere to go.

Whose fault was all this?

Well, after three–and–a–half years of legal action in Sydney, the other investor and I were impoverished but none the wiser.

Despite encouraging sounds about the excellent prospects of legal success and the issuing of writs, the mounting legal costs and seemingly endless legal procedure completely destroyed our faith in the court ever dispensing justice within our lifetimes.

These files have remained carefully hidden in my archives until 1999 when, on hearing that Renée Geyer and her band were visiting Perth, I wrote a letter to her Perth venue, suggesting that on the strength of my filling an ocean liner with food and honouring the contract with her band by payment in full, she might send me a ticket or two to her Perth concert, and even buy me a beer.

No response!

This RockCruise adventure was not only a hard-luck story, but a lesson in what traps lurk out there for simple souls like us when we go in search of investments and adventure.

Warren Buffett once described such traps: ‘They say the chains of habit are too light to be felt until they are too heavy to be broken. The chains you put around yourself now have enormous consequences as you go through life.’

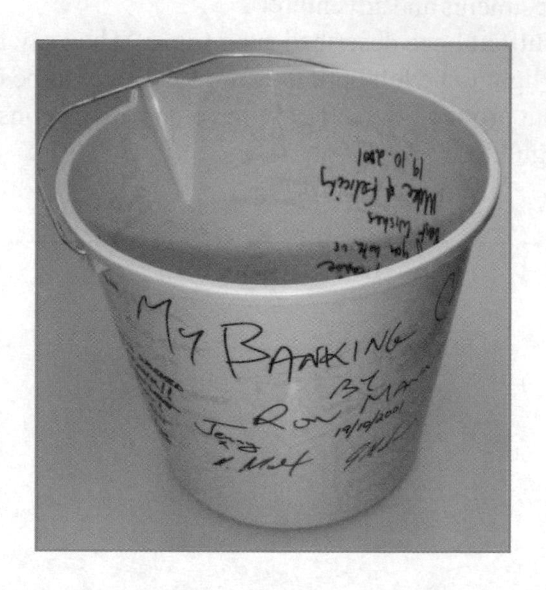

A Few Words in Defence of "Money Laundering"

How times have changed!

In the 1970s there was a degree of respectability, if not nobility, in the money laundering profession.

It was simply a matter of individuals putting some of their own hard-earned money out of the reach of a rapacious government.

Whilst now, three decades later, through the use of a process of language and thought control, anyone wishing to do the same thing, is treated as a 'drug lord' or an 'Islamic-extremist terrorist'.

Could this be another example of our disappearing economic freedom?

A Brief Banking Career

(Buckets of money at the Nugan Hand Bank)

As a brief background, let me give you a mental picture of the particular era in which this story is set.

It started on January 8, 1977 and continued through to Australia Day, January 26, 1980.

It was only three years, but now, three decades later, I am still scratching my head and saying:

"What the hell was that all about?"

All events should be judged against the political fabric of the time. Australia was just recovering from the Whitlam era. The Whitlam Government's main achievement was to take away the rewards from those who produced something and give it to those who produced nothing but votes.

It was an era when the business community was battered and bruised to the extent that it was common to see on office notice boards a sign saying:

**WILL THE LAST BUSINESSMAN
LEAVING AUSTRALIA,
PLEASE TURN OUT THE LIGHTS!**

The prospects were bleak and many people were leaving the country. Anyone with any significant income was involved in so-called "bottom of the harbour" tax schemes, which were quite legal at the time.

John Howard, as Federal Treasurer, brought in his "retrospective legislation" (retrospective, or retroactive legislation as the Americans call it, is generally unconstitutional in most free countries, but somehow it managed to become law in Australia). Its effect was to turn law-abiding citizens into criminals, by back-dating legislation.

On the home scene, I was President of the Kalgoorlie Chamber of Commerce, so I had a pretty good idea of the level of local difficulties.

Kalgoorlie was geared up for a continuing nickel boom but that was well and truly at an end.

I was personally fatigued from continuous attacks from the Tax Department. They were continually misunderstanding the Taxation Act with respect to my prospecting activities.

There was no point in earning any income in Australia as it would simply be seized, so I became an "odd job man" running a hotel in Bali and looking for nickel in Indonesia (as outlined in previous chapters).

It was in this context that opportunity knocked on my door in the form of this 1977 advertisement from the *Bulletin* magazine (see page 60).

A career in banking? Why not?

Remember, these were the days when banking was a well regarded occupation. Despite Australia having produced several political and business scandals, the banking industry was still seen to be relatively clean.

Apart from my rampant curiosity, there were two other prophetic indications why I should take this advertisement seriously (see page 59).

- The advert was dated 8 January, 1977 (my 41st birthday).
- On the same page, someone had written a letter to the editor agreeing with an earlier letter of mine.

So away went my job application to Hong Kong, complete with a rapidly assembled CV (which looked pretty good for a person without a proper job). Back came the reply from the *Swiss Pacific Bank and Trust* in Hong Kong, expressing interest in my application and offering me an interview in either Hong Kong or Sydney (see page 61).

Naturally, I accepted both.

A fancy brochure and international currency chart (see page 62) was all the background information I received.

The chart was interesting in that it showed various currencies charted historically against the Australian dollar.

Particularly interesting was that anyone switching from Australian dollars to Swiss Francs in January 1971 would have been 45 per cent ahead by December 1976.

It also explained the international connections of this interesting bank (see page 63).

titled *Exercise for Stretched Skin* (November 11). Perhaps he should keep a look out for the RSPCA.

Your Art Critic's childish enchantment with the Biennale is so pathetic it is embarrassing and one must ask: "Has this sordid and ludicrous situation in the Arts come about because the masses (albeit all classes) are unaware that CULTURE glides collectively on the complex, though controlled, machinery of inverted snobbery?"

SYLVIA HOLMES
Wahroonga NSW

Paper doing well

Your story about Rupert Murdoch (B, November 6) mentions this company and implies that we are "not doing so well."

Your information is wrong, and we would appreciate a correction.

In our second year of publication ending September 30, 1976, we have announced a net profit of $102,000.

For a new newspaper competing against a 107-year-old rival in a sluggish economy we think we've done damned well!

PHILIP HARKNESS
Publisher Fiji Sun Suva Fiji

Showing the flag

Since John Singleton's article on the Bureau of Census and Statistics and now Ron Manners' letter (B, December 11) it seems that we can bring another inconsistency of government departments to light.

The organisation of which we are directors is a private rehabilitation project for a handicapped husband and father – medically handicapped, that is. We had envisaged being able to, eventually, set up our own silk screen print shop and produce and market our own souvenirs.

To be on the safe side we wrote to the Prime Minister's office, which has also changed its name, and asked could we include the Australian national flag in tasteful souvenirs.

A reply told us that we could do this with regard to the royal visit this year but that it was forbidden for us to do it at any other time or to use the name of our organisation or "Souvenir of Gympie" on the items.

This would seem reasonable enough if it were not for the fact that one of the large variety stores sells carrier bags with the Australian and British flags printed thereon and, only today, a firm in Brisbane ran a full-page advertisement in the metropolitan Press with the Australian flag on a key ring.

One wonders what happens when others use the flag for advertising purposes apparently without asking the department concerned? Are they charged with any indictable offence? Can they be so charged?

Or is it simply a case of "not what you are but who you are" that matters with Public Servants and the nabobs of politics?

ALEX and CONNIE REHARDT
International Flag Gallery Gympie Qld

Right-left coalition

You neglected to mention Australia's largest union (B, December 11) with its 260,000 members, $650,000 in membership subscriptions, $20 million travel company and enormous assets and that is the Australian Union of Students (AUS).

Your correspondent's comments on big unions are especially pertinent to the AUS. He is entirely right when he points out that the collegiate system of voting in unions is vastly less democratic than direct elections of union officials, and that conservative or right-wing support

$60,000 A YEAR MAN?

IS THIS YOU?

- Strong desire or willingness to live and work in an overseas country for 2 years or more.
- Pioneering type who enjoys the challenge of breaking new ground and is not afraid to get out and sell.
- Strong sense of integrity, high personal standards, reliable, single minded, independent.
- History of achievement — result oriented.
- Larger vision of ability to succeed than is presently being realised in Australia.
- Capable of negotiating successfully at all levels — from the labourer to the Chairman of the Board.
- Able to work effectively without constant motivation.
- Physically fit, healthy, aged between 25-40, well regarded in the community.
- A keen awareness of what running a business is all about, an understanding of capitalism, a desire to accumulate.
- Excited by the genuine proposal of earning upwards of $60,000 a year (from which would be deducted cost of living and taxes as applicable in the country of residence).

THIS IS US

- We are a small though rapidly expanding Banking Group.
- Our affiliates have recently formed a new Bank and have requested that we recruit and train personnel to operate Representative Offices for selected overseas countries.
- The prime aim of the new bank is to attract substantial high earning medium term (5 years) deposits. The Bank will as well offer a full range of Banking and Trust Services.
- The Representative will be required to render the above services in conjuction with local experts in the appointed country, commencing as a sole operator and expanding as progress dictates.

If you feel you qualify for the above please write giving full particulars of your background in the terms of this ad to:

General Manager,
International Division,
P.O. Box 8282 General Post Office,
HONG KONG

You may be assured your letter will be treated with complete confidentiality.

6 THE BULLETIN, JANUARY 8, 1977

Advertisement from 'The Bulletin' January 8, 1977

$60,000 A YEAR MAN?

IS THIS YOU?

- Strong desire or willingness to live and work in an overseas country for 2 years or more.
- Pioneering type who enjoys the challenge of breaking new ground and is not afraid to get out and sell.
- Strong sense of integrity, high personal standards, reliable, single minded, independent.
- History of achievement — result oriented.
- Larger vision of ability to succeed than is presently being realised in Australia.
- Capable of negotiating successfully at **all** levels — from the labourer to the Chairman of the Board.
- Able to work effectively without constant motivation.
- Physically fit, healthy, aged between 25-40, well regarded in the community.
- A keen awareness of what running a business is all about, an understanding of capitalism, a desire to accumulate.
- Excited by the genuine proposal of earning upwards of $60,000 a year (from which would be deducted cost of living and taxes as applicable in the country of residence).

THIS IS US

- We are a small though rapidly expanding Banking Group.
- Our affiliates have recently formed a new Bank and have requested that we recruit and train personnel to operate Representative Offices for selected overseas countries.
- The prime aim of the new bank is to attract substantial high earning medium term (5 years) deposits. The Bank will as well offer a full range of Banking and Trust Services.
- The Representative will be required to render the above services in conjuction with local experts in the appointed country, commencing as a sole operator and expanding as progress dictates.

If you feel you qualify for the above please write giving full particulars of your background in the terms of this ad to:

General Manager,
International Division,
P.O. Box 8282 General Post Office,
HONG KONG

You may be assured your letter will be treated with complete confidentiality.

Job Advertisement The Bulletin *January 8, 1977*

Swiss Pacific Bank and Trust Company

Representative Head Office: 1110 Connaught Centre, Hong Kong.
Telephone: 262321. Telex: HX83499.

11th February, 1977.

Mr. R. B. Manners,
45 Brookman Street,
KALGOORLIE. WEST AUSTRALIA. 6430

Dear Sir,

Thank you very much for your reply to our advertisement headed "Is This You - $60,000 A Year Man".

We have been literally inundated with responses and are trying to interview in sequence of response all persons whose background seems most suitable for the project.

We look forward to meeting you as soon as possible and hope to be in touch within the next two to four weeks.

Yours faithfully,

J. M. GILDER.

Banking Services

International Certificates of Deposit

Bank issued Interest Bearing Certificates of Deposit, at the most attractive prevailing rates of interest available internationally, may be arranged in any major world currency at current rates of conversion.

Certificate of Deposit accounts may be opened by mail and deposits may be made and withdrawn by mail, telex, or telephone.

The client receives a fixed interest International Certificate of Deposit which is not subject to variations in interest rates.

Periods of deposit may vary from 6 months to 15 years.

Numbered accounts and special arrangements as to payment of interest are available and absolute banking secrecy and confidentiality are guaranteed by Cayman law.

World Currency Movements

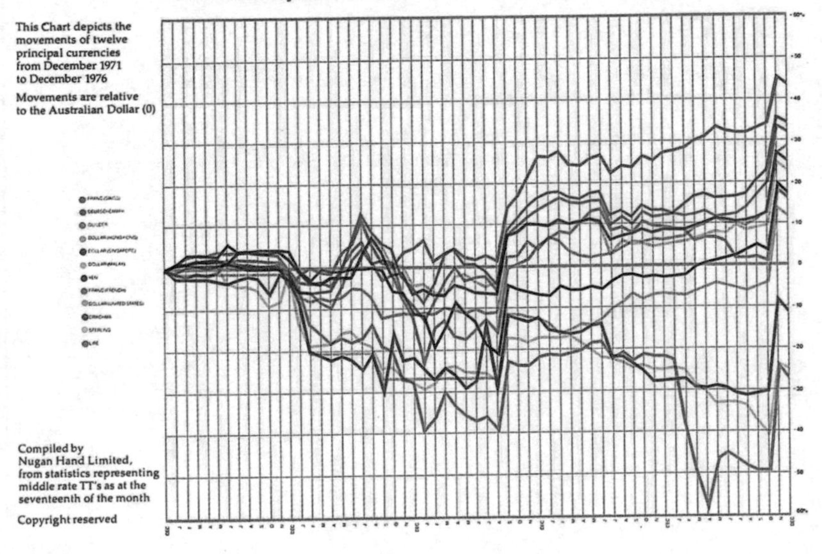
This Chart depicts the movements of twelve principal currencies from December 1971 to December 1976
Movements are relative to the Australian Dollar (0)
Compiled by Nugan Hand Limited, from statistics representing middle rate TT's as at the seventeenth of the month
Copyright reserved

Currency Chart

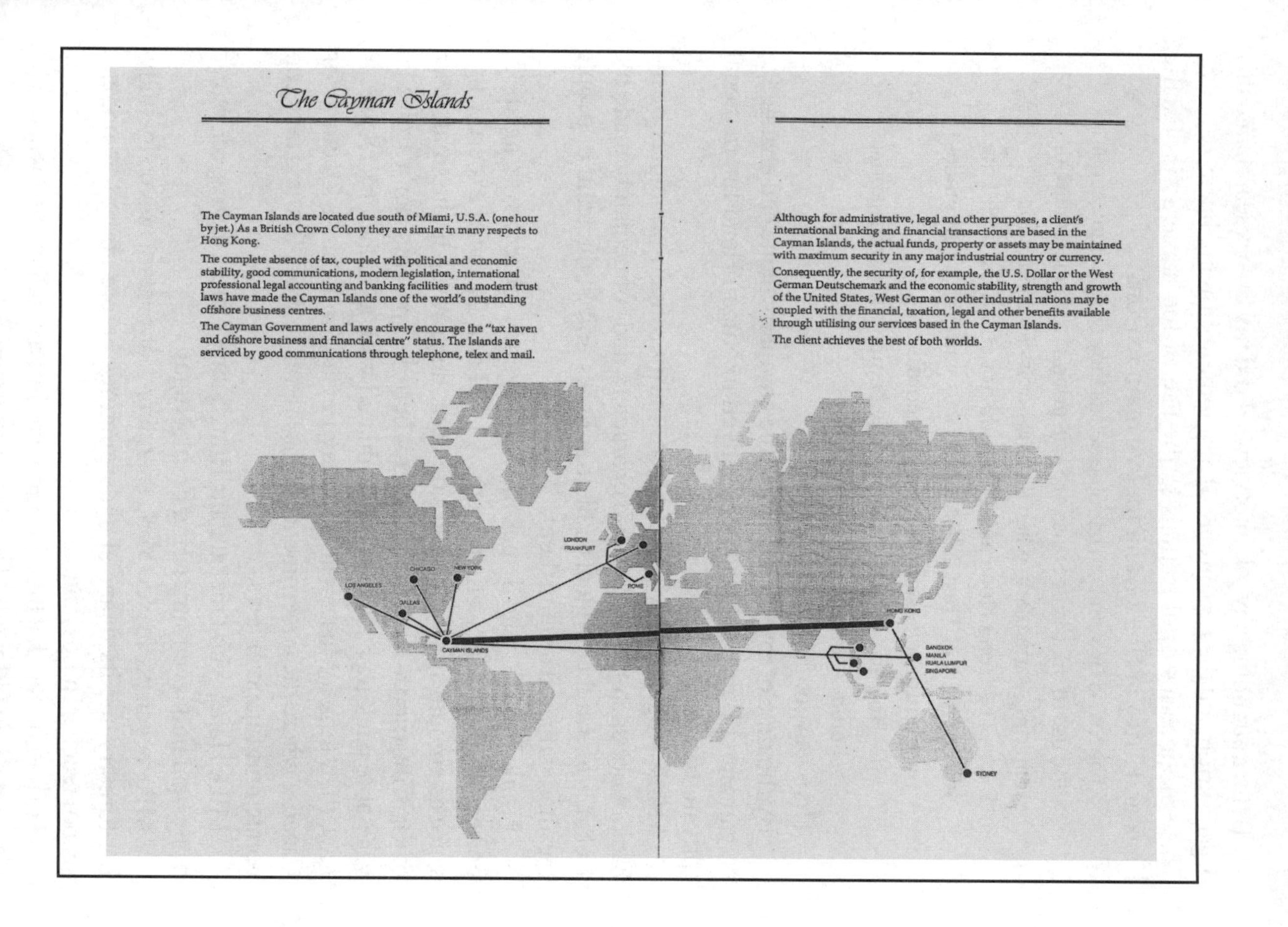

The Cayman Islands

The Cayman Islands are located due south of Miami, U.S.A. (one hour by jet.) As a British Crown Colony they are similar in many respects to Hong Kong.

The complete absence of tax, coupled with political and economic stability, good communications, modern legislation, international professional legal accounting and banking facilities and modern trust laws have made the Cayman Islands one of the world's outstanding offshore business centres.

The Cayman Government and laws actively encourage the "tax haven and offshore business and financial centre" status. The Islands are serviced by good communications through telephone, telex and mail.

Although for administrative, legal and other purposes, a client's international banking and financial transactions are based in the Cayman Islands, the actual funds, property or assets may be maintained with maximum security in any major industrial country or currency.

Consequently, the security of, for example, the U.S. Dollar or the West German Deutschemark and the economic stability, strength and growth of the United States, West German or other industrial nations may be coupled with the financial, taxation, legal and other benefits available through utilising our services based in the Cayman Islands.

The client achieves the best of both worlds.

Bank's International Connections

Before attending any job interviews, I did my own research into this organisation and the response read along the following lines:
There are a series of objections to the use of the name Swiss Pacific Bank and Trust in Hong Kong for two main reasons.

> The Swiss Government has objected as they feel strongly about the use of the words Swiss or Switzerland in connection with banking, particularly when there is no Swiss connection.
>
> The Hong Kong authorities do not allow the use of the words Bank or Trust unless it complies with very strict guidelines and a well established track record.
>
> However in view of the people behind the organisation, it should still be taken seriously.

That was good enough for me.

By the time of my job interview, the company name had changed to Nugan Hand Bank. It was later changed to Nugan Hand International (private bankers). (See page 65.)

Frank Nugan and Michael Hand, the two main principals of the bank, were each larger-than-life characters and immediately made me feel at home and confident in their abilities and in the team of people they had gathered around them.

Frank Nugan, who I met in their Sydney office, was aged 35, powerfully built and well dressed. A legal and financial expert with a voice as smooth as a well-oiled safe door, he grew up in the small town of Griffith (north-west of Sydney) where his parents ran a fruit and vegetable packing business. He graduated with a Bachelor's Degree in Law, then took a Masters at Berkeley in California and a Doctorate in Canada, where the government put his talents to work framing new corporate and financial laws.

Mike Hand, who I met at their Hong Kong office, then aged 36, had a physical bulk even surpassing Frank Nugan.

Mike began life in New York, spending four years at university studying forestry and its financial underpinnings before going to work as a school teacher in Los Angeles.

He mentioned that his education was interrupted in 1964 when "Uncle Sam decided I would look better in green."

Nugan Hand International

The Nugan Hand International group includes an Australian firm of investment bankers, two international private banks, a Hong Kong investment banking company, and commercial advisory and trade service companies.

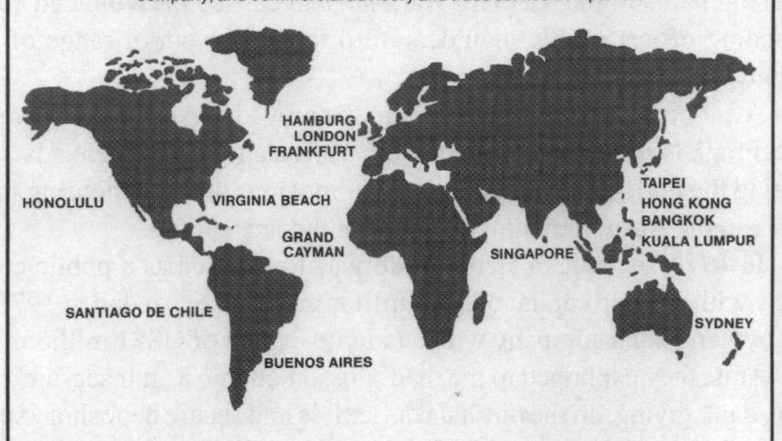

Australia—
Nugan Hand Limited
8Fl., Bennelong House, 55 Macquarie Street,
Sydney, Australia
Tel: 27-3311 Telex: 27127

Germany—
F.A. Neubauer Bank (est. 1841)
Neuer Wall 25, 2000 Hamburg 11, Germany
Tel: (040) 365-855/365-856
Telex: 2161750 Cable: fanbank

Cayman Islands—
Nugan Hand Bank
4Fl., Bank of Nova Scotia Building,
Grand Cayman, British West Indies
Tel: 92997/92648 Telex: CP302

Hong Kong—
Nugan Hand (Hong Kong) Limited
Nugan Hand Bank,
Representative Office
1110 Connaught Centre,
Hong Kong
Tel: 5-262321 Telex: 83499

Germany—
Nugan Hand Bank Representative Office
Mainzer Landstr.
49, D-6000 Frankfurt Am Main, Germany
Tel: 232-790 Telex: 7722413

Singapore—
Nugan Hand Singapore (Pte.) Ltd
Suite 806, Ocean Building, Collyer Quay,
Singapore 1
Tel: 917-255 Telex: 24157

Malaysia—
Nugan Hand (Malaysia) Sdn. Bhd.
10Fl., Oriental Plaza, Jalan Parry,
Kuala Lumpur 04-01
Tel: 209-258/201-734 Telex: 30641

Thailand—
Nugan Hand (Thailand) Limited
1010 Dusit Thani Building, Rama IV Road,
Bangkok, Thailand
Tel: 233-0407 Telex: 2314

U.S.A. Virginia—
Nugan Hand Bank, Representative Office
108, 88th Street, Virginia Beach,
Virginia 23451, U.S.A.
Tel: (804) 422-5559

U.S.A. Hawaii—
Nugan Hand Inc.
4910 Kahala Avenue, Honolulu,
Hawaii 96816, U.S.A.
Tel: (808) 732-6000

Chile—
Nugan Hand (Chile) Inc.
Casilla 15051, Correo 11, Santiago de Chile
Tel: 42056/383130 Telex: 40607
Cable: goyco

Argentina—
Nugan Hand (Argentina) Inc.
Lavalle 5562' Piso "D", Buenos Aires,
Argentina
Tel: 320989/329824

Taipei
Nugan Hand Inc.
1106 Shin Tai Bldg.,
106-2 Chung Shan N. Rd., Sec 2,
Taipei
Taiwan R.O.C.,
Tel: 551-0450, 561-2642
Telex: 11079 DAMEX.

G526

Brochure Nugan Hand International

He skipped officer's school and went to Vietnam two years later as a private in the US Special Forces. There he became a war hero and the holder of America's second highest gallantry award, a Distinguished Service Cross.

Records show that in 1966 he was one of only six survivors of a 200— strong unit which held out against 2,000 Communist troops at the Dong Xoai crossroads, 35 miles north-west of Saigon. This was the first big battle of the Vietnam War. He had carried his wounded commanding officer on his shoulders until they were out of range of the enemy.

After his discharge from the army he moved to Australia. There he met Frank Nugan and they started out as freelance investment advisors during the period when international companies were clamouring for a stake in the Australian mineral boom of the late 1960s.

In 1973, the Nugan Hand group was formalised as a public company with paid-up capital of A$1 million and then expanded in 1976 as a Cayman Island company with a paid up capital of US$1 million.

This, they explained to me, had blossomed into a 'full service' private bank giving, on the one hand a flexible and secure depository service for long and short-term funds and, on the other hand, access to professional services divisions. This was all built around a 70-strong task force of lawyers, accountants, management and business consultants, many of whom were cross-trained because of what Frank Nugan called 'a wonderful interchange of technical skills within the group'.

Their story was quite believable and it was pioneering banking work at that time.

Nugan Hand was the first bank to introduce money market operations to Hong Kong and they were beating Westpac by bringing money market operations into Australia.

I can't help smiling as I look back on some earlier notes from my meetings when it was explained to me what 'full service' really meant, specifically in relation to 'walking a client's dog' or 'washing a client's car'.

It is also important to remember these were the days before drug dealers and terrorists gave 'money laundering' such a bad name.

During my time with Nugan Hand I did not aspire to any particular title but showed particular interest in being a 'bagman' and 'special projects officer'. The 'bagman' activities of Nugan Hand could form a complete chapter in any book and perhaps be titled 'Life in the Laundry', but to give you some idea of how difficult it is for governments to stamp out 'money laundering' activities, let me explain that it did not involve getting on a plane with a suitcase full of bank notes.

All it needs is two complementary individuals, one here and one there, and please understand at that time there was no shortage of Australian money trying to get out of the country.

Similarly, there was no shortage of Indonesian Generals with money they could not explain. They were so keen to get their money to Australia, particularly to purchase a block or two of Sydney harbour-side apartments.

All it took was for the Australian dollar bank notes to be counted in Sydney and placed in plastic buckets.

Similarly, the Indonesian Rupiah were counted in Jakarta, to ensure equivalent value at that day's ruling exchange rates.

Settlement consisted of a single phone call and the money, complete with plastic buckets, didn't move, but simply changed ownership.

That sort of settlement works best when people are blessed with easily recognisable voices and I am told this was one of my strengths.

Conveniently, during these years, Jakarta provided banking with no currency controls to anyone other than an Indonesian national, so it was easy to direct money from Jakarta to anywhere in the world, but virtually impossible to do this from Sydney.

Plastic buckets were used as they were seen to be disposable and untraceable and each party actually brought their own empty briefcases to the settlement.

A fee of 8.5 percent was charged to each party and, as in all good transactions, everyone went home happy.

In respect to 'special projects', one into which I put a lot of work was the Minerals Exploration Project, where I formed a three-way joint venture with Frank and Mike by establishing a new company called Mining Resources (W.A.) Pty Ltd (see page 68).

The nature of this project was as outlined in Frank Nugan's letter of July 3, 1978 (see page 69).

These nine Kalgoorlie-based nickel and platinum prospects were all ready for exploration, to commence with a $500,000 annual budget (see page 71).

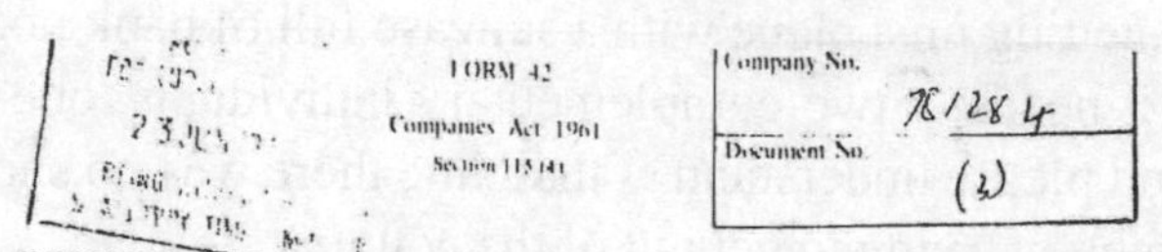

FORM 42
Companies Act 1961
Section 115(4)

Company No. 78/1284
Document No. (2)

LIST OF PERSONS WHO HAVE CONSENTED TO BE DIRECTORS

MINING RESOURCES (W.A.) PTY. LTD. ~~LIMITED~~

To the *Commissioner for Corporate Affairs*

I,* RONALD BROWN MANNERS, Company Director of 45 Brookman Street, Kalgoorlie, W.A., 6430.

one of the persons desiring the incorporation of

MINING RESOURCES (W.A.) PTY. LTD. ~~Limited~~, hereby

certify that the under-mentioned persons have consented to be directors of that company.

Name	Address	Description
Ronald Brown MANNERS	45 Brookman Street Kalgoorlie, 6430	Company Director
Francis John NUGAN	8th Floor, 55 Macquarie Street, Sydney, 2000.	Company Director
Michael Jon HAND	8th Floor, 55 Macquarie Street, Sydney, 2000.	Company Director

Dated this 14th day of June, 1978

* Insert name, address and description

(Signature) [signature]

MUIR WILLIAMS NICHOLSON & CO.

Lodged by or on behalf of *as agents for*
BANNERMAN LALOR & CO.,
ADDRESS Palace Chambers,
Maritana Street, KALGOORLIE.
TELEPHONE No. 21 2455

Lodged in the Office of the Commissioner for Corporate Affairs
23 JUN 1978
Commissioner for Corporate Affairs

CCR FORM 340

Mining Resources (WA) Pty Ltd

Nugan Needham

SOLICITORS

Francis John Nugan
LL.B., LL.M.
John Charles Needham

4TH FLOOR
55 MACQUARIE STREET
SYDNEY, N.S.W. 2000
TELEPHONE: 241-1401-3
DX 548 SYDNEY
TELEX AA27127

3 July 1978

Mr Ron Manners
Mining Resources (WA) Pty Ltd
45 Brooklyn Street
KALGOORLIE WA 6430.

Dear Ron:

We didn't get to use the work we have done on mining between you and I in the 1977/78 tax year for a number of reasons. Firstly, the legislation to defeat the very cheap and easy Curran scheme deductions came very late and most potential Australian tax minimisers went on in a fools paradise hoping the legislation would not be "retrospective". Although I sent it through to Germany, the people we have so far spoken to in Germany (where I thought it would be appropriate) do not believe they can get deductions on overseas exploration expenditures. I believe they can, and have seen a very substantial scheme similar to the ones I envisgaged for us, under which Firestone the rubber company's German subsidiary, achieved some $6 million worth of paper deductions over three years by purported joint venture exploration expenditures on mineral claims external to Germany.

I do genuinely have very high hopes for utilising the work you have done and the Company we have formed between us in this 1978/79 financial year. Ted Harland is working on the benefits arising from the re-introduction of 23P exemptions and that bona fide prospectors are exempt for tax in respect of the proceeds of sale of mining areas.

What I would like to do now in the first month of this new financial year, is to have you write a "review" on where we stand in terms of having a corporate structure, alot of areas on which there are existing geological reports etc., an assessment as to the sort of amounts that might superficially be believed to be adequately committed to "exploration expenditure" assuming we can find half a dozen new joint venture partners.

I feel certain that sometime over the next six months between you and us we will be able to start on the programme and profitability that I laid out for you when we first discussed this new exploration company venture between yourself, Mike and I.

Ron if you could send us your review as outlined above, then over the next month Ted and I will study how to use that structure to best effect for tax purposes for clients.

Kindest regards to you and your wife,

Frank Nugan's letter July 3, 1978

This was a significant figure in 1978 and, more importantly, times were "tight" and a lot of consultants and geologists were looking forward to this exploration programme. I am sure that we would have produced results from these prospects.

Well, apart from the 'nuts and bolts', there were some highlights on the social events side and I recall one interesting day at Frank Nugan's home in 1978.

Frank had a luxurious home in Vaucluse Bay, right down to the water, with its own pier and private beach.

Frank suggested I spend a Saturday with him as he said he had invited a group of influential friends I should meet.

About the only person I had met before was PLS, a well known Sydney company promoter. The others I knew by sight or reputation and they included senior figures from the New South Wales State Labor Party, plus a few very high-profile Federal Australian Labor Party (ALP) figures. (Names deliberately omitted.)

Some of the senior ALP figures made very appreciative comments to me about how Frank Nugan had arranged their taxation affairs in such a way they need not make further payments to the Tax Department. I recalled these interesting comments later when the ALP campaigned and brought intense pressure on the Liberals for having permitted widespread use of these 'bottom of the harbour' schemes. Risky of them to throw stones when so many of them lived in large 'glass houses'?

Especially when the Deputy Leader of the ALP later turned up the heat on these 'bottom-of-the-harbour' schemes as a way of embarrassing the Fraser Liberal Government.

If any group of people had something to fear from the information that Frank Nugan carried in his head, it was this group of senior ALP figures.

However, my Nugan Hand relationship came to a sudden end on the Australia Day weekend of 1980 when I received a phone call to say that Frank Nugan had been found dead, with his brains splattered all over the inside of his Mercedes, on a deserted country road near Lithgow, NSW.

Whilst his death was set up to look like a suicide, I had several doubts, as did others.

Nugan Needham,
4th floor, 55 Macquarie Street,
SYDNEY. N.S.W. 2000

Mr. F.J. Nugan

August 25,'78

Dear Frank,

As requested in yours of July 3, we now provide a summary of exploration prospects completed, ready for the venture.

Copies of these are enclosed and you alraady have a copy of the Whitehead Prospect.

PROSPECT	EXPLORATION BUDGET
Whitehead Prospect	19,997
Gindalbie Platinum Prospect	70,200
Rotorua Copper-Nickel Prospect	49,400
Bandya Nickel Prospect	29,904
Dromedary Nickel Prospect	190,000
Narracoota Proppect	9,939
Randalls Prospect	13,450
Karara Well Copper-Nickel Prospect	5,150
Jack Hills Nickel Prospect	65,000
TOTAL	$453,040

Looking forward to proceeding as discussed.

Regards,

R.B. MANNERS.

P.S. I'll be in Sydney for the World Money Analyst Seminar on September 9/10 and will contact you and George on Monday September 11.

Exploration Prospects - Letter to Frank Nugan

- I knew Frank well enough to rule out suicide. Some people may be suicide-prone but Frank, like myself, was not of such inclination. In fact he specialised in setting people up with new passports, giving them a pep talk and sending them on their way to a fresh start.
- There were no fingerprints on the rifle, or at least, no check was made.
- The death inquiry was handled by a country coroner whose comments indicated that from the way Frank was shot and the position of his body that "he would have had to been a contortionist for it to have been suicide".
- There were several strange aspects in respect to an insurance policy for $5 million on his life. If you take out such a policy, it has to run 13 months pre-suicide for it to be effective. Frank's secretary, Patricia Swan, had failed to meet one of the instalments and the policy was reinstated in September 1979. Frank was shot only a few months later, hence there was a lot swinging on the fact of the suicide versus murder decision.
- On the day of Frank's death, there was a $US100 million transfer to take place, arranged through the person who set-up Philippines' President Marcos politically and financially. No-one is quite sure what happened to this transfer.

Well, Frank's death certainly wasn't good for business and I have followed the ensuing events with a great interest, but from a safe distance.

All hell broke loose, with shredders operating in the Nugan Hand offices 24 hours per day.

Claims of gun running activities and links to drug dealers and the CIA were daily features of the media for several years (see page 73).

- Gun running? ...... OK!
- Money Laundering? ...... OK!
- Developments of islands to receive asylum seekers? ...... OK!

But despite the media claims, I doubt if Nugan Hand was involved directly in the drug trade.

Following Frank's death, the continuing operation was run by Mike Hand, who imposed a reign of terror over his staff. There was constant

Nugan

• FRANK NUGAN: Dead. A 38-year-old Australian. His body was found in his silver Mercedes in January, 1980, on a lonely road near Lithgow, west of Sydney. Official verdict: Self-inflicted gunshot wounds.

Two names that may be behind the most scandalous cover-up in Australia's history.

• MICHAEL HAND: Disappeared. An American in his late thirties. Strong ties with the CIA. The mastermind behind the bank's illegal dealings. Last seen in a cheap apartment in a seedy part of Sydney in June, 1980. Last reported in the Philippines.

Hand

World's biggest heroin push in '70s

THE Nugan Hand Bank may have been the largest single heroin dealer in the world during the 1970s, it was alleged this week.

One shipment alone organised by the group involved more than 250kg of high grade heroin worth about $100 million.

During the Vietnam War, the Nugan Hand group smuggled a massive amount of heroin into the United States. Much of the white powder, between 10-20kg of pure heroin at a time, was sewn into the bodies of dead American soldiers being shipped home for burial.

These claims were made this week on a national television news show by convicted drug runner Andrew Lowe, a Sydney-born Chinaman.

He said that back in May, 1977 the Narcotics Bureau had information that partners Frank Nugan and Michael Hand were "bigger than anything ever seen here in the heroin game".

That statement was repeated in Federal Parliament by Opposition Leader Bill Hayden, adding from a secret document that "if you caught these blokes, all hell would break loose".

Mr Lowe said on television that he and his family used to do "straight" business with the Nugan Hand Bank.

Later, he had taken several leaders of the notorious Chinese Triad, who were visiting Sydney, to see Michael Hand.

Hand had assured the Chinese he had secure methods of bringing drugs into Australia.

"Michael Hand told them he had connections whereby he could trans-ship huge quantities of heroin through Australia for eventual distribution in the US," Lowe said.

One of the methods used was shipping container loads of machinery from the US to Singapore, from Singapore to Sydney, back to Singapore and the US.

"The trick was that those containers never left the ships. But in Sydney, several containers would be damaged 'accidentally' and would have to removed from the ship to be repaired.

"This was the time when the heroin was either slipped out of, or slipped in to, the false sides of the containers or into the heavy equipment itself."

Lowe spoke of his association with Thai opium warlord Khun Sa, whom he introduced to Michael Hand.

Hand then worked out a deal which gave him direct control over the heroin shipments from the Golden Triangle.

"He re-organised, streamlined and sophisticated the whole organisation so the heroin came from the one source rather than four or five different groups, competing against the other and doing their own runs."

Lowe said he knew so much about the operations because he had interpreted every conversation between Michael Hand and the various Chinese and Thai leaders.

THE Sydney-based Nugan Hand merchant banker had peak assets of more than $1000 million, only a few short years after it opened its doors in the early 1970s.

By 1980, the bank had collapsed. Frank Nugan was dead and Michael Hand had disappeared.

This week, Deputy Prime Minister Doug Anthony has been shooting from the hip after forcing Opposition Leader Bill Hayden to withdraw accusations of a cover-up involving Anthony.

Now a royal commission in Sydney is trying to piece together a myriad of interwoven allegations linking the bank with the American Central Intelligence Agency, laundering millions of dollars of "black" money, gun running and drug dealing on an unprecedented scale.

QUESTION: "Why should we believe what you're telling us now? After all, you're a convicted drug dealer."

ANDREW LOWE: "I started telling the authorities these things in 1976, when I first started reporting to the Narcotics Bureau.

"I've been doing that up until the present day. I've seen a lot and some very funny things with people in high places.

"Now things have come to a head and people should be entitled to know what's going on.

"There's simply too much suppression. There's been cover-up after cover-up."

'Sunday Independent' March 21, 1982

Boss threatened to carve up wives

SYDNEY: Directors and employees of the Nugan Hand Group of Companies were told by Michael Hand that if they disobeyed him their wives would be cut into several pieces and sent back to them in cardboard boxes, a witness told the committal hearing of a conspiracy case yesterday.

The missing director and part-owner of the failed Nugan Hand Bank had said this several times following the death of his partner, Francis John Nugan, according to the witness.

Stephen Hill, a former director and company secretary of Nugan Hand Ltd and now unemployed was one of two witnesses called at the hearing.

Michael Hand, Patricia Mary Swan and Michael Jon Moloney are charged with having conspired to pervert the course of justice and contravene sections of the Companies Act.

Swan and Moloney are also charged with having falsely sworn oaths relating to the disappearance of documents of the Nugan Hand group of companies.

Mr Hill said that at one of the meetings held in the offices of the Nugan Hand Group in Sydney, in the week following Frank Nugan's suicide on January 27, 1980, Michael Moloney said: "I know what's been going on in these companies and you'll all be going to jail for 50 or 60 years."

Mr Hill said a senior partner of the auditors for Nugan Hand Ltd, George Brincad, told Hand and Moloney on January 30, 1980, that the internal bills of the company were about five million dollars and recommended that the company be liquidated.

Following the death of Frank Nugan, the principals of the Nugan Hand Group met on Monday, January 28, a public holiday.

Mr Hill said he had removed the cash book, journal and ledger of his two companies, Illerengi Investments and S. L. Notwist.

He said he saw Ted Harland, another senior employee (who has since died), and Ken Nugan remove documents.

Article Sunday Independent October 11, 1981

Whilst writing this chapter, these questions were never far from my mind.

- Why was the focus of police enquiries simply to ensure it was Frank Nugan in the grave?
- Why no interest in finding the murderer?

media harassment and Mike Hand was paranoid that some of their secrets would be revealed.

Then, on June 6, 1980, Mike Hand himself mysteriously disappeared. A half-eaten meal was still on his table and all of his clothes were still in place, and there were rumours that a professional killer had arrived in the country with a contract on his life (see page 76).

Meanwhile, throughout 1980, there were constant reports of Frank Nugan sightings around the world and, just before Christmas, the New South Wales Corporate Affairs Commissioner approached Inspector Harry Tupman of the Homicide Squad with a request to exhume Frank's body for further identification.

His original burial, apparently, was a complete shambles. At first, police said he had been cremated but later changed their story. No dental records were checked and the only person identifying him seemed to be his brother, Ken, who said, "This must be Frank because he has webbed feet." [I always thought Frank Nugan may have been a hobbit.]

The exhumation went well and there was general agreement that the body may have been Frank's. He still had webbed feet.

The publicity around this time was intense as there had just been a break-in at the Tax Department's Sydney office, apparently aimed at gaining access to confidential Nugan Hand Bank documents (see page 78).

One would assume that there were some secrets that were causing discomfort in high circles.

After the Nugan Hand bank collapse, the AMRO Bank came out from Holland specifically with the intention of taking the Nugan Hand Bank over from the receiver. They intended to take over all the operating divisions and pay out all creditors.

Prime Minister Malcolm Fraser refused to permit the transfer of the banking licence.

The offer letter from AMRO Bank stipulated the licence as a condition, so they could not proceed with the deal.

This misdirected "nationalism" from our politicians damaged a lot of people and later we saw history repeat itself with the Ansett Airlines collapse.

Missing bank chief feared dead

SYDNEY, Sat. – Frank Nugan's partner in the $20 million Nuhan Ltd merchant-banking crash, Michael Jon Hand, is feared to have been murdered.

Hand had been hiding in Sydney and his sudden disappearance has led his lawyers to fear for his safety.

Rumors point to contract

From our bureau

He last contacted the lawyers on June 6 when he telephoned them, apparently from a house in the city's inner suburbs.

A friend who visited his refuge found it deserted.

A half-eaten meal and Mr Hand's clothes were still there.

Mr Frank Nugan was found shot dead in his car near Lithgow, NSW, in January.

The $1000 million Nuhan Hand merchant banking group was found to have failed after Mr Nugan's body was discovered.

A five-day inquest on Mr Nugan found he had committed suicide.

Mr Hand is understood to have left his plush Darling Point unit and to have gone into hiding about six weeks ago.

There were rumors a professional killer had arrived in the country with a contract on his life.

Mr Hand was expected to attend a hearing in the Equity Division of the NSW Supreme Court on Friday where the court was to adjudicate on a number of applications concerning the appointment of liquidators to his company, Nuhan Ltd (in provisional liquidation).

But he failed to contact his lawyers, and all efforts to find him have been unsuccessful.

In his evidence to the inquest, Mr Hand claimed Mr Nugan had "fraudently misappropriated a vast amount of money from the company without my knowledge".

He estimated the amount at "up to $3 million" but said it could be substantially higher.

The provisional liquidator of the Nuhan companies, Mr K. Shirlaw, estimated the Nuhan and associated companies had deficiences of $19.3 million.

Also in Sydney the chairman of Australia's biggest privately-owned fruit and vegetable packing group, the Griffith-based Nugan Group Ltd, Mr Kenneth Nugan, and three of the company's employees, were committed for trial on conspiracy charges.

'Sunday Times' June 29, 1980

Patchy rain

DAILY NEWS

Perth, WA, Friday, February 6, 1981

Phone 321 0161

AIR

NUGAN: ALIVE OR DEAD?

IN LOVING MEMORY OF
FRANCIS JOHN NUGAN
DIED JANUARY 26 1980
AGED 37 YEARS
BELOVED HUSBAND OF LEE
& FATHER OF NICOLE & JOHN

◆ The plaque . . . removed as a security measure.

Decision today on grave riddle

SYDNEY, Today: Mr Ken Nugan said today that he was certain a body to be exhumed from a Sydney grave later today was that of his brother Frank, a former banker.

Mr Nugan said he had identified the body in January last year because of plastic surgery on the nose and the distinctive jaw line.

He said that he had asked police if he could carry out the identification simply by looking for the webbed toes that he knew his brother had.

Police had declined his request, asking him to make a facial identification.

Mr Nugan said that he later confirmed that the body he had identified did have webbed toes.

Mr Nugan said he had seen the body hours after his brother was found shot dead in his car at Lithgow, NSW on January 26.

"There is no way that is not my brother," he said.

"It was Frank I saw on the slab."

Suggestions of a conspiracy to cover up the fact that his brother might be alive were far-fetched, Mr Nugan said on the Willesee 81 television programme.

◆ Frank Nugan

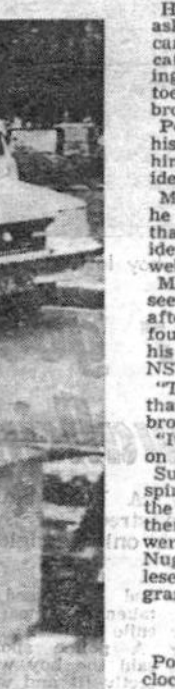

◆ A police patrol car guards the area of the Nugan grave.

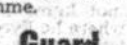

Guard

Police set a round-the-clock guard on the Nugan grave in North Ryde cemetery late yesterday.

It is shadowed by 30-metre high gum trees and surrounded by red roses in full bloom.

The NSW Supreme Court yesterday granted an application by the State Attorney-General to hold a new coroner's inquest and exhume the body.

Last year a coroner had found that Francis John Nugan committed suicide.

His partner Michael Hand, who co-founded the multi-million dollar Nugan Hand bank, vanished last year.

An unnamed businessman told the court yesterday that he had spoken to Frank Nugan in a nightclub in Atlanta, Georgia, in the United States, on November 16 last year.

City coroner Norman Walsh signed an exhumation order late last night to be carried out as soon as possible.

When the body was dug up, it would be taken to the city morgue at Glebe for an autopsy, he said.

Wife cries herself to sleep

From John Chenery in Nashville, Tennessee

More than a year after her husband's presumed death, Mrs Charlotte Nugan still cries herself to sleep "almost every night."

In an exclusive interview from their home in Nashville, her mother, Mrs Nicole Sofge told of her daughter's anguish.

"Why don't they just let Frank rest in peace?" she said when told of the planned exhumation of Nugan's body.

Told that the NSW Attorney-General, Mr Walker, was "99 per cent sure" Frank Nugan was alive, Mrs Sofge said: "He'd better have a look at the other one per cent."

Mrs Sofge said the family would be "delighted" if Frank Nugan was alive. "But we know it's a lot of baloney."

She said: "Frank adored his wife and children.

"Even if he was on the run from the law, he would have let them know he was all right."

Since her husband's mysterious disappearance last year, Charlotte and her two children have been living with her parents in Nashville, where she grew up.

Her mother says Charlotte still has not recovered from the shock and will not speak about it.

"This new thing about Frank being alive has just reopened the wounds," Mrs Sofge said.

"Charlotte has seen photostats of the autopsy report and pictures. There is no way she thinks Frank is still alive.

"Why would Ken deceive her? It's just not possible."

[Nugan's brother Ken, identified the body as his brother after it was found in a car on a deserted road in western NSW.]

Mrs Sofge said she feared the new developments in the tangled Nugan-Hand case would cause her daughter emotional harm.

"She doesn't say very much, but almost every night she can't sleep at all—she just sits there and cries," Mrs Sofge said.

"Frank was the first man she ever loved—and I think the only man she will ever love.

"I loved him too—he was everything you could ever want for your daughter. But we all accept the fact that he is dead."

Mrs Sofge said her daughter had not been interviewed by the FBI since leaving Australia after her husband's funeral.

Continued Page 2

'Daily News' February 6, 1981

Page 10—Sunday Independent, January 4, 1981

Tax Department burglars on trail of bank documents

NUGAN HAND BREAK-IN REVEALED

THE Australian Security and Intelligence Organisation has been called in to investigate a night break-in at the Tax Department's Sydney office apparently aimed at getting access to confidential Nugan Hand Bank documents.

The office broken into — the Investigation Section — held detailed records of Nugan Hand's foreign remittances and confidential interviews with the bank's senior executives.

Investigators believe these records of large amounts leaving Australia for overseas tax "havens" could help them unravel the operations of crime syndicates which "laundered" black money through the failed bank and dealt in gold and drugs.

By GRAHAM GAMBIE

The raid has forced the department to change all the locks in its offices at Centrepoint, install heavy combination-lock security cabinets and introduce armed patrols at night.

The Nugan Hand papers have now been placed under maximum security in a safe and only the most highly placed officers have access to them.

The raid on the Taxation Department's Investigation Section, which is highly security conscious, is one of the great previously untold crime stories of 1980.

Although the raid happened several weeks ago it was kept such a secret that not even the Nugan Hand Liquidator, Mr John O'Brien or the spokesman for the NSW Attorney-General, Mr Walker, knew about it.

ASIO and Federal Police have prepared a report on the break-in for Prime Minister Malcolm Fraser and Treasurer John Howard.

The Nugan Hand papers in the Investigation Section are completely separate from the bank's normal tax returns.

Only about 30 people are understood to have known about the existence of these documents. Because of the highly secret code of the Taxation Department there were no duplicate copies available to any

•JOHN HOWARD . . . receiving a report on the break-in.

other government agency or the police.

Investigations following the break-in have raised even more baffling questions:

• WHY did ASIO agents and Federal Police refuse to take fingerprints from the plastic folders when requested by the Taxation Department officers?

This has led to speculation that either the Federal investigators were so incompetent that they could not be bothered to take fingerprints at the scene of a major crime, or even that the break-in may have been the work of Intelligence agencies themselves.

• HOW did the Department's cleaning staff come to have a set of keys to the office without permission?

• WHAT is the truth of allegations by Taxation Department officers that Centrepoint management did nt know how many sets of keys there were to the Taxation Department office or where all the copies were? It was this fact that caused the Department to change all the locks in its office.

• WHY were 10 desks rifled, and two minor documents taken from another file, when Taxation Department officials are sure that the real object of the break-in was to examine or photograph the Nugan Hand documents?

"The security cabinets had been opened by keys and some other papers had been stolen, but we are pretty sure that this was just a front to cover tracks," a Taxation Department officer said.

"What they were really after were the Nugan Hand records. We refer to the incident as the Nugan Hand break-in.

"We are pretty sure it was an inside job or at least it was done with inside contacts.

"It was very embarrassing, especially happening in the Investigation Section.

"Even if someone had gone through all the records and photographed the lot we wouldn't know."

The Nugan Hand papers covered applications by the failed bank for tax clearance certificates to move large sums of money overseas to individuals and accounts in foreign tax havens.

The flow of this money was essential to "launder" black money collected in Australia and finance the operation of syndicates buying gold and drugs overseas.

Private accounting firms told the recent Williams Royal Commission into Drugs that the drain on Australia's overseas holdings through these gold and drug purchases was more than $100 million a year.

The records in the Investigation Section also cover extensive interviews with senior officials of the Nugan Hand Bank concerning the movement of this money out of Australia.

It is not known whether these interviews are also with the late Frank Nugan and Michael Jon Hand, the merchant bankers whose financial empire is in ruins with about $50 million missing from their overseas operations alone.

Hand has been missing since last June and there is a warrant out for his arrest.

After the break-in the Taxation Department took extraordinary precautions to prevent it happening again.

But as one officer said: "It's like closing the stable door after the horse has bolted."

Now only Class 7 officers or higher are eligible for security duty and they must check the security safes first thing in the morning and before leaving at night to see they are locked.

While the cleaners are inside the office they are now supervised and at night an armed guard makes two patrols. All locks in the office were changed and Centrepoint management given a limited number of copies.

"All these measures were introduced because of the break-in," the officer said.

The liquidator of the Nugan Hand bank companies, Mr John O'Brien, said he had 13 filing cabinets full of papers in his office and this was only a small proportion of the total.

Most of the documents were being investigated by Corporate Affairs investigators.

"I suppose we should secure our cupboards a bit tighter as well," Mr O'Brien said.

A smaller collection of documents from the bank was being held by combined Federal and State police inquiring into allegations of massive drug deals financed though the banking empire.

A spokesman for the Attorney-General, Mr Walker, said four Corporate Affairs investigators and two special police officers were working on the Nugan Hand inquiries, some part-time and others full-time.

SUNDAY INDEPENDENT

Tony Barlow

Lobby group named as . . .

NUGAN TIE WITH WA POLITICS

A WEST Australian political lobby group

•THE Nugan-Hand trail — what the Sunday Independent found.

'Sunday Independent' January 4, 1981

The West Australian *February 17, 1981*

Both Nugan Hand and Ansett were severely damaged companies, and if someone else comes along and offers to perform a miracle, we should let them do so.

Incidentally, the sightings of Frank Nugan ceased following his reburial, but Mike Hand "sightings" have been a regular event ever since and, ten years later, Brian Toohey (*The West Australian*, April 1, 1991) traced his movements without much trouble and wonders why the authorities did not do likewise (see page 81).

Four other writers have attempted to summarise the Nugan Hand saga.

1. John Pilger, in *A Secret Country* (Vintage Press p203–204) wrote this about the bank:

> One of Nugan Hand's distinctions was that its managers had virtually no experience in banking. But they did have considerable expertise in other fields, and were described as 'of a calibre and number to run a small sized war'. They included US Air Force General LeRoy Manor, Chief of Staff of the US Pacific Command and a specialist in counter-insurgency; army General Edwin Black, the Commander of US forces in Thailand; Rear-Admiral Earl Yates, former Chief of Staff for Policy and Plans of the US Pacific Command; and Patry Loomis, a CIA officer who helped Edwin Wilson recruit a team of Green Berets to train Libyans. There were numerous others who, in one guise or another, had worked for and were still working for the CIA.
>
> Notable among these was William Colby, who until 1976 had been the Director for the CIA and previously had set up the CIA's Operation Phoenix program of political assassinations in Vietnam.
>
> 'This thing is so big, it's bigger than you can imagine,' a former Nugan Hand executive told the Washington investigator, Nancy Grodin. The links between international crime and the intelligence services are, of course, not new. In its assault on Castro's Cuba, the CIA used Cuban exiles organised by the

THE WEST AUSTRALIAN MONDAY APRIL 1 1991

Half-hearted attempt to round up fugitive

SHOULD Australian authorities have trouble arresting fugitive banker Michael Hand at his home in Washington State, they could always get in touch with his wife, Helen.

Hand has been planning to join his wife, who is now using the name Helene Davies, in France in the next few months.

A former Central Intelligence Agency contract employee, Hand has spent the past 10 years eluding the feeble efforts of Australian authorities to execute a warrant for his arrest after the collapse of the Nugan Hand Bank in 1980.

As was revealed in The Eye magazine last week, Hand and his wife have been living in Bellevue in Seattle.

Hand left Australia on a false passport in June 1980 while his wife, who still travels on an Australian passport, left in 1983 to join him after stopping off in France.

The couple lived in Phoenix, Arizona, and in Coeur d'Alene, Idaho, before moving to Washington State.

The West Australian has learnt Helen Hand (Davies) is now living in France where she is attending the Institute of American Studies on the Rue du Bon Pasteur, 13625 Aix-en-Provence.

She used her Australian birth certificate to get her passport renewed for her most recent trip to France. She has also used the passport to return to Australia within the past year.

Earlier, money was transferred from Sydney to an account she operated at the First Interstate Bank in Phoenix.

None of these activities, however, seem to have caught the attention of the Australian authorities who might have been expected to keep an interest in her movements if they wanted to catch up with her husband.

Even if Australian authorities were unaware of her movements, it seems inconceivable that the American authorities did not know Hand had returned to the US.

The Australian Federal Police, which has officers stationed in the Australian Embassy in Washington DC, is supposed to maintain close liaison with the FBI while our intelligence services boast about even more intimate relations with their US counterparts.

Yet not a word appears to have been passed along the intelligence or police channels about Hand's presence in the US.

The warrant for his arrest was issued after documents were destroyed in the wake of the collapse of the bank he had co-founded with Frank Nugan in the mid-1970s.

The collapse occurred after Nugan was found shot dead in January 1980 — the official verdict was suicide.

One director later said on oath that Hand had warned: "If we didn't do what we were told, and things weren't handled properly, our wives would be cut into pieces and put in boxes and sent back to us."

Millions of dollars were discovered to be missing from the bank, which had specialised in shifting "black money" around the globe.

Customers included drug dealers, such as the Murray Riley and Mr Asia syndicates, and tax evaders, intelligence agencies and gun runners.

Tax evaders were a particularly easy mark — a matriarch of one of Melbourne's most prestigious families handed over $800,000 in cash in a suitcase, never to see it again.

True to form, leading Australian banks and international auditing firms had given Nugan Hand the thumbs up until its questionable activities became too glaringly obvious.

Unhappily for the Australian law enforcement system, no one has ever gone to trial in the wake of the Nugan Hand collapse.

The failure to nail those responsible for the missing millions (let alone for anything else) sent a clear signal to the cowboys of the corporate world that it would be open slather for the rest of the 1980s.

If tough action had been taken on Nugan Hand at the start of the decade we might have been spared at least some of the corporate skulduggery that ensued.

Both the NSW Corporate Affairs Commission and a joint Federal-State police task force made a good start on investigating the bank before the job was handed over to a royal commission conducted by Justice Donald Stewart.

Although not a single prosecution resulted from the royal commission, Justice Stewart later was promoted to the position of inaugural head of the National Crime Authority.

As royal commissioner he spent considerable time criticising the earlier work done by the CAC, the police and the media, paying particular attention to attacking claims about Nugan Hand's intelligence links.

Nevertheless, a highly regarded Wall Street Journal writer, Jonathon Kwitny, had no doubt about the links, writing a book on the topic called "The Crimes of Patriots".

Many of the key Nugan Hand figures were later revealed as deeply involved in the Irangate scandal, involving the sale of arms to Iran to help finance Contra rebels in Nicaragua.

Apart from the revealing fact that documents on Nugan Hand sought from the American FBI under the Freedom of Information Act were withheld on national security grounds, detailed information about the bank's intelligence connections has been provided by several ex-CIA officials.

The former head of covert action in the agency, Ted Shackley, told Australian police that Hand worked for him in the CIA in Indochina after leaving the US Special Forces in the late 1960s.

Justice Stewart was given a copy of this record of interview yet overlooked this admission when dismissing claims about Hand's links to the CIA.

In discussing William Colby, the former head of the CIA whose business card was found on Nugan at the time of his death, Justice Stewart repeated the official "cover story" that Hand worked for the State Department in Vietnam.

Mr Colby was not so coy, freely stating in his autobiography "Honourable Men" that he had been the CIA station chief in Saigon.

Justice Stewart's inability to see any Nugan Hand intelligence connections has taken another blow with the recent publication in the US of new material in a book called "Kiss the Boys Goodbye" by Monika Jensen-Stevenson, a former producer with the American 60 Minutes program, and William Stevenson, author of "Ninety Minutes at Entebbe" and "A Man Called Intrepid".

There should be nothing surprising about the "dirty tricks" side of the CIA using an organisation such as Nugan Hand.

Yet, while Justice Stewart was busy trying to rebut these revelations, the bank was allowed to get away with behaviour that became a model for much of the corporate roguery later in the 80s.

Brian Toohey is editor of The Eye magazine.

'The West Australian' April 1, 1991

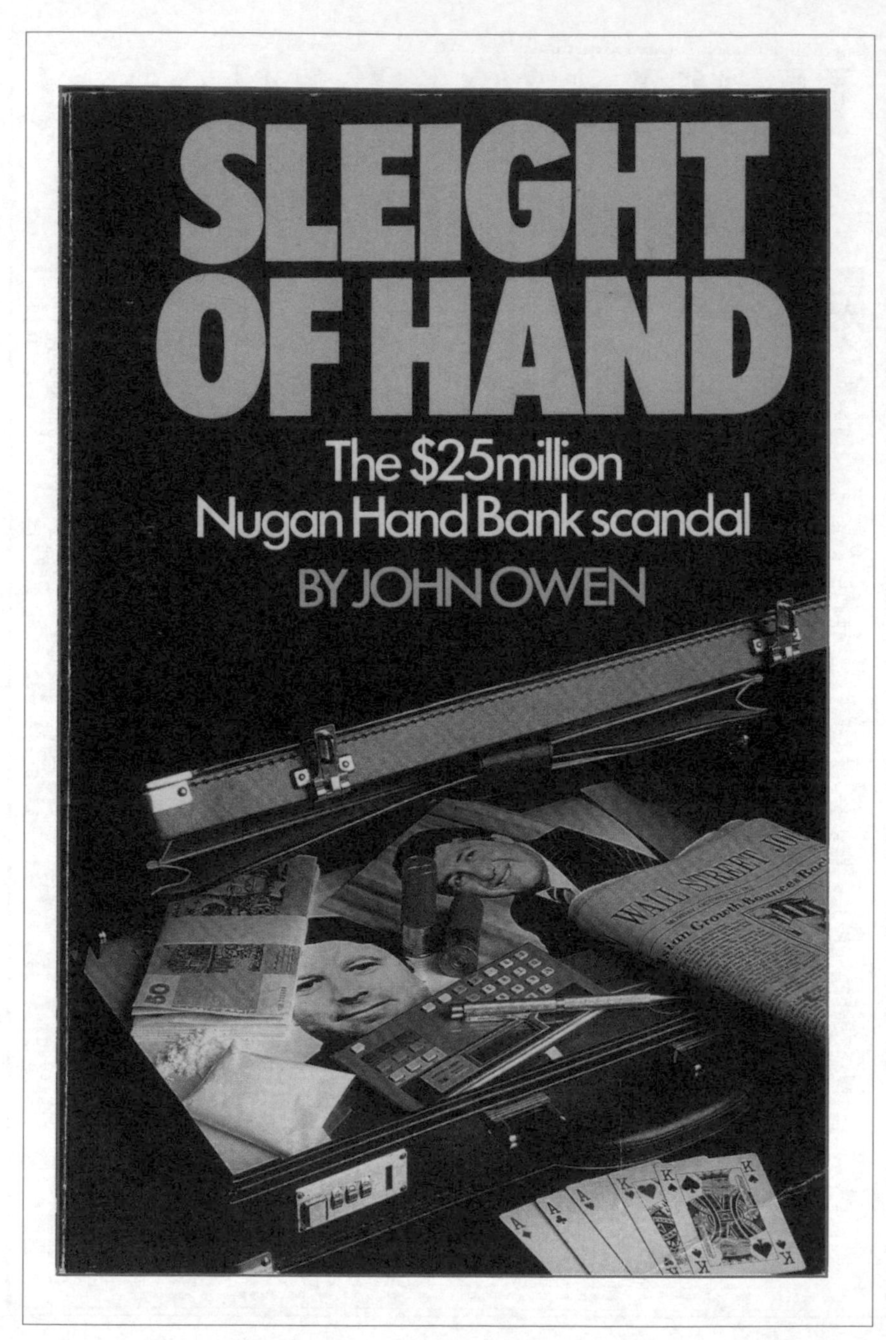

Cover Page Sleight of Hand *by John Owen*

Mafia. Nugan Hand's influence extended well beyond a hive of crooks. It was, in intelligence jargon, a 'conduit': an influence felt by Australian politicians, trade union officials and journalists, some of whom were unaware of the course of favors and of disinformation.

Former Nugan Hand principal Karl Schuller provided evidence that the CIA transferred a 'slush fund' of $A2,400,000 to the opposition parties in March 1973, four months after Whitlam's election. Schuller made this admission to South Australian Corporate Affairs investigating officers who were convinced he was telling the truth. Former CIA officer Victor Marchetti confirmed that the CIA had funded both opposition parties. Schuller pointed the investigators to documented sources; but none could be found. This was not surprising as thousands of documents were destroyed following the mysterious 'suicide' of Frank Nugan himself.

Incidentally, this book was suspiciously "sold out" and I was only able to obtain a photocopy of one of these rare editions.

2. Another book produced by a senior Nugan Hand executive, John Owen, with the clever title *Sleight of Hand* (Colporteur Press) [see page 82] hit the book stores, but was withdrawn following legal action. I have one of the few copies of this book and author Owen, like most of the Nugan Hand team, was curious as to just what it was 'all about'. His book would certainly make a great movie.
3. Yet another intensely interesting book was published, this time called *The Crimes of Patriots* (Norton Publishers) by Jonathon Kwitney. Kwitney covered the Nugan Hand story for the *Wall Street Journal* as it unfolded after Nugan's death. His pursuit of the story took him to Saudi Arabia, Hong Kong, the Cayman Islands and the Bahamas. Kwitney followed people in paper trails all over the world to document the complexity of the Bank's illegal operations. He found that an unsettling number of the people involved with the Bank were now dead.
4. Back here in Australia, Trevor "Pierpont" Sykes did some research of his own and, in his inimitable style, gave them this award:

> Company Of the Year: Nugan Hand Bank, in a walkover. This obscure black-money dealer was known to only a handful of people until it hit the limelight following the death of Frank Nugan. It now appears that this little-known bank had a turnover of $3 billion, not much less than the annual turnover of BHP. As 1980 closes, one partner is dead, one is missing and the Nugan Hand deficiency is anywhere between $14 and $50 million. A clear-cut winner, and Pierpont doubts whether 1981 can produce such champions.
> *The Bulletin*, January 6, 1981

Later, in 1986 (*Australian Business*, January 1, 1986), Trevor Sykes did a more detailed analysis where he stated:

> In preparing the 1974 accounts, various artifices were used to make Nugan Hand appear healthier than it really was. Through a "round-robin" of cheques its paid capital was stated at $1,000,005 when only $105 had been subscribed. Deposits were overstated and a profit reported, although it should have been a loss.
>
> A 'round-robin' is a device whereby cheques are exchanged simultaneously to give the impression of large transactions …
>
> If the cheques are deposited and cleared simultaneously at a bank, each company will appear to have done $1 million of business although nothing has happened in practice.

Trevor Sykes had access to the findings of the Stewart Royal Commission, to which I was summoned.

On March 1, 1985 I received a phone call from Les Peet and Brian Molloy, of the Stewart Royal Commission, stating that they wished to visit me in Kalgoorlie to ask some questions about Nugan Hand.

Coincidentally, I had just been putting away some old Nugan Hand press clippings and this one was fresh in my mind (see page 74).

With a very clear recollection of this particular press clipping I simply said to these gentlemen, "I only did a bit of prospecting work for them and nothing really ever came of it." Fortunately I didn't ever hear from them again.

One task remained, however, and that was to resolve the board of directors structure of Mining Resources (WA) Pty Ltd. A difficult task given that one of my co-directors had been murdered and the other was missing. So I held a board meeting on my own, and visualised receiving resignations from the other two. I also took that as an opportunity to resign myself.

The new directors, Peter Munachen and Geoffrey Stokes, were duly appointed in our place and the company went merrily on its way (see page 86).

A lot has happened since that Nugan Hand adventure closed in 1980. It gave me an opportunity to experience an environment where things were not quite as they were originally represented.

It was with some relief that I returned to the more open and rewarding world of the Australian mining industry.

There are just as many surprises in mining as there were at Nugan Hand, but the outcomes are usually beneficial to all parties.

This is one of the fantastic things about our mining industry, there doesn't need to be a victim for you to succeed.

Unlike war, where the strong overcome the weak, in our business as in most ethical businesses, the strong imparts strength to the weak.

You see this proliferating throughout so many industries. The thousands of joint-ventures where each party contributes their own unique strengths ensure that the combined entity gains momentum.

> Winning may not be
> everything, but losing has little
> to recommend it.
> .... Dianne Feinstein

In revisiting the Nugan Hand Adventure it reminded me of "Vertical Burial"and "Dubious Land Title" which now follow in Part 2.

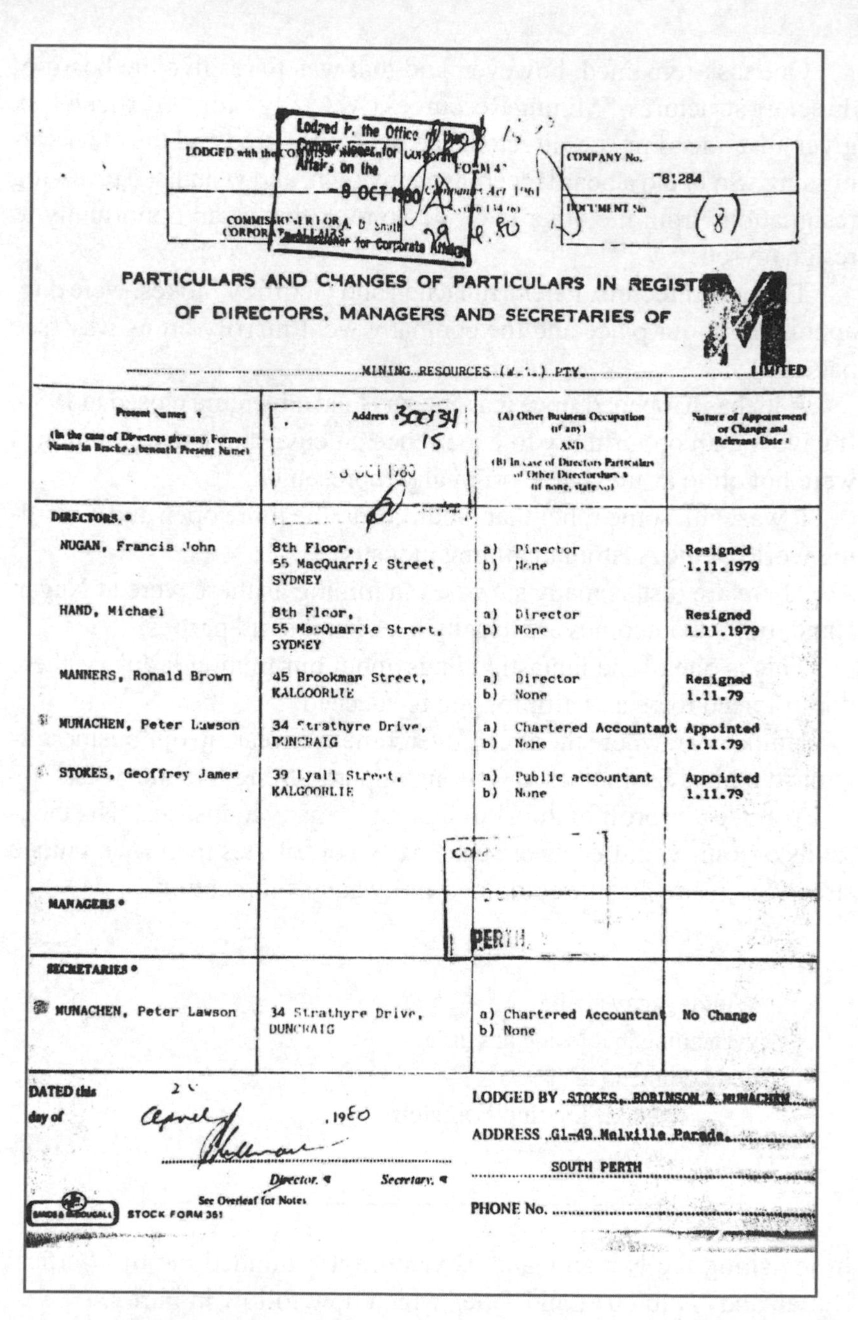
LODGED with the COMMISSIONER FOR CORPORATE AFFAIRS

Lodged in the Office of the Commissioner for Corporate Affairs on the —8 OCT 1980

A. D. Smith, Commissioner for Corporate Affairs

FORM 4
Companies Act 1961
Section 134 (6)

COMPANY No. 81284
DOCUMENT No. (8)

PARTICULARS AND CHANGES OF PARTICULARS IN REGISTER OF DIRECTORS, MANAGERS AND SECRETARIES OF

MINING RESOURCES (W.A.) PTY. LIMITED

Present Names (In the case of Directors give any Former Names in Brackets beneath Present Name)	Address	(A) Other Business Occupation (if any) AND (B) In case of Directors Particulars of Other Directorships (if none, state so)	Nature of Appointment or Change and Relevant Date
DIRECTORS			
NUGAN, Francis John	8th Floor, 55 MacQuarrie Street, SYDNEY	a) Director b) None	Resigned 1.11.1979
HAND, Michael	8th Floor, 55 MacQuarrie Street, SYDNEY	a) Director b) None	Resigned 1.11.1979
MANNERS, Ronald Brown	45 Brookman Street, KALGOORLIE	a) Director b) None	Resigned 1.11.79
MUNACHEN, Peter Lawson	34 Strathyre Drive, DUNCRAIG	a) Chartered Accountant b) None	Appointed 1.11.79
STOKES, Geoffrey James	39 Lyall Street, KALGOORLIE	a) Public accountant b) None	Appointed 1.11.79
MANAGERS			
SECRETARIES			
MUNACHEN, Peter Lawson	34 Strathyre Drive, DUNCRAIG	a) Chartered Accountant b) None	No Change

DATED this 2 day of April, 1980

Director. Secretary.

See Overleaf for Notes

STOCK FORM 351

LODGED BY STOKES, ROBINSON & MUNACHEN

ADDRESS 61-49 Melville Parade, SOUTH PERTH

PHONE No. ....

Register of Directors, Managers & Secretaries–Mining Resources Pty Ltd

Taxation and Survival

Perhaps we are all orchardists at heart.
Having prepared the soil, nurtured the vines,
patiently tending the trees.

Watching our fruit slowly ripen,
Evidence that our labours were meaningful.
Suddenly from the dark clouds, swoop scavengers,
to pick the eyes and decimate our fruit.
To remain as bystanders would be,
in neglect of our responsibility.

Surely we have but two choices:
Shoot the bastards; but perhaps they would
quickly be replaced by even more.

Instead, let's swiftly gather the fruit,
and store it out of reach.

That way the decision still remains with us,
of how we should share
the products of our labours.

RBM 1979

Touching

Touching, before the event,
is an investment.

Whilst afterward,
it is a pure gift.

RBM–2002

PART 2

Other Misadventures **Page**

Ron Manners addresses W.A. School of Mines–Curtin University, May 24, 2002

Build Your Bridge to the Moon*

It is a great honour for me to be with you in this capacity tonight. For 100 years, our School of Mines has changed a lot of lives for the better—and long may it continue to do so. This is certainly something to celebrate tonight and it also serves as an opportunity to acknowledge the untiring efforts of Sir Laurence Brodie-Hall and the other key players who managed to keep this School in Kalgoorlie. Many of those players I see here tonight.

I am happy to see Peter Wreford with us tonight, as he has served our mining industry with distinction over many years. The other night it was my pleasure to be seated with Peter at an Anzac Day dinner. I asked him at the time if he had ever considered writing a book on his experiences in the industry and his reply was, "My gift to posterity is silence!"

Bearing that in mind, I must work hard tonight to ensure that my speech is at least as good as Peter's silence.

Seriously, I know what Peter meant. If we are not careful, we can get bogged down in the past and that will stop us from moving forward.

So what I will do tonight is distil the essence of the past, which is experience; and connect it to the future, which is opportunity.

The task of properly connecting the two—the past and the future—is made easier for all of us with the wisdom that is the common gift bestowed on those of us who have known the Kalgoorlie School of Mines from the inside.

In this very brief word-picture, I will leave you with three things:

---

*Centenary address to graduation ceremony–W.A. School of Mines–Curtin University, May 24, '02

- Some quick “snapshots” of an earlier School of Mines that was simply dedicated to producing useful people.
- A brief explanation about why I am an optimist.
- Some concluding thoughts on leadership.

Let’s get on with it!

Looking Back

In the 1950s and 1960s, it was common for students to leave the local High School at the age of 15, after passing their Junior Certificate and then complete the normal two-year Leaving Certificate (T.E.E.) in one year, at the Kalgoorlie School of Mines. This had the effect of getting students into “useful subjects” a little earlier, and some of my friends were entering the mysteries of geology in this way. They were discussing this at our home one day when my mother started asking them some geological questions.

They “freaked out” at this display of knowledge from an unexpected quarter and the word quickly got around that “Ron’s mother knows all about geology!”

Several years later, when I enrolled at the Kalgoorlie School of Mines, it was pointed out to me that my mother was the first woman to study geology and chemistry there (from 1923 to 1924) and that she received credit passes.

She had difficulty enrolling, as there was some concern about the bad language she might hear in the classroom. However, she promised not to listen—so they let her in.

When I signed up for the first time, in 1956, please remember that these were the days of part-time education, when we worked in our day job and then spent three hours per night, five nights per week, at the School of Mines.

A lot of us had trouble staying awake during the classes. I developed some serious bumps on my forehead, caused by my head hitting the desk each time I dozed off.

That’s when I started smoking a pipe in class, so that the sound of the pipe hitting the desk would wake me mid-fall just as my head approached the desk.

There was an interesting bunch of “students” in the various classes, from all age groups, many of them already in senior positions; many others just starting out.

There are three vivid memories of my second sojourn, 1958–61. All relate to "out of the classroom" activities.

At one stage I was the Vice-President of the Students' Association and Editor of the School's Sigma Magazine. I nearly got run out of town with my report of the union belligerence that we witnessed on a sponsored inspection of wharf–loading facilities at Kwinana.

The following year, 1961, I stuck to less controversial matters such as developing a case for increased efficiency in local graveyards by adopting a method of vertical burial.

The following year, Doug Daws took over as Editor and somehow got his edition past the censors, but it was withdrawn from circulation the minute the Director, "Hobby" Hobson, saw his copy.

Some of the jokes were too colorful and the magazine's publishing team were forced to affix replacement jokes over the top of the offending sections. Some of the copies were corrected in this way and sold at the regular price of 3/- per copy.

The others that somehow avoided the sticker treatment became collectors' items and were sold for £1 each.

This resulted in a very reasonable donation to our favorite charity, the Lorna Mitchell Special School, that year.

Most of our activities were actually run at a profit, and I see from the Balance Sheet of the 1959 School of Mines Charity Ball that we donated £127.14/- to the same Special Education Centre.

Another vivid memory was a School of Mines annual dinner at the Palace Hotel.

The dinner started well enough, but unfortunately they ran out of food half way through the dinner. Being practical souls, we simply took up a collection and a few of us went over to the "Hot Spot" and brought back about 100 hamburgers which we unwrapped and ate at the meal table.

Ces Murphy, the hotel's proprietor, reacted violently to our initiative and became somewhat abusive.

I think we were beyond caring at this time and some of the more exuberant members then started pursuing the waitresses upstairs.

Some of the lecturers then felt it was about time to leave. This included Mr Andy Wells, a Metallurgical Lecturer who was also Metallurgist at the Lake View & Star Gold Mine.

As a bit of a joke, a student had tied Mr Wells' front bumper to one of the Palace Hotel veranda posts, obviously with a view to his leaving the front bumper behind as he backed out from the curb.

Instead it pulled the veranda post down and the balcony started sagging seriously. I think I left about this time so I am not sure what actually transpired, but I can remember that for some obscure reason we were forced to find another venue for the following year's dinner.

A final vivid memory was a deputation of three of us from the Student Council to Director "Hobby" Hobson, where we put forward a strongly reasoned case for increasing the academic standards of the School to that of a University. (A novel idea in those days.)

After we had exhausted our case, the Director said, "let me tell you what we try to do at this school".

He then explained that universities produced a very high percentage of "dropouts".

Here at the School of Mines we only produce "useful" people who go back to their industry, or their region, or their countries, and make a significant contribution.

If we ever see that people run the risk of not attaining their initial objectives, we then modify their course structure, often resulting in them achieving a Certificate Level rather than an Associateship. By doing this, I feel we are serving the students, our industry, and the country in a most satisfactory fashion.

Our deputation left that meeting in full agreement with Director Hobson, and we learnt that night that there is a lot of power in a well-reasoned argument, and his case was certainly well-reasoned for those times.

This was also useful early management advice for correctly positioning personnel and skills throughout any organisation.

We were all grateful that the School gave us this opportunity to "catch up", and I am still "catching up". And that's even after having three separate periods at the School, and perhaps a fourth in my future.

The first was in 1959, when I intended only to do a one-year electrical course. Our family company was electrifying many of the old steam-operated mine winders on the Golden Mile.

It was important that I knew which wires to twist together so that the cage or skip went in the right direction and stopped at the right place.

I was happy with my "single subject", but the very forceful "Hobby" Hobson thought otherwise and felt that this should be the beginning, rather than the end, of my useful education, and he eventually cajoled me into returning a year or two later. Mind you, it completely demolished my social life for what I considered three long years of my life.

Twenty-five years later, when I was about 50, I ended up back at the School of Mines doing a couple of geology subjects.

I needed just a little extra knowledge because I found myself running a couple of mining companies for other people, and I really wanted to get one going myself.

Countless hordes of useful people have been produced from this School of Mines and any time I travel I meet them because they are out there operating significant projects in every part of the world.

Each of my three periods at this School were great years, and I feel as though I have joined one of the world's greatest clubs just by being part of that "catching up" experience.

The School has certainly moved on since those days, as has the whole of the mining industry, and it is now far too safety-conscious to have blokes like me twisting wires together.

Yes, the School of Mines has moved on, now being part of Curtin University. This leads me to ask, "What is a university?" It is important to understand what a university actually is.

A useful discussion on this question came from noted scholar Michael Novak who expressed it in these words:

> The best answer to that may be to ask today's graduates: What changes have been wrought in you by your four years at this university? What is a university? It is what has changed you. And you, fellow parents, you may want to know what is a university—what is it that you have so sacrificed to pay for?
>
> A university is not a library. Were that all a university is, you graduates could have gotten it free, for the cost of a connection to the internet. A university is also not, although you will find this harder to believe, the search for a parking place. It is not, really, classrooms and laboratories. It is not a basketball court and a music hall and a chapel.

> A university is a blessed place, a sacred space in which persons converse in the pursuit of universal knowledge. In universities, mind speaks to mind, and (over time) heart speaks to heart. For what we learn from one another in our talks together, our lectures and seminars and discussions and question periods and exchanges, is how individual humans go about making judgments, what they count important, what they set aside as trivial or irrelevant, what they laugh at and what they take seriously, what is false even if it seems attractive, what is true and to be clung to even if it is unpopular and despised, and what is worth dying for.

So what of the future?

Why am I an Optimist?

Well, I was thinking about that this morning, when I realised that I felt more adrenaline flowing from having dinner last night with our own management team of 20 executives than I did from spending last week in Queensland at the Australian Institute of Company Directors' Annual Conference, where 500 of Australia's captains of industry were gathered.

Why was this?

I think that Australia's corporate captains feel that they have already reached the "dizzy heights", and are preoccupied 90 per cent of the time with compliance issues with only 10 per cent devoted to creativity issues.

With our team, we are all still on the way up, with much more yet to achieve, so we focus 90 per cent on creativity issues and only 10 per cent of our time on compliance.

This is not to denigrate compliance with the myriad of regulations, but if you let them take over, then nothing will be discovered or produced.

Some Concluding Thoughts on Leadership

In these days of continued erosion of trust and confidence in those who present themselves to us as our leaders, where can we really look for leadership and example?

This is something that worries me a lot, as some of our leaders have completely lost touch with reality (I could expand at greater length but will not do this tonight).

Let me suggest to you that you will find better examples of exemplary leadership much closer at hand than you might expect.

The more remote and removed from the creative process, the more the tendency is for these so-called leaders to indulge in misguided virtue.

In such a situation we have one of the major initiatives of the larger mining companies now described by Professor David Henderson(1) (Westminster Business School) and Phillip Crowson (formerly Chief Economist for Rio Tinto) in a joint report published in the April, 2002 issue of the Mining Journal,(2) summing up with these words:

> "It is surprising, and perplexing, that the industry has gone out of its way to sponsor a venture so deficient in its conception and its execution."

To you new graduates, please engage vigorously in policy matters within the industry and, most importantly, understand and learn to defend the significance of our industry, an industry that produces 42 per cent of Australia's export income.

We have the difficult task of creating enterprises. This is largely done by low-profile people with plenty of self-esteem (like ourselves), but it is those who tear down enterprises that are always striving for maximum publicity as they voice their shrill messages.

Don't ever let these detractors deter you from your productive challenges. Anyone without a clear vision of their future, ceases to live.

One of my favorite philosophers, Henry David Thoreau, once said:

> "Youth gets together the materials for a bridge to the moon, but later the middle-aged man decides to make a woodshed with them."

As you embark on your careers, don't let lesser people turn your "bridges to the moon" into any "old woodshed".

Let your visions shape your destiny, and if anyone like this gets in your way—run right over the bastards!

Endnotes:

1. Author of "Misguided Virtue – False Notions of Corporate Social Responsibility". Publisher: *The Institute of Economic Affairs* www.iea.org.uk
2. Available at www.mannkal.org, click on "Publications".

Cremate and save carbon

Roger Dickson

Thursday, February 19, 2009

CARBON offsetting of cremations could become the next big green thing in Cairns with ashes used to grow a memorial tree and dispose of the carbon.

The concept developed by Green Funerals at Kewarra Beach includes five other trees being planted on Cairns Regional Council land, meaning a person's death also can help reduce global warming.

Rod Putna, of Programmed Solutions, said when a person was cremated about 160kg of greenhouse gas was emitted.

"Each green funeral will reverse the carbon pollution caused by the cremation process within three years," Mr Putna said.

"After the six trees reverse the detrimental process, they live on for another 100 years and help reverse global warming."

Mr Putna said the process, a local idea, included logging the location of a person's memorial sapling on to the internet where people could log on and learn of the deceased's history.

"We GPS the tree and place a pipe in the ground and the ashes are placed inside," he said.

"The tree absorbs the ashes through the root ball and your body carbon becomes incorporated into the tree."

Pet ashes also can be absorbed.

The council discussed the green funeral concept at a meeting yesterday and legal advice as well as research into suitable sites will be conducted to determine the proposal's feasibility.

Mr Putna said Mayor Val Schier and Cr Sno Bonneau were big supporters, having quickly recognised the environmental benefits.

Cr Schier said the memorial trees could be planted to beautify or revegetate sites that offer easy access, such as public parks or walking trails.

"No memorials or plaques would be used to identify the trees in any way," Cr Schier said.

2009 may be remembered as the year that the climate alarmists' shrill messages reached crescendo. Concepts were promoted by carpet-baggers of all kinds, all promoting fantasy as a replacement for science. The business community disgraced itself by lining up in Canberra with begging bowls, seeking special favours and subsidies, instead of questioning the epidemic of nonsense.

Vertical Burial

(An idea whose time has come?)

The *West Australian* headline "Headstones to go from old graves to allow more burials" (October 16, 2004) reminded me of an early interest of mine in holes and efficiencies during my time at the Kalgoorlie School of Mines (late 1950s/early 1960s). By digging into my archives I managed to exhume a light-hearted thesis I published as editor of the 1961 Kalgoorlie School of Mines Magazine (Year Book) on the matter of *Vertical Burial* (sub-titled, *Why is That Headstone Smiling at Me?*)

Headstones to go from old graves to allow more burials

DAWN GIBSON

Thousands of headstones will be removed from old graves to make room for more burials at Karrakatta Cemetery, much to the dismay of families of people already interred there.

The Metropolitan Cemeteries Board says there is no new land left at the cemetery and it has no choice except to move headstones if the cemetery is to remain open.

But this is cold comfort to hundreds of families who have already been affected by the cemetery's renewal program, which has been under way since 1970, and hundreds more who will be affected as the program continues.

About a third of the cemetery will undergo renewal in the next 25 years to allow more bodies to be placed between existing graves, resulting in thousands of buried bodies being separated from their headstones.

The headstones are moved elsewhere in the cemetery or stored until families decide what to do with them.

WA Genealogical Society secretary Wendy Bloomfield said the practice was a form of desecration.

It also made it difficult for people researching their family histories, who relied on graves for crucial information.

"There's a lot of land around the city where cemeteries can be made. They should go and make a cemetery somewhere else," she said.

Metropolitan Cemeteries Board spokesman Bill Bullock said although the pressure on land had eased recently because of the rise in popularity of cremation and the opening of new cemeteries, there was still a strong argument for keeping Karrakatta open.

"If we close down the cemetery, it will just go into disrepair and we figure that is more disrespectful than what we are doing to keep the cemetery operating and keep the areas upgraded and beautiful," he said.

"If we closed it, there would be no money coming in to maintain it."

In WA, families buy the right to a grave for 25 years, which can be renewed for a further 25 years on expiry. But after 50 years, the cemeteries board can refuse to extend the lease so it can carry out renewal work.

The situation is slightly different for plots created before the current Cemeteries Act came into effect in 1986. Because plots before this date had various lease terms, the Government decided that all old plots would expire in 2012, 25 years after the new Act was created.

One of the thorniest issues is the fate of graves for which a lease has not been renewed. The rights then revert to the cemetery board, so headstones can sometimes be removed without the families' knowledge.

Mr Bullock said the board tried to contact families to give them the opportunity to lodge a written submission in favour of retaining a grave, but it was not always possible.

"A lot of graves are very old and the contact details we have are very out of date," he said.

He urged people who had relatives buried in the cemetery to keep the board informed of their contact details.

A spokesman for Local Government Minister Ljiljanna Ravlich, who took over the portfolio from Tom Stephens four weeks ago, said she had requested a briefing from the cemeteries board.

Protest at path over the dead

Like many Irish women of her generation, Margaret Nora Lyons believed walking on somebody's grave was bad luck.

So it is ironic that Mrs Lyons' remains are now buried beneath a path, along with the remains of her husband William and her infant son Mattie, as a result of the renewal program at Karrakatta Cemetery. Hundreds of visitors to the Catholic section of the cemetery now unknowingly walk over the bodies of the Lyons family, whose headstone has been moved about 40m.

The situation has angered Mrs Lyons' granddaughter, Gay O'Neill, who visited the grave yesterday for the first time since the move.

Armed with a cemetery map and the grave plot number, it still took her 20 minutes to find the moved headstone.

"I understand that the remains have not been removed, but it is the sacredness of it," Mrs O'Neill said. "We trust that when we bury our loved ones they will be there longer than 50 years."

Metropolitan Cemeteries Board spokesman Bill Bullock said the board had been unable to get in touch with any of the Lyons' descendants when the decision was made to renew that section of the cemetery.

ard to find: Gay O'Neill is upset that the tombstone of her grandparents has been moved 40m. Picture: Barry Baker

Headstones–'The West Australian'–October 16, 2004

In 1961 this idea may have been ahead of its time, but now, with the crisis at Karrakatta Cemetery, it reminds me of that quotation from Victor Hugo:

> "You can defeat an army but you can't defeat an idea whose time has come."

It seems that I was uneasy at the lack of efficiency exhibited at the local graveyard and I noted that in order to bury one human body (cubic displacement approximately two cubic yards[(1)] boxed) the authorities were shifting 11 cubic yards of earth. Also, further on the debit side, nine cubic yards of this earth had to be replaced. The overall displacement efficiency was 15 per cent.

I proposed that with Vertical Burial, in close proximity to the surface, a displacement efficiency figure approaching 100 per cent might be obtained.

My hopes for realization of this objective crashed upon discovery of a Council bylaw containing the clause "minimum depth – six feet below the surface". To conform with this bylaw, total depth for Vertical Burial would be 12 feet, thereby reducing the efficiency figure to 50 per cent and greatly increasing the danger of striking oil (which would necessitate heavy concrete ballasting of the "interred" lest it repeatedly float to the surface).

These investigations were coming to a dead end but were resuscitated after experimentation with some of the newer rigid plastics.

These were considered to be an ideal way of preventing decomposition of the deceased.

Furthermore, results from this new "PVC Plastic People Dip" were surpassing all expectations and, with recognition of the potential of this new encasing method, we approached local authorities who agreed that this new coating afforded sufficient protection against the elements, hungry canines and vandals.

This breakthrough paved the way for obtaining maximum efficiency in the graveyard.

Having gone this far, we wondered at the possibility of going beyond the ultimate goal of 100 per cent efficiency.

As I put it in the magazine:

"Yes," said one student to their dismay
"Drop them down only part of the way."
Efficiencies reached by using this plan
would ensure its acceptance by civilized man.

Their heads and shoulders transparently cased
Set with expressions, some pleasantly faced.
Headstones of stone, there would be no more.
Epitaphs now moulded below the jaw.

In fact, it seems in reality
headstones for ever they would be.
For tourists our town would be a must
Now somewhere to sit, up out of the dust.

Seated on heads in circles arrayed
With assorted expressions gaily displayed.
Many an hour they could spend each day
discussing the merits of those passed away.

This one, it seemed died in great pain,
he'd taken Chem. I, and been driven insane.
The man on our right had taken Maths II,
from the look of delight, he'd surely scraped through.

Plain to see he's an engineer,
the look on his face is so sincere.
Higher efficiencies may be made,
by using a Ramset instead of a spade.

The bodies are sorted and the tall and slim
may be loaded in Ramset and driven straight in.
Now that you've heard all about our plan,
we hope you'll all die, just as soon as you can.

RBM 1961

Now, lest you feel that I was being irreverent about the dead, let me quote the well-known philosopher Woody Allen, who once said:

> "The difference between sex and death is that with death you can do it alone and no one is going to make fun of you."

The only reason I mentioned the Vertical Burial Project, devised so many years ago, was to suggest that it may have been a Heroic Misadventure then, but now, over 40 years later, it must be an "idea whose time has come".

The idea is not patented but, as vertical holes for vertical burial could be a way for the drilling industry to diversify in times of mineral turndown, I'll simply leave that thought with you.

Endnotes:

1. Cubic yards in 1961, since replaced by cubic metres as unit of measure.

Freedom and Advertising

We expect freedom in Australia.

Freedom to choose the way we meet the challenges of life.

Freedom to compete, to risk, to fail, and to succeed.

No resource is more precious than freedom.

It enriches our personal lives and the lives of those around us.

And yet it can be taken away if we allow it,
By the same government that can assure our personal freedom.

Something to think about as government spends our money trying to influence us to its way of thinking.

RBM - 1979

Hong Kong Land Title

Dubious Land Title

(Land Access & Property Rights)

In 1979 I purchased a block of land in Hong Kong. I still have the title *(see facing page)*, headed "Document of Land Ownership", and it certifies quite clearly that "Ron Manners, the above named honourable person, is a purchaser of a square centimetre of land in the British Colony of Hong Kong entitled under this document."

It was purchased from China Square Inch Land Ltd.

Now let me compare that with an application in Western Australia for an Exploration Licence, Prospecting Licence or a Mining Lease.

Neither these applications nor the China Land Title give me useful access or rights.

The essential difference is that when I purchased the square centimetre of Hong Kong land I knew it was a joke, simply a clever tourist gimmick and I never had any expectations of claiming the rights to my so called 'title', for which I paid very little.

However, with the Mineral Tenement Application, that was different. I paid good money with the expectation I could proceed to explore and produce.

The scandal which confronts us now is that any of us applying for a mineral tenement would be lucky to live long enough to go through the various procedures that will give us the access, when in the past we could simply "get on with our job".

I despair at the outcome (or lack of any outcome) of what is mistakenly called Native Title.

Australian Aborigines do not have any title as a result of this and, simultaneously, the system of mining titles that previously gave good title is now severely diminished.

The Act was not well thought through and is poorly drafted. With all due respect to our High Court and Parliamentary scribes, I'm amazed how they can have had so much knowledge, but so little wisdom.

Since the High Court judgements, property rights have not only been reallocated without compensation for people's losses but, worse from an economic perspective, they have been stripped of any useful function —destroyed!

What is called Native Title is inalienable, and therefore cannot be sold or mortgaged.

Native Title is unclear as to ...

- ownership
- geographic extent
- rights that it confers

It is of almost no use to Aborigines and an absolute nightmare to investors who must steer clear of uncertainty.

It has cost our nation around $60 billion(1) in lost production, lost opportunities and lost employment and gives Aborigines no rights whatsoever other than to hold projects up.

Let's think for a while just what momentum and excitement Australia's mining industry could develop under the rule of law and some form of property rights, where we could quickly drill a few holes on exploration tenements.

No-one wants to talk about the land access problems that plague Australia and have caused so many Australians to seek employment overseas. These are people whom we desperately need to tempt back home.

I raised the question of the badly drafted Native Title Act with our Deputy Prime Minister at a public meeting in October, 2001 and, as someone said later, "I didn't realise that politicians could run so fast!"

ENDNOTES:

1. Native Title "lost opportunity" cost between $60 - $90 billion.

   A figure of $30 billion was the estimated opportunity cost of the Native Title legislation in its reduction in the value of mining projects, quoted in a paper delivered to the Securities Institute

Seminar on Native Title in Perth on June 4, 1996 by, Coopers & Lybrand Partner, Wayne Lonergan (now at Lonergan Edwards & Associates).

In delivering the paper Mr Lonergan said, "this is not a comment about the underlying social policy—it is a comment on a tragic and unnecessary waste of money."

Only a fraction of this lost value will flow to successful Native Title Claimants. Most of the lost value simply disappears because of the statutory time delays and the increase in risk created by the Native Title Act.

I have extrapolated his 1996 figure of $30 billion through to 2004 as "between $60 - $90 billion" for the following reasons:

Although my extensive files (see photo below) trace the development of Native Title since July 1977, the effects of the Native Title Act were only starting to make themselves felt in 1996 and opportunity costs have compounded since then.

No other detailed study of this nature has been conducted since 1996, to my knowledge, simply because it would not be regarded as politically correct to identify such lost opportunity costs to our nation. (Perhaps we need a study to identify the opportunity costs of "political correctness".)

Files on the Native Title Fiasco

Maluka Ranch ploughing, 1963

Ian Manners, the junior fencing contractor

Some days it just rained

Forty Years of Farming*

(The bureaucrats got me in the end)

My father, Chas Manners, trained for the land at the Ballarat Agricultural College with a view to running the Manners' family farm at Denmark, Western Australia.

Dad was pulled out of college prematurely in 1913 to run the Denmark farm when his father, WG Manners (WGM), returned from three years in South Africa to discover that one of his sons had made a complete mess of the farm.[1] Dad, the second son, then was given the task of running it (plus attend World War I) until WGM got cancer in 1924. That's when Dad returned to Kalgoorlie to take over his father's engineering business. This business still thrives but it is continually changing and is now based in my West Perth office.

Despite the ups and downs of the mining industry, Dad always had a yearning to get back and "tackle the land".

I saw an opportunity for us to do this in the late 1950s when the State Government started releasing Conditional Purchase land in Esperance at two shillings (20 cents) per acre.

That sounded "dirt cheap" and the attached conditions didn't sound all that difficult. You simply had to clear 20 per cent of the land each year and convert it into productive farm land. These responsibilities had a crippling compounding effect if you didn't have a solid cash flow from elsewhere to finance your farming.

However, this didn't worry us and we applied to the Land Board four times, each time being resoundingly rejected. The investigating panel had no difficulty recognising our inability to meet these financial conditions.

---

*Based on comments at an Esperance dinner with friends, marking a 'retirement from rural activities', on July 4, 2001

Not to be outdone by the bureaucrats, I found a second way around this challenge when I met an Eastern States farmer who had been granted a block of land and was experiencing difficulty meeting the conditions. His name was Jack Jehu. He had no hesitation in assigning his commitments to us. Of course the agreement stated that we had to pay him a healthy cash sum once we had completed our development commitments and converted the land to freehold.

I think one of the problems with this agreement was that it was highly illegal to transfer one's commitments in this way, and the bureaucrats once again became involved in what normally would be seen to be a voluntary transaction between consenting adults.

Opportunity number three came along when I found another 1,000 acres (405 hectares) of violently undulating countryside, relatively close to Esperance. It was just over the other side of Pink Lake and almost stretched to 11 Mile Beach. An American farmer, Jesse Skoss, and his wife, Rosemary, had been doing their best to farm this land but had continuously been defeated by the aggressive wattle re-growth, and an unwilling Shire Council which wouldn't provide an access road from Pink Lake Road.

After a few years of doing battle with this same aggressive re-growth and still being without an access road, I started casting around for some slightly more friendly land.

I knew the land around Esperance extremely well as I had attended school in Esperance when I was eight or nine. Not much notice was taken of the attendance record and this gave me lots of opportunities to roam the countryside on a borrowed horse.

I remembered galloping all over interesting, but relatively uninhabited land surrounding the old race course. In my memory this land had always been called "Pop Hancock's farm".

Pop Hancock had earlier been a prime land owner in the main street of Esperance.

A title search showed that Pop Hancock had "passed on" and the land was now held by a Perth-based solicitor, Charles Hopkins.

After spending a few days wandering around this land and finding everything in a general state of disrepair, with most of the fences either burnt or pushed over by marauding shooting parties, I took myself off to

Perth after phoning and making an appointment with Mr Charles R. Hopkins.

I arrived for the appointment in an appropriate "poverty" suit.

Mr Hopkins was curious about my visit but expressed a quickening interest when he realised I may be prepared to make an offer for this "useless bit of land that obviously he was unable to farm from Perth, and how I might be able to run a few stock there simply because I was based in Esperance and didn't have anything else to do".

Hopkins explained to me that although the property was in his name, he wasn't the beneficial owner but simply acting for the owner(2) as a trustee.

He explained that the owner had been talked into purchasing it by a person in Esperance who didn't have sufficient money at that time, and despite many promises, the Esperance person had not yet repaid the "loan" to the owner, even though the Esperance person had taken possession of the farm.

Hopkins had not seen the 1,600 acre (648 hectare) property himself, nor had the present owner, however their Esperance "partner" had been recently telling them how this land was not up to his original expectations and that he had intended to make something of a token offer to the beneficial owner in an endeavour to ameliorate his losses in the transaction.

I was heartened to realise that they didn't appear to have any positive plans for the property so I encouraged him to ring the beneficial owner and mention my interest.

He did this and I heard the owner say, "Well the young fellow's description of the land pretty much matches Mick's description, so you'd better grab his money while you can, but I suppose you should phone Mick Lalor in Esperance and at least let him know what's happening."

Hopkins then tried to ring Mick Lalor and was told that he was out of Esperance for a few days. He turned to me and said, "What should we do now?" To me it seemed pretty simple — they should accept my modest offer as it appeared there was a very willing seller receiving advice that the land was no good and that I was a reasonably willing buyer.

Hopkins thought this was a good idea so he asked me to wait outside "...but don't go away", while he dictated a Contract of Sale to his secretary. This was ready for my enthusiastic signature half an hour later and I was back after lunch with the borrowed deposit.

I bought a bundle of aerial photos from the Lands Department and then travelled back to Kalgoorlie that night to proudly show my father our latest acquisition.

A couple of weeks later I went back to Esperance and was walking up the main street when Mick Lalor saw me from a distance and he loudly proclaimed me to be 'a bastard'. I was curious enough to approach him and enquire as to his reason for the compliment and he mutteringly questioned me, "Who the hell told you what I was up to?"

Although I had no prior knowledge of Mick Lalor's involvement in the land itself, it seems he had the opportunity to purchase it but didn't have the cash at the time so he got this other person involved and then had been terrorising him with talk of how rotten the land was in the hope of picking up a bargain at about the same time as I walked into Charles Hopkin's office.

Each time Mick saw me after that he repeatedly expressed disbelief that I wasn't somehow "in on the plot".

Over the 40 years of ownership of that piece of land, known as Maluka Ranch, it has played an important part in our family's life. Mainly happy, but not always.

It was on that property that Dad died in 1966 when herding sheep from one paddock to another.

We used to run stock there ourselves, as in the early 1960s there wasn't much happening in Kalgoorlie and we were able to spend time in Esperance. So I know the joys of buying stock at the top of the market and selling at the bottom. We were continuously advised to get out of sheep and into cattle, and vice versa. Just after getting out of sheep, I remember John Crisp (our farm manager) picking up a destitute bunch of sheep for 20 cents each. He ran them on our place for a while and made an absolute fortune. I admired his timing.

One interesting diversion for me occurred in the early 1960s when I took on the challenge of confronting the extreme salinity on some parts of the farm, in particular one 32–acre paddock which didn't contain even one good acre.

I had read in an overseas farming magazine of a new species of salt-tolerant seed that had been developed in Turkey.

This Puccinellia species was said to grow vigorously on salt affected land and its sturdy stem, when trodden on by animals' hooves, created a suitable surface mulch which enabled other plant species to germinate.

I managed to import a limited quantity of this expensive seed from Turkey and the planting was so successful in this 32 acre paddock that I was soon harvesting the seed with a Victa lawnmower hanging off the back of my yellow Jeep (World War II vintage).

Fellow Esperance farmer, Ian Hay, was one of my first clients and I understand that he had considerable success with his own planting.

I am only mentioning this because, a couple of years later, I was selected, ahead of fierce competition, for the Duke of Edinburgh's Study Conference.(3)

I was always mystified as to why I had been selected but, many years later, when I again met one of the selection panel members, the late Senator Dorothy Tangney, I found out why. She remembered me clearly which led me to ask if she could remember why I had been chosen. She quickly said, "Yes, you were that bright young bugger who decided he wasn't going to be beaten by a bit of salt land so you went out and found a solution. That was the first Puccinellia in Australia and we thought this was a good example of problem solving and, as such, should be encouraged".

So, you never know where your curiosity might lead you!

During this 40–year farming experience on Maluka Ranch I appeared to be constantly persecuted by members of the bureaucracy.

I remember one occasion when a drunken shearer travelling home from the pub one night ran into a cow near our property. He may have been drunk, but not too drunk to cut off the cow's ear. It wasn't long before I received a Summons accusing me of permitting my stock to stray on the public road.

We never found the cow's ear. This may have helped identify whose cow it was. However, I had an interesting day in court as the Shire sued me personally on the assumption that the cattle and the farm were my own personal property.

Fortunately, I brought to court our company balance sheets which showed that the cows were company property and, as I was self-defended, I suggested the charge be dismissed.

However, the Shire Council's solicitor succeeded in gaining a 20–minute adjournment while he raced back to the council offices and did a title search to find in which company name the farm was held.

The re-energised solicitor then re-presented his case to the Magistrate and I thoroughly enjoyed perforating the solicitor's pomposity by agreeing that the farm may have been held in the name of Chasmann Properties Pty Ltd, however the balance sheets proved that the cows in fact were the property of Mannwest Pty Ltd.

The Magistrate did not hesitate to dismiss the case and award costs against the Shire Council.

I never heard what happened to the drunken shearer.

Still on the matter of the bureaucracy, I have several files in which I have been gathering evidence which shows that the Esperance Shire Council may be the worst Shire Council in the world.

When they succeeded in impeding the flow of water through the Coramup Creek, resulting in considerable flood damage to my farm and my neighbour's farm, it took all manner of legal action to make them face up to their responsibility to rectify the damage.

They knew they were guilty, and their senior staff admitted this to me, but their solicitor advised them to deny any liability.

It was only after two vigorous actions from me that they met their responsibility to clear the creek again. (One of their truck drivers had blocked off the creek with a load of gravel so that he could get his truck to the other side; and that's the way he left it.)

First, we had to get the State Government's investigator to pull them into line and, second, they suffered the indignity of being nominated (by me) for the 'wooden spoon' award for the most disgusting performance in that year's National Landcare Awards.

They did unblock the creek but never contributed to rectifying the damage done to my main paddock by their environmental vandalism.

However, all that aside, for over 40 years Maluka Ranch has acted as a friendly banker to our family and to our mining activities.

Each time we had trouble paying the creditors, or feeding the family, or paying for some exploration, or drilling a few holes, or underwriting a mining company float, we would sell off another bit of the farm.

When I got caught up in the spiralling interest rates in the early 1980s, while we were building home units in South Perth, we were rescued by being able to sell off another 13 sub-divided lots as Maluka Estate.

Then, a couple of years ago, we were able to sell our Golden Pond block on the east-side and this furnished our South Perth home and covered the cost of us shifting from Kalgoorlie to Perth.

That just about brings us right up to date but the final remnant area of the farm has been the subject of considerable farming activities, generally conducted under the watchful eye of rugged individualists such as John Crisp, Ian Cooke, Alister Syme and, more recently, Keith Hood.

To these people I would like to pay tribute as they assisted in so many ways. They have all been very patient with me.

Now, with 40 years of hindsight, I would say that Maluka Ranch has performed better as a residential subdivision than as a farm. It is currently home to 48 families.

For the last eight years my goal for the remaining 403 hectares was to adopt a detailed plan prepared by Whelans (town planning surveyors) in conjunction with Graham Gath (surveyor). They had carefully identified the various soil types and separated the fragile land from the lake system and from the more robust land classifications.

The robust land was to have provided us with another 47 sub-divided small holdings and a large area to be contributed as public open space, including all the fragile wetlands.

All this had taken seven years of battling with various branches of the bureaucracy and eventually we managed to obtain approvals from five of the required six bureaucratic entities.

The Department of Conservation and Land Management's (CALM) approval was still not forthcoming and, after an 18–month delay, we received a negative response. During a heated phone conversation with the relevant officer, I ended up giving him a lecture on property rights.(4)

In most civilised countries, when you own freehold title, you can do what you like with the land as long as you don't violate the rights of others.

He didn't seem to understand this so I suggested that if they wanted to make decisions about the land as though it was their own, they should be adult enough to simply purchase it outright. Then they would own the "property rights" and they could develop a whole new generation of endangered species if that's what they wanted to do.

There followed a strange silence at the end of the phone before he said, "Would you really sell it to us?"

Naturally, I didn't mind who I sold it to, as long as I could get a break from dealing with the bureaucracy. So a sale was quickly concluded.

So, here we have the end of an era, and this will be the first time in 70 years that the Manners family doesn't own property in Esperance.

Without any fences to fix, trees to plant, rabbits to shoot or creeks to unblock, my wife Jenny and I will be confronted with this new experience of enjoying the best beaches in the world and learning how to fish.

More importantly, we can simply enjoy the company of the nicest bunch of people that we are fortunate enough to call our friends.

Meanwhile, here is a quotation from William Butler Yeats that I dedicate to all bureaucrats, in the hope that in an enlightened society their powers may be diminished:

> I have spread my dreams under your feet;
> Tread softly because you tread on my dreams.

A gardener who cultivates his own garden with his own hands,
unites in his own person the three different characters,
of landlord, farmer, and labourer.

His produce, therefore, should pay him the rent of the first,
the profit of the second,
and the wages of the third.

—Adam Smith (1723–1790)

Endnotes:

1. The Denmark farm experience is explained by W G Manners in *So I Headed West*, ISBN 085 905 1234, pages 143-147. Pages 170-172 cover the farm's demise.
2. Later identified as a senior Perth business figure.
3. Refer to Appendix—www.heroicmisadventures.com
4. The right to acquire property is enumerated in many, if not all, of the State constitutions as one of the natural, inherent, inalienable rights of men—one that is not surrendered to government—one which government has no power to infringe—one which government is bound to respect and secure. And this right to acquire property off each other, only by such contracts."—Lysander Spooner.

   "Over the past century, Americans who own property—homeowners, landlords, businesspeople of all kinds, even non-profit organizations such as churches and charities—have found themselves increasingly entangled in a web of regulatory restrictions that have limited what they can do with their property. Imposed in the name of an amorphous "public interest", those restrictions have often been unwarranted and severe, resulting in untold personal and financial losses. By the last century's end they had led to the birth of the property rights movement and also to a call for both legislative and judicial redress. The movement is likely only to grow in the 21st century".

   From *The Birth of the Property Rights Movement,* a CATO Institute publication, June 26, 2001 by Steven J. Eagle.

Ron & Scott inspecting farm erosion damage caused by Esperance Shire Council (Photo April 23, 1991)

Farming; a family affair.

1964

Jenny, 1988

1982

Sarah, 1988

Ian, Scott & Craig Manners pegging the sub-division, 1988

A 'one page' history of Esperance

"Think Tank" (1974) left to right: Henrik? Kerry McCormack or Joy Lackmann, Merilyn Giesekam (Fairskye), Patrick Brookes, Mark Thier, Shirley Prosser, Bob Howard, Ramon Barros, Maureen Nathan, John Starink, John Zube

Party Naming Ceremony in Western Australia's Pilbara Region (1974) left to right: Dr Neil Scrimgeour, John Singleton and Dr Duncan Yuille (photo taken by the author).

Our Very Own Political Party

Up The Workers! - *(Heroic Misadventure* or part of an ongoing revolution?)

Picture the Australian political scene back in early 1974.

Australia was limping along under what could best be described as the worst Federal Government in its history.

The Whitlam Labor Party Government, in its persecution of entrepreneurial spirit, had successfully driven many productive individuals offshore.

Australia had emerged from a relatively stable political environment under Menzies' Liberals, where interest rates had averaged around five per cent, except for the brief 1961 Credit Squeeze (see page 14).

Menzies' successors then turned on the "printing press" and had interest rates up to six per cent. Then Gough Whitlam took over in 1972 and we quickly saw interest rates rise to 25 per cent by 1974.

The Liberal / Country Party Coalition provided no valid alternative philosophies, so throughout Australia there appeared groups of young people drawn together by an internationally emerging limited-government philosophy based on classical liberalism. Their focus was on ndividual rights, individual responsibility and limited government involvement in most aspects of our lives.

Most of these young people were introduced to this philosophy through reading the books of Ayn Rand (*Atlas Shrugged,* etc.) and some groups were simply called "Ayn Rand Discussion Groups".

Having been introduced to "limited government concepts" in the 1950s by Leonard Read's Foundation for Economic Education Inc. (see page 8), I was naturally connected to a similar Western Australian group. Though we were well aware of what was happening globally, we knew little of any other Australian groups.

Cover of 'Free Enterprise' magazine, First Edition
October 1973

Then, in 1974, I read an impressive Letter to the Editor in the *Bulletin* magazine signed by a John Whiting of Adelaide, describing himself as the President of the "Movement for Limited Government".

I met him in Adelaide on August 23, 1974.

Dr John Whiting saw a book protruding from my briefcase, written by Austrian Economist, Ludwig Mises. "Have you read that book?", Whiting said to me. When I said yes, Whiting responded, "Well that saves us about five hours, so let's get right down to it."

He suggested that I meet a bright group in Sydney who were moving toward forming a new Australian political party—Dr Duncan Yuille, Bob Howard and Mark Tier.

I joined this group's two-day meeting aimed at developing a political platform and found an inspirational collection of engineers, artists, lawyers, architects, pharmacists and the like, not only disenchanted with Australia's political and economic direction, but, more importantly, prepared to do something about it (see top photo page 120).

There was a larger audience at a subsequent meeting. Viv Forbes was given the job of organising Queensland, where he lived; Greg Lindsay was given the job of running a Sydney suburban branch; others were "sent" to Tasmania and Victoria to do similar jobs and I was assigned to putting together a Western Australian branch. I conveniently knew Lang Hancock, who was a strong advocate of smaller government and often saw bureaucratic obstacles in his project planning.

The Sydney working group was producing a magazine aptly named *Free Enterprise*, with the first edition produced in October 1973 (see facing page).

The three initial editors were Merilyn Giesekam (artist), Patrick Brookes (architect) and Tony Bryan (economist), with Maureen Nathan (pharmacist) as co-ordinator and George Carver in charge of distribution.

This excellent, modest magazine clearly stated the editors' positions on the benefits that would flow to all Australians from a dramatic reduction in government interference. However, apart from recruiting an ever-increasing range of thoughtful people such as Bob Howard (later editor of *Free Enterprise*) and Mark Tier, they were frustrated about not reaching a wider public audience.

MURRAY N. ROTHBARD
215 WEST 88TH STREET
NEW YORK, N. Y. 10024
—
SCHUYLER 4-1606

August 12, 1974

Mrs Ian Nathan
11B Redan St.
Mosman, 2088, NSW
Australia

Dear Mrs Nathan,

Thanks very much for your phone call. It was certainly exciting news that Libertarians are forming a party in Australia, and I wish you the very best of success.

I feel at a bit of a loss in answering your plea for advice. I am scarcely an expert on Australian political problems. However if your situation is anything like the U.S. the major political issues for the foreseeable future will be economic, and "middle class" issues: such as high taxes, galloping inflation, the welfare state, and swollen government budgets. If conscription is an issue there, then that should also be stressed. It should be pointed out that the mass of the public and of the poor do not benefit from the "welfare state". On the contrary, they lose through high taxes and inflation as well as the crippling restrictions and subsidies on the economy.

If you have any more specific questions, I'll be happy to try to answer them when I get back from Europe at the end of September. Once again, all good wishes on your endeavors.

Sincerely yours,

Murray N. Rothbard

MURRAY N. ROTHBARD
41 EAST 42ND STREET - SUITE 500
NEW YORK, N. Y. 10017

TELEPHONE
(212) 687-4247

December 4, 1974.

Mrs. Maureen Nathan

11b Redan Street

Mosman, N.S.W. 2088

Dear Mrs. Nathan:

Thank you for your letter of the 23rd November. I am delighted to hear that the Independence Party has been formed and I am looking forward to reading the Platform. Best of luck to the first Libertarian party outside of the U.S.

Thank you very much for inviting me to speak in Australia. However, I will not be able to travel to Australia at any time in the forseeable future. If I should ever do so, the Independence Party would certainly be my first port of call!

Best of luck again with your endeavors.

Sincerely yours,

Murray N. Rothbard

Murray N. Rothbard

MNR:lw

They noticed that advertising executive, John Singleton, had made several public statements that matched their own thoughts and on June 3, 1974 Maureen Nathan wrote to him, following up her phone discussion, and advised that she had "taken the liberty of giving your name and address to Bob Howard so that he can deliver the *Free Enterprise* magazines to you personally".

Bob then met John and explained that their group had ideas of starting a bookshop as a way of influencing people and broadening the scope of their magazine.

John's response was, "A bookshop, be buggered, let's start a political party".

Things were starting to move quickly and on August 8, 1974, Maureen Nathan held a dinner party at her home to which she invited John Singleton, Bob Howard, John Slade and Patrick Brookes. On that evening the founding of the new party was taken one step further with discussions about the need for consistency in ideology and the dangers of being politically expedient by resorting to compromise.

John Singleton asked if they could produce a written political platform within the next three weeks so that planning and publicity could start.

The challenge was accepted and that's about the time this new limited-government movement became a national organization.

The first step in assembling a platform was taken by Maureen Nathan who spoke to Prof. Murray Rothbard in New York. Rothbard was the economics and philosophic guru of the Libertarian Party of America.

Though aroused from sleep, through a miscalculation in time zones, Murray Rothbard proved cordial and offered to assist as he explained that this Australian initiative would be the world's second Libertarian Party (see facing page)

Why The Workers Party?

At that stage, the preliminary name for the new party was "The Independents Party" and over the next few weeks several other names were proposed and discussed.

Maureen Nathan recollected for me, on September 11, 2007, the background to one of the early suggestions:

The Sydney Morning Herald, Tues. March 23, 1976

Right-wing anarchists revamp libertarian ideology

By GRAHAM WILLIAMS

The Workers Party — the anar-

ment finds it cannot pull out of Big Government," he says.

"At the same time their socio-cultural libertarianism is attractive to the New Left with its pro-drugs, pro-abortion, anti-censorship and anti-conscription attitudes."

The party's radical permissiveness on socio-cultural issues, which shocks the Maoist puritans as much as it does

rial control if he wishes to exercise it.

"A great fan of Sir Robin Askin, the former Premier of NSW, John Singleton's personal philosophy seems to be a mixture of ultraconservatism admixed with an increasing measure of libertarianism and ockerish hedonism."

The fringe Right 2

Ayn Rand on capitalism

"We are fast approaching the stage where the Government is free to do anything it pleases, while the citizens

The Advertiser

Friday, February 7, 1975

But it alienates traditional … charms the New Left with its policies … inalising drug use, prostitution, … pornography.

All this is part of its policy of … dividual freedom. As party memb… Geisekam puts it, "Love of freedom is …

OPINION

Workers Party is 'not just a funny flash in the pan'

By JOHN MILES

DR. JOHN WHITING, suave, smooth-talking, smartly dressed, is not everybody's idea of a worker, though he does work hard as a general practitioner at Dulwich.

He is also foundation president of a new national political group called the Workers Party, started in Sydney two weeks ago.

His friend, Mr. Peter Kentwell, was introduced to me by Dr. Whiting as provisional president of the Workers Party in SA.

Mr. Kentwell is not anyone's popular political definition of a worker, either. He is works manager of a manufacturing firm. A production engineer, he is

piloted Lancasters over Germany and Italy and came home with a DFC, restless.

He became a worker, if a roaming one. He worked as a deck hand, in a chocolate factory, in a garage, as a salesman and even in public relations for the glossy … of British films.

social system in which a government could not take money from hard-working, productive people by force and threats of gaol, and give that money to people who might not deserve it.

The party was against involuntary charity, as practised by social welfare, but not against voluntary charity. Taxation would eventually be reduced to a minimum and replaced by fee-for-… and by private … over many of the … of government.

… process of de-con… would be whit… a limited authority … of police, defence … courts to protect … rights.

… all this be done?

… start with a crash programme for the …said Dr. Whiting.

…dney already we are get… hundreds of members to … meetings.

… will start here with key … cell meetings here in my … They will form groups of … own. We will spread through … advertisements to public meet…

"I am fully prepared to stand … Parliament at the next Fed… election. We will offer other

The Sydney Morning Herald

SATURDAY, OCTOBER 19, 1974

RAND FANS BELIEVE IN EVERY MAN FOR HIMSELF

'A beautiful time to be starting a new party'

By GAVIN SOUTER

BY REWRITING its platform, the Liberal Party stands to gain a certain amount of new support. At the same time, its qualification of such shibboleths as free enterprise and anti-communism may well break a few faithful hearts on the far Right.

This is the sort of climate in which new parties emerge, so it is not surprising to hear the muted sound of platform carpentry. The carpenters have yet to choose a name for themselves, but the most likely choice seems to be the Free Enterprise Party.

The initiative is coming from a hard core of "Rand fans" — disenchanted Liberals and others whose primeval vision of free enterprise and laissez-faire finds its best expression in the works of the Russian-American author Ayn Rand.

Others interested in this embryonic party are Mr John Singleton, managing director of the American…

eventually also from health, education, transport and communications. Taxes would come down, and …

National Service …

Initial Sydney & Adelaide media coverage (1974)

What is a Worker?

At dinner in my parents home in 1972, the discussion was heavily into political philosophy. One of the dinner guests, Thea, had come to Australia from Germany after WWII. Her husband was a furrier. They had adopted my family when we arrived in 1960 and our families had done some real estate investing together.

We discussed at length the various "-isms". Thea was adamant that Capitalism was not moral. In an effort to explain to her that she was a Capitalist, I posed several questions:

Q: Thea, you came to Australia with nothing?

A: Yes.

Q: You and your husband work for other people?

A: Yes.

Q: You have saved over the years?

A: Yes.

Q: You own your own home?

A: Yes.

Q: You own rental investment properties?

A: Yes.

Q: You have other investments that give you capital gain and/or return?

A: Yes.

Then I said triumphantly, "Well if you work, own and invest, then you are a Capitalist!"

"No, no," she replied very forcefully, "I am a Worker!"

In 1974 we only had a working name for the fledgling party. We had earlier talked about the political philosophy which recognizes the worth of people whether they work with their head, their hands, or the money they have come by previously. I had related the story of "I am a Worker" to the team, including John Singleton. For me the obvious name, appropriately marketed, was "The Workers' Party."

SATURDAY 23rd AUGUST
GOLDEN BALLROOM AT
SHERATON HOTEL 8.00 PM
(Attendance $1.50 Person)

The Workers Party

WESTRALIAN BRANCH
Invites YOU to Listen to and Question

JOHN SINGLETON

WHEN HE ANSWERS THE QUESTION

Why Workers Party?

ARE YOU CONTENT TO SIT BY AND WATCH CREEPING SOCIALISM TAKE OVER?

ALSO ADDRESSING - MR. BOB HOWARD
- NATIONAL SPOKESMAN FOR WORKERS PARTY

There is no longer a political void in Australia - THE WORKERS PARTY IS THE POLITICAL ALTERNATIVE FOR THE INDIVIDUAL WHO DOES NOT CONSIDER HIMSELF REPRESENTED BY THE SOCIALIST DOMINATED POLITICAL PARTIES IN AUSTRALIA.

ENQUIRIES - The Secretary,
Westralian Workers Party,
P.O. Box 148,
MT. LAWLEY, 6050.
TEL: 71 3040

Election Poster - 1975

To my surprise and delight, it was chosen instead of titles including Libertarian, Freedom, etc. To my total upset, the marketing was in the form of full page, fine print tabloid advertising. I had believed the campaign on consecutive weeks should have been:
Week 1: Do You Work?
Week 2: Do you work with your Head?
Week 3: Do you work with your Head or your Hands?
Week 4: Do you work with your Head or your Hands, or the money you have come by honestly?
Week 5: If you work with your Head or your Hands, or the money you have come by honestly, the Workers Party is for you.

My involvement continued in the West, having made contact with Lang Hancock who showed mild interest in some fresh thinking about the political problems.

Dr Duncan Yuille and John Singleton met Lang with his friend Dr Neil Scrimgeour, who was interested in the "new party". Lang flew them to the Pilbara, collecting me from Kalgoorlie on the way. A four–day visit from December 15, 1974.

We five discussed the platform and principles of the new party and, as Lang rather liked the name "The Workers Party", we officially named it that during a spell in Lang's pool following a hectic tour of iron ore operations and exploration areas in Western Australia's Pilbara.

During that Pilbara visit, details were finalized for the official launch of the Workers Party at the Sydney Opera House on January 25, 1975 to coincide with the Australia Day holiday.

Lang, although quite happy to be our keynote speaker at the event, declined membership or any official title as he modestly described himself as being "lead in the saddle" and a disadvantage for our new Party.

Though he encouraged us and gave periodic advice, he didn't contribute financially, later explaining why. He told me one of the books we gave him, as early briefing, was Murray Rothbard's *For A New Liberty (The Libertarian Manifesto)*[1] and in the corner of the front dust-cover was a small black Anarchist flag. This worried Lang, as without

Happy guests at the inaugural dinner
of the Workers Party at Sydney Opera House–January 25, 1975

any government at all, who would grant the mining titles? Lang had a valid point and I pointed out that Rothbard wasn't an Anarchist, but a realist in the sense that to achieve minimal government, one needed to aim for no, or almost no, government, with a view to landing close to your chosen level of government involvement.

Land titles, law courts and the justice system were, of course, all included on our list of "legitimate Government activities".

I'll always remember this example of how easy it is to lose supporters by pushing the envelope too far.

The official launching of the Party, at the Sydney Opera House, went well, with considerable media coverage by this time (facing page).

An extensive range of candidates was recruited in all Australian States, including regional areas.

Among the very high profile and influential spokespersons and candidates were Maxwell Newton and Sinclair Hill, ensuring media coverage of our message.

How did we go as a political party?

> Only fools seek power, and the greatest fools seek it through force—Lao Tsu

No, we didn't get any of our "own" elected as Prime Minister or gain "control", but many benefits did flow from a positive point of view. We, as members, all gained from the overall experience of learning the finer points of what we believed in, to the point of defending what, in many ways, has become known as "Western Civilisation".

This is a fair description as, apart from some fragmentary thoughts attributed to the Chinese philosopher, Lao Tsu, almost all the ideas of liberty are Western: individual rights, secure private property, freedom of speech, freedom of the media, freedom of association, freedom of religion, freedom of trade, separation of powers, equality before the law, and so on.

As so capably explained by Bob Howard, "As far as we were concerned, as long as you left other people alone you could do what you liked. This meant that we opposed such actions as theft, murder, rape, fraud, assault and trespass. It also meant that we considered taxation theft, and therefore all things financed by taxation immoral."

New party favours free enterprise

SYDNEY, Today: Most members of the newly-formed Workers' Party were either members or supporters of the Liberal Party, Mr John Singleton said last night.

Mr Singleton, chairman of the party, and managing director of an advertising agency, was speaking on the ABC television programme Monday Conference.

The Workers' Party which has a free enterprise, laissez-faire philosophy, wants government eventually reduced to controlling armed forces, police and courts.

This would mean no taxes, no tariffs, no subsidies or bounties and no welfare payments.

Mr Singleton said that when he and his supporters looked at supporting the Liberal Party they did so not because they had any belief or strong feelings about its policies.

"In fact we can't define exactly what their policies are," he said.

"We thought it does seem strange in a country as young and virile as Australia and so potentially rich that nobody within the Liberal Party has either the foresight or the courage to promulgate the only way these riches can be potentialised, and that's through a free market economy.

"There are two ways you can do this—you can hope to join the Liberal Party and reform it, or help to reform it; or you can give people an intelligent alternative.

"That's the course we've elected to take."

Mr Singleton said he thought most public servants were non-workers.

"The reason we chose the name Workers' Party was to hammer home to people the fact that the Labor Party exists not for the worker but for the non-worker—the person who wants to live on handouts and kick-me-downs," he said.

"One in four of the work force is a public servant.

"We work two days in three for the government but I don't think we get two days in three back."

'Daily News', February 11, 1975

Our preference was for governments to charge a "fee for service" for the few things left for them to do.

In short, we favoured a *voluntary* society rather than one of *compulsion* and *command.*

We were more of an idealistic or ideological party than a popularity contest, as we were pushing some very radical policies at that time—for example, privatisation of government bodies such as Telecom (Telstra), the Post Office (Australia Post) and rail and bus services.

Subsequently, many of our research files on 'Privatisation' were borrowed by the Australian Labor Party, along with our 'Victimless Crimes' files (where crimes having victims are to be given police priority to solve, ahead of civil disobedience matters where there is usually no sign of any victims).

Many of our policies have since been adopted by subsequent governments, even though the ideas took years to germinate— for example, floating the dollar.

The Role of the Doctors

As mentioned earlier, my introduction to the Australian Libertarian Movement was via Dr John Whiting and there was a significant group of medical doctors behind this movement for limited government. It continues to the present time with the magazine *The Australian Private Doctor* (www.privatedoctors.com.au) which remains one of Australia's finest libertarian publications under the capable editorship of Brian Bedkober.

They continue to strive for direct relationships between doctors and their patients, rather than dealing via government intermediaries.

The August, 2007 edition of *The Australian Private Doctor* featured articles covering the early involvement of Dr John Whiting in the Workers Party to mark his recent death at age 86.

These words from that magazine explain the leadership role taken up by the doctors at that time:

> John realized that "the problems of doctors were, in essence, the problems of butchers, bakers, carpenters, farmers, manufacturers, architects and all other such productive workers." John was a co-founder and Chairman of "The Movement for

JOHN SINGLETON
with
Bob Howard

Limited Government" which was one of the precursors of the free-market "Workers Party" of which he was also one of the founders and its President. He gave the inaugural address for the party at the Opera House on January 25, 1975. In 1975 he also stood (unsuccessfully) for the Senate—not because he wanted to be a politician but because he believed that Australia was in deep trouble under the Whitlam socialist government and that the opposition Liberal Party under Malcolm Fraser was only marginally better.

John was one of those "small but committed nucleus of men and women worldwide who manage to keep the philosophic concept of individual liberty alive."

John Whiting also leaves for posterity his three books:

Be In It, Mate!

Wake Up, Mate!

and his internet accessible *Are They Crooks or Fools?* (www.crooksorfools.com)

From the ranks of Australia's medical doctors came many of the candidates and branch organizers for the Workers Party, and many still play a continuing role in Australia's freedom movement.

Looking back, it was interesting to note that we were without a great range of "literature for liberty" and had to develop our own, largely guided by the books of Murray Rothbard and, in particular, Dr John Hospers' excellent *Libertarianism (A Political Philosophy For Tomorrow).*

One of the significant books produced from the Workers Party era was the most readable John Singleton and Bob Howard book, titled *Rip Van Australia,* which has become something of a collector's item.

In the past 30 years, there have been complete libraries published, full of libertarian literature, so that future Libertarian Parties would have a policy headstart—although whether that gives them additional votes is another matter.

Sunday Independent, April 29, 1979—Page 9

Sign stands victorious

GEOFF McNeil's sign has shown up a council's bureaucrats.

There were red faces under the bowler hats when they took him to court over it — and lost.

The sign saga started when Geoff put up his "Vote for..." sign outside his dental premises in Canning Highway, South Perth.

Triumphant Geoff told the Sunday Independent: "The South Perth Council did not mind at first — then someone complained and they told me to take it down. I refused — it was on my own land and it was an issue of personal freedom.

"Then I got a letter threatening a summons. That was in November 1977. I heard nothing more until May last year when I was standing as a candidate for the council."

The legal wheels ground on until Geoff was finally taken to court. But magistrates dismissed the case.

"I was defying the law for the sake of a bit of common sense. They told me there was a by-law to say I could not have the sign, even on my own land. They wanted to know if I had permission — so I told them 'yes — from myself'.

Better

"It is all so stupid. Do these petty-minded bureaucrats have nothing better to do? Why don't they do something useful?

A spokesman for South Perth Council said: "The case was dismissed on a technicality. There is a law to say signs cannot be erected without permission."

Did we get any members elected to parliament?

The simple answer is 'no'. However, in 1978, one candidate, dentist Geoffrey McNeil (Greenough, Western Australia), scored 14 per cent of the votes, coming within 50 votes of the Australian Labor Party candidate.

One sitting Liberal, Dr Peter Richardson (Federal Member for Tangney, Western Australia) defected to the Progress Party (successor to the Workers Party), so we did have a very capable and articulate representative in parliament.

In Dr Richardson's media release of October 14, 1977, one paragraph read:

> The choice then was to become an Independent or to join the Progress Party. A group of Independents offers little hope as an effective alternative party. I have adopted the Progress Party as reflecting most nearly the ideals for which I originally stood. It has often been regarded as a controversial party, but I believe very many people are in favour of its principles.

There were many other sitting members of all parties who often espoused policies either identical or similar to the Workers Party/Progress Party. Such an example was the Queensland National Party Senator, Dr Glenister Sheil, who also joined Viv Forbes and an Australia-wide group in forming the Foundation for Economic Education (Australia), with the approval of the original Foundation for Economic Education Inc.

We were always receiving interesting electoral feedback, an example being during the campaign for Farrer in the Riverina. There, Wal Fife, the incumbent, said to Workers Party candidate Maureen Nathan, "Thank you, you yell out loud what we can only whisper".

Reflecting back on that period, I recall that members of the major political parties often expressed envy at the quality of the writing in the various libertarian publications.

We had some "quality writers" and policy people such as Gary Sturgess(2) and Tony Rutherford, sometimes writing under his pseudonym Hamish Kirkcaldy.

Taxation/Inflation Protest.

Attend public meetings to hear:

.... from a 1976 Workers Party brochure

Author's mental 'flashback' from 2009:

I first met Maxwell Newton, one of the giants of journalism, when I was enjoying a very minor role as Kalgoorlie correspondent for *The Australian Miner*.

The hierarchy of writers linking me to Max (the big boss) included Ian Huntley, David Haselhurst, Ross Louthean, Peter Samuel and Jules Zanetti.

Our next encounter was when Max was appointed Director and Economic Spokesman for the Workers Party in 1976 where he introduced a vital new dimension.

Our third encounter(s).... throughout the 1980s was during his period as Rupert Murdoch's 'man in New York'.

One aspect of his tumultuous life to touch me in a permanent way was his infinite capacity to unravel the intricacies of economics, human action and politics and to explain all this in words that the rest of us 'foot soldiers' could understand.

I often wonder if I would have spent so much of my life 'figuring things out' if it had not been for Maxwell Newton's ability to expose so many 'clothe-less emperors'.

Max, always the master of the colorful phrase, as his daughter Sarah Newton quoted in her biography, *Maxwell Newton* (Fremantle Art Centre Press, 1993), "But as Maxwell would have said, 'Enough talk! Come on you buggers — time to get going and write! 'You gotta pound those keys, son, pound those keys. Spin it out — like a spider spinning it out of its arse.' "

THERE ARE FOUR WAYS FOR INDIVIDUALS TO ACHIEVE REAL POLITICAL & ECONOMIC FREEDOM, WHICH DO YOU PREFER?

THIS BOOKLIST IS DIVIDED INTO FOUR CATEGORIES:

1. BOOKS ON FREEDOM AND FREE MARKET ECONOMICS. (Education is a pre-condition for any meaningful increase in Freedom)
2. ECONOMIC SELF-PROTECTION AND SELF-PRESERVATION (How the individual can protect himself against inflation and other government policies)
3. NON-VIOLENT, PEACEFUL FORMS OF CIVIL DISOBEDIENCE (Against government and bureaucrats. When they go beyond their legitimate functions)
4. POLITICAL ACTION AND ITS USE TO ROLL BACK THE POWER OF THE STATE AND RESTORE THE RIGHTS OF INDIVIDUALS.

BOOKLIST, 1979

From

LIBERTARIAN BOOKSHOP

P.O. BOX 33, KALGOORLIE,
WESTERN AUSTRALIA, 6430.
PHONE (090) 212 728

PRICE LIST AND ORDER FORMS AT REAR OF CATALOGUE.
(Further copies available on request)

'THE POLITICIAN'S IDEA OF HELPING THE POOR TO BECOME HELPLESS IS NO ACT OF KINDNESS.'

L.E. READ.

One of several bookshops that flourished in the 1970s.
(The four choices, which do you prefer?)

The View from 1975

The View from 2009

Comment by author ....

It was an interesting exercise, tracking down so many of the early instigators of this Political Party.

Thirty years later, many had not lost their zest for living.

One example being orthopaedic surgeon, Barry Bracken, now 83 years old but still involved in medico-legal work as well as running his Hunter Valley winery.

Apart from trading some fine Hunter Valley red wines for some quality Western Australian red, Barry commented as follows:

"It was good to hear from you and it really made me think a little about the old Workers Party and Progress Party and what they might have achieved. I think we can take quite a bit of credit for making both the Liberal and Labor people think about what we were proposing at the time. The attitudes we were trying to push were reinforced by dear old Margaret Thatcher when she hit the ground running with copies of Hayek's books under her wing. Most of the economic changes were adopted and although we failed to reduce the size of government and failed on the flat tax front we sure won the battle of privatisation which has gone from strength to strength. I think there is still some hope in respect of flat tax as it has been adopted in Russia and other areas of Europe."

What penetration did we get on university campuses?

Not as much as we expected. We expected there to be considerable interest in the link between absolute economic freedom, absolute social freedom and absolute civil liberties. Perhaps we were just seen as yet another conservative party in disguise, or perhaps our intolerance of government grants and the conditions that come with government funding made our message a "hard sell".

However, interestingly enough, there was a resurgence of interest on campuses for our libertarian ideas some 12 years later.

This resurgence was presented in a scholarly fashion in a 60–page Honours Dissertation for the Department of Politics at the University of Western Australia, October, 1987, by William J. Stacey (studying under Professor Patrick O'Brien).

The title of this study is *Libertarianism in Australia's New Enlightenment,*[3] and in his introduction he comments:

> Libertarianism is a contemporary version of political philosophy which has been given considerable attention, at least since the publication of Nozick's, *Anarchy, State and Utopia* in 1974. Coincidentally, it is at about this time that groups of people emerged in Australia, who at first tentatively, engaged in political activity to promote a libertarian free-market economy and a minimal state, which was to abstain from virtually all interference in people's lives. Most of these people had never before taken an active interest in politics. They were motivated by a belief in the ideals which they held, and the confidence that in politics and all realms of human action "ideas count". A decade and a half later many of these ideas are firmly entrenched at the centre of political debate.
>
> This paper looks at libertarian ideas and the means by which people, who were at least initially novices in political activity, have over a long period of time promoted their vision of the good society, with at least some degree of success.

Then, a further decade later, in 1997, another published paper appeared, this time from Ernesto Zanatta, titled *Grail Quest: the Libertarian Enlightenment and the Australian University.*[4] He commented in his two opening paragraphs:

The 'West Australian' –Monday November 3, 1975

"Any of you fellows interested in joining the new, dynamic Workers' Party?"

'The Bulletin'–February 22, 1975

Once upon a time, during the mid to late 1980s and the early 1990s, while classical liberal ideas were sweeping through the broader intellectual agenda like a strong gale driving out stale air, a libertarian enlightenment spread out across the university campuses of Australia. In this enlightenment, the most intriguing and radical ideas offered by libertarian thought came to be entertained, discussed and debated as a matter of routine, as something to be taken for granted.

That this would happen is not surprising. Undergraduates tend to be encountering ideas and philosophies for the very first time, no matter how old those ideas might be. Consequently, these ideas always appear new and innovative. For undergraduates, learning about political philosophy, those with curious and enquiring minds are going to be drawn to philosophical belief systems such as libertarianism, ideas which are both more interesting and more morally uncompromising than the pragmatism of the liberal-democracy and democratic socialism which are usually taught in modern political theory courses.

What brought the Workers Party to an end?

In most Australian States, having to constantly explain the reason for choosing the name "Workers Party" became fatiguing, resulting in much internal debate about a name change.

In some States the name was changed to "Progress Party", in others a new party was formed as the Progress Party, issuing a simplified Policy Document.

Further candidates were run, with limited success, but I think that what really brought the curtain down was Malcolm Fraser's Liberal Coalition victory, with a record majority, in December, 1975. As Prime Minister, Malcolm Fraser expressed some interest in the philosophies of Ayn Rand.[5]

His election speeches were indeed refreshing and gave many of us the feeling we could "pull up our political tent and go back to work" as the country would be in safe hands.

THE LAND OF THE FREE

by Viv Forbes

ONE day in the land of the strong and the free,
John Rover said, "Brother, this job's not for me.
All I do for my pay,
Is file forms every day,
I'll resign and produce for my fee.

"I'm strong and determined, I'll get me a farm,
I'll build with the brawn of my arm."
But alas for John Rover,
His quest was not over,
For his lawyer was filled with alarm.

"You've no permit for dairying, you've no quota
for eggs,
You've no licence for honey-or pigs.
You can't trade in wheat,
They're closing down meat,
And there's levies on apples and figs.

"Not to worry," said John "I'll work with
my hands,
I can build, I can paint or drain land."
But the council said, "No,
Such a man has no show,
Till he's licensed and numbered and planned."

"Forget it," said John "I'll go work in in the mine,
They need men who are willing to sign."
But the men on the picket,
Said, "Show us your ticket,
Or there's no work for you on this line."

So John packed up his bluey and went back
to town,
"There's one place they won't turn me down.
I'll rejoin the department,
And forget where my heart went,
I'll be sure of good pay with the crown."

John Rover now sits at a desk, sipping tea;
He handles the permits and fees.
When they speak of their schemes,
He still thinks of his dreams,
Of what could be in the land of the free.

A visit to Prime Minister Fraser's office at Parliament House on August 26, 1976, when I introduced him to Eugene Guccione (Editor of the US-based *Mining Engineering* magazine), showed us that he was simply "just another politician", as Guccione commented.[6]

Several years later, when it became apparent that Malcolm Fraser had neither written nor understood his election speeches, we made some effort to find out who actually wrote them. Dr David Kemp was the author and a member of Fraser's staff at the time.

On reflection, the three terms of the Fraser Liberal government produced very little other than the fine work of a group of backbenchers known as the 'Dries' — Bert Kelly, John Hyde, Peter Shack and others.

Their outstanding work on policy formation for deregulation and freeing up the economy was totally overlooked by the Fraser Cabinet, but enthusiastically activated by the subsequent Hawke Labor Government.[7]

The opportunities missed by the Fraser Liberal Government caused many of the original Workers Party/Progress Party team to continue their political activities, focusing mainly on bringing free-enterprise concepts to an ever-widening audience. Outstanding performers in this field were various Adam Smith Clubs in several States; Elaine Palmer, Nadia Weiner, Graeme McKinnon and John Clemitson with their widely circulating magazines *On Liberty, Optimism* and *The Optimist,* and their Centre 2000 bookshop in Sydney; Michael Darby and his regular magazine *Free Market;* and Dr Hal Soper with his regular *Progress Party Newsletter.*

In Melbourne the main torch bearers continue to be Prodos Marinakis (www.prodos.com.au) and The Institute of Public Affairs (www.ipa.org.au) although not bred from libertarian roots, has always been a strong supporter of free markets and limited government. A great team of activists continues in Western Australia.[8]

Announcing A Brand-New Australian Libertarian Party

In September 2007 a new libertarian party was federally registered in Australia, run by a new breed of libertarian activists. The Liberty and Democracy Party (LDP) was started by John Humphreys in 2001 and has run twice in the ACT as the Liberal Democratic Party, receiving

Greg Lindsay, AO (left) continues his freedom philosophy career with his Centre for Independent Studies (www.cis.org.au) and the Mont Pelerin Society. Pictured here with the author, selecting which sake Barrel to open.

Both photos from the Mont Pelerin Society General Meeting - Tokyo 2008. Professor Hiromitsu Ishi, Greg Lindsay, AO and Professor Victoria Curzon Price, performing 'Kagami-biraki', a ceremony performed at celebratory events in which the lid of the sake Barrel is broken open by a wooden mallet and the sake is served to everyone present. Kagami refers to the lid of the sake Barrel and biraki means 'to open' so kagami-biraki literally means 'opening the lid'. Because of the lid's round shape, the kagami is a symbol of harmony. The kagami-biraki, therefore, represents an opening to harmony and good fortune.

one per cent (2001) and 1.3 per cent (2004) of the vote. The name was changed in 2007 when the bureaucracy decided that the Liberals have a monopoly on the word "liberal".

Like the Workers Party, the new group of libertarian aspiring politicians come from a range of backgrounds including lawyers, economists, insurance brokers, software engineers and farmers. The party is currently lead by businessman David McAlary and the federal executive includes David Leyonhjelm, Terje Peterson, Justin Jefferson, Mark Hill, Peter Whelan and John Humphreys. The party has membership throughout Australia, but is concentrated in Queensland, NSW and the ACT.

The LDP is currently preparing for future federal elections and is currently seeking candidates to help give libertarian ideas the maximum possible exposure. Their policies include low flat tax, the abolition of the minimum wage, decriminalizing both marijuana and euthanasia, relaxation of shooting regulations, privatisation of the ABC and other government assets, school vouchers, free trade and expanded immigration, voluntary voting, restoring real private property rights, rejecting the Kyoto protocol and the excessive anti-terrorism legislation, opposition to an ID card and generally promoting free markets and individual liberty. Their website can be seen at www.lpd.org.au. If their efforts produce another bumper crop of advocates for economic and personal liberty, it could be a timely exercise, and I wish them well.

The Educational Method vs The Political Method

Several of us subsequently directed our activity entirely toward the educational method of spreading ideas rather than the political method of direct political engagement.

The notable success in the educational field has been Greg Lindsay. His Centre for Independent Studies (www.cis.org.au) celebrated its 30th anniversary in 2006 and Greg Lindsay was featured in the *Bulletin* magazine (September 28, 2004) as "perhaps the most influential man in Australia."

An early recruit and supporter of the Workers Party was Sydney businessman Neville Kennard who stood on their Senate ticket in the

ON LIBERTY

AUSTRALIA'S NEWSLETTER FOR ADVOCATES OF CIVIL AND ECONOMIC LIBERTY

incorporating OPTIMISM

Volume 1 | November 1979 | $12 per year

A DIFFERENT VISION

I read some verse by Darlene Bridge,
About the government our protector.
Politicians and bureaucratic fat-cats,
And regulators from the public sector.

Dictate your rules,
To one of those sheep.
I was born with a right
I intend to keep.

Your smile is kind,
You wish me no harm
But this body is mine.
Let go of my arm.

You seem to care
And perhaps you may;
But you don't understand.
Get out of my way."

She sees it clear, lovely fellows all,
Paving the road to hell with good intention.
But the results are the problem,
Don't embarrass them by making a mention.

Their vision is,
"Keep the serfs in their place.
Decisions are ours,
The superior race."

Is it presumptuous,
Of all of us others,
Ever to think,
We could care for our brothers?

How could we ever,
Permit such a thought,
After all what rights,
Are ours without being bought?

They tell us none
Unless we acquire,
A government license,
Guaranteed to expire.

It's only our lives,
Our labor, our cash.
Too bad they believe,
Our independence is brash.

Seems we should,
Have more room to breathe.
In fact we should manage,
To do anything we please;
With our lives and our property.
But one thing we should know,
We must not harm our neighbor.
He too has the right to grow.

So, sounds easy.
If no victim, then no crime.
Simple as that,
And all in one rhyme.

Say! What would we do
With those fat-cats and regulators?
We could give them a job,
As feedstock for alligators.

But seriously though,
With the Country moving again,
There would be gainful employment,
For each of those reformed men.

The energy of freedom,
Would again be on stream.
Responsibility of individuals,
A reality and no longer a dream!

Ron Manners

'no person or group of people has the right to initiate the use of force, fraud or coercion against any other person or group of people.'

1975 election. Neville, at that time, was the first financial supporter of the Centre for Independent Studies and the first CIS Chairman.

Neville Kennard recently recalled that era. "They were heady days in 1975, with the Labor Party rushing towards socialism and destroying the economy, the blocking of supply, the sacking of the Prime Minister, the [false] promises of Malcolm Fraser, the naive optimism of the Workers Party ...."

Other success stories are Viv Forbes, whose *Common Sense* articles continue to be published, and Ronald Kitching, a prolific author who wrote *Understanding Personal and Economic Liberty*.[9]

Perhaps the most outstanding archive of Australian Libertarian material has been compiled by John Zube (http://users.acenet.com.au/~jzube/). John would say that mine may be heavier by weight and volume, but his archives are being meticulously digitised.

There have been many interesting people I've met during this Libertarian adventure, all with their own individualistic way of "sticking up for themselves", one example being Mr Adam Dollar (see page 155).

My own non-political efforts with the Mannkal Economic Education Foundation (www.mannkal.org) continue and are dealt with elsewhere.

That brings us up to 2009. So to conclude this chapter let me quote the final two paragraphs from Ernesto Zanatta (see page 141).

> In such a time, people are more likely to take their rights for granted, and less inclined to think about what those rights are based on, or to be interested in libertarianism.
>
> However, I cannot help but think that these things do come and go in cycles, and that the pendulum may swing back some time in the future to another genuine libertarian enlightenment in the universities. For now, I feel that it was a privilege to have been a participant in it, and I find the words of F. Scott Fitzgerald in *Echoes of the Jazz Age* to be a fitting conclusion:
>
> '..... and it seemed only a question of a few years before the older people would step aside and let the world be run by those who saw things as they were — and it all seems rosy and romantic to us who were young then, because we will never feel quite so intensely about our surroundings any more.'

Endnotes:

1. I noticed that subsequent editions of *For A New Liberty* were printed without the small black Anarchist flag on the dust-cover.
2. Now Gary Sturgess AM, described by the WA Chamber of Commerce and Industry as "one of the world's leading experts on public sector reform and development of markets for public services. Gary ran the NSW Cabinet Office in the Greiner Government and was one of the most innovative public servants that State, indeed Australia, has seen. He is currently Executive Director, Serco Institute; a U.K. think tank, owned by Serco Group plc, dedicated to the study of competition and contracting of public services. Serco Group plc is one of world's largest service contractors with 40,000 employees delivering services to government and private clients in over 30 countries and revenue of in excess of $3 billion in 2006. Serco was awarded the contract to operate WA's Acacia Prison in 2006."
3. Accessible at: http://209.85.173.132/custom?q=cache:3qOxDWedJC0J:www.mannkal.org/downloads/guests/stacey.pdf
4. Ernesto Zanatta's and Alan Dungey have contributed introductions to William J. Stacey's paper, available on link referred to in reference (3) above.
5. When a reporter asked Malcolm Fraser about reading Ayn Rand, Fraser replied, "Yes — and I've read Karl Marx too, but that doesn't make me a Marxist."
6. Eugene Guccione's two-page interview with Prime Minister Fraser appeared in the January, 1977 edition of *Mining Engineering.* On pages 16-19 of the same magazine Eugene Guccione wrote a perceptive article on Australia's ability to be a major player in world uranium markets. An excerpt from this article is reproduced on page 230.
7. The full story was later published and is available as a book *Dry — In Defence of Economic Freedom* by John Hyde, published by the Institute of Public Affairs. For further information go to: http://www.mannkal.org/bookshop.php.
8. In some towns the Workers Party/Progress Party branch members even exceeded that of the major parties. Apart from those already mentioned in this chapter, the activists included James MacDonald, Clive Prosser, Maurice Brockwell, Valda Harris, Dieter Kops, Maxine Cable, John & Julie Maxwell, Mike Byrne, Christine Maher and so many others; they are all part of this great libertarian adventure.
9. Copies of *Understanding Personal & Economic Liberty* are available from http://www.mannkal.org/bookshop.php.

The Spectator

Are you down among the players when the game gets really rough?
Are you standing for the victim when the bully boys get tough?
When the herd-men bay in unison, is yours the "No" we hear,
or are you in the grandstand with your esky full of beer?

When a modern-day dictator says your life belongs to him,
do you risk your safe position by not bowing to his whim?
Do you laugh at mass opinion when you know that it is wrong,
or do you think that truth is learned by listening to the throng?

When "democrats" are shouting that you can't tell right from wrong,
When the law depends on circumstance and bends before the strong,
When "National Interest" demagogues are ranting on the street,
Is yours the one dissenting voice, or are you hiding from the heat?

Is your name among the builders when they write the book of life?
Would you be called a helper when your friends are having strife?
When your child is seeking guidance, are your answers straight and clear,
or do you say "Please count me out, I'm needed over here?"

Do you believe the state cocoon that binds men till they die
is just a crutch that keeps them weak and pays them not to try?
Will people say "At least he tried" when someone shoves the knife,
or are you just a viewer at the silver screen of life?

—Viv Forbes, Sept. 1980.

We hear from astute sources that already the Liberal Party is scared of us.
— Mark Tier of the newly formed Workers' Party

What do you think of Labor rule?

Paul Hogan saying a few words

DON'T MISS the unique opportunity to praise or criticise the Labor Government currently being offered by The Bulletin.

As we said in last week's issue an entire section is being set aside in a future issue for your answers to the question: "What has the Whitlam Government done for Australia?"

Already personalities as diverse as Sir Robert Crichton-Brown, president of the Institute of Directors of Australia, and the entertainer/humorist Paul Hogan have written their views for us.

We want to hear from students, businessmen, the unemployed, academics and teachers, pensioners, artists, writers, laborers, professionals – from everyone with a point of view.

The shorter you can keep your letters the greater the range we shall be able to publish. But don't be discouraged – if you need space to present your views you can have it.

The Bulletin, Feb. 15, 1975

In response to your invitation for letters on "What the Whitlam Government has done for Australia", I submit the following :

THE WHITLAM LAW OF SUPPLY & DEMAND

The Whitlam Government has been successful in creating a class of people who are permanently dependent. In doing so they have proved that the free-market law of "supply and demand" applies to their compulsory welfare programs - i.e. if you supply the demand for welfare recipients, the supply of welfare recipients will rise to fill that demand!

Yours faithfully,

R. B. MANNERS

Kalgoorlie,
West Australia.

All their own work

Led by the silver-tongued mountebank Whitlam with an army of charlatans and quacks behind him, we are seeing the destruction of the foundations of economic growth in our country and we are seeing its possibilities of great wealth being frittered away in an appalling display of profligate government spending whose sole significant result will turn out to have been to throttle economic growth and to put man against man, brother against brother, in the unseemly and disgusting rush for more and more gluttony at the trough of public funds.

— Journalist Maxwell Newton to the Workers' party in Sydney.

The Bulletin, June 7, 1975

"THE LIBERTARIAN MOVEMENT IN AUSTRALIA" -

a five minute address given by V.R. Forbes to a special meeting of the Mont Pelerin Society Meeting in Hong Kong, September 1978.

In the short time available I'd like to emphasise just one message for libertarian politicians -

"THERE IS NO EASY WAY"

Every day I'm earbashed by someone trying to convert me to his plan for instanteous political success.

For example, on the boat yesterday, I was told -

"The only answer is to work through the established political parties." - My answer - "Fine, which one are you going to join?"

Today I was told -

"The secret is to stick to education of the opinion makers" - my answer - "fine, which one will you work on?"

And almost everyday someone says -

"Why don't we concentrate all of our resources on one state, - electorate, project or whatever and really give it a trouncing?" - my answer - "fine - where would you like to concentrate your effort?"

All of these views are examples of what I call "THE MYTH OF CONSTANT RESOURCES".

They all assume that there is a fixed amount of human and monetary resources available to the libertarian movement which some wise leader can manipulate like a pawn on a chess board.

I have learnt that the resources available are not constant - they depend on what activities are carried out - the more activities - the more resources will be available.

For example, there are people who believe that there is no value in entering politics at all. If this is the only avenue available these people will not work - their energy and their resources will be lost to the movement. If a non-political avenue did exist, RESOURCES AVAILABLE TO THE MOVEMENT WOULD INCREASE.

Therefore to maximise our resources, we must let people work in all fields. We should encourage free enterprise and individual initiative in politics.

In Australia, the libertarian effort is occurring in about 4 areas. They are, in ascending order of aggressiveness -

1. EDUCATION
2. LOBBYING
3. INFILTRATION
4. DIRECT POLITICAL ACTION

1. In Education we have the Centre for Independent Studies which is doing a great job spreading the word among the academics and intellectuals. The director, Greg Lindsay, is here. We also have an infant Foundation for Economic Education which is an Australian replica of Leonard Read's organisation. FEE distributes books, shows films, arranges lectures and seminars.

The Bulletin, June 7, 1975

2. In the Lobby area we are taking over or setting up special interest lobby groups whose aims agree with ours. eg We -

- . set up NFC (National Firearms Council) - opposing confiscation and registration of firearms
- . set up PRAG - (Property Owners Action Group) - opposing compulsory acquisition of land
- . control part of - RTW (Right to Work Association) - opposing compulsory unionism
- . set up - Ratepayers Association - reduced rates
- . sit on - Taxpayers Association - reduced taxes
- . have close contacts with the - Cannabis Research Foundation - morality and effectiveness of prohibition
- . hold executive position - Civil Liberties Group
- . also in Chambers of Commerce, Chamber of Mines, IPA, Small Business and Self Employed Association, etc

3. At the third level of aggressiveness we encourage infiltration of other parties. We welcome members of other parties as members or as subscribers to our mail list. Our mail list now includes several members of parliament and prominent members of older parties. This builds a fifth column within the other parties.

4. The fourth area of activity, direct political action, appears to be the most effective. It generates publicity and it makes politicians listen. I believe politicians will only listen when you kick them in the ballot box, good and hard. And to do this you need direct aggressive political action.

Each state of Australia has its own autonomous libertarian political party. We use the name "Workers Party" in South Australia and "Progress Party" everywhere else. The Progress Party is two years old and has contested a federal election where we got an average 2-4% and about 4 state elections where we got 5-10% with several candidates getting 15% or better. The best result was 19% of the primary vote. About 3 members have been elected to local government positions.

Because of the preferential voting system in Australia any party that can attract 5-10% of the vote can determine the result of elections. Thus the Progress Party is already a growing political force especially in the frontier states where it does best.

For the future, I see persistence as the only key to success. We must keep on sowing the seed.

Only the government can reap without sowing. We must sow before we can reap.

To put it in military terms I see a three pronged strategy -

(1) Fight on all fronts

(2) Press on, no matter what the outcome

(3) Don't stop for casualties - you can lead a thousand men but you can't carry two.

And to those who believe they have an idea which will guarantee the success of the libertarian movement I say -

"Ideas without action are but words on the wind."

Who is Adam Dollar?

Introduction to Adam Dollar's book by, long-standing friend and associate, Ron Manners:

Adam Dollar knew exactly what he believed in. That marked him as a rare individual as I often meet members of the human race who are still coming to grips with who they are, what they stand for and why.

That made Adam, the individual, a pleasure to deal with.

I became aware of his existence when reading a magazine at my sister's home. It contained a "letter to the editor" from Adam Dollar. The letter lucidly explained his position on a seemingly complex issue that had confused another letter-writer.

I was electrified by the letter and reached for the phone book to see if such a person as Adam Dollar really existed. He did and his response to my congratulatory phone call was equally surprising, "Well, you should like my letter. I wrote it using material from the books I've been buying from your Kalgoorlie Libertarian Bookshop over the past ten years."

Suddenly I realised that my book client, Dollar Rent-A-Car, was the same entity as Adam Dollar.

From that point onward, Adam had all my car-rental business each time I visited Perth.

One morning in November 1985, fresh from the airport, I arrived to collect my car from Adam to find that he was in the process of being arrested by the Federal Police on charges of defacing the currency. He had affixed on the notes a rubber-stamped message: "As government expands, liberty diminishes!"

Realising that he had been set-up, I quietly asked what he was doing about his court defence. His reply was that he was happy to defend himself, caused me some concern as I knew exactly how they could tie him in knots with their pompous "legalese". Adam accepted my offer to engage and pay for an appropriate defence lawyer.

I chose Ron Cannon as he had earned a first-class reputation in defending murderers, rapists and drug dealers and I knew that they would pursue Adam with equal vigour. Mr Cannon's eloquence was a guarantee that the Crown Prosecutor would meet his match. .....

The day in court turned out to be sheer pleasure with Ron Cannon entering into the true spirit of the occasion.

THE WEST AUSTRALIAN SATURDAY NOVEMBER 23 1985

The message which landed Adam Dollar in court.

Dollar's dollars cause trouble

FIVE words — "as government expands, liberty diminishes" — landed a Perth business man in court yesterday.

Adam Dollar (62) stamped the words on money that came into his Belmont business, Drive-A-Dollar car rentals, and yesterday was in court on four charges of defacing the currency.

He was arrested on Tuesday after a customer complained to the federal police about receiving notes stamped with the message.

Mr G. Rutherford, for the Commonwealth, told the Chief Stipendiary Magistrate, Sir Clifford Grant, that Dollar informed federal police that he believed in minimal government interference.

Dollar had told police that he believed that by stamping the money with this message he would make people think about their loss of liberty.

Mr R. W. Cannon, defending, said that Dollar believed that the business of government was not business.

Dollar had told police he stamped the notes to make people think about their loss of liberty as government expanded with each law that was passed.

Dollar had also stamped his message on business correspondence. He was not aware that it was an offence to do so on currency.

Sir Clifford said he had not come across such a case before but he could not encourage others to follow suit.

He fined Dollar $15 on each charge and ordered him to pay $60 costs. — Susan Faull

Adam Dollar outside court after being convicted of defacing currency.

At every opportunity Mr Cannon asked the Magistrate what was the message stamped on the notes, to which the Magistrate was caused to repeat, "As government expands, liberty diminishes!"

Then, on about the tenth repeat of this message, the Magistrate paused and addressed the courtroom, "Hey, that's not a bad message." "As a matter of fact, I can't see any harm in that at all and I think the prosecution is simply wasting the court's time." The Magistrate then dismissed the case and ordered Adam to pay the minimum fine of $15 plus court costs of $60.

Adam and I continued as firm friends right through to the time of his death in 2000. It's been my pleasure to assist in finalising the writings of Adam with his editor, Kerri Lane, in Sydney and to bring this publication *Who is Adam Dollar?* to completion.

In 1984, as a protest against government 'destruction' of the Australian dollar, we flooded the market with 57¢ notes, in the colour and size of the $1 note of that time.

The government policies continued so the following year we devalued our next print-run to 55½¢. Pictured is the official launching of the note on June 12, 1985.

Two years later the clarinet player, at the opening of the Jones Family's Boulder Block Hotel, recalls being paid in these 55½¢ notes; which by that time had become collectors items.

LIBERTARIAN CRASHES MEETING OF SOCIALIST INTERNATIONAL

By Ron Manners/ISIL Member/Australia

If you were present at the Socialist International Conference in Sydney, Australia last March, you would have seen me there in the back row fitted up like all the other delegates with the mobile earpiece translating device.

I had some difficulty getting in without documentation, but when interrogated by the gaunt-faced registration attendant I admitted to being a ``poet of the revolution".

She still wanted to see my identifying documents, but accepted my reply that ``poets of the revolution don't carry identification".

My interest in attending was simply to see what they have planned for us.

You would have seen **Gough Whitlam, Bob Hawke, Gareth Evans** and other prominent members of the Australian Liberal Party and you would have followed the general discussion that as Communism is generally seen to be losing credibility around the world and that their switch to the word Socialism is also losing credibility, they have now redefined their plan under the general terms of ``social democracy", and all the various Communist Parties in the countries represented at that conference now call themselves ``Social Democrats". As a matter of fact in some of those East European countries the word Communism is in such low esteem that the Communist Party by that name has been outlawed – but of course the communist bureaucracy lives on and it is keen to expand membership – so they have devised a new recruiting scheme: members who recruit a new member are excused from membership fees for a year. Members who recruit two new members no longer need to remain members themselves. Those who recruit three new members are presented with an engraved silver plaque which states that they were never members in the first place.

They may change their name but they haven't changed their philosophy, and it's the consistency of their philosophy that has enabled them to do so much damage.

Australia's **Gough Whitlam** was a raging success when measured by their standards. He transformed Australia in the vision of **H.C. Coombs** and the other back room socialists so that over the three years of Whitlam rule, although productivity rose only 1%, wages rose 70%, the size of the public service rose 12.6%, parliamentary salaries increased by 36%, Federal spending by 80% and inflation to 20%.

He had bought the minds and souls of the public sector and their hangers-on who now represent one in three of those termed employed, as defined by our official statistics.

INTELLIGENCE GATHERING IN ENEMY TERRITORY–1993
The above faxed article appeared in the U.S. publication
'Freedom Network News'—Jan.–Mar. 1993

"Find out everything you can about possible antagonists. Anticipate what they are going to do and then change the rules of the game to something they simply won't understand." *The Next Whole Earth Catalogue p.304*

PART 3

Refer to website—**www.heroicmisadventures.com;** also featured will be short articles on some Remarkable People–Leonard E. Read / John Hospers / H.R.H. Prince Philip / F.A. Hayek / Milton Friedman / Murray Rothbard / Peter Bauer / Hernando de Soto /Antony Fisher / Margaret Thatcher / Keith Parry/ C.R. (Bert) Kelly / Prof. Geoffrey Blainey / H.M. (Harry) Kitson.

No amount of political activity or electioneering will ever establish the idea of human freedom until the idea has taken possession of the minds of man. It is in the field of education and not the field of politics that the primary battle must be fought and won.

—Frederic Bastiat—*A Man Alone*

There's no way to rule innocent men. The only power government has is the power to crack down on criminals. When there aren't enough criminals, one makes them. One declares so many things to be a crime that it becomes impossible for men to live.

—Ayn Rand

When you see that trading is done not by consent but by compulsion —when you see that in order to produce you need to obtain permission from men who produce nothing—when you see that money is flowing to those who deal not in goods but in favours—when you see that men get rich more easily by graft than by work, and your laws no longer protect you against them, but protect them against you—when you see corruption being rewarded and honesty becoming a self-sacrifice—then you will know that your society is doomed.

—Ayn Rand—*Atlas Shrugged*

When buying and selling are controlled by legislation, the first things to be bought and sold are legislators.

—P.J. O'Rourke

On “Doing Business”

“There is a time when work and need are one, when avocation and vocation are united.”—Robert Frost

The more I find out about “doing business”, the more I find that it is similar to life itself in that it is a delicate mixture of the past, the present and the future.

We carry the past as a guide to our present and the way we conduct ourselves in the present has a great bearing on our future.

Another similarity is that the ultimate outcome has a lot to do with the company we keep and the values we share as we travel through life.

We all should remain forever vigilant and aware of how delicate and fragile our business is, as it is tossed around on the turbulent economic ocean of today.

In that sense business is very much like the concept of freedom. If you substitute the word “business” for the word “freedom”, as in this quotation from the much admired, late President Ronald Reagan, you will see the similarity ...

> Freedom is a fragile thing and is never more than one generation away from extinction. It is not ours by inheritance; it must be fought for and defended constantly by each generation, for it comes only once to a people. Those who have known freedom and then lost it have never known it again.

May you run your business, or your life, successfully and train well those to whom you pass the torch in life’s wonderful relay race.

Small Business Lemmings

Here we go marching,
one two three,
Willingly paying each
fine, tax and fee.

We seem to have forgotten,
that freedom was respectable,
until the government licenced it,
which is morally unacceptable.

They dish it out sparingly,
now freedom's in such short supply,
you're doomed you know,
until for that licence you apply.

Why do you act as unpaid tax collectors?
when you would never dream,
of burdening either friend or foe,
with such a dreadful scheme.

Government plays the game,
to a different set of rules,
we deal with voluntary exchange,
while their gun points at our crown jewels.

Nothing much will change it seems,
till you get your knees up off the floor.
Stop begging for protection from competition,
that's just a perversion of the law.

The problem's solved if we all stand upright,
and decline their invitation.
Let **them** collect the taxes,
if **they** want to run the nation.

(Written for the State Conference of
The Federated Chambers of Commerce of W.A. Inc.
October 15–16, 1983)—RBM, 1983)

The Challenge for Chambers

(Freedom rather than favours)

In March 1995, former Presidents of the Kalgoorlie-Boulder Chamber of Commerce & Industry Inc. were invited to comment on their time with the Chamber.

My comments as President, 1976–78, were generally as follows:

- How did I get involved?
- Our start on the long journey to expand Kalgoorlie's role as a regional service centre.
- Our continuing challenge.
- How we had a bit of fun along the way. (The "Royal Visit" of 1977 and Mona the Madam.)

How I Became Involved

I will never forget that day in 1976 when four representatives from the Chamber of Commerce[1] burst into my office, unannounced, and said, "We want you to be President of the Chamber." Equally clearly I recall my response, "I'm not even a member of your Chamber as I don't like the way you avoid competition by hiding behind government regulations."

Their answer was equally memorable, "Good, that's why we want you to be President."

What could I say?

Because there were four of them and only one of me, I consented on the condition that I didn't have to go to any meetings, but when they took off their coats, I agreed to go to some of the meetings.

When I look at the minutes of the first meeting I attended it reminds me of how tough those times were.

> In submitting the Executive Committee report, Dieter Kops said, The previous 12 months has seen a number of drastic

changes in the Kalgoorlie/Boulder region and those changes had their effect on commerce in this area. Some of the more pronounced changes were:

- The closure of gold mining at Fimiston (the Golden Mile) in 1975;
- The Federal election in December 1975;
- The proposal to move the School of Mines to Perth;
- The reduction of air services between Kalgoorlie and Perth; and
- The scheduled closure of the Mt Charlotte operation, the last of the gold mines in Kalgoorlie.

A Regional Service Centre

For the next two years I thoroughly enjoyed working with a group of stimulating and energetic people who set about to prepare the community of Kalgoorlie for its emerging role as the Mining Service Capital of the World.

If any of you doubt this description of Kalgoorlie, then you haven't visited the world's other mining centres. I assure you that the breadth of service industry and suppliers in those centres is almost nonexistent when compared to Kalgoorlie.

I give credit to the dedicated group who saw that vision and doggedly went for it.

We quickly re-affiliated the Kalgoorlie Chamber with the Federated Chambers of Commerce as we realised that we would achieve our objectives quicker as part of a larger group.

One of our early tasks was to identify the impediments and regulations that hindered Kalgoorlie's development and then to devise ways of having these impediments abolished.

We decided that it was far more challenging to have these bad laws abolished as opposed to simply breaking them.

This was spearheaded by a two-day economic seminar at which we unveiled many plans to achieve these objectives. They included the proposal for a northern highway to the Pilbara. We also drew attention to the potential for the region if we could only remove the obstacles confronting mining and commerce.

By relentlessly ridiculing the perverse consequences of much of the existing restrictive legislation, we showed how the results of these restrictions were often the opposite of their declared intention.[(2)]

Our efforts actually had more effect than we ever imagined at the time. However, as usual, we underestimated the timeframe involved.

The documents we produced before and after the seminar were referred to in two speeches which the late iron ore pioneer Lang Hancock gave in 1978.[(3)]

> In Kalgoorlie there is a little company owned by Ron Manners.
>
> Working through the Chamber of Commerce, Ron Manners has produced a document called *Australia Lookin Good, Feelin Awful* (or you could call it *The Case for Governments Getting Out of the Way*). He has followed up with a specific 15-step policy on how the government could best get out of the way or "release the handcuffs", as he terms it, from the Mining Industry.
>
> It is impossible for Canberra to knock over the logic presented in these documents and more difficult for the government to reply to his demands for monthly reports on what progress they are making along these lines.
>
> In the year following the publication of the document Manners has been inundated with requests for copies, as they are forming the basis of strategy for many other industries in other parts of Australia, to push the case for deregulation of their various industries and regions.
>
> They are using the same tactics as Manners in showing how every government intervention into peaceful private activity tends to make things worse rather than better.
>
> By bombarding Canberra with logic in this fashion it is putting the bureaucracy on the defensive and making them think twice about erecting any more hurdles so, with a bit more pressure of this kind we could even have them dismantling some of the existing hurdles.

As Manners reminds them, "A predatory government, casting a pall of toxic uncertainty, will not revitalise investment in the Australian mining industry."

Why don't more of us challenge what Manners called the arrogance of officialdom? Why don't we set up communications between organisations and trade associations, to rally others to come to the aid of an individual like that? Or to an industry or profession when they're threatened by the barons of bureaucracy (who have forgotten that we are their employers)? Government by the people works when the people work at it. We can begin by turning the spotlight of truth on the widespread political and economic mythology that I mentioned.

One of the severe impediments facing the Goldfields was transport.

Do any of you remember that in the mid–1970s, it was illegal to transport any items of furniture or personal possessions, that you purchased elsewhere, if you brought them back to Kalgoorlie in your Holden utility?

The reason it was illegal was that it apparently created "unfair" competition against the government–owned railways.

I had an earlier confrontation with these stupid rules when I had a contract to mine and export optical glass quality quartz from the Goldfields town of Menzies to Sumitomo in Japan.

Brambles quoted an acceptable commercial rate for trucking the material from the site near Menzies to Fremantle, so I concluded the contract with Sumitomo.

Brambles then told me I had to obtain permission from the Western Australian Government Railways (later renamed Westrail so that it didn't look like a Government Department). Of course they refused, saying it would compete with an existing service. They expected me to put the mined material on a truck, take it to Menzies, put it on a train to Kalgoorlie, transfer trains via a truck (as the rail gauge was of a different width), rail to Fremantle, then finally truck from the rail head to the ship.

This caused me to write back to Sumitomo saying that I was unable to fill the contract because of this absurd government regulation.

They wrote back saying that they had heard our Government was "encouraging exports" but unfortunately I had to write back to explain that sometimes governments tell lies.

Out of our economic seminar came the State Government's South-West Transport Study, to examine the suggested benefits of allowing a bit of healthy competition. It scared the hell out of the WA Government Railways; so much so that they nominated a "spy" to sit on our Executive Committee.

We subsequently had considerable effect on that "spy" as he developed into a valuable member of our community and later became our Executive Director for several years.

Our Chamber was right on the crest of the deregulation wave which continued to gain momentum.

Often, when we got down to the serious business of achieving our objectives, we seemed to upset some of the local incumbent "leaders".

Some of them didn't know the difference between economics and politics, or management and politics.

Then, as now, I sympathised with them, however my sympathies still don't extend to patience.

Writer Ayn Rand's earlier words were appropriate for our Chamber's challenges, "Unjust laws have to be fought ideologically; they cannot be fought or corrected by means of mere disobedience and futile martyrdom."

Our Executive Committee was a lively bunch, always venturing beyond our region in quest of new markets.

Our Economic Sub-Committee, of Jim Keogh, Chris Fyson and Andre Gedes, covered all the mines in the Pilbara and brought back a lot of business, both for themselves and the many other emerging service groups.

Many of us at the time were providing more than 50 per cent of our goods and services outside the immediate Kalgoorlie region.

Following that same trail, in more recent times, Kalgoorlie has now "gone global".

These plane-loads of Kalgoorlie business people and contractors are our region's greatest ambassadors in so many parts of the world.

The Chamber's 1977 and 1978 years were not always as serious as the events mentioned.

There were several light-hearted incidents that I'll cover in the following pages:

- The "Royal Visit" of 1977
- Mona the Madam

Meanwhile The Challenge Continues

There is a further challenge left for all of us who work through Chambers of Commerce or similar industry organizations. That is for us to maintain the respect of the community.

This is doubly important when the integrity of so many groups in the community is being queried: from the politicians, the police, the teachers, through to the public servants.

The general public wants a break from all of this.

They know that when we persist in regulating the number of competitors who can enter the market place, limiting the number of hours that a man may work and manipulating the wages and prices which may be charged, we demonstrate our absurd belief that limiting people's freedom to produce and compete will somehow make us all wealthier.

Every such limitation weakens the marketplace and the increased costs are passed on to consumers.

Consumers are aware of all this and they are demanding higher standards of both service and ethics.

It is our challenge to meet these expectations.

Footnotes:

1. Chris Fyson, Dieter Kops (Woolworths Manager), Brian Williams (Jordan & Jackson) and Peter Munachen (Accountant).
2. See Appendix and www.heroicmisadventures.com
3. To the Executives Association of Australia, Sydney, September 22, 1978 and the Australian Retailers Association, Melbourne, September 25, 1978.

THE EXPRESS REGIONAL NEWS, Friday November 21, 1980

LOCAL FIRMS TRY FOR AWARD

Three Goldfields firms have been nominated for small business awards--a programme jointly sponsored by the Federal Government, the Confederation of Australian Industry and Australian chamber of Commerce.

They are Bob Muirhead Electrical Pty Ltd, of Boulder-rd, Kalgoorlie, Hainault Tourist Gold Mine at Fimiston and Libertarian Bookshop, of Brookman-st, Kalgoorlie.

Presentation to the five WA finalists will be made in Perth by Honorary Industrial Development Minister, Mr Barry MacKinnon, on Monday.

The Libertarian Bookshop provides books and data to small businesses and individuals, to assist in economic survival against government policies including inflation and excessive intervention, "protection" and regulation.

Proprietor, Mr Ron Manners, said a new service contributing to the success of the bookshop was a standard "sub-contractor" contract form. By using the form it was possible for employers to avoid the penalty of payroll tax imposed for creating employment.

Mr Manners said the Libertarian Bookshop was operating in a growth sector of the economy and he was confident of continued expansion in view of the dramatic increase in government interference in commerce.

WHY PAY PAYROLL TAX?

Why should employers be fined for creating jobs?

You can legally "AXE" payroll tax!

For particulars send stamped, self-addressed envelope to:—

LIBERTARIAN BOOKSHOP

PO BOX 33 KALGOORLIE

WEST AUST 6430

"GOLDRUSH COUNTRY"
ROYAL VISIT
1977

The Man Who Beat The Bureaucracy

The remarkable story of Prince Leonard of Hutt

("The Bulletin", May 17, 1975)

IN THIS JUBILEE YEAR IT IS FITTING THAT WE SHOULD WELCOME ONE OF THE NOBLE SONS OF "GOLDRUSH COUNTRY", WHO VENTURED FORTH AND STARTED HIS OWN COUNTRY.

THE HUTT RIVER PROVINCE FORMALLY SECEDED FROM AUSTRALIA ON 21ST APRIL, 1970 IN PROTEST AGAINST OPPRESSIVE WHEAT QUOTA RESTRICTIONS IMPOSED BY OUR NOTORIOUS BUREAUCRACY.

ROYAL PROGRAM

Thursday June 30, 1977

8.10 pm	Arrival on M.M.A. flight and public welcome at Kalgoorlie Airport.
8.30 pm	Press conference at Palace Hotel.

Friday July 1

9.30 am	Official opening of Hutt River display in "Markets Arcade" (This display will remain open on Friday and Saturday morning)
10.00 am	On-air discussion with students, Kalgoorlie School of the Air.
11.00 am	Visit to "Little Sisters of the Poor".
2.00 pm	Underground T.V. filming at Hainault Tourist Mine.
4 - 5 pm	Available to meet the public at the Hutt River display.
7.30 pm	Dinner meeting at which Prince Leonard will describe the interesting events leading to the creation of the Hutt River Province. Those wishing to attend should phone 21 2728 as soon as possible.

Saturday July 2

10.30 am	Hannan Street parade.
2.00 pm	Special guest of the Kalgoorlie-Boulder Racing Club.

Sunday July 3

Royal visit to Coolgardie with "Goldrush Country Tours".

The "Royal Visit" in 1977

(Why not start your own country?)

The Queen was visiting Australia in her Jubilee Year and she was going everywhere in Australia, except to Kalgoorlie. We were naturally disappointed.

As a result, our Chamber of Commerce organized our own "royal tour", with big banners proudly displayed in all the shop-fronts: 'In this Jubilee Year, the Royal Tour comes to Kalgoorlie'. Then in a smaller print: 'Prince Leonard from the Hutt River Province[1] (near Kalbarri, Western Australia) has been invited for four days for a spectacular royal tour!" We organized a wonderful tour.

The event had a special relevance because Prince Leonard was born and raised in Kalgoorlie. We had both attended Kalgoorlie Central School. (My mother, Nancy, was a teacher there in 1929.)

Consequently, we had great connections with the Kalgoorlie Central School. So I telephoned the Head Mistress, Mrs Henderson, to advise that we had her most famous student coming back to Kalgoorlie. He had even gone out and started his own "country", something no other student had done.

As a part of his royal tour he'd like to come back to Kalgoorlie Central School and address all the students. Mrs Henderson was thrilled and organized for all the students to gather on the quadrangle at 10 am so Prince Leonard could address them.

At that time I owned a Volvo with a sun roof. This was perfect for Prince Leonard who was able to stand on the front seat with his head and shoulders through the sunroof waving to all the students.

One of the carpet distributors in Kalgoorlie gave us a roll of red carpet which we had laid out from the car right through to the school.

HRH, Prince Leonard of the Hutt River Provence, signing a "Trade Treaty" with the "People of the Goldfields, with Ron Manners, the then President of the Kalgoorlie Chamber of Commerce, Inc. (At the Palace Hotel, June, 1977.)

The Tuart Hill, S.H.S. Concert Band giving a command performance for Prince Leonard in the Hutt River Province.

Hutt River Currency
Could this even be developed as a "sound alternative" currency? See Appendix—www.heroicmisadventures.com

Hutt River Treaty
(Between the Hutt River Province and the People of Kalgoorlie)

Prince Leonard had co-operated completely with this ceremony and sent us hundreds of miniature Hutt River flags which all the students waved as Prince Leonard arrived to address them.

Everyone was thoroughly enjoying themselves.

Suddenly, there was a telephone call from the Minister for Education who wanted to speak to Mrs Henderson. The Minister advised her that under no circumstances was "this fellow, Len Casley, posing as Prince Leonard", allowed to go to the school, address the students or be referred to as Prince Leonard.

Mrs Henderson acknowledged "she had a problem" and quickly returned to the presentation just as I was helping Prince Leonard into the Volvo. Not a student was in sight.

After questioning me as to where all the students had gone, I replied, "Leonard got carried away, he thought he was Sir James Mitchell or some similar early State Governor. He gave such a good speech and then declared it to be a half-day holiday and sent all the children home."

Mrs Henderson said, "Mr Manners, I think I'm in big trouble."

Prince Leonard urged her not to be concerned and presented her with a Hutt River "visa", assuring her that if she needed somewhere to go then he would welcome her as his Minister for Education at the Hutt River Province.

All in a day's work.

Endnotes

1. See page 170.

Visitors Gavin Bunning & Will Loader hearing the remarkable story of the creation of the Hutt River Province (June 19, 2009)

The foundation stone

The Hutt River Province chapel

Entrance to the Hutt River Province, via Western Australia

Thirty–two years later, we meet again. HRH Prince Leonard receives a signed copy of 'Never A Dull Moment', from the author—June 19, 2009.

A small selection of the international memorabilia as presented to Prince Leonard in his travels.

Mona The Madam

(When is a brothel not a brothel?)

Prostitution has always been an integral part of mining towns which can be pretty rough places at times, especially for barmaids who expand their horizons.

Well remembered is one barmaid at the mining town of Broad Arrow.

She stayed there 12 months, served the thirsty during the day and the love-hungry at night. When she decided to quit and return to the coast, a large crowd of prospectors turned up at the station to wave goodbye.

One pretty hard case in the mob said, "You must be going away with a pretty good bank balance. How much are you worth?"

She looked at him with a gentle smile and said, "If I had another shaft on the lease I could have put through another 2,000 crushings."

I realise that writing about such delicate subjects as prostitution, in this "politically correct" decade, should cause me to give a disclaimer to the effect that writers simply write about their own observations, neither sitting in judgment nor making any recommendations.

Political correctness has damaged our language in a way that currently causes "drug addicts" to now be referred to as "victims of substance abuse".

On the same basis brothels are probably no longer brothels, but instead are "houses of negotiable happiness".

This reminds me of Mona, the leading Goldfields Madam of the 1970s, who always referred to her establishment as a bordello.

I first met Mona when I was the President of the Kalgoorlie Chamber of Commerce and enjoyed our discussions immensely.

Although she was about twice my age she maintained an elegant vitality which caused me to ask of her on one occasion, "Mona, are you still active, in that sense, anymore?"

She said, "Oh, Mr Manners, not so much these days but when some of the young School of Mines students come in for the first time they are a bit shy with the younger girls, but with me it's different, it's more the mother image."

Mona had this fabulous player piano (yes the old style with large pedals and Pianola music rolls) in her central service area and I asked her, "Mona, what's this doing in here?"

She replied, "Well it's the greatest investment that I've ever made because the boys come in here and then they go into the bedrooms and then they come out and we give them a cup of tea and then they play the piano and, with all that leg work, before long they are back in the bedrooms!"

Actually, it was just after being elected as the President of the Chamber of Commerce, that Mona first made contact. I was in my office one day attending a meeting and the phone rang—it was Mona. She said, "Mr Manners, I wish to ask you a question." I replied, "Mona, I'm a bit busy, can you ask it quickly." She said, "Yes, what is it we call a prostitute's vagina?"

I don't know if anyone else in my meeting heard but I said, "I don't know Mona you'll have to tell me because I'll never guess!"

She chuckled and said, "I'm ringing you because you are now the President of the Chamber of Commerce and we call a prostitute's vagina a Chamber of Commerce!"

The next day I called her back and said, "Mona, you are not even a member of the Chamber. You really should become a member if you wish to call about Chamber business." She replied, "I can't be a member because you haven't got a category for me." I said, "We have." She said, "What is it?" I said, "Here it is - Essential Services!"

Mona said, "Well I know what I can do for you guys but what can you do for me?"

I said, "Well if you are ever in trouble with the bureaucracy, come and see us?"

About three months later she rang me and said, “Mr Manners I need your help, I’m having trouble with the Kalgoorlie Council.”

She’d lodged a building application for a long transportable house and included as description “residence”. It had three doors along the front.

The Mayor, Ray Finlayson knocked it back and she’d lost her $10 building application fee. The Council advised that she could not build a “residence” in Hay Street, Kalgoorlie because it was zoned ‘industrial’.

Mona explained to me that all she was trying to do was to bring Kalgoorlie up to modern standards to cope with the expansion. The Council, unfortunately, was preventing her from moving forward in this way.

So, Mona brought the plan around to me and asked what she should do.

I advised that we would fix it. I got a pen, drew another five doors on the front,and then crossed out “residence” and wrote ‘hatchery’.

She delivered this back to the Council with a note saying that we would phone the Mayor direct.

She came into my office the next day to make the call. The Mayor said, “This is very embarrassing because Mona is going to lose a second deposit because all you’ve done is put a few more doors on it and changed ‘residence’ to ‘hatchery’.

I replied, “Mr Mayor, it now fully complies with the industrial zoning.”

He said, “Well, what do you mean, hatchery?”

I replied, “It’s a hatchery by definition because Mona raises a thousand ‘cocks’ a week.”

Well, without any further complications, she got it through the Council and that building, complete with multiple doors, became famous as the ‘starting stalls’.

> Life is full of misery,
> loneliness, and suffering - and
> it’s all over much too soon
>
> —Woody Allen (who apparently never visited Mona’s)

THE KALGOORLIE MINER, FRIDAY, OCTOBER 17, 1980 3

A new transportable house has been installed in Hay Street, Kalgoorlie. It is yet another indication of Kalgoorlie's current prosperity, though some would say it is a dubious sign of growth. The Kalgoorlie Town Council recently approved the transportable house as meeting local authority requirements.

The Hatchery

The Kalgoorlie Miner–October 17, 1980

The barmaid with a balance

Mining towns can be pretty rough places at times, especially for barmaids. I remember one barmaid at Broad Arrow. She stayed there twelve months, served the thirsty during the day and the love-hungry at night. When she decided to quit and return to the coast, a large crowd of prospectors turned up at the station to wave goodbye. One pretty hard case in the mob said: "You must be going away with a pretty good bank balance. How much are you worth?"

She looked at him with a gentle smile and said, "If I had had another shaft on the lease I could have put through another two thousand crushings".

****

Achieving Balance in Our Lives*

(Perhaps we can have too much balance?)

Balancing the various priorities (mostly other people's priorities) can be enough to fill our day. How easy it is to become confused between sundry duties to others (grouped together as society).

Let's look at two quotations:

> Duties are not performed for duties' sake, but because their neglect would make the man uncomfortable. A man performs but one duty—the duty of contenting his spirit, the duty of making himself agreeable to himself.
>
> —Mark Twain

> Society is joint action and cooperation in which each participant sees the other partner's success as a means for the attainment of his own.
>
> —Ludwig von Mises

In our pursuit of happiness, let us indulge in excess to the point where we become "notoriously happy".

Nothing is balanced about happiness and we are certainly not much good to anyone else unless we cultivate our own "notorious happiness".

Philosopher Ayn Rand got it right when she coined the phrase "rational selfishness", best demonstrated by the airline in-flight announcement that "in the event of loss of oxygen, mothers should firstly go for the face mask and then they will be in a position to help their children".

---

*Based on my after-dinner comments to the annual dinner of The Chamber of Minerals & Energy of W.A. Inc.–The Hannans Club, Kalgoorlie–October 19, 2001

Rational selfishness is the opposite to "self-destructive altruism".

Several years ago I thought about "balance in our lives" when attending the funeral of my Uncle Bill (89 years old) where his son Garry, in the eulogy, described Bill's job satisfaction at being the horse racing writer for the *Sunday Times* for so many years.

Old Bill once said, "I must be the luckiest man in the world to be paid to go to the races".

If we are paid for doing what we love doing, there's not much chance of us being out of balance in our careers.

However, the balance in our home lives is perhaps the greatest challenge of all, due to our ladies being programmed with an entirely different set of priorities.

We know when we are in balance in our careers, but for the family end, this needs input from someone far wiser than myself.

Actually, I met someone of such superior wisdom recently, sitting alongside me on a plane.

When I asked her what she did for a living she replied, "I bring balance to the lives of people like you." After further interrogation she admitted to being a "fully participating sex therapist", providing a select group of men with warmth and passion which they were no longer receiving in their, otherwise normal, marriages.

Among the memorable thoughts she left with me was, "You guys create your own problems with your focus on time management, slotting in an hour for so many specific tasks. Your wives can't handle it on that basis, but it suits me."

Perhaps this inspired me to pen the following poem:

Dining Well?

Marriage is simply not a menu
in this restaurant of life.

In this complex task of professionalism
that we often call husband and wife.

We can't just tick a few
selected items here and there,

and always expect the weather
to remain warm and fair.

It's a well rounded challenge,
that we need to aim for

if a marriage is to endure
the end result's in the score.

I know there are countless specialists,
whose talent is provide the bits missing,

but simple things that vanish over time.
are conversation, laughter, tenderness and kissing.

When the specialists excel,
many marriages can make do this way.

But we can be happy day and night
if all courses at the same cafe!

RBM, 2001

The more we study and understand the human condition, the more effective we become in management and as individuals. It might even help us to become more aware of the vital part that our loved ones play in creating that essential balance in our lives.

The part that our life-companions play is so important that unless we've got things 'right' at home, we are not much good to anyone.

A vote of thanks may be appropriate for the "home front".

HOW CLOSE WE ARE

Close friends are we,
with so many shared feelings.

The years have been kind,
by watching over our many dealings,

From fire-fighting to tree-planting,
from grave-shifting to dog-walking.

Every adventure something unexpected,
but always companionably rewarding.

You have brought me a new dimension,
and these years have been my best.

That's why I call you,
my darling treasure chest.

RBM, 2001

Prospecting to Mining to Investing

(One thing leads to another)

At a writers' seminar some years ago, each participant was asked to write a poem about any of the Goldfields paintings that were currently displayed at the Boulder Town Hall.

I wrote this little piece which was based on a John Sztermula painting, showing a bush road.

It is, in many ways, a metaphor for the life of all prospectors:

"I took the road less travelled by
and that made all the difference".

Robert Frost wrote the lines
so many years ago,

but they just came back to me
as down the road I go.

Just when I'm about to solve
the reason for these tracks

I come to this fork in the road
so another mystery will unfold.

what was on these old-timers' minds
in their quest, to seek and discover gold.

The next few pages are a brief skip-through the past 40 years of active involvement in prospecting, mining and investing.

This is a journey that I've travelled with so many truly remarkable people—and that is the 'fortune' that so few people actually find.

THE KALGOORLIE MINER, FRIDAY, DECEMBER 21, 1984

Bonanza at Siberia find recalls 1893 gold rush

The recent bonanza from Sundowner Minerals' gold find at the Siberia Consuls mine, 100km north-west of Kalgoorlie, revived memories of the rich crushings which sparked a rush in October, 1893.

Details of the rush are contained in a paper prepared by Coolgardie historian Mr Harry Ware, and makes interesting reading:

With the passing of the years and the decline in prospecting, many of the once prosperous and important mining towns are now deserted, the history of them going with the passing of the pioneers and early-day prospectors.

In many cases a heap of broken bricks and a ruined chimney indicate where once stood a bakery or a cellar-hole, and broken glass marks the site of what was once a hotel.

Reminders

Alluvial tailings heaps and mullock dumps are mute reminders of the hard earned reward for the prospector and the miner.

My informant, prefers to be known as an "Old Timer."

The gentleman who came to Coolgardie early in 1894, followed several 'rushes' before going to Siberia in January, 1897.

Messrs Frost and Bonar discovered Siberia in October, 1893.

A severe drought was prevailing at the time on the Eastern Goldfields, and water in the area was scarce.

When the find was reported at Coolgardie, nearly 100km to the south, a wild rush set in as was usual in those hectic days.

Water

Many of those who set out for the new find either perished of thirst before reaching their destination, or did so on the way back to Coolgardie – Wongine Soak, a few miles to the west, being totally inadequate to supply their needs.

Thus the find earned the title (and doubtful fame) of Siberia.

When, later a townsite was surveyed and a State battery erected there it became known officially as Waverly.

In addition to the surface alluvial found by Messrs Frost and Bonar, there were rich "deep loads", the most notable being the Noah's Ark, the Camperdown, and the Pearling Grounds.

'Very rich'

The Siberia Reward, found by Messrs Christie and Downie shortly after the original find, was very rich.

"Old Timer" recalls that when he went to Siberia in January, 1897, a new rush had set in after the discovery of alluvial gold in the gullies west of the Reward, and the earlier finds on the northern end of the field.

At the time there was a population of about 500, and it remained about that figure for several years.

General stores were conducted by Paul Bros, J.S. Christie, who was also the mail contractor, W. Sheppard (later owned by Albert Tyler), Joe Cooney and McKee (who had been at Kunanalling earlier), Crowley Bros, who also had a bakery, Dick Mason and Alec Courage.

There were two hotels, the first – the Siberia Hotel, owned by Rene Bertox, a Frenchman – being removed from Wongine Soak, and the second, the Reward Hotel owned by Jimmy Kirkham, which was shifted from the Carnage.

This hotel was later bought by the late Mr Jim Correl, who conducted it for many years.

Post office

The first post office was a tent, and the first post master was a Mr Ryan. Later a wood and iron building was erected, the post master then being Mr E. Woods.

There never was an official school building erected, but a Miss Thornton did conduct classes for a short while.

A mechanics' institute, built by Mr Dave Stenhouse, was the social centre.

Two sports meetings were usually held each year, and there was an active rifle club.

Alluvial mining gave way to "reefing," and in November 1904 a State battery was erected.

This ceased operations in 1924.

The first battery manager was Mr A. Cale, others being Messrs Neil Irvin (1906), who later died on the Gold Coast, M. Quick, J.O. Kelly, Jim Halligan, and Kennedy-Smith who managed the Ora Banda State battery at that time also (1924).

Siberia had seen the best of its years before the outbreak of the Great War, but many thousands of ounces of gold had been won, both from alluvial sources and from mines, including The Consuls, The Cave Hills, The Majestic, The Bonnie Doon, The Missouri, The Prince Foote, The Pole, The Merriwee King and others.

"Old Timer" recalls the finding of The Consuls, a very rich mine.

At an extensive alluvial patch, known as the Four Mile, Messrs Jim Correll and his brother-in-law, a man named Nolan, had put a long costean across the head of the alluvial workings.

They found traces of gold at the end of the costeen, which they widened and deepened, but did not extend.

'A salt'

They came to the conclusion that the gold was a "salt" from the alluvial workings.

Correll left the Four Mile and acquired the Pole Mine from Nat Freedman, and Nolan left the district.

Some months later Messrs Framco and Adams extended but a short distance the costean dug by Messrs Correll and Nolan and struck it rich.

A 14-ton parcel from their find, crushed at the Siberia State battery, yielded 1357oz. of gold, and as "Old Timer" put it, their next parcel was a poor one, 60 tons being recquired to produce 1250oz.

A company was formed to work the mine, and several hundred tons of ore averaging about 2oz. per ton was produced, but the mine reverted back to the original prospectors.

Mr Correll acquired the interest of one of the shareholders, and among other returns shared a 600oz. "patch" – some reward at least for his original costean.

Mounds

Adjacent to the townsite and not far from the Reward Mine is a well fenced area marked by regular mounds, covered in orderly manner by white quartz stones.

It is the last resting place of a dozen souls who had "pegged their last claim," and earned their "just reward."

These do not include any of those unfortunates who perished in the first wild "rush" to Siberia.

Names

The names of those buried in the Siberia cemetery, given by a man who was there from 1897 till 1942, and who vouches for the accuracy of the details of the occupation and circumstances, are: David McCormick, fever; James Anderson, speared by natives; William Reid, condenser owner; William Byrne, dropped dead; William Dawson was on the Fair Adelaide, Xmas reef locality; Thomas Lee' Walter Betts, found dead; John Kirkham, natural causes; William Graves, one of the original shareholders in the Mexico (later, the New Mexico), Xmas reef locality, and producing rich ore; Nils Bengston of Swedish nationality, finder of the Little Hero slug, on the Pilbarra fields, the largest slug found in Western Australia up to that time, 333oz. 18 dwt.; John Dillon, buried about 1923 or 1924. There is also the grave of one infant, whose parents were Mr and Mrs Kirkham.

The names are in rotation from the southern end.

Plan
Shewing Mining Leases at
SIBERIA
WESTERN AUSTRALIA.
Compiled by G. A. Harris, C.E. L.S.
Published by Harris & Besly, Perth, W.A.
Scale 20 Chains 1 Inch

REFERENCE

Nº	Lessee	Area	Name of Mine	Diagram Nº
134	J.E. Burbank & Ors.	12 a	Birthday Gift	4/164
289	Cornish & Ors.	9 -		4/28
290	- - -	12 -		4/29
366	Rowles & Ors.	24 -		4/33
398	A.E. Cauliffe & Ors	12 -	Sebastopol.	4/37
399	Chambers & Ors	12 -	Muggetty Gully.	4/38
418	Wisdom - -	12 -	Glen Isla	4/41
436	Stewart - -	6 -	Montrose	4/45
615	J. Kittleby	12 -	Bonnie Doon	4/49
727	H.T.C. Lamb	20 -	Siberia Extd.	4/74
874	A. McPherson	20 -	McPherson	4/85

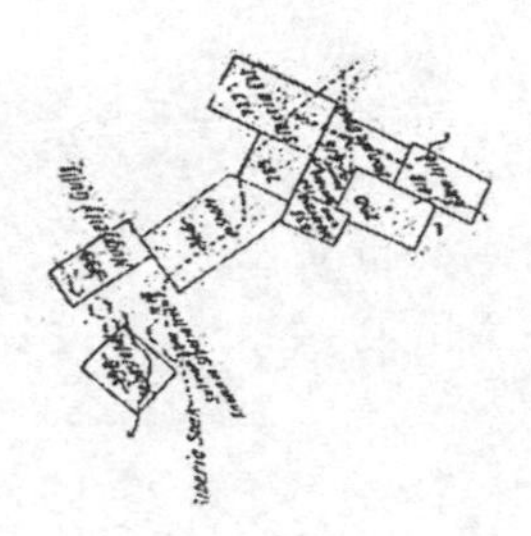

THE KALGOORLIE MINER, FRIDAY, DECEMBER 21, 1984

Bonanza at Siberia find recalls 1893 gold rush

Full report see facing page ....

My first 'Nickel Boom' prospecting area was pegged over the old Siberia Goldfields, north west of Kalgoorlie, in 1966.

That Siberia area led to my involvement in the Westralian Nickel Syndicate which subsequently became the successful public company, floated as Westralian Nickel N.L.

This in turn led me to a long-winded dispute with the Australian Taxation Office, who had a very poor understanding of Section 23P(a) of the Australian Taxation Act.

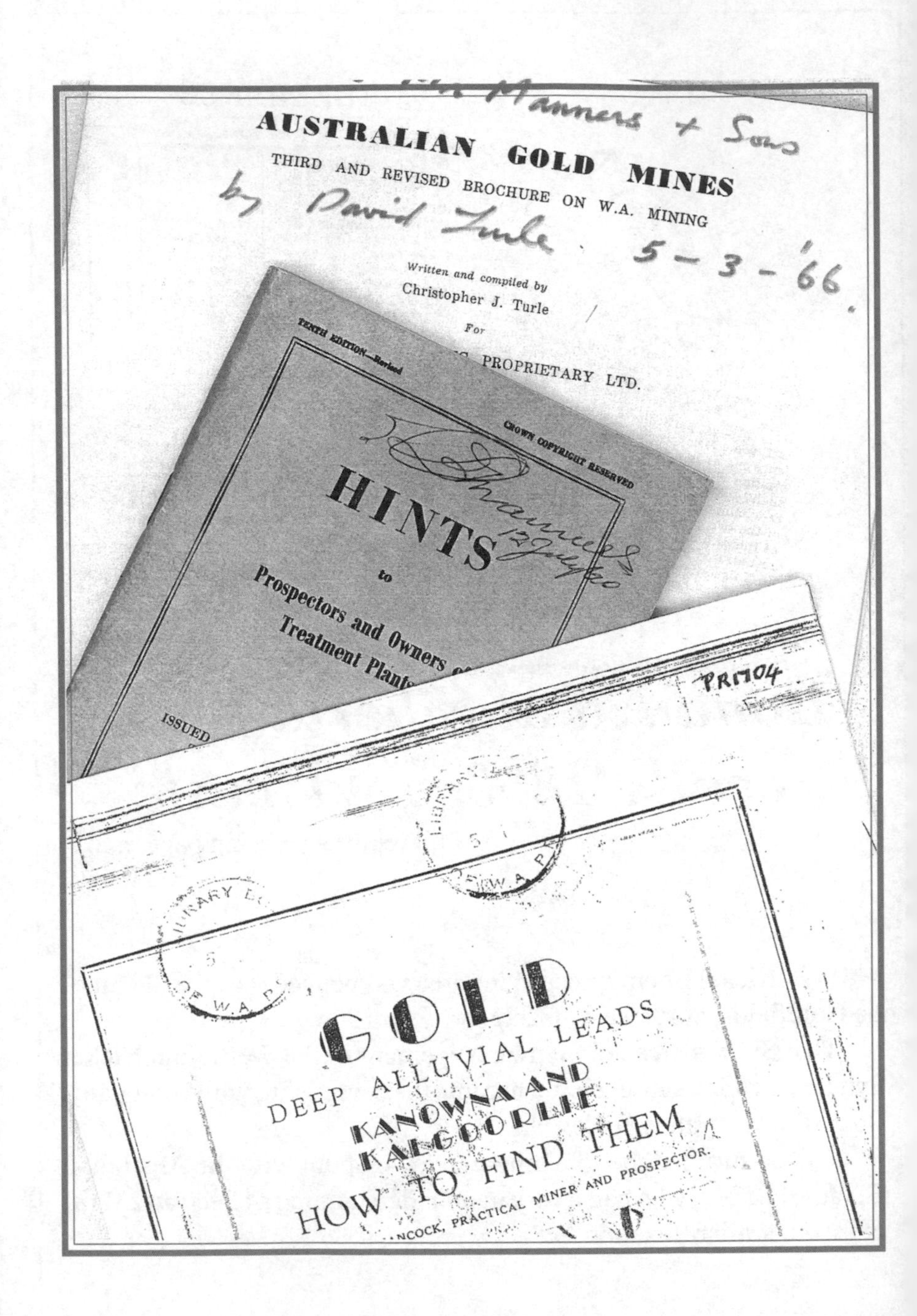
Manners + Sons
AUSTRALIAN GOLD MINES
THIRD AND REVISED BROCHURE ON W.A. MINING
by David Turle 5-3-'66.
Written and compiled by
Christopher J. Turle
For
PROPRIETARY LTD.
TENTH EDITION—Revised
CROWN COPYRIGHT RESERVED
HINTS
to
Prospectors and Owners
Treatment
ISSUED
PR1704
GOLD
DEEP ALLUVIAL LEADS
KANOWNA AND
KALGOORLIE
HOW TO FIND THEM
PRACTICAL MINER AND PROSPECTOR.

Prospecting: a way of life

You must love the crust of the earth on which you dwell
more than the sweet crust of any bread or cake.

You must be able to extract nutriment out of a sand heap.

You must have so good an appetite as this
else you will live in vain.

– Henry David Thoreau, *All Nature is My Bride*

For the early part of my life, in the Kalgoorlie Goldfields, there wasn't much prospecting going on.

There were at least two reasons for this.

First, the gold price was 'fixed' by the Federal Government and costs had overtaken the official selling price.

Second, the world's appetite for base metals hadn't risen to the point where there was much commercial interest in exploring the vast natural resources of the region.

Fortunately, some of the Goldfield's early prospectors had kept the 'art' of prospecting alive by running occasional seminars to share their knowledge, in the hope that gold and other metals would again be eagerly pursued. (See facing page.)

I admired these old-time prospectors, who were always generous with their time when expounding theories (gained from first-hand observations) on where the next 'Golden Mile' may be hiding.

Patience was their foremost quality. As the Californian writer, Dorothy Bryant, described it: "Like an old gold-panning prospector, you must resign yourself to digging up a lot of sand from which you will later patiently wash out a few minute particles of gold ore."

Almost all the subsequent, very substantial mineral discoveries in Australia, with the exception of Olympic Dam in South Australia, have been made as a result of earlier visits by prospectors, who carefully recorded their observation for others to follow up with their more recently developed sophisticated exploration tools.

It was in this easy-going "unhurried" 1960s that significant stirrings occurred in iron ore (the Lang Hancock–Peter Wright Partnership, Charles Warman, Stan Hildich, Don Rhodes and many others) and the outstanding work of Western Mining Corporation (WMC) sowed the seeds of 'something big coming on'.

WMC's discovery of nickel sulphides at Kambalda (south of Kalgoorlie) in 1966 which ushered in a new era of base metal exploration in Australia, followed by Poseidon's discovery of nickel sulphides in 1969 at Windarra (near Laverton, north east of Kalgoorlie), led to Australia's original 'nickel boom' (inaccurately reported on facing page.)

This nickel boom lasted only one-and-a-half years. Despite initially giving the impression that everyone would make a discovery, it ended with the realisation that significant discoveries are few and elusive.

From a personal point of view, I rate the original nickel boom, not just on the value of Poseidon shares, that ranged from 2.5 cents to $280 and ultimately into liquidation, but also on the number of people I employed in our mining equipment company, W.G. Manners & Co.

There were four of us in 1966, 48 in 1970 and by the late '70s we were down to four again.

The first nickel boom was so exciting that I became very involved in floating publicly listed companies. To mention only four: Westralian Nickel N.L. which developed from the Westralian Nickel syndicate (a bunch of 'hard-core' prospectors), then Mining & Associated Industries Ltd of Brisbane, then Theseus Exploration N.L.(1) (Greek scholars will remember that Theseus was the illegitimate son of Poseidon, who was called Neptune by the Romans.) Finally, there was Kalmin Exploration Ltd.

I wouldn't have believed anyone if they had told me then, that Kalmin would be the last company floated in the nickel boom and that it would ultimately be transferred to the industrial board on the Australian Stock Exchange and become a home-builder (Bellcrest Corporation).

Statistics from that period were never reflected by smooth gradual graphs.

Manners saved for the Palace

STICK a microphone in the hand of mining industry stalwart Ron Manners and you can be pretty sure you're in for a good yarn.

So stayers at the Australian Nickel Conference closing cocktail party in Perth this week re-ordered drinks and settled in when big Ron took the stage to reminisce about the heady days of the Poseidon nickel boom.

He told how with 350 companies exploring in and around Kalgoorlie, and an unwritten rule that any company which did a deal had to buy champers for the bar at the Palace Hotel, he often went days, if not weeks, without going home.

"One of my kids (we're not sure if it was stockbroker Craig or Sons of Gwalia PR flak Sarah) once told me I'd neglected them because I spent so much time at the bar," he sprouted.

"I had to tell them, you only get one nickel boom in your lifetime, but you can always have more kids."

Manners went on to say how the lack of quality directors (nothing's changed Ron!) meant you had everyone from drinking pals to fishing buddies filling board seats.

"We had guys nicknamed Mirror and Vomit. Mirror was always "looking into it" while Vomit would always "bring it up at the next board meeting".

THE WEST AUSTRALIAN SATURDAY SEPTEMBER 18 1999

At the time there were 350 Australian and international companies looking for nickel in Kalgoorlie, Western Australia.

Kalgoorlie, in 1970, hosted the highest number of geologists in the world.

Interestingly enough, the second highest population of geologists was in New York city.

Of the 350 companies searching for nickel around Kalgoorlie, how many of them actually made a profit from mining nickel?

Two.

They were Western Mining Corporation (WMC) and Metals Exploration N.L.

When the 'tide went out' in 1972, none of us 'true believers' could imagine that it would be another 17 years before nickel would again pop its head up.

Just as the Australian economy was 'rescued' by the Japanese in the early 1960s and again by China five years into this century (who will rescue us next?), the remnant prospecting, exploration industry was rescued by the resurgent gold industry in 1980 and we were all 'back in the saddle' riding a brand new race again.

It was a good feeling, to be back in active exploration again.

My old private exploration company, Mannkal Mining Pty Ltd, was vigorously reactivated and at the same time I took on a series of 'odd jobs' as Exploration Director of several listed companies, including a most enjoyable period with one of Peter Briggs' companies, Coopers Creek Mining & Exploration N.L.

Each time I needed $100,000 for a drilling programme, I headed off to London to 'make a share placement', having outlined our expectations.

It was during one of these successful trips to London in January 1980 that the gold price spiked at US$850, virtually granting me celebrity status in London.

However, during the long flight back to Australia, the gold price, equally miraculously, dropped US$150, but we were still able to bank the money and proceed with the drilling progamme.

Endnotes

1. Theseus Exploration N.L. is still trading as Uranium Equities Ltd.

My prospecting years (1969–1987), were a blur of countless prospecting, court battles, drilling, joint-ventures, discoveries, travel and adventure. These photos/clips capture several small segments.

Underground at the Golden Rainbow Mine, 1984

John Elkington 1971 following up radioactive indications on our uranium joint-venture with Utah Development Corp. Prospecting with a land-yacht on salt lakes.

Jenny Manners with John Elkington and Kim Robinson at Forrestania – 1986.

John Elkington when we revisited (2004) our original 1974 Forrestania prospect.

One of the many discoveries in 1980 as the increased gold price encouraged more prospecting (cont. on facing page)...

Dogger's became reality

AN 80oz gold nugget picked up by two Kalgoorlie prospectors has sparked off an intensive exploration programme near the town of Menzies.

MENZIES SEARCH STARTS

Kalgoorlie dogger Karl Srb and his partner Ron Manners picked up the nugget late last year while prospecting near the town, which is half-way between Kalgoorlie and Leonora.

They pegged the area and decided to take a closer look.

When they did, they found differences between the surface gold in the area and the surface gold they had seen elsewhere.

The partners managed to get a large English company, Charterhall Ltd, interested in the areas.

"So far they have spent about $200,000 on the areas and they intend to spend a further $1.1 million," said Mr Manners.

"The geologists claim the surface gold is not surface gold, but was formed exactly where it is lying. They say it has not shifted its position.

"If this is the case then it could indicate large reserves of gold under the surface."

Charterhall can earn up to a 51 per cent interest in the areas by spending up to $1.3 million.

The 49 per cent interest will remain with Messrs Manners and Srb. According to Mr Manners, Charterhall Ltd are anxious to start drilling as soon as possible to prove up the leases.

Mr Srb is only a part-time prospector. His main job is as a dogger for the Agricultural Protection Board.

He has the freedom to roam through thousands of square miles of the Kalgoorlie, Coolgardie and Menzies shires, trapping and shooting dingoes. But freedom was one thing he didn't have earlier in his life.

He was a teenager in Communist Czechoslovakia and had to run the gauntlet of border patrols to escape to West Germany in 1949. He migrated to Australia in 1950 and for 30 years he has worked in the outback, fencing, shooting brumbies, kangaroos, rabbits and now dingoes.

He lives in Kalgoorlie with his wife and four children and spends 10 days out on patrol and four days off.

A Kalgoorlie geologist, Mr George Compton (above, left) and a local business man, Mr Ron Manners (right) sign a joint venture agreement with CRA Exploration covering their Princess Royal East gold prospect at Norseman. The Australian-listed company Coopers Creek Mining and Exploration, have acquired the Compton-Manners interest in the joint venture. Mr Manners said that the terms of the joint venture allowed CRA to earn a 60 per cent interest in the venture by expenditure of $470,000 on exploration. The agreement then allowed for conversion into a joint mining operation at the time of declaiming the prospect to be commercially mineable. He said Compton-Manners would retain a five per cent carried interest.

Kalgoorlie Miner–February 12, 1980

dream

BUSINESS RESOURCES REVIEW

KARL Srb holds the 80-ounce nugget which he and partner Ron Manners picked up near Menzies and (right), Karl armed and ready for a day's work.

The prospecting bug hit Karl as it has many of the locals and about 18 months ago he started looking out for unpegged areas that might turn up something promising.

There aren't many areas unpegged in the Goldfields but he found a spot near Menzies and came up with the goods, a piece of ore rich in gold. He christened it "Dogger's Dream".

The nugget has been sold and now he's back in the bush, working for wages and a $5-a-head bonus for each dingo scalp.

1962–Inspired by Benny Goodman taking his clarinet to Moscow on a 'cultural exchange', I took my clarinet to Laverton, Western Australia.

1983–Another successful court battle over the Masterkey Mine. Bob Rogers, Chris Lalor (Solicitor), Ron & Craig Manners.

Interesting Dinner Guests

Jules Zanetti (1928–1997)

There were so many interesting visitors to Kalgoorlie during the heady Nickel boom in 1969 that we could choose only the most interesting to 'take home' for a meal.

One such guest was finance journalist Jules Zanetti.

Zanetti had lost an arm in a Bass Strait helicopter accident (oil drilling platform) that killed several reporters, about four years previously.

As the bearded Zanetti was elegantly fitted out with a stainless steel hook as a limb replacement, I had taken the liberty of briefing our four young children that; "Tonight, we are having a real live 'pirate' to dinner. At the first sign of any bad behaviour, he will simply reach over with his hook and rip your throats out!"

Well, we all listened intently to Jules' stories of his extensive travels and the next day he remarked to me, "Manners, you have the best behaved children I have ever seen in my whole life."

I explained the reason for this, which he took in good grace and we maintained regular contact over the next few years when he set up his own public exploration company, Zanex N.L.

When the Nickel boom fell apart, so did Jules' fortunes and our last contact was when he was running *People* magazine, where the focus was more on nipples than drill core.

Mining: The Productive Process

(Leads to Canada, Mexico, Brazil & Turkey)

Mining with King Croesus

(Based on notes made in 2004)

In the mid–1970s I experienced some difficulties with the Australian Taxation Office (see page 15) which prevented me from working effectively in Australia for a few years.

These were challenging years for me but more challenging for Australia in general as this was the period when politics moved from benign to malignant.

I had just completed a slim volume titled *The Alienated Australians*, being interviews with 27 Australians who had been driven out of the Australian workforce by the heavy hand of the bureaucracy. They were all enjoying successful careers in other countries where they were able to move much faster without the bureaucratic burdens of Australia.

Many of them shared a common motto: "If Socialism Works, I Won't." Socialism has never worked because socialism is parasitic and needs a fresh supply of victims to exist. In the long term it just runs out of victims and that was happening in Australia. (It took another fifteen years for the same thing to happen in the Soviet Union.)

During a break from my travels I wrote politely to the Commissioner for Taxation in the early 1980s, and suggested that if they tore up our tax dispute files I would be prepared to re-enter the productive workforce and allow them to pursue their speciality of plundering yet another pay-packet.

They found this offer too good to refuse and this gave me the opportunity to reactivate some almost forgotten skills[(1)] such as regional prospecting and floating a publicly-listed mining company which I called Croesus Mining NL. While Croesus Mining was coming together I was also on three other public company boards: Mistral Mines N.L, Great Central Mines NL and King Mining Limited.

Croesus Mining began trading on the Australian Stock Exchange in 1986, having raised $2.5 million. After nine months of exploring we were down to $0.5 million with no sign of any cashflow so we made a $20.3 million acquisition from Rio Tinto (then called CRA) of their gold interests in the Kalgoorlie region.

Smaller Companies Use More Innovative Financing

I recall that Rio Tinto wouldn't initially talk to us in the tender process because we had no 'credit rating' and their insistence was that we fronted up with a Letter of Credit from our bankers.

Our bankers, Westpac, were understandably unwilling to give us a Letter of Credit for $20 million so I asked how much they would charge if we only wanted to "borrow" a Letter of Credit for the morning. Their answer was $25,000 and I had to promise to have it back to them by noon.

This enabled Croesus to be included on Rio Tinto's tender list; but it was a bit embarrassing when Rio Tinto asked to keep the Letter of Credit. They eventually settled for keeping a photocopy and I managed to get the original back to Westpac at two minutes to noon.

SHORT-TERM LETTER OF CREDIT

Our first gold bar was ceremonially passed to John Oliver (left) and Bob Rogers (right).

John Oliver (another School of Mines mate who, in the late 1960s, had co-ordinated WMC's Kambalda nickel operations right through to production) was my adviser and this enabled us to justify a bid of $20.3 million.

John had good connections with Bank National de Paris (BNP) and we brought this bank's senior executive from Sydney to Kalgoorlie to look over our proposal. They agreed to finance us.

BNP took a copy of all the data and despatched it to their head office in Paris where they confirmed that, technically, our courageous bid was sound.

Subsequently our bid won the tender and later that day I phoned BNP in Sydney (just before they went home). Their Australian Manager said he would immediately telephone their Paris head office which would just be starting their day. He phoned me back saying that they were delighted and that their mining engineer would be visiting Australia in about nine months, at which time they would then be in a position to discharge funds.

As we had to have the ten per cent deposit ($2.03 million) into Rio Tinto by noon the next day (remembering we only had $0.5 million left ourselves), with 21 days to pay the balance, I somehow knew we were wasting our time talking further with BNP.

My main concern at that moment was not only missing out on the deal but also how I was to explain to the auditors the $25,000 payment to "borrow" a Letter of Credit.

Anyway, after about an hour in the toilet, I received an abusive telephone call from London, Rod Whyte, a stockbroker friend of mine had read on the Reuters' wire the details of the transaction and was upset at not being given the opportunity to participate. I said, "Don't worry, there is still time. If you place some Croesus shares right now with your UK clients, and if you promise to have $2.5 million deposited in our bank account by 10 a.m. tomorrow morning, you can be part of this exciting story."

Thankfully this worked and getting the other $18 million together over the next 21 days, in a mixture of share placements and loans, was equally exciting. Only with a lot of help from some very supportive friends and colleagues, we managed to get the transaction over the line.

My father always told me, "Never borrow money to bet on horses or look for gold", but I felt comfortable about borrowing money against the proven gold reserves actually in the ground.

We paid off all debt within nine months by mining that gold.

More recently, in 2002, Croesus jumped a few similar hurdles when we took over Central Norseman Gold Corporation.

Our bankers asked if we were really serious when we set out to borrow $60 million which, they reminded us, was "twice our current market capitalisation."

We got this away okay, having since repaid all debt and emerging with a market capitalisation of $150 million.

Now [in 2005], Croesus employs about 420 people and has paid 11 dividends, totalling in value about $28 million, as a result of mining and pouring 1.275 million ounces of gold, with a total value of about $1 billion at recent values.

We know that we will only be able to succeed and take advantage of the exciting opportunities in the future if each one of us continually reinvents ourselves as a way of coping with the challenges and impediments we are likely to confront.

Author's Note

For more details, earlier and subsequent challenges, spanning my 20–year involvement with Croesus Mining, refer to the separate publication "Turning Ideas Into Gold Bars".

During my 20 years with Croesus Mining I was fortunate to have competent people, such as the late Harry Kitson, to look after my private company interests so that they didn't intrude during my 'Croesus years'. I always paid for my several secretaries/personal assistants out of my own pocket even though 90 per cent of their work was on Croesus matters.

I believe it is always best to keep things tidy like this. However, such practice would be regarded as quaint these days. Similarly was my preference for flying economy class (so I didn't have to sit next to politicians).

In 1995, the Canadian company Eldorado Gold Corporation acquired my major shareholding in Croesus and I joined the Eldorado Gold board to become involved in gold mining adventures in Mexico, Brazil and Turkey.

My contract was to remain as Croesus Executive Chairman only for six months, as I was moving to Perth to expand our private Mannwest Group Pty Ltd into property and other mineral investments.

Eldorado's plans for Croesus were to expand into the South East Asian region, in particular Indonesia, which was caught up in 'Bre-X Fever' where the Canadian company Bre-X was seen to have discovered the world's largest gold mine at Busang.

Two events then occurred which completely changed Croesus' direction.

Firstly, the Bre-X 'boom' came to an ungodly end when their chief geologist jumped or was pushed from a helicopter, and it was subsequently found that their discovery was a 'scam' of gigantic proportions.

Secondly, Eldorado was effectively 'taken over' by the South African company Gencor (Billiton) and were discouraged from any further Australian involvement.

Croesus then entered a period where it really had no significant major shareholder and I remained as Executive Chairman until 1998, continuing as Non-Executive Chairman, and then retired from the Board in 2005.

The mid–1990s were my favorite years with Croesus and I valued the complete honesty and integrity of my hand-picked team. When I stepped down as major shareholder of Croesus, in 1995, I personally contributed financially to the team's visit to Hong Kong (to address a major group of shareholders) to express my gratitude for the years that we had spent together building such a team.

I didn't really enjoy the subsequent non-executive years as, apart from having a first-class board, I missed the direct engagement with company personnel. I felt that its corporate culture was changing dramatically, from a 'team culture' to a 'corrosive culture'. We were plagued by unfortunate events such as a suicide of one of our senior operators and by an epidemic of 'alleged gold stealing' and what in hindsight we found to be 'rubbery reporting from site', where management experienced difficulty in delivering on their own budgeted figures.

The Board suspected (correspondence dated August 9, 2004) that over-optimistic estimates were submitted to us, simply to enhance management salary review proposals.

Subsequent Board investigations were unable to cast any light on our suspicions.

In hindsight, it could be likened to one having an alcoholic spouse or a drug-afflicted child; they get very clever at concealing any evidence.

All this of course does not absolve the Board from their responsibility as custodians of the shareholders' investments.

What had been a 20–year grand adventure was at that point reduced to just another 'Heroic Misadventure'.

On June 23, 2006, Administrators were called in to restructure the company. They did a remarkable job and the company was recapitalised and 'back on board' by May 9, 2008, renamed Sirius Resources.

Hopefully, those who follow on can conclude 'the Croesus story' on a more upbeat note.

The following "piece" on Croesus' earlier years was presented by the author on February 21, 1994 to a Brisbane lunch, jointly sponsored by The MacArthur Club and Ernst & Young.

A Golden Opportunity

Now, when floating a mining company, why pick a name like Croesus, a word very few can pronounce let alone spell? Croesus was the King of Lydia, now Western Turkey, between 560 and 546 BC. He was noted for his great wealth, hence the term "rich as Croesus".

Anywhere in the world where there is mining there is always a Croesus Hill or a Croesus Nob or a Croesus Shaft and, in Kalgoorlie there is a Croesus Street. This was where we lived and the company actually had its registered office and operating staff based in our kitchen for the first couple of years of its life.

There are two other aspects of King Croesus I would like to mention as they still have relevance today: he had some good survival strategies, but overlooked a few small details, and he had a keen sense of the correct role for government in money matters.

As a means of survival through good and bad times he formed many joint ventures with neighbouring countries in much the same way as we currently joint venture our mining properties. It gives us tremendous leverage.

By doing deals with many of these partners he raised Lydia to the peak of its power, conquering Greek coastal cities and extending his empire to the Halys River in Central Asia Minor.

In one of the stories of how he ultimately met his end, Croesus and some joint venture partners were waging war against a neighbouring King alongside one of the corner pegs between the two nations. The record has it that there was a huge fire right near the corner peg and at the last minute one of his joint venture partners pulled out of the deal and joined forces with another. They quickly ran a spear through Croesus who fell on the fire and that's how they invented shish kebabs!

Another more scholarly version is that, around 546 BC, a young Persian corporate marauder, who later became known as Cyrus the Great, was having a great deal of success with his corporate takeovers because he had developed the technique of allowing conquered people to keep their jobs and their own corporate identity.

This technique was noted by King Croesus in Lydia who took it as a sign that the time had come to add a few more tenements to his own Kingdom.

He sought advice from the Oracle of Delphi on how to proceed and was informed that if he attacked he would destroy a great empire. The Oracle had given a typically enigmatic message, as it later turned out.

Croesus' first battle on open ground with Cyrus the Great did not go well for him and Croesus retired to his homeland for the winter, as was customary.

On his way home, Croesus alerted the Egyptians, the Babylonians and the Spartans that, come spring, they would all march together and destroy this "upstart" named Cyrus.

Cyrus wasn't in the mood to wait for spring. As Croesus' army was beginning to disband for the season the Persians marched up to the gates of Sardis, the capital of Lydia.

Although Croesus' defenders were always ready for attack, Cyrus tricked them as he had a secret weapon.

Instead of riding to the attack on horseback, his soldiers were mounted on camels, the sight and smell of which spooked the more traditional mounts of the Lydian cavalry and the defending army was driven back into the city.

Sardis was widely regarded as the most impregnable city in the world at the time, because of its location at the top of a steep hill, and Cyrus thought he was beaten. However, after more than two weeks of the siege, an odd accident gave Cyrus the key to the city. Watching a point near where the hill was steepest and least protected (because it was considered unclimbable) one of the Persian soldiers was surprised to notice a sentry on the wall lose his helmet over the side and, rather than go to the quarter-master for a new one, he scrambled down the hill to retrieve it. This revealed the presence of a secret pathway.

Following this route the next morning, before light, the Persians entered the city in single file, killed Croesus and claimed his legendary treasures. The "Great Empire" to which the Oracle had referred was Croesus' own.

So often a whole corporate empire has crumbled because it has not practised Total Quality Control and insufficient investment has been made in training every single staff member.

Even the best survival strategies can come unstuck because of a lack of attention to one tiny detail.

Shared or Stolen

A point worth mentioning about King Croesus is that he was the first ruler in the world to mint gold coins.

The single action in recognising gold as honest money, untouchable by politicians and government officials, could rank equally in importance with Adam Smith's contribution when he was credited with having explained the moral foundations for "free enterprise" over 200 years ago.

Adam Smith gave us some guidelines, later refined by Frederic Bastiat, Ludwig Von Mises and FA Hayek, as the basis of a government's job specifications.

Identifying the correct role of government and controlling governments so that they stay within these bounds is the key to our personal and corporate survival.

This presents a continuing challenge for us all. So what can we do about it?

There appears to be total confusion in this country as to the correct role of government; but the problem is worse than that. There appears to be total confusion as to what our personal roles should be and what our corporate responsibilities are.

The problem goes back to our early training. We are not conditioned for the real world.

For example, how many of you have developed an automatic response you will use when you are confronted with a physical "mugging" from one individual?

Of course the success of a perfect automatic response depends on surprising your assailant so, naturally, I can't divulge the secret to you — but you really should know it already.

The root of this conditioning problem goes back to childhood and can be related to a recent incident that I witnessed.

It was at a family gathering at Christmas. This family had small children and their three-year-old was playing with a new toy he had received, a truck which came with a number of smaller pieces including a plastic water tank fitted on the back. Smiling, he carried his treasure into the living-room where other family members sat. Immediately his two-year-old cousin came over and seized the tank from the back of the truck.

Naturally, the boy tried to take back the purloined tank. Just as naturally, his cousin twisted away and clutched his prize more tightly to his chest. Plaintively, the boy looked up with a pained expression on his face and pointed to the small plastic tank. Sternly two or three of the adults in the room—including his mother—told him in no uncertain terms that he must "share".

I cringe at this brief drama as it exemplifies one of the basic problems with our society. This incident and countless others like it have helped establish the underpinnings for a moral assault on our free society, the sanctity of private property and individual responsibility.

There is, of course, nothing wrong with sharing. But there is something wrong with stealing, and what happened in that living-room was stealing not sharing.

These messages learnt in childhood are often the most enduring and they are unthinkingly adopted before we have the intellectual ability to analyse them. Buried among forgotten childhood experiences, these principles frequently guide our adult actions without ever having been exposed to the light of rational questioning. Eventually we will face the negative consequences of faulty ethics and ask, bewildered, "Why did this happen?"

"Sharing", because someone makes you do it, is just as much a self-contradiction as the notion of "forced charity". The redistribution of income applauded by most politicians, the cries of our citizens for "entitlements" and social welfare programmes to fulfil personal needs or desires, the idea that government interference in our private lives is proper, and the contention of taxation are all destructive beliefs and actions; the roots of which can be traced back to the mind-set which says to innumerable and defenceless small children, "You have to share," when their toys are taken.

The good intentions of parents and adults do not alter the damage they are doing any more than the possibly good intentions of our politicians when they wildly throw our money at their favourite vote-buying schemes.

If each of us can break away from any such early programming problems, it will help us understand the problems which are coming at us from every direction and help us understand the legitimate role for government, individuals and companies.

Let's start with the easy bit first.

What is corporate responsibility?

This is a question which involves the nature of business itself. Very simply, a business produces a product or provides goods and services to people who want them.

By law, a business corporation is authorised to act in place of a person, even though it may be owned by many. The profits belong to all who invest in expectation of earning a return. Doesn't it follow that the profits of a corporation be reserved for the benefits of the owners?

Of course, the owners have a duty and obligation to consider how they will dispose of their profits. The matter is simple in a proprietorship or partnership with a small number of owners. The parties may meet and choose to give to worthy causes. It gets more complicated in the case of a so-called public company which may have thousands of shareholders. How can all be consulted about the disposition of the profits? I think the solution is very simple—pay out the profits as dividends and let the owners (shareholders) decide what to do with the money.

However, in recent years, corporations have learned from politicians to become very skilled at giving away other people's money while making themselves feel good about it. Many arguments are raised to justify corporate giving. People are moved by pure motives to contribute and this is commendable. A second argument is that the needs are so great that they require corporate rather than individual resources. A third justification is that giving creates goodwill in the community.

This view is based on the idea that it is important for corporations to be good citizens and to contribute to the community. This sounds appealing until one realises that it is possible to give back to the community simply by lowering prices or expanding operations and increasing employment opportunities.

The current buzzword in corporate giving is "enlightened self-interest". If you make the world a better place, people will buy more of what you have to sell. Enlightened self-interest also creates good public relations. Whole textbooks have been written on this kind of "cause-related marketing".

Huge public relations departments create photo opportunities for corporate heads to shake hands with leaders of local charities and hand them cheques. The results of this kind of philanthropy are measured by the good it does for the company, not the good it does for the recipient. Now, all this sort of giving may be acceptable for a company which sells something to the public as such expenditure can form part of their advertising budget.

Unfortunately, there is also a great deal of peer pressure for non-selling companies to conform in this way. If a worthy cause is in need and most of the community is giving to that organisation, a company which doesn't becomes conspicuous by its absence. So corporate philanthropy could help avoid "trouble". Dozens of special interest groups routinely target corporations and issue the threat of a boycott in order to secure contributions. Often these contributions are in reality just like "protection money" which businesses are forced to pay to the underworld or to governments in the form of occupational licence fees in return for the government protecting them against competition.

Corporate Social Responsibility[2] has become a catchword of the Left, an excuse for ever-expanding government control of business. It's time that business fought back and explained that it has no more social responsibilities than anyone else.

Corporate philanthropy has also funded hundreds of legitimate causes meant to solve our nation's problems. But the poor seem to get poorer, and many citizens have become more and more dependent upon government. Corporate philanthropy has often helped foster this dependence.

It is also clear that corporate philanthropy has been a poor substitute for personal philanthropy. Not only has it been widely perverted by businesses and special interest groups, it has also not been very effective in addressing the problems it seeks to solve. In this context it is more important than ever to develop guidelines for personal philanthropy.

Here is what I suggest :

- Support people and causes with which you are personally involved. Give more than just money to those you are helping—stand with them and help them personally. It is often the dynamic energy of the corporate world that is needed to help these people achieve their worthy aims.
- Do not wait until you are established in the world; you never will be "established" in the world. You will never reach a point at which you have "arrived" and can begin giving.
- Give privately, not seeking recognition for your work. It is for others' benefit that you are giving, not your own.
- Be a cheerful giver. The joy of helping others far exceeds the joy of helping yourself.

Now having said that, what does a company, based within a community, do when they receive these various letters of request from worthy causes?

Here are single paragraphs from two recent letters received by our company:

> A permanent honour board will be suitably placed to recognise those firms who give their support. Our approach for funds is to those firms who enjoy the fruits of Kalgoorlie, be it through stockmarket activities, mining or the service and supply industries.
>
> Croesus Mining and the Mystery Mint Mine are an integral part of Coolgardie and I invite you to consider helping us with our advertising budget.

How many times are we, in business (or politicians for that matter) faced with these demands for money, which is not ours to give?

Is there a way of combining acceptable corporate philanthropy with private philanthropy to avoid any of the problems I have mentioned?

It's about as far as we can go as a compromise.

I believe there is and, having canvassed many companies for ideas, we have adopted a scheme based on a concept developed by Delta Gold NL.

When they started making a profit in 1991, Delta were inundated with requests for help and they faced the dilemma of how to respond. They developed what they call their "Matching Plan" where Delta matches every dollar given by its staff members to their chosen charities. Naturally, such a plan would only apply when a company is making profits as it would be quite immoral for an exploration company to dip into its exploration budget to assist causes, no matter how worthy.

This is a good system for screening out requests such as any that have little merit such as any anti-business cause. In this way, the company supports its staff by giving them the choice and responsibility of choosing where such funds are allocated and it effectively doubles their contribution and increases their personal involvement as that person usually goes on that charity's committee to inject management skills as well.

Now, wouldn't it be good if we could impose a strict set of controls on the way our various governments give our money away?

It might prevent these continuing scandals, one example from 1993 when Federal Sports Minister, Ros Kelly,[3] with her "sports rort", gave away $30 million of your money and then rubbed all the details off her white board.

Now $30 million may not seem like a lot of money to Ros Kelly, because she regards it as other people's money, but it does to us as it is *our* money.

These are the very same people in Canberra who set up committees to control the behaviour of the corporate sector.

I laughed heartily when I read of Labor MP Stephen Smith, formerly of the party's Left wing and now Chairman of the Federal Parliament's ASIC and Stock Exchange watchdog committee, commenting: "The committee is in the business of spiv-watching."

We know who the spivs are, but unfortunately most of us are too busy working on our economic survival to find time to control these political spivs.

The writer P. J. O'Rourke recently said, "A little government and a little luck are necessary in life, but only a fool trusts either of them."

In a company, when critical mass is reached, it is a good thing because it then becomes self-sustaining and profits can be reinvested in exploration or research and development and everyone wins.

Unfortunately, when a government reaches critical mass and starts behaving as we now see in Australia, there is no stopping them because government is out of control. It consumes the economy, crushes freedom and individual rights and then ultimately self-destructs as we have recently seen in the East European countries.

What Government Actions Are Legitimate?

This brings us to the challenging bit. What is the correct role of government?

Government's role is essentially a negative one and in many ways the less they do for us, the better it is for us.

Henry David Thoreau may have been cynical, but he was correct when he said, "Government may best assist by the alacrity with which it gets out of the way."

Government should be regarded as a necessary evil (and therefore be kept very small), and given the job specification of simply protecting the lives, liberty and property of individuals who constitute society.

This ideal job specification came from the Founding Fathers of the United States of America who, unfortunately, did not build in sufficient controls to prevent the political process from taking over.

Good political systems are designed to protect us from our leaders.

The Swiss have the solution!

When Switzerland adopted its constitution in 1848, it was inspired by the United States' Constitution and its republican system which, among other things, incorporated much of the great body of English common law. However, even in 1848, the Swiss saw that in the American system of representative democracy the representatives of the people had already become corrupted by power and their Congress was being ruled by vested-interest lobbies (this was in 1848—look at it now!)

Switzerland opted instead for a decentralised state with a very small central government in which most of the power was devolved to many small regions, or cantons.

Their system is characterised by their reliance on numerous referenda and initiatives and includes the power to recall corrupt politicians and to veto legislation.

For the most part, Switzerland has been successful in avoiding the problems which have plagued centralised federal states around the world. Even though the Swiss have a great potential for conflict, with many religious and ethnic divisions within their borders, their policy of regional autonomy has assured a high degree of social harmony—not to mention stellar economic performance. Switzerland is still at the top of the list of the most desirable places in the world to live.

The people have also provided a successful formula for limiting the size and powers of government.

Back in Australia, there is no mystery as to why we have more than one million people unemployed and why Canberra continues to pursue policies which will increase that figure [in 1994].

We have [in 1994] a Federal Government whose policies and supporters are largely enemies of economic growth. These policies and people are on a collision course with anyone trying to create real jobs.

Things will not change until their policies change and the socialists cease their relentless war against mining and development.

The combined efforts of the Native Title nitwits and the environmental fringe dwellers, with their well-orchestrated pressure on vote-seeking politicians, has cost our nation dearly (refer 106).

I heard a story about Moses the other day and, if it wasn't so serious, it could be funny. It goes:

Moses was leading the children of Israel across the Red Sea. "I have some good news and some bad news for you," said Moses. The good news is I will lift up my arms, the Red Sea will part and we will be able to walk across on dry land. The bad news is that we have to wait for the Environmental Impact Statement."

Wouldn't it be interesting if Native Title nitwits and the environmental extremists, before pursing their self-interest projects, had to first fill out not only the Environmental Impact Statement we have to, but also an "Economic Impact Statement" to show the Australian people the exact cost imposed on us by the impediments they attach to any development projects? I call them "Barnacles on the Backside of Progress".

The costs would be hard to quantify because exploration, for example, is the seed capital of future mining development. If the seeds are not planted, there are no future crops. The damage being done today will not affect existing mines but it is their replacements over the next five, ten or twenty years that will be missing. [Note the lack of recent discoveries for 2008.] These missing mines will be missing revenue, missing taxes for Australian Governments and missing jobs for the Australian workforce.

Well, this must all sound very depressing.

So why haven't we shifted to Chile, Indonesia or Africa, where 24 of Australia's largest explorers are spending 25 per cent of their exploration dollars?

I estimate that there is over $1 billion of Australian investment money going into overseas exploration this year [1994]. This is amazing when we consider our one million unemployed back home [1994]. Two Australian companies, Rio Tinto (CRA) and Mount Isa Mines, are considering another $1 billion investment in Argentina alone.

Croesus Mining receives deputations from these countries and the offers of 'red carpet' treatment sound tempting. We have opened files on many of these opportunities and there may be a time in the future when we will be more than tempted.

Why are we still here? The reason we are still based in Kalgoorlie, Western Australia, is that I wouldn't miss out on what is happening in Australia right now, despite how many tempting offers may be made.

I am an optimist.

"Crisis means opportunities", as the Chinese say and, as many of Australia's larger companies have diverted funds and attention overseas, it has created a whole new range of opportunities for small-to-medium size companies here in Australia.

All I ask of governments is that they keep out of our way and leave us with the economic freedom to explore and produce. I know we will only hold these freedoms as long as we have the courage to fight for them. Courage is like love; it must have hope for nourishment.

May I wish you courage to expand your own freedoms and responsibilities within your chosen profession. This can be done if we take seriously our responsibilities as a free people, which means never conceding to politicians and bureaucrats the right to run our lives.

But always remember that no matter what may happen, changes bring forth opportunities and, no matter what politicians and government officials may do to us, the secret of economic success is to be ready for opportunities when they come.

Endnotes

1. Being no stranger to public company boards, having been a director of 'Poseidon nickel boom" companies, Theseus Exploration NL, Mining & Associated Industries Ltd and Trendline Traders Ltd, prior to floating what was probably the last of the Poseidon boom companies, Kalmin Exploration Ltd.
2. For a later submission on Corporate Social Responsibility, go to: http://www.mannkal.org/downloads/submissions/sub20050929.pdf
3. The whiteboard was Ros Kelly's preferred administrative tool—(as Labor's Sports Minister)—while working out how to dole out $30 million in grants to sporting, cultural and recreational bodies before the 1993 election. The "sports rorts" affair, as the scandal was alternatively

known, grew out of Opposition complaints that the money had not been distributed on the basis of need or due process, but to buy community favour in sensitive electorates.

There was a damning Audit Office report about the lack of proper process, followed by an even more damning House of Representatives inquiry.

During one parliamentary censure motion against Ros Kelly, John Howard called her "pathetic", "stupid", "dishonest" and "dead meat". He was right about dead meat. At the end of February 1994 Kelly resigned.

....as reported, Margo Kingston's Webdiary–smh.com.au

4. See also 'What Would Shakespeare Think of Our Mining Industry?' - See page 257.

Lang Hancock
(1909–1992)
Flying over the Hamersley Ranges–1974
(Photo by the author)

Gina Rinehart, daughter of the late Lang Hancock (who is credited with being Australia's iron ore pioneer), phoned me to explain that she was inviting a few friends on November 22, 2002 to celebrate the 50th anniversary of Lang's iron ore "discovery flight".

"Ron, as you had a special friendship with my father, could you give a little talk to the guests please?" she asked.

Like most things in my life, I left my preparation a little late and expecting a dinner party for ten or so people, thought I could get away with some impromptu comments.

To my amazement, a gathering of 700 guests were assembled for this celebration and what follows is a transcript from my impromptu attempt to cover so much in such limited time.

1952
Nov 22

Discovery flight with wife, Hope, whilst flying from their Nunyerry mine to Perth

1953

Returning to discovery area, landing in spinifex and collecting samples for more than 50 miles and sending to Perth for analysis.
After analysis, realisation he had found an iron ore zone of possible world significance.

1955

Established family company, Hancock Prospecting Pty Ltd

1963-1964

Arranged and hosted the visit of the world's then richest man, Daniel K Ludwig, and interested him in presenting a cost saving proposal to the West Australian government for the building of a large central port and unified railway system to service the entire Pilbara iron ore region, to enhance the region's competitiveness.

1966

Tom Price commissioned, and Port and town of Dampier established.

1969

Established with WPPL the newspaper "The Sunday Independent"

1970-1971

Hanwright explored with the co-operation of Mr Hancock's brothers in law Jim and Bill Nicholas, and friend Don Rhodes, the West Angelas, which Mr Hancock named after E.A. Wright's daughter, but these areas were then confiscated by the West Australian government, and later given to a competing company.

1972

HPPL and WPPL established with TexasGulf the Iron Ore (Rhodes Ridge) Agreement with the West Australian government.
HPPL and WPPL established with the Iron Ore (Wittenoom) Agreement with the West Australian government.
HPPL and WPPL established with MIM, Utah and Consolidated Goldfields the Iron Ore (McCameys) Agreement with the West Australian government.

1973

Paraburdoo commenced production

1974

Acquired HPPL Perth headquarters in Nedlands and named the building "The Angelas" as a reminder of the importance of prospecting, together with the security of title. Established the nationwide "National Miner" newspaper. Gained jet pilots license at age 65, acquired first Lear jet and utilised for overseas visits to promote Australian mineral developments and to show executives, politicians and others the Pilbara's potential.

1994

Marandoo commenced production

1997

Pre-feasibility study for Hope Downs finalised and bankable feasibility study commenced.
Gina hosted visit of Chairman of Iscor of South Africa and senior executives to Pilbara.

1998
Jan 29

Announcement of participation of Iscor Limited to develop the Hope Downs Iron Ore Project with Hancock Prospecting Pty Ltd.

1999
June 10

Naming of Hancock Range in the Pilbara in honour of Lang Hancock and the Hancock family, and their pioneering history in the North West region.

2000

Established program with the Notre Dame University to commence the Hancock Free Enterprise Lectures.

2001

Opening of the Hall of Fame for Prospectors and Miners and establishment of permanent display in recognition of Lang Hancock's contribution in the Prospectors and Mining Galleries.

2002

Finalisation of the technical feasibility study for Hope Downs - production due to commence late in 2005 or 2006. Fifty year commemorative plaque and rock sculpture established in West Perth, in conjunction with the Perth City Council.

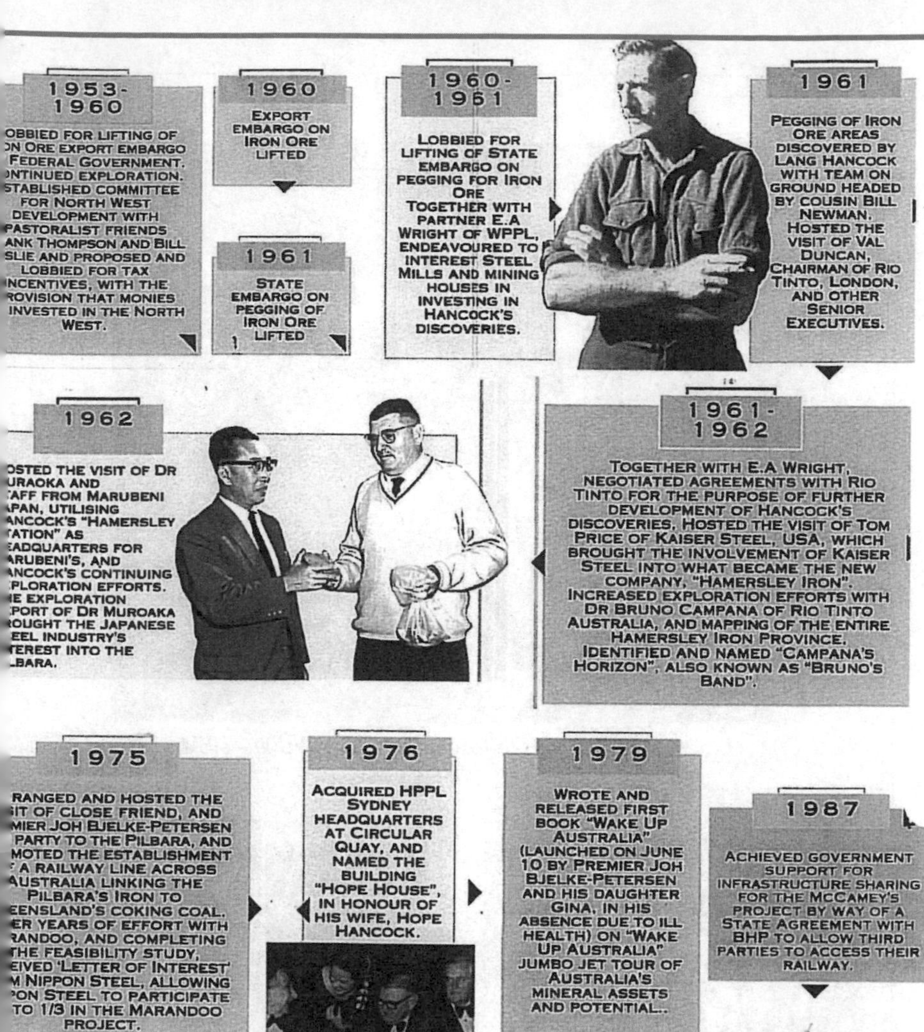

1953-1960
OBBIED FOR LIFTING OF
ON ORE EXPORT EMBARGO
FEDERAL GOVERNMENT.
ONTINUED EXPLORATION.
STABLISHED COMMITTEE
FOR NORTH WEST
DEVELOPMENT WITH
PASTORALIST FRIENDS
ANK THOMPSON AND BILL
SLIE AND PROPOSED AND
LOBBIED FOR TAX
INCENTIVES, WITH THE
ROVISION THAT MONIES
INVESTED IN THE NORTH
WEST.
1960
EXPORT EMBARGO ON IRON ORE LIFTED
1961
STATE EMBARGO ON PEGGING OF IRON ORE LIFTED
1960-1961
LOBBIED FOR LIFTING OF STATE EMBARGO ON PEGGING FOR IRON ORE
TOGETHER WITH PARTNER E.A WRIGHT OF WPPL, ENDEAVOURED TO INTEREST STEEL MILLS AND MINING HOUSES IN INVESTING IN HANCOCK'S DISCOVERIES.
1961
PEGGING OF IRON ORE AREAS DISCOVERED BY LANG HANCOCK WITH TEAM ON GROUND HEADED BY COUSIN BILL NEWMAN. HOSTED THE VISIT OF VAL DUNCAN, CHAIRMAN OF RIO TINTO, LONDON, AND OTHER SENIOR EXECUTIVES.
1962
OSTED THE VISIT OF DR
URAOKA AND
AFF FROM MARUBENI
APAN, UTILISING
ANCOCK'S "HAMERSLEY
TATION" AS
EADQUARTERS FOR
ARUBENI'S, AND
ANCOCK'S CONTINUING
PLORATION EFFORTS.
HE EXPLORATION
EPORT OF DR MUROAKA
ROUGHT THE JAPANESE
EEL INDUSTRY'S
TEREST INTO THE
LBARA.
1961-1962
TOGETHER WITH E.A WRIGHT, NEGOTIATED AGREEMENTS WITH RIO TINTO FOR THE PURPOSE OF FURTHER DEVELOPMENT OF HANCOCK'S DISCOVERIES. HOSTED THE VISIT OF TOM PRICE OF KAISER STEEL, USA, WHICH BROUGHT THE INVOLVEMENT OF KAISER STEEL INTO WHAT BECAME THE NEW COMPANY, "HAMERSLEY IRON". INCREASED EXPLORATION EFFORTS WITH DR BRUNO CAMPANA OF RIO TINTO AUSTRALIA, AND MAPPING OF THE ENTIRE HAMERSLEY IRON PROVINCE. IDENTIFIED AND NAMED "CAMPANA'S HORIZON", ALSO KNOWN AS "BRUNO'S BAND".
1975
RANGED AND HOSTED THE
SIT OF CLOSE FRIEND, AND
MIER JOH BJELKE-PETERSEN
PARTY TO THE PILBARA, AND
MOTED THE ESTABLISHMENT
F A RAILWAY LINE ACROSS
AUSTRALIA LINKING THE
PILBARA'S IRON TO
EENSLAND'S COKING COAL.
ER YEARS OF EFFORT WITH
RANDOO, AND COMPLETING
THE FEASIBILITY STUDY,
EIVED 'LETTER OF INTEREST'
M NIPPON STEEL, ALLOWING
PON STEEL TO PARTICIPATE
TO 1/3 IN THE MARANDOO
PROJECT.
1976
ACQUIRED HPPL SYDNEY HEADQUARTERS AT CIRCULAR QUAY, AND NAMED THE BUILDING "HOPE HOUSE", IN HONOUR OF HIS WIFE, HOPE HANCOCK.
1979
WROTE AND RELEASED FIRST BOOK "WAKE UP AUSTRALIA" (LAUNCHED ON JUNE 10 BY PREMIER JOH BJELKE-PETERSEN AND HIS DAUGHTER GINA, IN HIS ABSENCE DUE TO ILL HEALTH) ON "WAKE UP AUSTRALIA" JUMBO JET TOUR OF AUSTRALIA'S MINERAL ASSETS AND POTENTIAL.
1987
ACHIEVED GOVERNMENT SUPPORT FOR INFRASTRUCTURE SHARING FOR THE MCCAMEY'S PROJECT BY WAY OF A STATE AGREEMENT WITH BHP TO ALLOW THIRD PARTIES TO ACCESS THEIR RAILWAY.
1993
HOSTED VISIT BY
MIER MR RICHARD
RT AND PARTY TO
PILBARA.
UNE 10, A NEW
NET, DISCOVERED
R CANDY, NAMED
N PERMANENT
NOUR OF LANG
HANCOCK.
1992
JUNE-
BROCKMAN COMMENCED PRODUCTION. DECEMBER - HPPL ACHIEVED THE IRON ORE (HOPE DOWNS) AGREEMENT WITH THE STATE GOVERNMENT.
1992
MARCH 27
PASSED AWAY UNEXPECTEDLY, DESPITE STRONG WILL TO LIVE.
1989-1991
ACHIEVED FIRST TONNAGE TO BE MINED AT MCCAMEY'S
1990
JANUARY
CHANNAR COMMENCED PRODUCTION.

Background profile of Land Hancock—copied from the commemorative brochure for the guests November 22, 2002.

Lang Hancock with fellow pilot, Keith Wilkin–1974

John Martyr, MHR Swan, Gina Hancock (later Rinehart) and the author–1974

The rugged Pilbara terrain–1974

Remembering Lang Hancock

Thank you Michael (Darby), you're very kind and I respond well to kindness. Michael has given me a great list of the dignitaries here tonight and I will simply say that I welcome you all.

Tonight is called "Remembering Lang Hancock". Where does one start? I thought about this around midnight last night and I came to the conclusion I could only fit in five points. They are:

1. The time in 1963 when Lang probably saved my life without his knowing that this was the case.
2. Eventually meeting Lang personally some years later.
3. Everyone has a 'Lang Hancock story' to tell.
4. So who is the real Lang Hancock?
5. Concluding remarks.

Going back to 1963, life was very simple, as I recall, and I'll have to give you the background to this so you can understand Lang's involvement in this incident.

Then based in Kalgoorlie, two mates and I wanted to sell some mining equipment to a copper mine at Thaduna, way up north, somewhere between Meekathara and Darwin. We then wanted to call into Wittenoom to look at the asbestos mine. The first thing we did was get a map. Finding it was too far to drive in a couple of days we said, "Let's hire an aircraft." So we did. The plane's owner looked at the three of us and said, "Do any of you know what you're doing?" One of us had a pilot's licence and I said, "That's okay, he can fly the thing and I've just bought a new map, so we'll be okay."

So away we went. We found Thaduna, no trouble at all. We had a good tour of the mine. Rodney Fletcher and Malcolm Scott were running the Thaduna copper mine at the time. They were mining copper and concentrating it on-site before shipping it off to Japan in 44 gallon drums. Pretty pioneering stuff back then in 1963. We finished the tour and asked, "Now, how do we get to Wittenoom from here?" "Well that's easy," Rod said. "You just need to go west and look out for Mt Bruce, it's the highest mountain in the State. Once you get to Mt Bruce, just circle around in ever increasing circles and you can't miss Wittenoom."

A few hours later we saw a couple of high mountains on the horizon. We had a guessing game about which was the highest of the two and it was unanimous that one was higher than the other, so off we went to Mt Bruce. However, we picked the wrong one (see page 221).

We got there, circled around and around in increasing circles, but there was no sign of anything. Nothing at all. We did this for a couple of hours and then we heard the plane's engine go "cough, cough" and we said, "Well the fuel gauge is working ok".

By this time we turned the radio on, hoping we could talk to somebody. We got the Department of Civil Aviation (DCA), (I think it's changed its name since then). We explained to the fellow that we weren't travelling very well and he could hear the "coughing" of the engine. He said the best thing to do was to, "Try and set down somewhere".

We looked out the window and saw that we were hopelessly lost in the middle of the Hamersley Ranges. It was rugged stuff and we replied, "Well, that's a pretty good idea". He said, "Now, if you get down, radio us again, but as you go down, take note of any landmarks so you can describe where you landed."

We flew around a bit more, glided actually, and saw an area where an aircraft may have landed some years before. There were some scratchings, but there were a few trees in the way.

We landed there and took a few markings as we went down. There was no "black box" or anything on the plane so I took a few movies thinking this might be as good as a "black box" if anyone ever found us.

We got down and re-established contact by radio. It was getting dark and they said, "First of all, light a fire." So we lit a fire and within minutes we had about a thousand hectares of burning spinifex. We reckoned this would be clearly visible from the moon. At the least, any planes in the southern hemisphere were bound to see us. (In fact they did, and many reported seeing a serious fire, but they didn't fly close enough to see us.)

How to Get Lost by Following Instructions?

On page 220 I explained how we got lost in the Pilbara by using "Western Australia's highest mountain" as a reference point.

At that time (1963) all the maps showed Mt Bruce as being our highest mountain (1235.4 metres) and our colleague, Les Harrison, as a licensed pilot, was required to attend an inquiry as to the reasons for our becoming lost.

Our "error" was that we had "mistaken" Mt Meharry as being higher than Mt Bruce.

Four years after the inquiry (in 1977) following a re-survey it was discovered that Mt Meharry was in fact 13.5 metres higher than Mt Bruce and subsequent maps have been modified to show this.

So we got back on the radio and the operator said, "Well done!"

We described what we had seen as we came down and he said, "Look, there's only one person in Western Australia that can really give us any idea as to where you may be, so what we'll do is put you on hold and we'll ring him." So they rang through to Mr Lang Hancock. Lang was not at home at the time. However, a lady answered the phone and said, "No, Mr and Mrs Hancock have just gone to the movies."

The DCA person said, "What we'll do, if you don't mind, is ring back at 11 pm on the dot."

He said to us, "To conserve the battery on the radio, contact us every two hours and then particularly at 11 o'clock."

Well, we had no other plans for the night!

They rang Lang Hancock's home, Lang answered the phone, they explained the problem and he asked a few more questions. Yes, there was a creek across one corner of what had been an abandoned strip. Lang said, "Hold on, I don't know how you got down there but that was my strip but I haven't used it for years and years. If you want to take off tomorrow, whatever you do, clear a few trees out of the way, because the strip is in pretty bad shape."

Lang told them exactly where we were.

They arranged for the Flying Doctor to come out the next morning and he had a bit of trouble landing even after we removed the trees, but he got down. The first question he asked was, "Have you got a jerrycan so we can shuffle some petrol across from my plane to yours?" Actually, when we took off from Kalgoorlie, the last thing on our minds was to take along a jerrycan! Who takes a jerrycan on a flight? The only possible container available was the doctor's little stainless steel urinal. You know, the one with the handle you see in hospitals. It took half a day to transfer enough fuel across to get us to Wittenoom.

I have a very clear memory of that night which we spent, lost in the Pilbara, huddled around that campfire. One of us commented, "Isn't it remarkable, that in a State of this size, there's only one person who knows where things are up here in the Pilbara?"

We all agreed and then one of us said, "Well I hope Lang makes it home from the movies okay."

We were lucky.

Three In Aircraft All Safe

A PIPER Cherokee aircraft, off course and forced down in the Hamersley Ranges last night, was found early today.

A Flying Doctor Cessna aircraft from Port Hedland landed beside the missing aircraft at 7.15 a.m. and reported that the pilot and two passengers were safe.

The aircraft was found on an iron ore exploration strip, at Mt. Pyrton, about 70 miles off course. Its location was pin-pointed by a Department of Civil Aviation course plotting crew who worked all night on the missing pilot's information.

THE map pin-points where salesman-pilot Leslie Harrison landed on an old airstrip near Mt. Pyrton in the Hamersley Ranges.

The aircraft had been bound for Wittenoom from Thaduna, a distance of 245 miles.

It became lost late yesterday afternoon and after following suggested courses by DCA, decided to land on an unidentified airstrip.

DCA advised the pilot to conserve his radio battery and to call base with information every two hours.

He was told to light a fire so that the smoke could be spotted from the air.

Late last night the Flying Doctor aircraft crew at Port Hedland was told to stand by to take off in a search early today. At midnight a preliminary search area was radioed to Port Hedland.

The Flying Doctor aircraft found the Piper Cherokee on the suggested course 110 miles inland from Port Hedland.

Meanwhile, a chartered DC3 aircraft, heading for another search area, was recalled to Perth.

The grounded aircraft was refuelled from the Flying Doctor aircraft and it continued on its planned flight towards Wittenoom.

Down safely, last light–1963

West Australian—*Wednesday August 14, 1963*

Can I just mention one more thing about that flight we had in 1963?

I just thought, this is a classic example of when you really don't want to believe everything in the newspapers. *The West* reported it this way:

> Three In Aircraft, All Safe: Its location was pinpointed by a Department of Civil Aviation course plotting crew, who worked all night on the missing pilot's information."

I skip forward now, about seven years to 1970, when there was a "nickel boom" happening in Kalgoorlie which took me out of the country a fair bit. Every time I travelled anywhere overseas, and people knew I was from Western Australia, they'd say, "Oh, you must know Lang Hancock." I was very embarrassed and I said, "No, I don't." They'd say, "But you must." They assumed there were only about ten people in Western Australia.

I put up with this for a few years. However, I was so embarrassed about this that one day I rang Lang from Kalgoorlie and said, "Mr Hancock, I'd like to meet you."

He said, "Why?"

I couldn't tell him the truth, so I said, "We may have some things in common, I'd like to meet you so we can discuss them."

He said, "I'll give you ten minutes and don't be late, 10 o'clock tomorrow morning."

I jumped on a plane and there I was. He said again, "I'll give you just ten minutes."

Well, I remember walking out of his office five hours later.

We found out that we did have a lot in common. I think it must have been something to do with Milton Friedman, his favourite economist, and F.A. Hayek my favourite economist, and Lang getting his secretary to photocopy things from book, after book and from many magazines. I walked out of his office five hours later with a great big carton containing almost a photocopied library of magnificent "stuff".

So we got to be good friends.

However, he was appalled at my ignorance of the Pilbara. I knew little of what was going on up there and what was about to happen.

He cured that. He took me up there a few times and gave me personally conducted tours, giving me some insight into what was happening and, more importantly, what tremendous potential the great State of Western Australia had for those who are prepared to take a few risks and "have a go!"

I felt he'd given me several comprehensive Pilbara briefings so I later brought him to Kalgoorlie and showed him what was going on there. I thought he might like to be part of the "nickel boom" but he said, "I'm a bit busy."

We had several visits north together and I could tell you lots of stories about those visits but I'll just move on to the next point, which is:

Everyone Has a Lang Hancock Story

Now, everyone has a story about Lang Hancock but I'll just tell you four.

How did Lang Hancock get the nickname 'Pedal Faster'?

I didn't know. I had to ask. It goes back to his early days on Mulga Downs station when he phoned up on the pedal radio. He sent a lot of messages back, took a lot of notes and he was pretty active on the radio in those days. After a little while though, his voice used to trail off and listeners on the other end used to yell out "Lang, speak up! Speak up!" Lang used to yell back, "Pedal faster! Pedal faster!"

Now I'd better explain, so you can get a mental picture. The "Flying Doctor" radio was a "pedal wireless" in those days with electricity generated from what looked like a stationary exercise bike.

Lang just wanted to use the microphone and do the writing so he called in one of his Aboriginal field-hands to go on the pedals. This poor guy, after about 20 minutes, absolutely exhausted, started slowing down, resulting in Lang's voice trailing off on the reduced voltage. "Lang speak up!" "Pedal faster!" Lang would call to his assistant and so they all knew him as "Pedal Faster" .

Another story involved Denis O'Meara. He was the Mining Registrar in Marble Bar during the '60s and he had a lot to do with Lang and his business partner, Peter Wright.

Denis saw Lang more as a tin miner because Lang and Peter were mining tin at Cooglegong, which wasn't far from Marble Bar.

While at a Warden's Court "hearing" one day for some proceedings Lang was talking to Denis. Lang reached into his satchel and brought out an air photo of Depuch Island and some overlays he had done himself showing how, with the provision of suitable infrastructure, the roads and the railway lines could bring the iron-ore down for export. All these things have since happened.

Very visionary stuff and Denis, who you can ask tonight yourself, saw the future. He saw the future of Western Australia through Lang's eyes and so many of us have had our eyes opened because of Lang's early vision.

The third story is about the "phantom pilot" but I'm not going to tell you that story because you'll have to buy the book. John McRobert has almost finished the official book of Lang Hancock and the story of the famous "phantom pilot" will be there in great detail. It's a fantastic story.

I will tell you one final story I have about Lang though.

It was one day in 1976 when I got a bright idea, again. I'd read an editorial in the American *Mining Engineering* magazine by the editor of that magazine, Eugene Guccione. His editorial was really promoting the benefits of mining and how, if we encouraged more mining now, we'd get more prosperity, more jobs and everyone would be better-off as a result of us being able to just get on with it.

He was addressing an American audience because, for those of you who can remember, in America mining came under attack many years before the "enemies of industry" moved to Australia. That battle was just starting in the US and Guccione saw all these signs. His article explained how this was going to affect us all.

I showed this article to Lang and said, "Lang, we've just got to have this guy, Eugene Guccione, here in Australia. Take him around. You can spend a bit of quality time with him, I can spend a bit of quality time with him. We'll take him to Norseman, Kalgoorlie, up to the Pilbara and Darwin. (Pan Continental had some very interesting things happening up there at that time.) We'll take him over to Mt Isa, down through Brisbane, Sydney and Melbourne. I'll take him along to Canberra and introduce him to Malcolm Fraser because, as our new Prime Minister, he needs a bit of help to understand how mining could benefit Australia."

Lang said, "How much?"

I said, "Lang, this won't cost you very much, it's like an underwriting. I've already phoned Eugene Guccione in America and he's happy to come. He's never been to Australia and he'd love to come. It's going to cost $15,000 in travel and accommodation but it won't cost you anything because you just have to underwrite it."

Lang said, "That's a lot of money, who's going to pay for it if I don't?"

I said, "All these other mining companies. We'll go and visit them and they will all get good value out of this visit. They'll recognise this and agree to pay a share."

Lang said, "You won't get a cent out of them and I'll be stuck with the lot."

I said, "No, no that's alright."

He said, "I don't believe you but we have to have him here don't we?"

So away we went and this guy had a great "royal Australian tour". Lang came and picked up Guccione and myself in Kalgoorlie and we had the Pilbara tour, then headed off to Darwin. Mt Isa Mines then sent their plane and picked up Guccione from Darwin, took him down to Mt Isa and then on to Brisbane, Sydney and Melbourne. I then flew across and we arranged to see Malcolm Fraser. At that time I thought Malcolm Fraser could turn out to be an exceptional Prime Minister as he was using all the right words.

As we emerged from the interview, which I thought had gone very well, Guccione commented, "I'm sorry Ron, but he's just another bloody politician with no principles. Let me play back the tape and I'll show you what I mean."

A couple of months after the Guccione visit, I assembled all the public relations stuff and all the newspaper and magazine articles generated by the visit and rang Lang from Kalgoorlie, once again.

I said, "Lang I'll come down with all the 'wash-up' of that Guccione visit." He said, "Oh, I know, I know, I'm ready for you."

I showed Lang all the magazine articles and he said, "That's terrific coverage, but now for the bad bit."

I said, "No Lang, relax. Everyone put in and it won't cost you a cent."

Now that's the first time I've ever seen Lang speechless.

However, I thanked Lang, because without him agreeing to "back" the visit, it just wouldn't have happened. That's the sort of guy he was. He gave you that little extra courage, some fire in your belly and a realisation that you could make things happen.

(Portion of Eugene Guccione reporting is on page 230.)

So who was the real Lang Hancock?

I think he was just as human and as fallible as all of us. However, the things that marked him as being different were first, that he insisted on getting his information direct from the source. If he wanted information about economics, he'd just jump on his plane and fly over to the U.S. and spend time with Milton Friedman, one of the world's leading economists. If he wanted information about science, he'd go and visit Dr Edward Teller.(2) If he wanted information on mining and the environment, he'd see Dr Petr Beckmann.(3) He'd go anywhere, but he wanted that information first-hand, so it wasn't recycled or reinterpreted by other parties. This was an interesting habit from which we can all learn. Just get your information first-hand; from the source.

He was also a person closer to nature than almost anyone I'd ever met. Several times, while driving me around the Hamersley Ranges, he'd get out of his 4WD and take me into a cave to show me some little bird's nest, or some small animal's nest, or some rock painting, or something similar.

He wanted to protect these from desecration, from tourism. He had a very strong conservationist nature. That was never featured in any of his numerous media interviews.

He also didn't see why he should await the pleasure of bureaucrats when he knew the information he had already assembled was in most cases superior to the information the bureaucracy was getting. It annoyed him that he had to stand in line, waiting for these people to go through their endless processes.

He clearly understood the principles of capital and labour, the resultant wealth creation that can come from fusing them together and how, without getting that right first, all the "redistributionists" of the world are simply "pissing into the wind".

But most of all, Lang was himself. He could do that, he could be himself, whereas most of us couldn't be. Whether you are from Rio Tinto, the Labor Party or the Liberal Party, you can't be yourself. You have to "toe the company line" or the "party line". I think this individualism used to drive them nuts with absolute, sheer envy. They didn't envy Lang for his money, which only came later in his life, they envied him for his free spirit. He could be himself and they couldn't.

Concluding Thoughts

Lang and a very select few entrepreneurs set the pattern for so many of us to follow. My own company motto is "Growth Through Persistence". Every time I use that word 'persistence' I think of Lang Hancock. 'Persistence' is an inspirational word that can bring success to everyone at any stage of their personal development, in every walk of life. You could also say that Lang and others like him "planted the trees" so that we could come along later and "enjoy the fruit".

We must remember that many of our achievements and our opportunities only became possible because of the human investment made by people such as Lang Hancock and his equally admired business partner Peter Wright.

Our humility in remembering this is an essential part of tonight's celebration.

Lang will always be a legend and an icon of Australia and I am proud to be included in tonight's magnificent celebration of this event, the 50th anniversary of Lang Hancock's discovery flight.

Thank you Gina and thanks, too, to the Rinehart family.

Endnotes

1. Eugene Guccione's observations on Australia in 1976—following pages.
2. For details on Dr Edward Teller click on:
   http://www.achievement.org/autodoc/page/tel0pro-1
3. For details on Dr. Petr Beckmann, click on:
   http://www.accesstoenergy.com/view/ate/s41p901.htm

Flashback to August, 1976*

Australia's Slow Entry Into The Nuclear Age

Australia could eventually become a major world supplier of uranium oxide—but how quickly that happens depends on the outcome of a highly complex and emotional battle among different special interests.

Australia has immense uranium reserves, of about the same size as those of the United States. But Australians seem undecided as to what to do with their uranium. Should mining be allowed or forbidden? [Three decades later and still undecided?]

The Environmentalists

The Australian Conservation Foundation (ACF), the most powerful pressure group in the country, has already concluded that uranium mining and nuclear power are "unsafe, unreliable, uneconomical and unnecessary". ACF, therefore, is fighting a bitter war to prevent Australians from ever developing their uranium resources. ACF is also advocating Zero Population Growth for Australia—a country the size of the continental United States (minus Alaska and Hawaii) with a population of 14 million, about two-thirds that of California.

It wasn't always like this. When ACF was formed in 1965, its executive council consisted of prominent public figures, businessmen and academicians. However, in late 1973, a group of radical conservationists took over ACF and threw out four key members of the executive council—which immediately lost seven more members who resigned in protest at the takeover. (Those who resigned, reports the *Australian News Weekly*, were replaced by such figures as Jack Mundey, former

---

*These are brief comments from the USA–based Mining Engineering magzine (January, 1977) following a visit to Australia by Eugene Guccione, Editor.

president of the Australian Communist Party and former secretary of the Builders' Laborers Federation of New South Wales; Kenn Carr, member of the Socialist Left of the Labor Party, and New South Wales secretary of the Furnishing Trades Union; and Bob Giles, the left-wing South Australian secretary of the Plumbers and Gasfitters Unions.) And so, since 1973 ACF has been more interested in advancing its own "progressive" ideology than in finding technological solutions to environmental problems.

Behaving as if it were a shadow government, the ACF in late 1974 passed a resolution "to refuse to export uranium to those countries engaged in researching or manufacturing nuclear weapons or generating power by fission or breeder reactions". Then, to put teeth in its resolution, ACF launched a joint campaign with various labour unions to institute a ban on uranium mining and export. When the Ranger Environmental Inquiry was formed under Justice Fox, ACF made known that it would continue to support the union ban on uranium mining regardless of the outcome of the Fox inquiry.

ACF warmly supports, morally and financially, the Australian chapter of Friends of the Earth (FOE). Last year, about 400 FOE members rode bicycles to Canberra from Melbourne and Sydney, holding meetings along the way to protest against uranium mining and nuclear power. FOE members also testified before the Fox commission, where they identified Friends of the Earth as an international organization with chapters in Australia, Belgium, Britain, Holland, France, Japan, Kenya, Mexico, South Africa, Sweden, Switzerland, the United States, and Yugoslavia.

Although ACF and FOE have had an immense amount of publicity, the most recent poll shows that 71 percent of Australians favor development of nuclear power for peaceful purposes, 70 percent favor uranium mining in the Northern Territory, and 50 percent favor the export of uranium.

ACF receives a $150,000 annual subsidy from the government, points out John Martyr, a member of the Federal Parliament in Canberra, who wants that subsidy stopped "because I believe that what the Australian Conservation Foundation does is diametrically opposed to everything that this government is trying to do."

Eugene Guccione, Editor of 'Mining Engineering U.S.A.' arrives in Darwin to investigate Australia's uranium potential —August, 1976 (Author is second from right.)

Eye-opening excerpts from 1976 speeches delivered by Eugene Guccione, chemical engineer and senior editor of *Engineering & Mining Journal*.

(a) Carbon dioxide. If we were to stop all combustion processes on earth—and thus plunge the world into the primitive state that existed thousands of years ago, before the discovery of fire—we would succeed in eliminating only about 2 per cent of the carbon dioxide emissions into the atmosphere. According to information provided by Environmental Protection Agency Director, William D. Ruckelshaus, the combined total of man's activity—world-wide —accounts for around 2 per cent of CO_2 production. All other living organisms, vegetable and animal, account for 98 per cent.

(b) If only men, and not nature, were the polluters, it would take them 47,000 years, to triple the present CO_2 level. And if you care to wait for 47,000 years, the CO_2 concentration in the atmosphere would still be less than one-tenth of one per cent.

(c) The true 'environmentalist' is the scientifically oriented individual who applies 'knowledge and reason' to the problems of environment. In the final analysis, the problems of pollution will not be solved by impractical, if well-meaning, environmental extremists. The problems will be solved, as usual, by the research and development man, by the technologist, by the engineer—all men of reason and knowledge—provided they are granted enough freedom to operate.

Australia's Mining Hall of Fame

Building an Aussie Icon

I should have known what I was doing when I said 'yes' to the invitation to be the Chairman of the Australian Prospectors & Miners Hall of Fame, put to me by Allan and Max King in 1996.

Not long before that, I had been asked to summarize the creation of the Museum of the Goldfields.(1)

Thirty-one years had passed since that project was conceived, enabling a reflective examination to diminish the many delays, disappointments and individual frustrations when that small band of activists experienced how long it took others to "share the ultimate vision".

As youthful members of the JAYCEE's (Junior Chamber of Commerce) in 1965, we had proposed the Goldfields Museum as a worthy community project.

Our original timetable was three months from inception to the official opening of stage 1.

In reality, the first official opening was eventually three years later, not three months from the original conception.

The final opening of the expanded Museum then took place a total of 23 years later and my compiled notes showed that the frustrations on the "way through" were from the very people from whom we expected maximum assistance. Those who procrastinated the most appeared to be those who felt threatened by a tourist attraction which they felt "may take some of their business away".

However, the final Museum project is judged a success and it is far grander than our original concept.

The many volunteers listed in my published summary can feel proud that they played a part in the development of this important Goldfields project.

THE DATUM POST

THE JOURNAL OF THE AMALGAMATED PROSPECTORS AND LEASEHOLDERS ASSOCIATION OF WESTERN AUSTRALIA INC.

Representing prospectors since 1904

June 2000 Vol.7 No.2

Rare Nugget for APMHOF

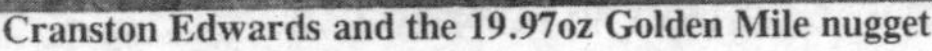

Cranston Edwards and the 19.97oz Golden Mile nugget

APLA members and prospectors Cranston and Donna Edwards have just made an incredible gift to the Australian Prospectors and MinersHall Of Fame for display in the form of a beautiful 621 gram (19.97ozs) gold in quartz specimen nugget.

As this nugget was found on the Historic May Lease on the southern end of Kalgoorlie-Boulders famous Golden Mile makes it extremely rare and very unique. All but a few hectares of the Golden Mile have been held by large companies for the last 50 years or more, and has virtually been off limits to prospectors, and with the rest of the Mile being swollen up by the Super Pit, it looks as though the chances of anyone finding any nugget on the Mile is highly unlikely.

But in 1991 Cranston and Donna managed to get a tribute to work the southern end of the Mile and this beauty was one of the nuggets from that tribute.

On handing over the nugget last week Cranston explained.

"When we found the nugget we thought it was something special as it was one of the last sizable nuggets found (legally) on the Golden Mile. During some of the tough years we fleetingly thought of melting it down but something held us back. We felt it would have been a crime because we considered it irreplaceable as the alluvial areas on the Golden Mile were all but gone due to the massive Super Pit. Having now donated it to APMHOF we do not consider it a loss. It was never meant to be an investment piece to us, we mainly held on to it because of the significance of it. Now after holding on to it for almost 10 years we feel we have found a worthwhile home for it in the Hall Of Fame, as a fitting tribute to prospectors, honouring their past, present and future, and also promoting our industry. We are grateful of the goldfields which has mostly been generous and good to us, and now we want to reciprocate and we feel this is the least we could do."

When you consider Cranston was and will probably be the last prospector to have a tribute to work the alluvial on the Golden Mile has to add to the uniqueness of this lovely piece of gold.

Taking into account that the 11.7gr Hall Of Fame nugget that was found on the northern end of the Mile recently fetched $1,600 per oz it could make this one worth around $32,000.

A very generous donation indeed!

The Mining Hall of Fame

This residual positive feeling convinced me to accept this new challenge, knowing that the vision of the finished product would ultimately block out the trials and tribulations of getting there.

As Cervantes once said,

> Time ripens all things; no man is born wise.

He then went on to say (in Cervantes, *The Impossible Dream*)

> Man scorned and covered with scars still strove with his last ounce of courage to reach the unreachable stars; and the world will be better for this.

Another motivation to become involved was that I had just published a book, *So I Headed West*, covering the period of my grandfather's involvement in the mining industry between 1881 and 1924, an era "when miners were heroes".

Such a different situation existed in 1996. The mining industry then appeared incapable of explaining its vital place in civilised society and was constantly under attack from the many "enemies of industry".

Perhaps I saw this as an opportunity to take part in the creation of a 'showcase' that would explain to all Australians how dependent we are on the mining industry.

Perhaps if we actually encouraged mining, we could actually have more of it—to everyone's benefit.

Okay, so I thought, "Let's give this Mining Hall of Fame project all we've got!"

How was this Aussie icon built, what does it represent and who made it possible?

The idea of a Hall of Fame had been around for a while. There are notes of a discussion at the "Balzano Barrowman Race" at Kanowna (October 10, 1993) when Peter Bridge and Bill Moriarty mentioned to Kris Laurie that they were looking at the Coolgardie Court House for that purpose. Kris supported that idea and offered her assistance.

Later, on April 21, 1994, an article appeared in the *Goldfields Magazine* indicating that the Prospectors Association were discussing a similar proposal. Max King and Lindsay Stockdale were keen supporters.

The early sequence of events was listed in the first annual report (see page 254).

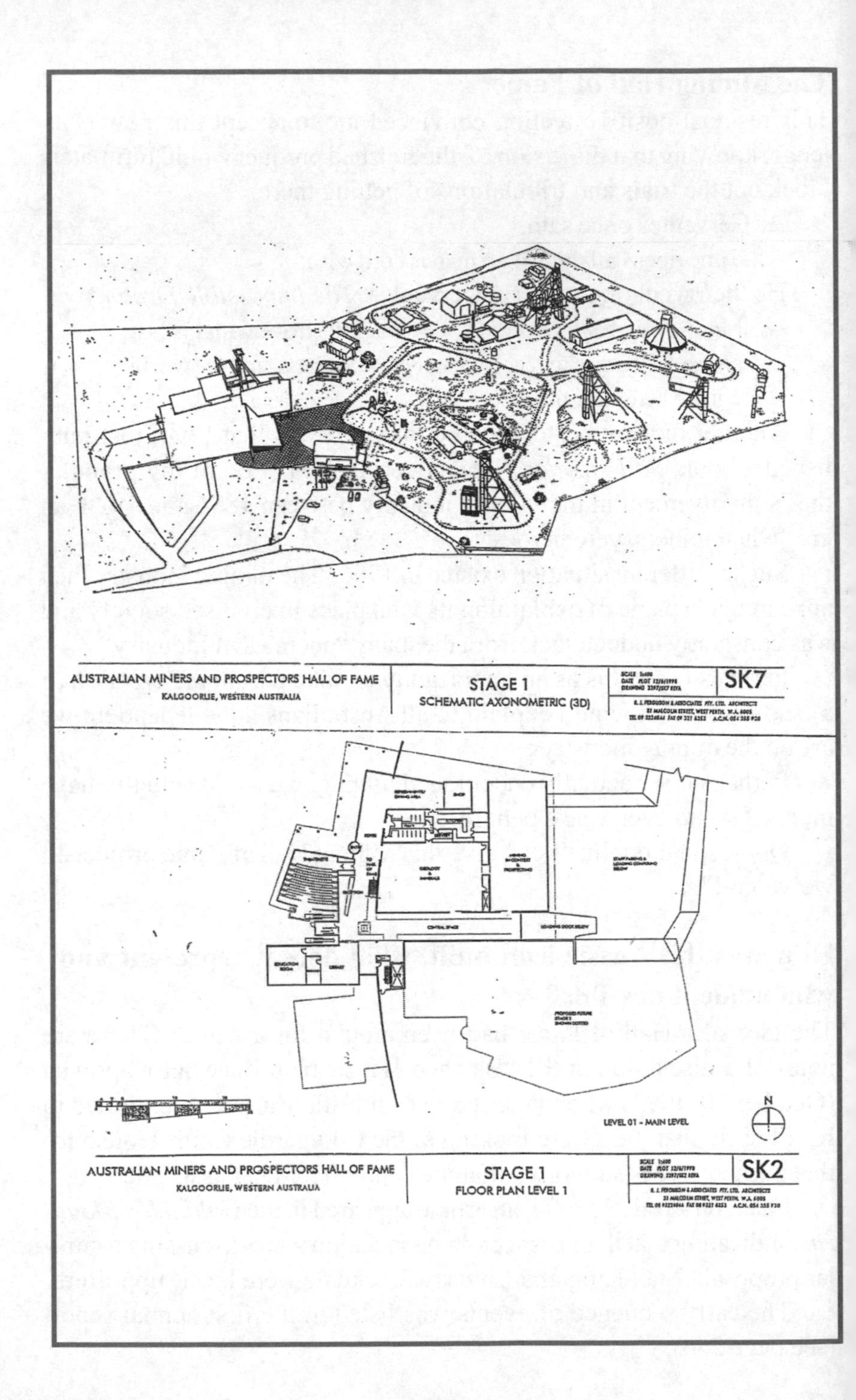
AUSTRALIAN MINERS AND PROSPECTORS HALL OF FAME
KALGOORLIE, WESTERN AUSTRALIA
STAGE 1
SCHEMATIC AXONOMETRIC (3D)
SK7
N
LEVEL 01 - MAIN LEVEL
AUSTRALIAN MINERS AND PROSPECTORS HALL OF FAME
KALGOORLIE, WESTERN AUSTRALIA
STAGE 1
FLOOR PLAN LEVEL 1
SK2

Then on July 1, 1994 a group of 28 volunteers (see page 253), selected and brought together by Kris Laurie, decided to put into action the idea that several people had mentioned over the years—namely, that of starting a Hall of Fame in Kalgoorlie, Kambalda or Coolgardie. Those at the meeting went to work and recruited an ever-widening circle of activists, much like the ripples created in a pond from a single stone.

Seven years later, at the official opening, it was my pleasure to thank all those people and the volunteers who shared the rapidly expanding vision and stepped forward to make it actually happen.

As you know, a good idea is worthless without action and the early financial supporters deserve special thanks. We did not have much to show them but they simply said, "Here's some cash, so just get on with it." This led to the formation of the company, the Australian Prospectors and Miners Hall of Fame Ltd, and to the appointment of a Board of Directors and the impressive patrons to our organisation. Those patrons, thanked on opening day, were Sir Arvi Parbo, Mark Creasy, Robert Champion de Crespigny and Jack Mackenzie plus those unable to be present, Professor Geoffrey Blainey, Sir George Fisher and Rt. Hon. Doug Anthony.

Once the company was formed, a national architectural competition followed which was won by Ferguson and Associates of Perth. (Gus Ferguson, Doug Harvey and Ahmad Abas attended the opening.)

This was accompanied by 14 months of negotiation with the Federal Government to have us included as a Centenary of Federation project. We had Premier, Richard Court, in there batting for us and the State Government adopted the project some months earlier than Canberra. We appreciated both Federal and State Governments for their significant support and, in particular, the enthusiastic assistance of Barry Haase and Nick Minchin.

When people realised that this project was not just about money, that it was really about leadership, our task became easier. Leadership should start at the top, with leadership by example.

A magnificent example of this was our initial campaign donation from our Patron-Mining, Sir Arvi Parbo.

Arm-wrestling for a good cause! Prime Minister, John Howard (June 1998) had to be convinced that a small portion of royalties and taxes should be "given back" in recognition of prospecting and mining's contribution to the nation!

Prime Minister, John Howard's original site visit (April 20, 1999) to the proposed Mining Hall of Fame was the first visit to the Kalgoorlie region by a Prime Minister for eighteen years.

We all knew that the standard set by him would be the example to be followed by so many.

He didn't disappoint us and told me with a smile, "Ron, I've never made a personal donation of this size before, but I know it's a good investment."

We then started taking fundraising seriously, with the formation of campaign committees in all States.

Our fundraising efforts reminded me of the words of Aung San Suu Kyi, "People will contribute hard work and money cheerfully if they are convinced that their contributions will truly benefit the public."(2)

Our two national fund-raising chairmen were David Reed, for Finance and Business, and Richard Tastula, for Prospecting and Mining.

The individual State campaign chairmen were Graeme Smith in Western Australia, John Horan in South Australia, Ross Fardon in Queensland, Sir Eric McClintock in New South Wales and John Barr in Victoria, with Dennis Gee in the Northern Territory and Harry Stacpoole in Tasmania.

They were, in turn, supported by 61 campaign committee members. A great team and a magnificent achievement.

Midway through the project we received a real boost when Normandy and Homestake donated the eight hectares of mining precinct and the operating Hannan's North End Tourist Mine to our project. Without the support of Normandy and Homestake, this integrated project would not have been possible. Likewise, the support of their Resident Mine Managers, Ian Burston, Bob Crew and John Shipp.

(There could also be another benefit in having ownership of the Hannan's North Mine; a colleague of mine, George Compton, assures me that on the four level eastern platt, there is a north-south quartz vein running 3.5 ounces of gold per tonne.)

Once our campaign gained sufficient momentum, we went out to tender. DeVaugh Pty Ltd of Bunbury were the successful tenderers. We enjoyed working with Merv DeVaugh and Graham Teed and our site representative, Andy George of Rapallo Pty Ltd, and the many contractors and suppliers who were also involved.

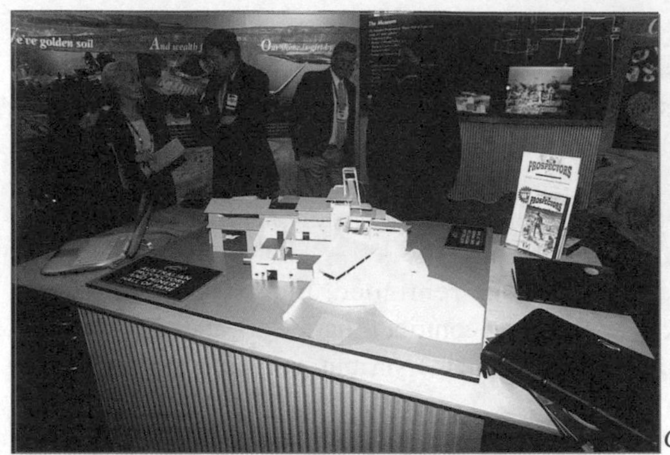

Conceptual model.

Foundations at July 22, 2000.

Steady progress

We received great local support. One example was the Kalgoorlie Rebel Road Builders who, seeing that we needed a new direct road, just turned up one morning and built it in true Kalgoorlie fashion.

Swift progress was made in the run-up to opening, with the gallery sponsors working with us on the exhibits. In particular, our Patron-Prospector, Mark Creasy, worked tirelessly with us on the Minerals Gallery. The work done by Mark and his team, including David Vaughan, Peter Clark, and Bob Noble, with further valuable input from Normandy, resulted in us being at the forefront of any mineral collection in Australia.

Two of our galleries were completed, namely the Mark Creasy Minerals Gallery and the Peter Wright Prospecting Gallery. The timetable for the other three galleries, the Business of Mining Gallery, the Mining in Context Gallery and the Energy Gallery, was displayed on our magnificent website, provided and supported by WMC Resources (www.mininghall.com). This site is updated regularly with the Rio Tinto-sponsored educational material. It is our prime mode of communicating. Our website is where we acknowledge all our supporters, including the many that I was unable to mention personally at the official opening. I desperately wanted to mention every one of our 306 donors as each donor is as important as the next.

The official opening ceremony was held in the Business of Mining Gallery and above the guests an aircraft was displayed, a similar Auster aircraft to the one flown by Lang Hancock over his Pilbara iron ore discoveries. Lang's daughter, Gina Rinehart, readily provided this display and a great deal of support.

Another exhibit was signed up during opening week: a pledge from the Simon Lee Foundation in conjunction with the WA Chinese Chamber of Commerce to establish a Chinese Garden of Remembrance on the south side between the building and our new entrance road.

This garden complex (completed in 2007) commemorates and tells the story of the significant role played by the Chinese community in every major Australian mineral field (see page 256).

Another last-minute inclusion for opening week was Alcoa World Alumina Australia who submitted an international grant request to the Alcoa Foundation in America. The Alcoa Foundation supported the

November 2001
$7.95 Volume 1. Issue 79
Australia's
Paydirt
Registered by Australia Post PP 643938/0071
The
Mining Hall of Fame
Our history—Our future
•NICKEL REVIEW
•NORMANDY NFM

Environmental Exhibit within the Business of Mining Gallery with a significant contribution over three years.

This was doubly significant as we were the first ever recipient of a grant from the Alcoa Foundation to a non-profit organisation in Australia. It also emphasised the international support that was an important feature of our campaign.

To summarize, had the project all been plain sailing? Pretty much—apart from the occasional cynics who are always there when an innovative and visionary project gets under way.

Things may have been moving too fast for them, so they decided to just sit there. They shouldn't have been so surprised when they got run over!

In true Kalgoorlie fashion, we also turned a $21 million project into a $25 million project by adding, among other things, an Energy Gallery. An option was held over this by the Australian Energy Industry. We were still about $2 million short to enable completion, so there will always be room for some more heroes to step forward.

What I enjoyed most about the project was the momentum it generated, driven by the directors who shared the load over the whole period.

I will mention, in particular, specific Board names: Deputy Chairman Dick Scallan, Vice Chairman Andrew Caulton, Bruce Harris and Martin Albrecht and the tireless Cranston Edwards, because the workload for them was intense during countdown to opening. In addition, all the former Directors and Alternate Directors over the seven years leading up to the opening.

A Key Figure

Norma Latchford was our extraordinary Project Manager and she continued with the project from day one, from that very first meeting on July 1, 1994.

I know of no other person who could have achieved so much on such a lean administrative budget.

Norma's complete belief in the continuing vision, and her tenacity, were an example to all of us. She maintained excellent communications with our enthusiastic bunch of volunteers while we were usually immersed in our "day jobs".

Norma earned our team's admiration and we gave her our full support to complete her tasks.

Some of the 680 guests at the Official Opening of the Australian Mining Hall of Fame, October 30, 2001. "History is the record of what we find was of note to past generations. We can use this knowledge as stepping stones to the future."—RBM

"The present is saturated with the past and pregnant with the future." — G.W. Leibniz (German Philosopher, 1646–1716)

Chairman's introductory 'thank you' at the Official Opening

October 30, 2001

Have any of you ever lost a pet or an animal? If you have, you will know how the two old-time prospectors felt when their donkey fell down an open mine shaft, not far from here.

It fell about 10 metres, but it was still alive and after a few moments started braying and snorting in anguish.

The two old prospectors had no chance of rescuing it but they couldn't bear to see it suffer, so they decided the right thing to do was to bury it by shovelling dirt down the mine shaft.

After an hour of shovelling, there was no sound and, with tears in their eyes, they looked over the side and peered down the shaft.

What they found, to their amazement, was that each time a shovel full of dirt landed on the donkey's back, he simply shook it off and stamped it underfoot to get him closer to the surface.

After two more hours of shovelling, the donkey gratefully scrambled from the filled shaft.

I am telling you this story today because our team at the Mining Hall of Fame feel, very much, like that grateful donkey.

When we set the target of raising $21 million to establish this spectacular building, people said that it couldn't be done.

We felt for a while that we were down that mine shaft without a ladder, but each time you gave us a cheque or any encouragement at all, it brought us closer to seeing daylight again.

Thank you for your time, your generosity and your spirit of leadership.

Conclusion: What is this project and why did we build it?

The opening of the Mining Hall of Fame on October 30, 2001 celebrated the most ambitious and visionary project of its type in the world. This project is a true reflection of the importance of the mining industry to the Australian and world economies and has the potential to change the way the world looks at minerals and their importance in everyday life. Like all successful projects, the Mining Hall of Fame has been born out of a vision, developed with a clear purpose and will prosper as it establishes a new level of communication between the mining sector and the general public.

The opening also celebrated the work and support of hundreds of people across Australia and, in particular, the small group of people in Kalgoorlie who have supported this from the very beginning, seven years earlier. Kalgoorlie itself is a living, breathing, vital community that clearly demonstrates what mining can do for a community and it is the ideal home for this national symbol.

The Mining Hall of Fame is a gift to the people of Kalgoorlie.

I hope they will accept it, use it and develop it because, if they do, it will repay their investment many times over by bringing hundreds of thousands of new visitors to the city on a continuing basis.

It is also Western Australia's first built, recognizable national icon, so it brings this added dimension to the State.

This truly national project will educate, entertain and explain the important role that Australia's mineral-rich regions play in improving the living standards of all Australians and how it brings opportunities and new employment choices to Australians of all ages.

The project is an extremely successful joint venture between the Federal Government, the State Government, the mining industry, and hundreds of supporters. It will bring all these parties together on a regular basis and promote the mutual benefits of removing some of the obstacles that prevent our industry from achieving its true potential.

My biggest challenge on opening day, as Chairman, was to thank everyone involved, particularly the 500 or so supporters, members and helpers who poured the cash, time and, most importantly, their enthusiasm into this exciting project.

In so doing, they have joined with the legendary heroes who have given us so much by providing us with so many new opportunities and career choices that will take our prospecting, exploring and mining industries proudly forward into this new century.

Footnotes

1. *See chapter "The Museum of the Goldfields" in Never a Dull Moment (www.mannkal.org/bookshop).*
2. *Letters from Burma*, Penguin, London, 1997; 17

MINING HALL OF FAME OPENING

A collage of photographs from the Mining Hall of Fame opening in Kalgoorlie.

NOVEMBER 2001 GOLD GAZETTE 23

On Reflection @ 2009

My nearly six years of full-on involvement with the Mining Hall of Fame was both a great honour and a privilege.

It gave me a six-year entree into any mining company boardroom in Australia, access to chief executives and a relationship with every mining industry organization in every Australian State.

This was a rare insight into the existing level of leadership within our industry at that time and its ability to withstand the constant attack of the various political, regulatory and dark-green extremists, all intent on denigrating our achievements.

All this was at a time when the industry was severely "stuck in the rut" of one of our regular downturns.

These many personal contacts proved invaluable for me in later years when giving advice to overseas investors.

I was often asked, "How is it that you appear to know everyone in the mining industry?"

For other reminiscenses of that period, refer to chapter *What Would Shakespeare Think of Our Mining Industry?* and *Corporate Alzheimers* (see page 251).

At the time of writing, my continuing non-executive involvement with the Mining Hall of Fame is simply as Emeritus Chairman and one of the Patrons, enjoying occasional contact with the subsequent Chairmen, Richard Scallan, Richard Tastula and Neil Warburton, the last of whom currently has the challenge of taking the project into the future.

He deserves full support, especially from the new generation of chief executives and the new crop of companies enjoying this industry upturn.

Ruffled Feathers

A wise man never fights with those whom he regards as friends and allies.

However, it's often instructive to hold up a mirror for those few with the courage to examine their reflections honestly as a guide to remove any blemishes caused by internal conflicts.

As the Mining Hall project steadily grew from being a "local idea" to being a "national project" so the "ownership" of the project changed as well.

Major contributors had little interest in donating to a project focused solely on fossickers and history as they saw the ongoing benefits flowing from contrasting those aspects with the modern educational and technological leadership role played by the industry of the present time.

This created all manner of friction with the local prospectors, some of whom refused to grasp the fact that "prospecting" is a vital part of the all-encompassing term "mining".

The originators, having handed the project over to a national organization, still had a sense of total ownership. As a result they harboured resentment to the point that many articles appeared in their official Amalgamated Prospectors and Leaseholders Association (APLA) magazine *Datum Post*. This example is from their June 2001 edition:

May I suggest that APLA disengage from its interest in the Mining Hall of Fame and concentrate on building up a project in Coolgardie. Alternatively, if we wait a few years until the government and mining companies get tired of financing a project that has little hope of financial viability, we could then take over the project on our terms and use it for the reason it was originally set up.......

I suppose their sense of "loss" was similar to seeing a private company progress to public company status. Nothing remains the same but the whole idea is that the benefits should outnumber the disadvantages.

Some of the funds raised for the project were also conditional on the Mining Hall being a "dynamic" and not an 'old fashioned' institution, so that any future efforts to turn back to its quaint beginnings would be counter-productive.

Fortunately, we were not running a popularity poll, we just had to get a complex project completed on time.

Interestingly enough, some of the "prospectors" who verbally abused me over this change of direction were unaware that my own membership of APLA was of longer standing than their own.

In response to this endless "static", our Project Manager, Norma Latchford, responded capably as follows:

Long before Europeans arrived in Australia, the indigenous people carried out mining operations. They mined to extract stone and ochre and traded their products over great distances. Were they miners or prospectors? Does it matter, as long as their activities are recognised and recorded?

Similarly, with regard to participants in the minerals industry today, it seems to me that inclusion is the most important element; making sure that the secretaries, the truckies, the communities and families are noted for their efforts, as well as the prospectors and miners.

No one person or organisation should take credit for the Australian Prospectors and Miners Hall of Fame. It was built as a monument to everyone in the industry, by everyone in the industry. Let us move forward.

Confronting a Case of Corporate Alzheimer's

Back in the year 2000, in my role as Chairman of the Australian Mining Hall of Fame, I visited the Melbourne head office of BHP (just before it became BHP-Billiton). I was trying to gain their support for the Mining Hall of Fame project.

They had a bundle of senior BHP people politely listening to my presentation and then at the conclusion they said, "Well we have decided not to support your project for the following reasons:

- BHP has never had any involvement in Kalgoorlie so we don't identify at all with Kalgoorlie.
- This seems to be a gold-oriented project and BHP hasn't ever had any interest in gold mining so there's little incentive for us to support it for that reason."

I was fascinated by this display of ignorance about where their company had or had not been and, in my most polite and humble way, pointed out that:-

- The actual site of the Mining Hall of Fame was known as the BHP Hannan's North End Mine right up until the time that BHP closed it around 1954.
- Then, for the next 15 years, the site was the WA Headquarters of the Titan Manufacturing Company, a BHP-owned company which, at that time, was supplying all of the underground rock bolts to Australia's mines.
- Then more recently, in the late 1980s, their corporate entity, the public mining company by the name of BHP Gold, was one of the most successful and active gold explorers and producers in this region and that company then merged with Newmont's Australian operation to form what has become Australia's leading gold producer, Newcrest Mining Ltd.
- Further, it they didn't believe my claims about BHP's involvement in the region, they could visit the Mining Hall of Fame and view the many framed photos that we had obtained from BHP's archives.

I mention this incident only to demonstrate what I call "Corporate Alzheimers"........

Now, I wouldn't expect anyone to have an intimate knowledge of their company's history but they must know enough to avoid making claims that are grossly inaccurate.

However, even when confronted with these facts, BHP (the "Big Australian") still declined any form of participation in the Mining Hall project.

This news wasn't received well by our hard-working fund-raising committee who had been relying on some leadership participation from BHP, especially as the South African company Billiton, with which BHP were discussing merger possibilities, had made a most generous unconditional donation, above and beyond the amount we had suggested from BHP.

One of our problems flowing from BHP's refusal was that one of the first questions put to us by potential donors was, "Well, how much is BHP putting in?"

Well, I felt that this was a situation that called for some strategic diplomacy.

From a past corporate life as a director of a Canadian company, ldorado Gold Corporation, I knew Brian Gilbertson (Billiton's South African CEO), as he had, as CEO of Billiton's Precursor, Gencor, acquired a 40 per cent interest in ldorado.

As I was in London shortly after BHP's refusal, I called in to see Brian at 4.30 on a Friday afternoon.

He found it hilarious that his South African company was a major supporter of 'Australia's Mining Heritage' while their Australian partner—The Big Australian—was not.

He offered to raise this anomalous situation at a BHP board meeting in Melbourne, the following week, with the suggestion that they might at least match Billiton's contribution.

His persuasion did bear fruit, with approval of this suggestion at that board meeting.

However, by the time the instructions were passed down to ground level, their matching donation had been reduced to the amount that we originally asked of them.

There were also many conditions attached to BHP's donation. Then, eight years later, I was pleasantly surprised when it actually arrived.

This particular incident served to enhance the status of all those smaller companies who volunteered those unconditional amounts that enabled us to complete the project.

That's why www.mininghall.com maintains a 'Roll of Honour' listing all those contributors who 'got us over the line' and who contribute to future expansion phases.

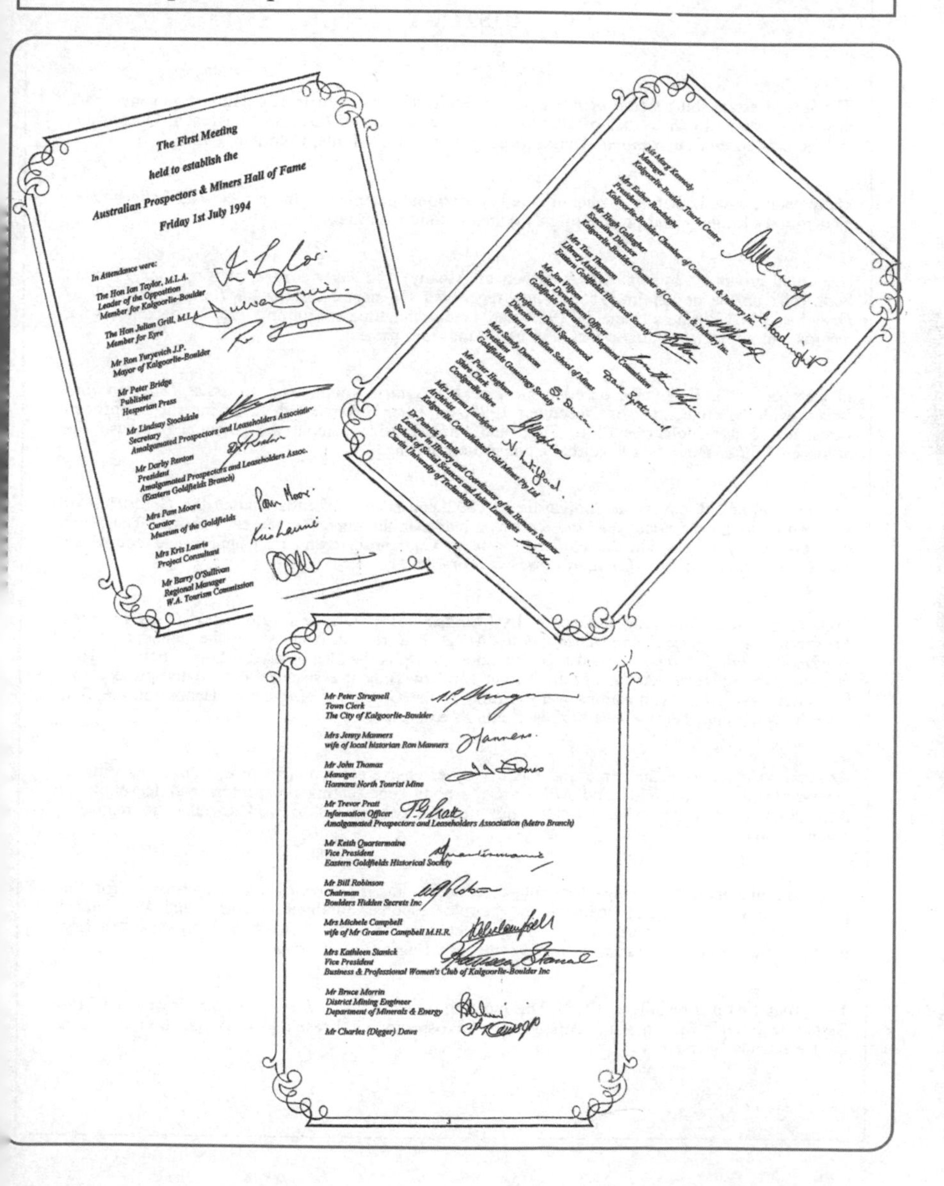

The First Meeting

held to establish the

Australian Prospectors & Miners Hall of Fame

Friday 1st July 1994

In Attendance were:

The Hon Ian Taylor, M.L.A.
Leader of the Opposition
Member for Kalgoorlie-Boulder

The Hon Julian Grill, M.L.A.
Member for Eyre

Mr Ron Yuryevich J.P.
Mayor of Kalgoorlie-Boulder

Mr Peter Bridge
Publisher
Hesperian Press

Mr Lindsay Stockdale
Secretary
Amalgamated Prospectors and Leaseholders Association

Mr Darby Renton
President
Amalgamated Prospectors and Leaseholders Assoc.
(Eastern Goldfields Branch)

Mrs Pam Moore
Curator
Museum of the Goldfields

Mrs Kris Laurie
Project Consultant

Mr Barry O'Sullivan
Regional Manager
W.A. Tourism Commission

Mr Marg Kennedy
Manager
Kalgoorlie-Boulder Tourist Centre

Mrs Esther Roadnight
President
Kalgoorlie-Boulder Chamber of Commerce & Industry Inc.

Mr Hugh Gallagher
Executive Director
Kalgoorlie-Boulder Chamber of Commerce & Industry Inc.

Mrs Tess Thomson
Library Assistant
Eastern Goldfields Historical Society

Mr Jon Viljoen
Senior Development Officer
Goldfields Esperance Development Commission

Professor David Spottiswood
Director
Western Australian School of Mines

Mrs Sandy Duncan
President
Goldfields Genealogy Society

Mr Peter Hughson
Shire Clerk
Coolgardie Shire

Mrs Norma Latchford
Archivist
Kalgoorlie Consolidated Gold Mines Pty Ltd

Dr Patrick Bertola
Lecturer in History and Coordinator of the Honours Seminar
School of Social Sciences and Asian Languages
Curtin University of Technology

Mr Peter Strugnell
Town Clerk
The City of Kalgoorlie-Boulder

Mrs Jenny Manners
wife of local historian Ron Manners

Mr John Thomas
Manager
Hannans North Tourist Mine

Mr Trevor Pratt
Information Officer
Amalgamated Prospectors and Leaseholders Association (Metro Branch)

Mr Keith Quartermaine
Vice President
Eastern Goldfields Historical Society

Mr Bill Robinson
Chairman
Boulders Hidden Secrets Inc

Mrs Michele Campbell
wife of Mr Graeme Campbell M.H.R.

Mrs Kathleen Stanick
Vice President
Business & Professional Women's Club of Kalgoorlie-Boulder Inc

Mr Bruce Morrin
District Mining Engineer
Department of Minerals & Energy

Mr Charles (Digger) Dawe

The Australian Prospectors & Miners Hall Of Fame Ltd

HISTORY

The idea of establishing a *Hall of Fame* on the Goldfields has been in circulation for many years, inspired no doubt by the decision to build a *Stockman's Hall of Fame* in Longreach, Queensland and the existence of the *National Mining Hall of Fame* in Leadville, Colorado, (USA).

Many people saw the heritage, scientific and educational potential of the project and believed that recognition of mining and prospecting activities is long overdue.

One small group led by *Alf Thomson* (then of Albany) and *Peter Bridge*, of *Hesperian Press* in Perth took up the notion in 1985. They registered the name *"Australian Prospectors Hall of Fame"* as a WA Business Name in 1989 and began the time-consuming task of deciding what records and artefacts should be included in the museum project.

In October 1993, Kalgoorlie based consultant *Kris Laurie* volunteered to assist *Thomson and Bridge* with the project, and in December 1993, on *Peter Bridge's* behalf, an informal approach was made to the Coolgardie Shire Clerk and Shire President about the potential to house the proposed *Hall of Fame* in a historical Coolgardie building.

Bayley & Ford's discovery at Coolgardie in 1892 caused the rush that started the Goldfields of Western Australia and established the State as a leader in the mineral resources industry. Therefore the opportunity to position the *Hall of Fame* in Coolgardie seemed an appropriate course of action. The response from Coolgardie was favourable.

In the meantime and quite independently, *Lindsay Stockdale and Max King (Amalgamated Prospectors and Leaseholders Association "APLA")*, were also inspired by the concept of the *Stockman's Hall of Fame*, and had recommended to *APLA* the idea of establishing a national Hall of Fame to prospectors. *APLA* began to look for Government assistance to fund the project and in March 1994 *APLA*'s intentions were printed in the *Goldfields Magazine*. Hence for the first time the two groups became aware of each other's existence.

As *Peter Bridge* owned the name and has a very extensive collection of prospecting and mining archives from the Goldfields, and *APLA* are the body representing prospectors and leaseholders throughout Western Australia, it made sense for the two groups to work together to realise a common objective.

Many discussions and meetings took place, resulting in *APLA* taking on responsibility for the project. However, a lack of financial and people resources inhibited progress, and *Kris Laurie* again volunteered her services to take the project into the public domain and organise the first meeting of the proposed *Australian Prospectors & Miners Hall of Fame*.

This group first met on July 1, 1994. The meeting was chaired by *Darby Renton*, President of the Eastern Goldfields Branch of the Amalgamated Prospectors & Leaseholders Association, and *Kris Laurie* acted as Secretary.

Comment from Bruce Harris, one of the project's instigators "I recall that at one of our early meetings, Kris Laurie made a presentation on the Stockman's Hall of Fame* .... the way it became established, the cost, the time it took to the opening and other interesting facts.

Those present scoffed at the thought that it should have taken the Stockman's Hall of Fame a full seven years from commencement to opening. It seemed such a tediously long time.

The Centenary of Federation was celebrated in 2001. I reflected only recently that the opening of the Hall of Fame was conducted in 2001, not just to celebrate the Centenary, but because it was only barely finished in time for that year and the opening.

It had taken a full seven years from commencement to opening."

*Author's Note:

The Stockman's Hall of Fame located at Longreach, Queensland, was opened by Queen Elizabeth in 1988 and has subsequently become a National Icon, symbolising the contribution to the nation by the outback pioneers of Australia.

The full, official name of this project is;

The Australian Stockman's Hall of Fame and Outback Heritage Centre but, of course, no-one calls it by that name.

The shortened term, simply **The Stockman's Hall of Fame**, is what it was renamed by the public and that's how it remains.

Similarly, **The Prospectors and Miners Hall of Fame Limited** was "as bit of a mouthful" so that was quickly shortened for practical purposes to the **Mining Hall of Fame** embodying, as it does, the multitude of participants involved in the industry.

That's how the popular name evolved, as did the transition from the old logo to the new logo.

Symbolizing the historic heritage

Symbolizing both gold panning dish & an open pit mine.

An Ongoing Project—Update to 2007

Michael Wright addressing the attendees at the official opening of the Chinese Garden of Rememberance, May 25, 2007

Neil Warburton, Chairman of the Australian Mining Hall of Fame with Puan Lee and Dr Eric Tan, AM

What Would Shakespeare Think of Our Mining Industry?*

(An independent second opinion)

Why ask the question of what would Shakespeare think of our mining industry?

Why Shakespeare?

Shakespeare was possibly the world's finest dramatist, giving us the ability to look at ourselves without being self-conscious.

This objectivity gives us the ability to learn something new about ourselves.

We are members of an industry who often find it difficult to talk to each other, but if Shakespeare was reporting on our activities, our responses would produce a highly entertaining version of the *Merchant of Venice*, particularly if he had been fortunate enough to have been the Chairman of the Australian Prospectors Miners Hall of Fame for the past five-and-a-half years.

Most of us have adequate knowledge of our own companies, but little of other companies, and some not even a clear view of the national significance of our own industry.

To facilitate and gather support for the Mining Hall of Fame, Shakespeare would need to study each company and in particular all those CEOs running them.

*Based on address–The W.A. School of Mines Mining Executive Development Group February 28, 2002

This would give him a clear overview of the quality of leadership, the vision and perception each CEO has toward their own company and the overall industry and its interlinking facets.

He would be fascinated to hear how these CEOs personally feel about this very vital and creative industry. Their lack of passion would have mystified him.

He would be staggered to hear comments such as:

"Exploration is a destroyer of shareholder value."

Or:

"We are dropping the word MINING from our company name as this will bring more investor support."

Or:

"We don't really think of ourselves as a mining company."

To these three CEOs Shakespeare would have asked what they are afraid of if they feel that:

> "To be direct and honest is not safe."
> —*Othello*

Shakespeare would enjoy putting in words the very precise correlation that charts so accurately the speed at which decisions are made; quickly in smaller companies and perhaps never in the largest.

Not only did smaller companies' CEOs identify faster with the Mining Hall's vision of presenting our industry in a more dynamic and youthful fashion, but they also put their own personal money into the project in addition to shareholder support.

Shakespeare's genius and patience would be tested in his desire to transform all this into a literary masterpiece.

In some cases he may have to borrow a phrase from my favourite writer Ayn Rand:

> "The verdict you pronounce upon the source of your livelihood is the verdict you pronounce upon your life."

Shakespeare would be impressed by Professor Geoffrey Blainey's overview of the industry, as they both have in common the appreciation that the industry's economics and ethics are not at odds, but in harmony.

This would be consistent with Shakespeare's other writings where he invites us to re-think the relationship between our economic and spiritual life.

Rising above any temptation to create a resentful "poor class", with unjustified feelings of entitlement, Shakespeare would enjoy our process of achieving improvements to knowledge, science and skills in a profession that cannot survive without honesty and integrity.

Hopefully, Shakespeare would be forgiving in his dealing with some of the executive pay packages and "golden parachutes" set up in such a way that the senior executives view their companies as being worth more to them as a "break-up" or "takeover target" than as a living, breathing entity worth nurturing and growing.

Greed is the killer of many good relationships, and Australia has recently been confronted with gross examples of corporate greed that diminish the corporate side of our industry.

Greed sits more comfortably with governments and unions but the corporate world is far too transparent when it comes to masking the true value of our endeavours.

Politicians may be able to fool some of the people, some of the time, but if we are to find mineral resources and economically develop these, we have to face the indisputable facts of nature and of natural science. As Sir Avi Parbo has said, "Nonsense cannot be pursued far in engineering."

Shakespeare would expand the theme so ably laid out by another of our mining industry legends, Charles Copeman*, in his masterful understatement from the introduction to his 1988 AusIMM Presidential Address:

> We come together because we have a mutual interest in improving what is done by the mineral industry, in all its aspects. It is this sense of continuing improvement, of doing better, of doing as well as we can, as our knowledge and skills improve, that unites us in creating and fostering a professional association of like-minded people.

---

*Charles Copeman almost single-handedly reshaped Australia's archaic industrial relations practices when he was M.D. of Peko-Wallsend/Robe River in the 1980s. "..... had the effect of boosting productivity 400% and elevating Robe River from a corporate basket-case into one of the world's most efficient iron-ore operations".—Tim Treadgold, *BRW*, April 7, 1997.

We know from our professional training and experience that enormous progress has been made, at an ever increasing rate, in the mineral industry, particularly in this Century. We know that the mineral industry has played a very major role in providing the means by which so many people survive to live longer, healthier and more interesting lives than ever before. Indeed together with the oil and gas industry, which is an integral part of the mineral industry but has achieved its own commercial distinction, it is fair to claim that the mineral industry has played the major role in providing the means for the advancement of the human quality of life.

We do not need to make any great claims on human society in consequence of our statement of these contributions. The facts, for those who are aware of them, speak for themselves. Our more modest interest, as members of our professional association, is to look to the future while conscious of our heritage as a guide to what more might be done in that future.

We certainly do not claim that this indisputable contribution made to human welfare by the mineral industry gives us some moral position of superiority from which to claim greater support or understanding from the wider community of people.

On the other hand, we know that as members of the mineral industry we have a responsibility to do what we can to help other people to be aware of, and to understand the significance of, those facts which will only speak for themselves if we take the trouble to make them known.

To which Shakespeare would respond:

> This above all: to thine own self be true, and it must follow, as the night the day, thou canst not then be false to any man.
>
> —*Hamlet*

During his various interviews with mining company executives, Shakespeare would have sensed that the industry has experienced, over the past 100 years, the best of times and the worst of times (with this cycle repeating several times).

The best of times being over 100 years ago at the turn of the last century When Miners were Heroes*. At that time the nation and its cities were being built on the back of the mining industry and the evidence was there for everyone to see.

Mining rescued Australia from the banking crash of the 1890s and again in the 1930s amidst Australia's depression-ravaged economy when mining was about the only fundamental employment on offer.

Then started the "great decline", to which Shakespeare would have quoted his lines from King Lear.

"This great decay."

Trevor Sykes (*Australian Financial Review*, November 17, 2001) described this era (briefly interrupted by the WMC and Poseidon nickel boom) as follows:

> Mining companies used to be run by engineers and geologists who were enthralled by the prospect of discovering an ore body and bringing a mine on stream. Whether they could sell the minerals they produced was almost an afterthought.
>
> That attitude was largely responsible for the industry's unacceptably low returns to shareholders.

The new generation of mining leaders then seized on the concept of controlling markets and production, closing off new competition to the industry, and hatched a plan to do just that.

Where they obtained their strategies from and the front-line people they employed to present this message will be ultimately judged by history.

---

*'When Miners Were Heroes', 1992 book launch speech by Ron Manners for *So I Headed West (Ballarat to Broken Hill to Kanowna to Kalgoorlie 1863–1924)*.

They sought advice from public relations firms with input from high profile "enemies of industry".

Shakespeare would have been fascinated at how we had developed a whole generation of "enemies of industry" who are more articulate and more dedicated to the destructive role, than the creative role of explorers and miners.

The shrill anti-development message from these "enemies of industry" had become widely disseminated throughout our education system, just as the Marxist approach to economics permeated our education system. Note the way they say:

"The products of mankind's labour are here; how did they get here?" "Some how!"

Well, this approach is not true for economics anymore than it's true for mining.

Shakespeare would have questioned the wisdom of us taking advice from such people, and would have summed this up by stating,

> Our doubts are traitors
> And make us lose the good we oft might win
> By fearing to attempt.
>
> —*Measure for Measure*

Certainly our mining leaders' actions were not moderated by economic advice such as that given by Julian Simon at the time: "Because we can expect future generations to be richer than we are, no matter what we do about resources. Asking us to refrain from using resources now so that future generations can have them later is like asking the poor to make gifts to the rich".

Many major mining companies, 27 in fact, came forward with what they called a Mining Minerals & Sustainable Development Project (being part of the Global Mining Initiative).

Most of their strategies were quite noble and practical, such as more clearly defining what was currently described as Best Practice, at that time. But, in the absence of any obvious spokesman from their own ranks, they enlisted the aid of Labour Union leaders and a former President and CEO of the US-based National Wildlife Federation to make the running as public faces for this new-look mining industry.

Part of the plan was to develop a standard set of "weasel words" that could then be replicated in every mining CEO's repertoire and we saw what Shakespeare may have described as .....

> A new generation of snivelling apologists, prattling on with replicated speeches, constantly referencing the same weasel words, to the point where it becomes a public turn-off.

Fortunately, this new "and second great decay" came to an end when a further generation of mining leaders took over. They realised that, having returned the industry to profitability (aided of course by China rescuing us in much the same way that Japan rescued the industry in the 1950s and 1960s, and having transferred the "Best Practice" right down through the whole chain of command in their companies), that there was nothing to apologise for. So now we see them adopting a fresh new "language of leadership this time".

This new "language of leadership" is serving the industry better at a time when we desperately need to recruit more people in a very competitive environment. It is imperative that our message must not only be good; it must be inspirational.

All creative writers, including Shakespeare, simply work with ordinary words to which they claim no intellectual entitlement.

They spend their lives making value out of combinations of words that have no economic worth in themselves, being common property, infinitely reproducible with no scarcity value.

Poets and writers, like Shakespeare, blaze a trail so that people such as us can fight our battles and tackle our challenges with a clearer perception of how we fit into the overall scheme of things.

As Shakespeare said in Hamlet:

> We know what we are,
> but know not what we might be.

Yes, Shakespeare would be ideal for the task of dramatising our industry with passion, but unfortunately he is not available. Therefore, we may have to step forward and take on this challenge ourselves.

To which Shakespeare may respond:

> "Though this be madness, yet there is method in it."
>
> —*Hamlet*, Act 2, Scene 2

Here I'm sure that Shakespeare was using the word "madness" in the same sense we often use it to describe that reckless "just one more" drill hole that so often makes that major mineral discovery.

So it's up to us now to infuse this sense of responsibility and unrelenting curiosity to the next generation as we continue on in life's relay race.

We will need enough courage to adopt these big goals and again Shakespeare would encourage us by saying:

> Be not afraid of greatness:
> Some are born great, some achieve greatness,
> and some have greatness thrust upon them.
>
> —*Twelfth Night*, Act 2, Scene 5.

And if Shakespeare could experience the current re-awakening of our mining industry he would marvel at how an industry could turn in a few short years from struggle-street to a four-lane highway, largely by circumstances outside of our control.

He would probably leave us with these words of encouragement:

> There is a tide in the affairs of men,
> Which, taken at the flood, leads on to fortune;
> Omitted, all the voyage of their life
> Is bound in shallows and in miseries.
> On such a full sea are we now afloat;
> And we must take the current when it serves
> Or lose our ventures.
>
> —*Julius Caesar,* Act 4, Scene 3

Is It Time For Another Revolt?*

The 150th Anniversary of Australia's Eureka stockade Rebellion.

I understand that our Prime Minister, Mr John Howard, was invited to address this significant 150th celebration of the Eureka Rebellion but that he couldn't come.

Well, I was invited and did come. As I've said to your President, Rita Bentley, "you couldn't keep me away", and over the next 30 minutes I want to give you something of value to take away with you.

This is what I'd like to cover with you today:

First, I'm going to share with you the three reasons why I'm proud to have been chosen to give this keynote address.

Then, secondly at President Rita's request, I'll tell you why I've enjoyed being a prospector since the early 1960s and how this has led me into a deeper involvement with Australia's mining industry.

I'll mention why I feel that access to land is one of the major challenges facing us all.

Then thirdly, we can look at the significance of the Eureka event, both then, 150 years ago and, more importantly to us, today, and then ask ourselves "are we due for another revolt?"

Will this be necessary to give us the kind of Australia that will fulfil its true potential?

These are the reasons that I'm proud to be here today:

In 1992, in Ballarat, I launched the book I put together about my grandfather, W.G. Manners.

---

*Based on my Keynote Address delivered in Ballarat, Victoria on December 4th, 2004)

The 'Time Capsule' laden with treasures for future generations, pictured with the organizers.

The 'Time Capsule' positioned in Ballarat's Eureka Centre

Eureka 150
Prospecting
Our Heritage & Our Future

This time capsule was placed at the Eureka Centre on 4th December 2004 by
Prospectors & Miners Association of Victoria
to provide a snapshot of our time.
It is to be opened on 3rd December 2054
by those continuing the tradition of prospecting and mining.

The book is called *So I Headed West* and it covers his journey west from Ballarat, where he was one of the first two engineering graduates from the Ballarat School of Mines. He then worked on the Ballarat mines before moving westward to Broken Hill and then subsequently to Kanowna and Kalgoorlie where he started his mining consulting business in 1895 which, after 110 years, is still operating.

I'm honoured to have a copy of this book go into the Eureka time capsule for opening in 2054.

His father, my great great grandfather, William Manners, left school in Scotland at age 8, became a shipbuilder and at age 26 took a job as a ship's carpenter, jumped ship and went looking for gold at Ballarat in September 1853, about a year before the Eureka event.

Another reason for him jumping ship was that he fell in love with a young passenger on the ship and they eventually married and she moved to join him in Ballarat just 9 days before the Ballarat Rebellion.

On the fateful Sunday morning of the Eureka stockade he was home with his new bride, but then became involved in the general pandemonium and had some contact with the police and troopers.

His wife's family downplayed his involvement, as there was not a deep understanding outside these fields of the issues and principles involved.

Now, with hindsight and contemplation, I'm extremely proud of his involvement.

William Manners continued prospecting and producing gold from his Queen Victoria Mine and later at the Smeaton Reserve Mine and lived out his life in Ballarat until his death in 1901.

My other grandfather, Pietro Tamo, from Switzerland, who also left school at age 8, became a builder and built the church in the Swiss town of Sonogno before leaving Switzerland at age 19 to search for gold. It took him 18 months to get to Ballarat, arriving in 1856, just too late for the Eureka event and too late for the early Ballarat opportunities.

However, he worked hard at prospecting from 1856, but found only sufficient gold to subsist and raise a family until he died of a heart attack aged 43.

As a commentary on the hardships of those times, these two Ballarat families of my great grandfathers produced a total of 15 children, of which 6 (more than a third) died at age eighteen months or younger.

All this tells you is that I've got some very deep roots planted over here at Ballarat and that those pioneers really "did it tough". These are the reasons I am honoured to commemorate the memory of all the Ballarat pioneers.

This is where I'm to mention how I got interested in prospecting and how things developed from there.

That's easy, I was born in Kalgoorlie, the WA centre of vigorous prospecting, so I just grew up with it.

I lived in a home full of rocks, where most visitors arrived with a rock in their hand, so they would have something to talk about.

My mother was the first female student to study geology at the Kalgoorlie School of Mines, so she, of course, knew much more about rocks than me or my mates.

Prospecting became my passion from the mid-1960s (predominantly in gold), then along came the nickel boom of 1968-70 where everything simply went into "fast-forward".

Ever since then, it's been a series of booms and busts in rapid succession, and I'm fortunate to have survived these extreme cycles.

My prospecting and joint-venturing developed into Croesus Mining NL in 1986 when we commenced with a staff of 2, including myself. Now, after almost 20 years, we've survived both good and bad periods, employ around 400 people and Croesus Mining has developed (2004) into Australia's 3rd largest Australian-controlled gold producer, approaching 300,000 oz of gold per annum.

I'm fortunate to be working alongside such a fine bunch of enthusiastic young people and I enjoy trying to keep up with them.

More recently, in 2000, I've also become chairman of DeGrey Mining Ltd, a company formed by my long-term prospecting mate, Denis O'Meara.

Denis started drilling these DeGrey prospects the day before listing in July 2002. From the continuing exploration success of so many companies we rely on new discoveries being made to contribute to our nation's prosperity.

Now that all sounds fairly positive, but I'm finding that more and more often we are being obstructed by multi-levels of bureaucracy in our pursuit to gain access to exploration ground. So I'd like to raise my concern with you about the attack on our property rights and land access. I see this is a growing impediment which calls for a battle into which we must all throw ourselves before it grinds us to a halt.

Land Access is one of the major challenges facing us all.

I've been adversely affected by governmental attacks on Property Rights, both as a farmer in Esperance (where the problem was rezoning and the multiple approvals process), and as an explorer in Australia, particularly since the advent of what is mistakenly called Native Title (dealt with in detail on page 106).

As I've mentioned before, when the eminent Economist, Hernando de Soto, visited Fremantle's Notre Dame University last year (2003), he pointed out that such unclear and unreliable property rights are the essence of "Third World" status.

Do I see this situation getting better?

No, not without a struggle, mainly because we haven't got enough votes between the lot of us to strike terror into the hearts of politicians, and because neither Liberal nor Labor politicians are willing to risk upsetting the Greens and their fellow travellers.

However, these land access problems are not exclusive to the exploration and mining industries. They equally affect farmers, fishermen, hunters, prospectors and property developers.

Their mutual concern is that another major threat, Environmental Fundamentalism, is denying them all their access rights, their property rights and their water rights.

Now I should also mention that 25 per cent of my time is spent running the Mannkal Economic Education Foundation in Perth and that, on November 9 (2004), we gathered a bunch of these concerned people together at a Land Users Symposium.

If I thought the problem was bad before we organized this symposium, I now realise that it's worse than we could ever have imagined.

There are so many people in Western Australia being crippled by excess regulation and destruction of their property rights that our very own State Government launched an inquiry into this and the Executive

Summary of their findings, consists of 683 pages—that's how serious the problem is!

Is the Western Australian Government going to do anything about it? No, because there is no political pressure to do so. That's the way the system works—they've had their inquiry, there's the information, the problem is really serious but there is no pressure to do anything about it.

The information we gathered from our Perth symposium was part of the national input to the Inaugural Eureka Forum held in Ballarat yesterday.

Yesterday's forum was organized by the Institute of Public Affairs. It saw 150 separate land user groups come together to identify the size of the problem right around the nation. An agenda for action and the sheer number of people involved has become obvious. This push is gaining momentum and if we all get behind it, we can make a difference.

Let me explain why we chose Tuesday November 9, 2004 as the date to hold our Land Users Symposium in Perth.

That date was declared World Freedom Day, as it was the 15th anniversary of the day that they tore down the Berlin Wall, without bloodshed.

As the late President Ronald Reagan had a lot to do with demolishing that particular wall, we started our symposium with a quotation from Ronald Reagan, and I'd now like to share it with you as it's as relevant today as it was 15 years ago. He said:

> You and I are told increasingly that we have to choose between left or right, but I would like to suggest that there is no such thing as left or right. There is only an up or down —up to man's age-old dream—the ultimate in individual freedom consistent with law and order—or down to the ant heap of totalitarianism, and regardless of their sincerity, their humanitarian motives, those who would trade our freedom for security have embarked on this downward course.

If Ronald Reagan were still alive, he'd identify today's environmental fundamentalists and our over-aggressive bureaucracy as those who were steering us on a downward course towards the ant heap.

The challenge is for us all to learn more about our property rights and the vital importance such rights play in the very survival of our wonderful and exciting prospecting and mining industry. In short, we must become activists for our own industry. This is a very worthy cause.

The significance of the Eureka Rebellion, then, now and the lessons for us

If we accept the challenge of honouring the memories of those pioneers, we must keep their dream alive.

Those diggers were confronted with an insurmountable problem and they had a choice: do something about it, or do nothing.

For us to judge this event, we must train our eyes to see the world as it was in 1854.

The monthly licence fee being extracted by force from the Ballarat diggers was equivalent to a week's wages. That's a tax of about 25 per cent with almost nothing offered in return.

They say that a fine is a tax for doing wrong; and that a tax is a fine for doing well.

But this tax or fine was being forcibly extracted and it applied whether you found gold or not.

It has been said that "taxation is the price we pay for civilization", but isn't the opposite really the case?

Taxation is the price we pay for failing to build a civilized society. The higher the tax level, the greater the failure.

A centrally planned socialist state represents a complete defeat for the civilized world, while a totally voluntary society represents its ultimate success.

So here in Ballarat, back in 1854, we had an intolerable situation, being badly administered.

It is difficult for anyone with an Australian sense of "a fair go" not to side with the diggers once they hear the facts….

- There were other issues, beside the Gold Licence Fee, including the right to vote, the ability to purchase land, democratic reforms and, in particular, the blatant corruption of the administration.

"Time for another revolt?"

"Yes!" said the enthusiastic Ballarat audience.

Always good to see a friendly face in the audience—(Denis O'Meara, OAM).

- Religion was always a powerful force on Australia's goldfields and it was seen as a sneaky manoeuvre when up to 300 well-prepared troops and police (both mounted and on foot) attacked the Eureka stockade at dawn on the Sunday morning when many of the diggers were away with their families.
- Only about 150 diggers were in the stockade, many of them unprepared.
- The ratio of those killed—30 miners as opposed to 5 soldiers—represents the imbalance of the battle.
- Public sympathy was such that the 13 arrested and charged with high treason were all found not guilty.

The influx of more than 100,000 miners to the Victorian Goldfields was an interesting mixture.

Nearly half were Irishmen being brought up on the epic and heroic tale of the 1798 rebellion at County Wexford near Dublin where 20,000 people were killed from a population of 120,000. There were many Americans, mainly from the Californian Gold Rush (with a tradition of their War of Independence behind them), while the rest came from all over Europe, some with first-hand or family involvement in the then current Crimean and Sebastopol conflict (where 600,000 people died) and earlier memories of the French Revolution, 1789-1799 (25,000 deaths).

These people had a tradition of achieving results through violence. They didn't have the benefit of excellent communications, the Internet or democratic votes.

There were almost no Australians at the Eureka stockade. In those days, we all came from somewhere else, all busy blending into the people we now call Australians. One hundred and fifty years later, the world is learning to appreciate us as a people, small in number, but who always manage to "punch above their weight". Our own Prime Minister, John Howard, was a classic example of that when he represented us on the world stage.

It's always constructive to accentuate the positive about what makes Australia special. Outside of the U.S., it is about the only country in the world where people can come from all over the world and become citizens of their adopted nation.

Before the dawn service—2004.

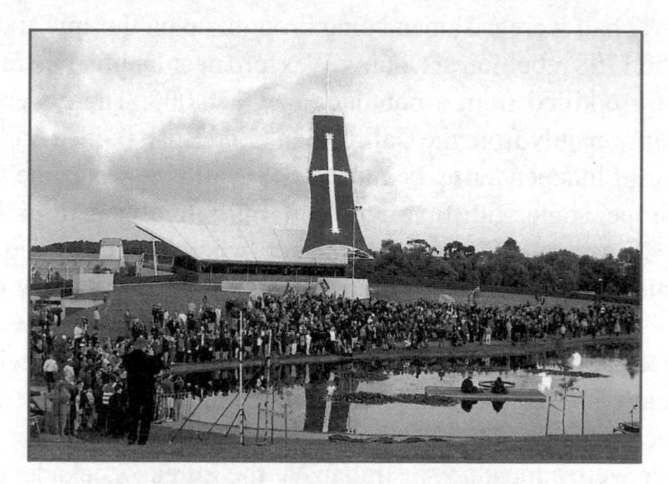

After the dawn service—2004

Posters displayed the theme and cause of the Eureka Revolt in 1854

You can't go to Greece and become Greek, or go to Japan and become Japanese, or Switzerland and become Swiss. Think about this and the many qualities that we have blended together by combining British law and property rights with the creativity and energy of such a wide mix of people.

The Eureka stockade memory and tradition has been very much a part of giving us this competitive edge.

The incredible thing is that, despite .....

the Eureka stockade being almost completely ignored by the government-controlled education syllabus;

that despite ......

the union movement hijacking the Eureka flag and devaluing its memory by presenting it as a symbol of mob rule;

that despite ....

the contemporary musical *Eureka*! defining the Eureka stockade as a politically correct revisionist absurdity;

that despite all that ....

the overwhelming majority of ordinary, intelligent Australians have understood the importance and the lasting significance of the Eureka stockade for the enduring nature of democracy in Australia—a country which is one of the oldest continuous democracies in the world.

The key to understanding and preserving democracy is to ensure that it doesn't degenerate into the "tyranny of the majority" where we allow pressure groups to impose their priorities on the rest of us.

I think the philosopher-writer Ayn Rand put it well when she said:

> Individual rights are not subject to public vote; a majority has no right to vote away the rights of a minority; the political function of rights is precisely to protect minorities from oppression by majorities (and the smallest minority on earth is the individual).

That's what she said and let me add that the "individuals" she spoke of are people like us, members of the creative class who are "turning ideas into gold", and there can be nothing more creative than that.

Never underestimate the importance of what you are doing as part of Australia's resource industry, often described as the "power-house of Australia".

The small band of people in the Australian resources industry is vital to Australia. We account for 27 per cent of the nation's exports (and considerably more if we include the finished products of mining).

We are responsible for 8 per cent of Australia's gross national product.

But despite that, we don't even rate a dedicated Minister for Resources either in Canberra or in any State Government.

We have a long way to go in making our presence felt.

Through your leadership and clear understanding of the problems confronting us, your Prospectors and Miners Association is an example for the rest of us. You have devised a focused strategy and it shows through in your excellent publication *The Eureka Echo*.

You know that you have to fight your own battles, that your concerns are not the concerns of the giant mining companies. I know the majors are not as concerned about the issues of land access as we smaller companies are, as access to land is our very life blood.

Each of us carries this responsibility on our own shoulders. As Thomas Paine once said, "those who expect to reap the benefits of freedom must undergo the fatigue of supporting it."

That's exactly why we built the $25m Australian Prospectors and Miners Hall of Fame in Kalgoorlie: to be an effective and easily recognized symbol and icon for your efforts.

Prospecting and mining have given this country such wealth and opportunity in raising the standard of living for all Australians, we felt it fitting that this symbol should be created to celebrate the past, the present and future of our industry.

The Hall of Fame would benefit from your support, just as you would benefit from creating a two-way link with the Hall of Fame. In that way, we can be part of keeping the Eureka legend alive.

So, in conclusion, let me say there are not many "trigger points", as we say in business, that acted as a catalyst for making Australians different.

Let me suggest that the 1854 Eureka stockade and the 1915 Anzac Gallipoli experience predominate, so let's take up the worthy baton in life's relay race and get on with the job of defending our rights and freedom to prospect, our freedom to explore and our freedom to produce, with minimum interference.

We have the modern tools to continue the Eureka Revolt; without spilling blood.

We have to work smarter at it, just as the enemies of industry are working smarter at closing us down.

We have technology, economics and morality on our side—so all we need is the physical courage and the moral courage to win.

Our livelihood depends on us winning these battles, but it goes beyond this.

If Australia is to achieve its potential, it depends more than ever on people such as yourselves relentlessly pursuing these strategies to keep the Eureka dream alive.

The Next Eureka Moment

(Celebrating the 150th Anniversary of the Eureka stockade Rebellion)

"Put some words
into the Eureka time capsule," they said—
Me?—who already has a headful of stuff
each time I go to bed!

"If you're still around
in two thousand and fifty four," they said,
"you'll be on the invite list."
Well, that was an invitation, I simply couldn't resist!

And so it got me thinking
about splitting two hundred years into four—
the last three groups of fifty years—
and the fifty yet in store—

Eighteen hundred and fifty four to nineteen hundred and four—
discovery dividends declared before the banking crash,
Australia finding its feet again—
brave moves were made—with some quite rash—

Then came the second quarter, 04 to fifty four,
when the very bad overwhelmed the best—
Two world wars and a depression made it
not just rough, but very tough for those who headed west—

1954 till now—bad start but hope towards the end—
restrictive policies discouraged—
some cautious experiments were made,
and enterprise, to our surprise, was actually encouraged—

So the next quarter is the one
for us to make a stance—
and we'll be in there fighting—
Yes! We still have a chance

Government's lofty plans for us
conflict with our own plan—
so can we shape our future now?
with time and thought and confidence, I reckon that we can!

So when they dig the capsule up
in two thousand and fifty four,
I'll come from the West, join Eureka's best—
and ready to write some more!

RBM (2004)

AUSTRALIAN

BUSINESS

AUSTRALIA'S WEEKLY FINANCE MAGAZINE $2.50* OCTOBER 12, 1988

ONE YEAR AFTER

Could it happen again?

*AIR DELIVERED COPIES NEW ZEALAND $4.50 INCL. GST

Do All Booms End in Tears?*

(Part 1 ... 1960 to 2006)

What are my credentials for writing on this topic of investing? They are simple but extremely relevant.

My qualifications are only that I've lived through so many violent market cycles that I feel myself fortunate to have survived to tell the tale.

Occasionally I pull out a few old files to try and get a further understanding of some of them. Each time my wife, Jenny, spends the next few days sneezing from all the old Kalgoorlie mining dust that escapes from these files.

So, after pulling these files out once more, let me give you a quick 'tour' of my personal experiences with such business cycles.

Let me take you back to the mid–1960s

This was a time in Australia when nobody appeared poor, but nobody seemed to have any money to spare. Everyone worked hard, to feed and educate their families.

That was about the time my father, Charles Manners, died.

I was 30 years old and helped my mother sort out Dad's affairs.

Among the bits and pieces Dad left to my mother was a thick file of share-certificates.

We lived in Kalgoorlie and I walked this file over to the local stockbroker's office, run by Ron Reed (father of David Reed), to see if there was anything in it that could help my mother re-establish herself in Perth so that she could be near my sister and her family.

---

*Based on my July 10, 2006 presentation to the Financial Markets Group at The Weld Club, Perth, Western Australia

He had a good look through the share-certificates and said, "Too bad Ron, they are all dead."

This was in fact a fantastic collection of historic mining share-certificates and in amongst this collection I also found a copy of a page from the *Coolgardie Miner*, May 26, 1896 [see panel]

The manager of a New Zealand gold mine recently sent an imperative demand to a shareholder for the payment of a "call," and received the following reply;—"Dear Sir,—I have your letter of this date, and note that your directors propose to proceed against me. Your prospectus stated that one of the objects of your company was to 'seek, win, and work gold in ——— and elsewhere.' Things not turning out well in ———, your directors apparently consider it their duty to seek, win, and work gold elsewhere, i.e., out of me. I can assure you, however, that I am not in an auriferous vein, the only lode I possess is a lode of debt, and as a gold mine I shall be a failure. Your prospectus estimates a yield of 1oz. of gold per ton on 30,000 tons of quartz crushed per annum. You may 'crush' me, but you will find that I will not yield nearly so much. My person (which for the purpose of this calculation may be considered quartz) weighs, roughly speaking, 10st., and if crushed immediately I estimate that it would yield as under:—Gold, nil; silver, 3s.; copper, 4½d.; total, 3s. 4½d. Deduct cost of crushing, say £5 5s.—Yours faithfully ———."

'Coolgardie Miner' May 26, 1896.

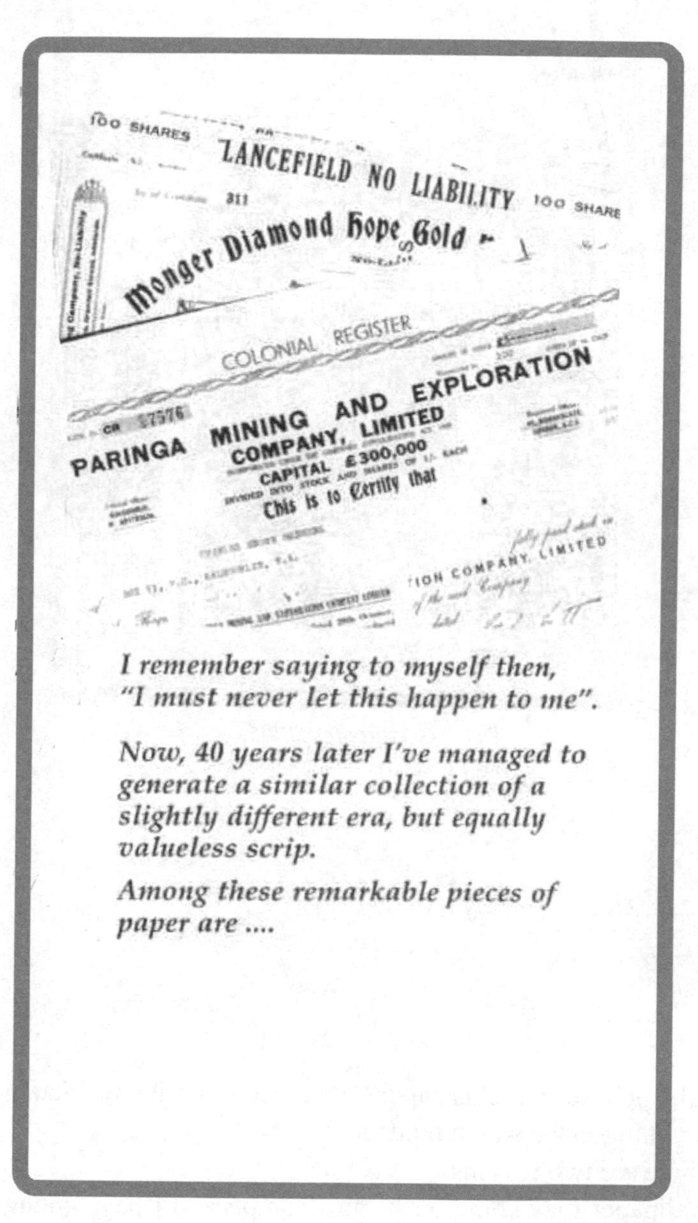
100 SHARES
LANCEFIELD NO LIABILITY
100 SHARES
Monger Diamond Hope Gold
COLONIAL REGISTER
PARINGA MINING AND EXPLORATION
COMPANY, LIMITED
CAPITAL £300,000
This is to Certify that
I remember saying to myself then,
"I must never let this happen to me".
Now, 40 years later I've managed to generate a similar collection of a slightly different era, but equally valueless scrip.
Among these remarkable pieces of paper are ....

Dead Certificates 1966

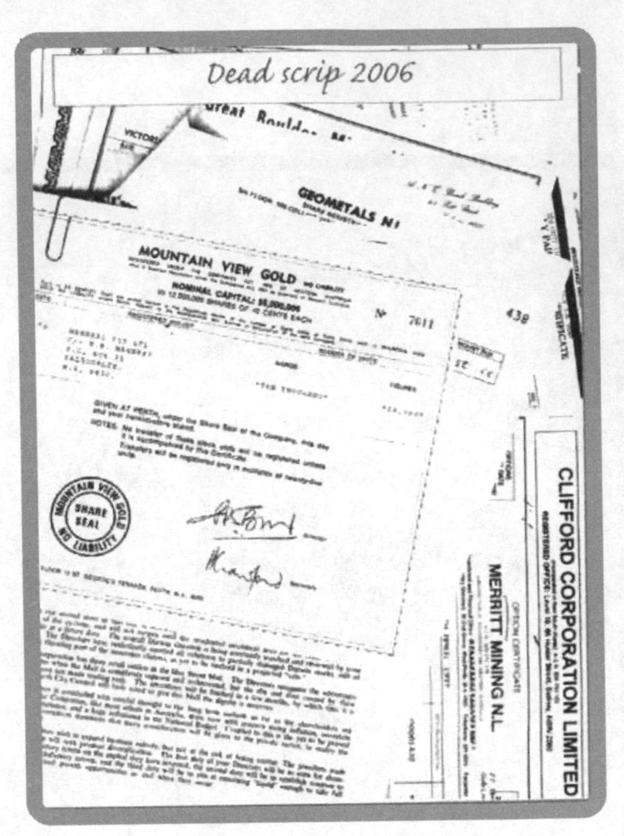

Dead Certificates 2006

Why do I keep all this paper? Is it just to remind me that history is a funny thing in the way it repeats?

There are two reasons:

- Wallpaper may come back into fashion and I have enough share scrip for a large room.

- Four years after taking my father's share scrip file into the stock-broker's office, I heard that the Hicks family was planning to breathe life into one of the companies from Dad's "dead scrip" file by recapitalising the company and involving it in the nickel boom. The company was called Spargos NL.

Their efforts were successful and it certainly helped my mother establish herself in Perth.

So the moral to that story is that 'tears may only be temporary'.

My first experience with violent financial cycles

This was Australia's 1960 'credit squeeze'. Possibly, some of you may have lived through this or heard of it.

It was the first example I came across of what I call 'government failure', and that's when I started a file titled 'Outcome of government actions' and how it is usually the opposite to their intent (it's become a fairly fat file).

I'll tell you about the government intent first as then we can analyse the actual results of the credit squeeze.

In November 1960, the Federal Government (Robert Menzies P.M. and Harold Holt, Treasurer) was confronted with statistics showing that imports were outstripping our exports and Australia was running out of foreign currency.

No Hedge Funds in those days, electronically moving funds back and forth trying to outwit the various business cycles. It was a totally regulated system in the 1960s.

The Federal Government overreacted and promptly announced a credit squeeze, that resulted in any companies with overdrafts being told by the banks to quickly reduce the amount by up to 50 per cent.

To further stifle business, Treasurer Holt announced that the interest payable on most business loans would cease to be tax deductible.

A Melbourne friend of mine, David Hains, was operating a very successful chain of retail stores at that time and explained the effect on retailers ...

> As most hire purchase companies were borrowing 10 or 15 times their issued capital and made profits that were small, after paying interest this of course turned profitable finance

operations into very substantial loss makers. This directive created a huge reaction, with investors rushing to withdraw funds from the finance companies and finance companies immediately restricting credit to retailers.

My own experience in Western Australia was similar.

The finance companies of the day, Esanda, Custom Credit etc., with greatly restricted funds available, could place all these funds easily, to selected customers from their head office. So, they promptly closed all branch offices, particularly in the country regions. This left retailers without finance facilities and, consequently, without clients.

Somewhere, I have statistics of how many thousands of firms 'went to the wall' as a result of this government failure.

Older Australians may remember some of the bigger names such as Cox Brothers, Reid Murray, H.G. Palmer and Eric Andersons. These were all big names in Australia's retailing of the 1950s and 60s, but there were thousands of smaller names that were forced to close their doors, resulting in mass retrenchments.

Those firms that did survive never trusted governments or finance companies again and it was quite normal for these survivors to open their own in-house finance companies. I know we had our own called Hentry (Aust.) Pty Ltd and that ran quite profitably right through into the late 1970s when, under considerable pressure from the larger finance companies, the State Governments introduced legislation licensing finance companies, imposing very high asset criteria and high license fees. This then wiped out another vital segment of an industry.

I always queried how consumers benefited from such licensing. If a finance company goes broke, it cannot adversely affect the consumers (in fact it may even be beneficial for them. That is, if the finance company vanished you may even avoid repaying your loans!) If investors in the finance companies lost money through fraud, the existing legal remedies were sufficient.

However, it was very clear to see how the larger finance companies benefited and how finance and leasing rates took an impressive upward hike.

That misguided government policy position of the 1960s credit squeeze was equivalent to a 'crash' and brought on widespread tears. I believe it set back Australia's emerging 'consumer society' by up to 10 years. The really sad thing about it was the number of businesses that were completely wiped out and who didn't have a chance to participate in the healthy recovery process.

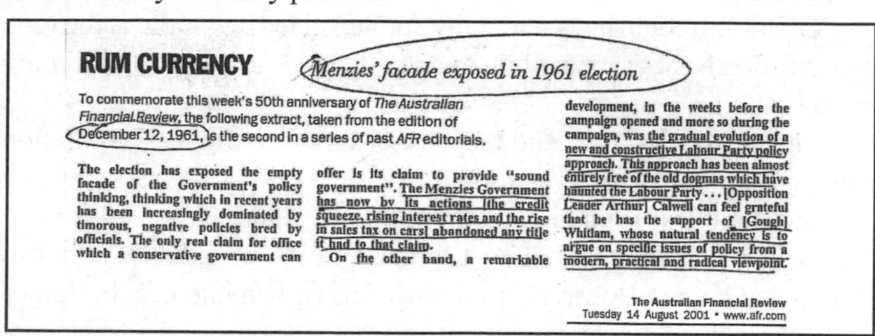

RUM CURRENCY

Menzies' facade exposed in 1961 election

To commemorate this week's 50th anniversary of *The Australian Financial Review*, the following extract, taken from the edition of December 12, 1961, is the second in a series of past *AFR* editorials.

The election has exposed the empty facade of the Government's policy thinking, thinking which in recent years has been increasingly dominated by timorous, negative policies bred by officials. The only real claim for office which a conservative government can offer is its claim to provide "sound government". The Menzies Government has now by its actions [the credit squeeze, rising interest rates and the rise in sales tax on cars] abandoned any title it had to that claim.

On the other hand, a remarkable development, in the weeks before the campaign opened and more so during the campaign, was the gradual evolution of a new and constructive Labour Party policy approach. This approach has been almost entirely free of the old dogmas which have haunted the Labour Party . . . [Opposition Leader Arthur] Calwell can feel grateful that he has the support of [Gough] Whitlam, whose natural tendency is to argue on specific issues of policy from a modern, practical and radical viewpoint.

The Australian Financial Review
Tuesday 14 August 2001 • www.afr.com

The first Nickel boom

The next experience I had with market cycles was the original nickel boom.

This was the original 1969 version.

That nickel boom, often called the Poseidon Boom, lasted only 18 months.

I chart that original Nickel boom, not just by the value of Poseidon shares. Poseidon shares, incidentally as retold and retold again in folklore ranged from 2½ cents–$280–and then ultimately zero as the company slipped into liquidation.

I chart it also on the number of people we employed in our mining equipment, engineering company W.G. Manners & Co., now Mannwest Group (still 'serving industry since 1895').

There were four of us in 1966, 48 in 1970 and by the late '70s we were down to four again!

The first nickel boom was so exciting I decided to float a company called Kalmin Exploration Limited.

I wouldn't have believed anyone, if they had told me that it would be the last company floated in the nickel boom and that it would ultimately be transferred to the industrial board and become a home-builder.

None of the statistics of that period were reflected by smooth gradual charts.

There were 350 Australian and international companies looking for nickel in the Kalgoorlie region.

Kalgoorlie had the highest population of geologists in the world at that time.

Interestingly enough, the second highest population of geologists was in New York City.

Of the 350 companies searching for nickel in Kalgoorlie at the time the question is: how many of them actually made a profit out of mining nickel?

The answer is—two, and they were, Western Mining Corporation (WMC) and Metals Exploration NL.

Mostly, it was tears for the other 348 companies.

Debt and leasing was almost unknown in the Goldfields, prior to that nickel boom. However, so many of us rushed into new buildings and acquired additional equipment and stock to service the frantic activity, that we found ourselves somewhat exposed when the tide went out.

Fortunately for us, the supply and engineering cycle always lags the commodity cycle by a couple of years, so, many of the unprofitable miners continued their efforts to succeed.

This included companies like CRA (Rio Tinto), Anaconda Inc. of USA and Newmont.

That's probably what saved us from some tears, but it didn't save us from the boredom of survival for the next 10 years until gold poked its head up again in 1980 (for a short while) and 16 years after the first nickel boom, the second nickel boom gathered steam, far more orderly this time and, thankfully, it's continuing with substance.

A percussion drill rig at Mt Windarra has plenty of enthusiastic onlookers.

MEMORY LANE

"We calculate the present value of Poseidon NL as between $300 and $382."
— London broker Panmure Gordon & Co, January 1970

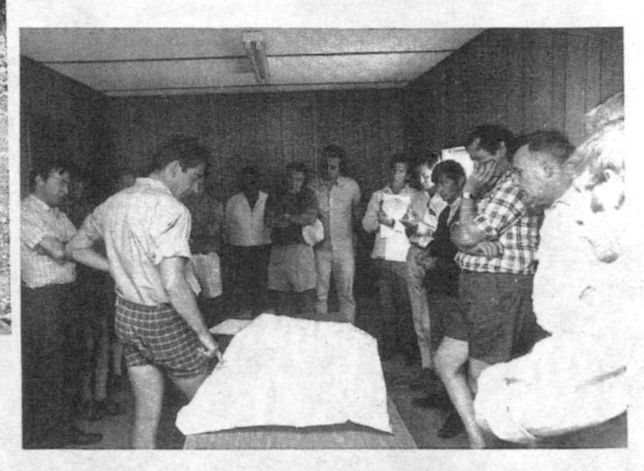

ABOVE: Norm Shierlaw is chipping away. RIGHT: Geoff Burrill gives a briefing — among the participants were Peter Andrews (extreme right), Norm Shierlaw (he hadn't changed his shirt!), John Cornell, television commentator John Hudson (holding papers), Lou Checker (white shirt in centre) and Ron Manners (extreme left).

... 20 YEARS LATER

A reunion for those who participated in Australia's greatest sharemarket run.
THE VENUE: The Hannans Club, Kalgoorlie - February 10, 1990.

Early in 1990 I had an idea!

Should we allow the 20th anniversary of the Poseidon boom (the stock market peak of the Poseidon shares) to pass without a celebration of some kind?

I felt we could gather together 15-20 of the original Poseidon participants which should guarantee a good night of reminiscences.

So out went the 'faxed' invitations.

Promptly, 52 acceptances were received, as the invitations had been 'passed on'.

A great night at Kalgoorlie's Hannans Club, followed with a star-studded evening of good humour, where at last, many true stories of those times were revealed.

Among those reporting on the event were Ross Louthean and Trevor Sykes, whose stories were incorporated into a commemorative souvenir and an airline magazine, both of which will be replicated in the Appendix ... www.heroicmisadventures.com.

See also the following page.

THE POSEIDON NICKEL ADVENTURE

Reliving the sharemarket's greatest adventure

Those at the reunion were: (kneeling from l to r) Aidan Keogh, Bob Berven, Barry Fehlberg, Colin Brooks. (seated) Ken Shirley, Norm Shierlaw, Basil Lewis, John Roberts, John Horan, Trevor Sykes. (standing l to r) David Reed, Jim Paull, John Willis, Jim Keogh, Derek Fisher, Alan Deans, Bill Trythall, John Burgess, Keith Biggs, Rod Fletcher, Kai Kjellquist, John Jones, Bill Humphrey, Don Leahy, Geoff Hynan, Chris Fyson, Ian Paynter, George Compton, Wally Unger, Tony Hall, Doug Wilkinson, Peter Andrews, Malcolm Mayger, Rob Bowden, Ross Louthean, Doug McGay, David Hedderwick, Harry Kitson, Ron Sheen, Ron Jones, Harry Davies Snr, Doug Daws, John Leahy, Ian Burston, Gordon Buller, Rod Black, Graeme McGarry, Ron Manners, Bruce Benny. PHOTO by Richie Hann.

by Ross Louthean

In 20 years the good yarns can get more romantic, the pain of lost fortunes can ease and the wounds of sour deals can heal.

The Hannans Club in Kalgoorlie, where many of the Poseidon era deals were struck, was host of the Poseidon reunion on February 10 and *Far Horizons* attended.

The only other media representative was the Poseidon boom's keenest observer, Trevor Sykes, who is executive editor of *Australian Business* magazine and also author of the highly acclaimed book "The Money Miners" (see page 6).

The reunion marked the day when the sharemarket stood bolt upright, on February 10, 1970, as shares in the small Adelaide exploration company Poseidon Ltd started the greatest share price rise in Australian history, which not only started an unbridled sharemarket stampede but also saw a large number of new companies floated.

So frenetic was the rush that geography became just as important as geology. Any company with leases close to Poseidon's Windarra property near Laverton could go for a price run.

Announcements of good surface grab samples, or early drill results that gave a sniff of nickel, provided the right sort of rocket fuel.

Everybody went pegging — the butcher, the baker and the candlestick maker.

One of the 52 reunionists was "the butcher" Keith Biggs who, as a young butcher and businessman in Leonora, hit the 1970 headlines as a perceptive buyer of Poseidon shares.

Keith now lives in Kalgoorlie and gets into the background of junior explorers. He is also principal of a drilling company and occasionally makes the headlines as a part owner of Paklani and other successful racehorses.

Near the end of the evening he was the successful bidder, with $2,000, for a hard cover copy of Sykes' out-of-print "The Money Miners". The money went to the Royal Flying Doctor Service.

The book had signatures of key players in the Poseidon share boom, including Biggs, who was a high profile prospector at the time and also regarded as one of

No tears in sight, even though some companies will perform better than others.

The current uranium boom might be different, but history tells us that it could produce a similar statistic to the original nickel boom, where two companies out of 350 ever became profitable.

Of the hundreds of uranium exploration companies, Paladin Energy Ltd is on the way to profitability where it is reported that "Paladin's Langer Heinrich Mine (in Namibia) is the first brand new conventional mine commissioned anywhere in the world for a decade." (www.fatprophets.com.au).

So, perhaps, plenty of tears ahead for the majority of uranium explorers.

Gold Boom of January 1980

The next boom and crash for me was the brief gold boom that peaked in January 1980.

At the time, gold had been moving up steadily from its fixed price of around US$38.

It's hard for us to imagine now, but during the years of the fixed gold price it was illegal for people to own gold.

I think it was around 1972 when President Nixon opened what they called the "Gold Window", and not many investors had actually seen gold or been involved with it—until then.

Several years after this we were confronted with the Oil Crisis when the oil price quadrupled, resulting in a massive transfer of funds from the Western world to the oil-producing countries.

One of the reasons why the oil producers so dramatically increased the price of oil was that they were tired of being paid in US$ paper currency that the US Government was printing like confetti at that time, guaranteeing an ultimate erosion of purchasing power.

As a way of diversifying and not reinvesting their surplus funds in US-denominated investments, many of the Arab nations plunged heavily into gold, sending its price rocketing to US$840 in January 1980.

For anyone with a dormant but clean company shell this was a perfect opportunity to refinance it and join in the new gold rush.

This single book explains the intricacies of the resurgence of Australia's gold industry

I was in London when gold was at its peak, raising funds for a small company called Coopers Creek NL. I was treated like a celebrity, simply because I was associated with our gold industry at that time. It was almost as good as being a winning World Cup Soccer player!

However, during my time in the air on the flight home from London, the gold price dropped by US$150 (off the US$840) and kept going down through until around 1982, when I think it got as low us US$280.

Not many tears that time as so few even got started.

Looking back I'm sure that mini-boom was somehow related to an almost follow-on boom in South Perth home units. It appears that anyone who made any money out of that gold burst decided to invest in countless blocks of home units being built in South Perth.

My first home unit experience, in partnership with my dentist, was so successful that we sold the development, even before we got around to demolishing the old houses on the blocks.

I was so excited by this success that I immediately doubled my bets.

Very exciting, highly leveraged, finance packages were readily available, and 'of course all the units would be sold off' before one had to bear the full impact of the astronomical interest rates of 17 per cent–24 per cent that were ruling circa 1982.

I didn't know then and still don't know now where all the buyers were supposed to come from, but they certainly didn't arrive.

I think my tears at that time were blood red and I can remember the light-hearted question that was often asked during that period ... "What's the difference between a home unit in South Perth and syphilis?"

The answer, or course, was ..."You can always get rid of syphilis".

My own father had always told me, "Never borrow money to go looking for gold, or to gamble." I always followed this advice but somehow thought the South Perth units were different, by being bricks and mortar. I was wrong and Custom Credit proceeded to sell one unit per month, just to pay off their interest payments. Not even reducing the principal. Times certainly change and the Perth property market is seeing better times.

Whilst, as I mentioned, the 1980 gold run-up didn't seem to come to very much at that time, it did however plant a lot of seeds in the minds of our mineral explorers who had been pretty much stranded since the

Geoffrey (Geoff) Stokes (RH) pictured with his colleague, John Langford, - July, 1982.

FIVE YEARS IN LIMBO

The great sharemarket crash of 1987 would have been less damaging if we had learned more from it, writes Trevor Sykes

Five years ago this week, the Australian sharemarket suffered its greatest collapse in history. On October 20, 1987, the market was marked down by 25% even before it opened for trading. Unlike the world's three leading sharemarkets – New York, London and Tokyo – it never enjoyed any significant recovery.

In Australia, the All Ordinaries index lost half its value between September and November 1987, a proportionately much steeper fall than that suffered in the other three markets. By mid-1989, the Australian sharemarket had regained about half its lost ground but that was the best it would do. Since then it has been moving sideways and in the past four months has lost some 15% of its value.

Gil Hoskins, managing director of National Mutual Life, says: "Australia was devalued and the devaluation seems to be permanent. However, as we were recovering from the crash we were subjected to a huge second shock with the crash of property values. The property market has gone off maybe one-third, or about the same as the equity market. That represents an enormous devaluation of the country's capital base.

"Then there was a third shock to the banking sector when loans that had been regarded as secure suddenly turned into property investments. These accounted for a great deal of the write-offs by the banks, which by now must be around $15 billion."

Ray Block, chief economist at SBC Dominguez Barry, believes the Australian sharemarket may have suffered worse than the three majors be-

INSIDE: TIM KNAPTON ON BROKERS' FUTURES .... 78 PIERPONT ON FEES 85

end of the nickel boom. Many of these groups then began working toward putting companies together, resulting in some great performers emerging through from 1982–1985.

These companies included Metana Minerals, Sons of Gwalia, Pancontinental Mining, Dominion Mining, Delta Gold and Croesus Mining.

There were many other companies that also participated in this run-up to the fantastic nine-month long 1987 gold boom, right up until the fever pitch and the famous …

Crash of 1987

Now that was one that was heavy on the tears because this time there was a whole new generation of punters who borrowed heavily to be part of something they didn't understand.

From memory, that major crash actually happened in London and New York, on a Friday night, 19 October 1987.

Also from memory, the London Stock Exchange closed its doors for a day.

On the Friday, our Australian market was thundering away and I can remember being in the late and great Bill Wyllie's Perth office with my Mannwest Co-Director, Harry Kitson. We were asking Bill's advice on whether we should accept a broker's invitation to list our private company Mannwest Group.

Bill had explained why he was not going to list his own Asia Securities private company and we parted company, without any real sense of foreboding about what was to happen about four hours later.

Back in Kalgoorlie, on Monday morning, from my office I heard all the bad news about what was going on with our Australian stock market.

Fortunately for the gold producers everything crashed except the price of gold!

That didn't collapse until the very next day, as gold-denominated assets were about the only thing left that people could actually sell to get themselves out of trouble.

I clearly remember then walking down Hannan Street, Kalgoorlie feeling somewhat numb and considerably diminished by this absolute wipe out.

I bumped into my friend, Geoff Stokes. Apart from owning Kalgoorlie's Palace Hotel and being my accountant, Geoff was also a substantial mining company promoter.

Geoff exploded with some expletives when he saw me and finished off with this question ... "Manners, do you know how much I've dropped since Friday?" "$21 million."

Well, up until then I was on the verge of tears, but my situation was, by comparison, relatively insignificant.

I suppose everything is relative, so that's about all that stemmed my tears on that occasion.

The next one was the DOT-COM Boom of 2000, when we saw many of the previously abandoned corporate shells, change names and head towards the universe of the Dot Coms.

This boom was difficult for me to understand. However, years previously I had read a book called "*The Madness of Crowds & Other Delusions*". It was therefore easy for me to see where this was all going.

The tears were shed by some pretty big fish when all this fell over and by the time some of the legal cases actually made it to the courts, they were judged by people who had little memory of the hysteria that accompanied that era.

I think very few winners emerged from this one and one of the serious outcomes was that it produced a whole generation of people who vowed never ever to buy a share again. Think of all the fun and adventure they would have missed out on if they did remain out of the game.

Australia is often called the 'lucky country' and just as we were rescued by Japan in the 1960s when their demand for iron ore and other commodities gave us some muscle, so there we were in 2007, being rescued by the Chinese this time.

We were calling it a new kind of boom.

"This time it's different" we said.

"Stronger for longer" was the term we used, not a concern in sight anywhere.

Then along comes a whole heap of new terminologies such as *Sub-Prime* and Wall Street's very clever packaging of its "toxic slime" which was cleverly repackaged and sold to unsuspecting investors all around the world.

The wheels completely fell off the code of trust which enables the international financial community to transact business with ease.

Nobody proceeds now without going through the hoops of labyrinthian legal layers and many quite reasonable transactions will simply grind to a halt with this added "lead in the saddle".

We were right! It was different this time, but not for the reasons we thought.

It was different in the sense that it was like an external seismic event that came close to spoiling our "resources boom party".

It was also different from earlier financial crashes, for at least two separate reasons.

Firstly, this one was widely predicted:

- As far back as 1948, Austrian Economist Ludwig von Mises said, "There is no means of avoiding the final collapse of a boom brought about by credit expansion. The alternative is only whether the crisis would come sooner ... as the result of a voluntary abandonment of further credit expansion; or later ... as a final and total catastrophe of the currency system involved."
- Again in Asia Inc. (June 1997) Professor Ravi Batra said, "The U.S. is on the brink of a financial disaster that could bring down its entire capitalist system. It's much worse than in the 1930s. Despite high employment, there are a record number of bankruptcies. Even more shocking is the fact that 50 percent of Americans have less than $1,000 in the bank .... The U.S. runs enormous deficits, yet it continues to prosper. Why? Because countries with trade surpluses invest their accumulated dollars in America. This keeps interest rates low, inflation modest and the stock market at record highs. But some time soon .... the stock-market bubble is going to burst."
- And again, more recently, in its cover story, *The Economist* (May 29, 2003) warned about "the biggest bubble in history." Here are four quotes from that article:

> The total value of residential property in developed countries rose by more than $30 trillion, to $70 trillion, over the past five years—eclipsing the combined GDPs of those nations.
>
> Consumer spending and residential construction have accounted for 90 percent of the total growth in the American GDP over the last four years, and more than 40 percent of all private-sector jobs created since 2001 have been in housing-related sectors, including construction and mortgage brokering.
>
> 23 per cent of all American houses bought last year were for investment and in Miami, one speculation hot spot, 70% of condo buyers are investors/speculators.
>
> Last year, 42 per cent of first-time buyers—and 25 percent of all buyers—put no money down.

And since that 2003 article, things have only got worse.

The second reason (this one is different) is that it is easier to find someone to blame this time.

- Put so well on January 12, 2008 by Bill Buckler (www.the-privateer.com):

> One cannot flout economic laws with impunity. The inevitable end result is always economic collapse. True, the "inevitable" sometimes takes a while, even a LONG while, but the end result is nonetheless inevitable. No system of "money" created by fiat and force fed into the "system" by means of "legal tender" laws and fractional reserve banking has EVER lasted. All have collapsed. History shows no exception.

- And even more recently on May 19, 2008 by Alvaro Vargas Llosa (director of the Center on Global Prosperity at the Independent Institute), when commenting on the Federal Reserve U.S. Government "bail out" of Bear Stearns and injecting cash into the financial system:

> These are the latest steps taken by the U.S. government to solve a problem created in large measure by the government itself. We have seen this movie before.
>
> As a reaction to the bursting of the dot-com and telecom bubbles at the end of the 1990s, the Fed inflated the currency through the actions of its Open Market Committee. By June 2003, the policy of easy money was reflected in the drop of the federal funds rate to 1 percent. The loose monetary policy was maintained, with variations, for almost five years. The result was a fiction economy in which millions of people borrowed and consumed too much. The fact that mortgage loans were turned into sophisticated securities traded internationally made the fiction global.
>
> Greedy investors and profligate consumers are but a symptom of the real problem, which is monetary policy. The history of the boom-bust cycle since the creation of the Federal Reserve in 1913 has been the deliberate increase of the money supply, the misallocation of resources due to the perverse incentives of inflation, and eventually the bursting of the bubble. It is the consequence of the Federal Reserve, a central bank that confers upon a chosen elite – the Federal Reserve governors – the monopoly of money creation and the power to decide what amount of money is appropriate for an economy in which millions of people are making decisions they cannot anticipate.
>
> The Fed was created as a response to the periodic bank runs of the late 19th and early 20th centuries. Some of the greatest economists have explained that part of that instability was caused not because private banks were free to issue currency (even as late as 1907) but because the government maintained a policy of rewarding irresponsible behaviour by rescuing financial institutions when they reached the verge of collapse. In any case, as Milton Friedman wrote, the instability

of the pre-Federal Reserve years was nothing compared to the booms and busts caused by the monetary authorities after 1913. Nobel laureate Friedrich Hayek, whose free-market ideas triumphed with the collapse of the Soviet Union, frequently denounced the connection between central banks and the boom-bust cycle. In an interview conducted in 1977, he said, "If it were not for government interference with the monetary system, we would have no industrial fluctuations and no periods of depression... The mistake is the creation of a semi-monopoly where the basic money is controlled by the government. Since all the banks issue secondary money (in the form of loans based on deposits), which is redeemable in the basic money, you have a system which nobody can control."....

In a system of free banking, institutions that do not protect the value of the currency simply collapse—and their collapse does not wreck the entire economy. Under a rule of law that punishes fraud and counterfeiting, the risk of failure without bailouts is enough to guarantee a more stable system. And in such a system, it would be harder for the government to spend as much money as it does now—a major factor in the devaluation of the dollar—because it could not create money, only tax and borrow.

Advocating the abolition of the Federal Reserve, an institution people take for granted, seems too radical for most people, who think financial crises are the result of too little, not too much, government regulation. So the knee-jerk reaction, as exemplified in so many editorials and statements on the campaign trail nowadays, is to scream in favour of government intervention—the reason why bank rescues and the pumping of new money is the government's sacrosanct policy.

It is time to think more boldly. If abolishing the Federal Reserve is politically inconceivable right now, there are less dramatic measures that can be taken on the road toward a definitive solution. The most obvious one is to simply stop using the Federal Reserve to inflate the currency.

> If a crisis in which at least $400 billion has already been lost and millions of people have been badly hurt is not enough to set minds thinking audaciously, nothing will."

There is absolutely no mystery about the cause of this international imbalance.

Americans *borrow* and *spend,* while many other countries are saving and investing.

The latter countries produce real things that are in demand, and they will continue to prosper and the international centre-of-gravity will move in their direction.

Like any good race, it will make sense to back a winner.

So what was the effect of this latest burst of "government failure" on Australia's greatest resource boom in living history?

It "knocked the stuffing" out of our Australian banking and financial sectors, which had previously been described as our "defensive investments."

On the other hand, our "resource sector" previously having been thought of as only for risk-takers, simply shrugged like the legendary Atlas and continued flexing its muscles.

The process of new companies listing continues, bringing back many memories of having seen all this before, and I cannot help wondering how many of these new iron ore listings will progress to the stage of being profitable entities?

If the fact that the original nickel boom produced only two profitable companies from the 350 active participants is a guideline, then we might have another six profitable iron ore miners.

If these six companies go on to become BHPs or Rio Tintos, it will be a very satisfying outcome for everyone who has bought a ticket to ride this great resource train.

I'm encouraged, because this is the first time in my memory when such a broad range of mineral commodities are in demand.

Even lead, as a metal, is sexy!

Tag this onto the very substantial property development market in Western Australia and we have a very buoyant platform to underpin our efforts in whatever field we choose to specialise.

Perhaps it's too soon to call 2008 a boom but once again everyone is telling me that "This time it's different."(1)

We thought it was a mining boom in 2004 when, as Chairman of the Australian Mining Investments Group, we brought a collection of Australian companies to Hong Kong. Admission to that seminar was free and we had trouble filling the conference venue. Now, 4 years later, I'm attending a similar conference which is sold out at a US$1,500 entry fee.

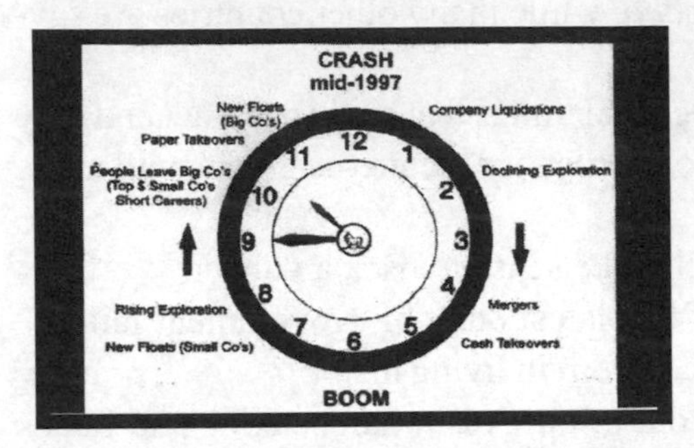

Journalist Tom Holland quoted me at that time (*Far East Economic Review*, May 6, 2004) as having said, 'Never in my experience has there been a rise like this in commodity prices across the board,' says Ron Manners, a 67 year old veteran of the metals and mining industry who sits on the boards of a clutch of Australian mining companies.

The increases have been exacerbated, especially in the market for minerals, by a legacy of underinvestment."

Four years later those comments still hold true.

So if it has the feel of a 'boots-and-all' boom, how will we know if this one is a real boom?

Perhaps we should refer to the Robin Widdup Clock Face Predictor (often called the JBWere Clock Face Predictor as Robin Widdup was working with JBWere at the time he developed the clock theory.

Here are two things that might minimise future tears:

- If you work with several stockbrokers, try running your own in-house Broker of the Year competition. This can be most revealing on the true value and quality of their advice.

- Ensure that your own loved ones, i.e. wives, and children, understand how to handle money and preserve capital and benefit from investing.

This is a harder task than it was some generations ago, mainly due to the pervasive popular culture of TV / movies which tends to diminish the role of parents as 'head of the house'.

I was probably lucky to be part of a generation where we actually took more notice of our parents than is the case today. However, I'm still aware that much of the passed-on wisdom from my parents simply went straight over my head, because at the time it was seen to be of no consequence.

I do, from time to time, remember their wise sayings and I've already referred to my father's comment, *don't ever go looking for gold or go gambling with borrowed money.*

It is instructive to observe how other people pass on their wisdom.

One example from a friend of mine consists of a three page list of tightly condensed—36 points— has titled *Old Fashioned Advice to Siblings*. These are short, sharp, single sentence items which they can easily carry with them, which they do.

Another friend wrote a comprehensive 551-page book with a detailed index.

I completed this task for him after he died of cancer, but from observation there was far too much information for his family to absorb, so they never really appreciated its value and I doubt that they ever opened the book.

Remember, when tackling this task that *brevity will win.*

In these words I hope that I've provided you with sufficient evidence that I'm a serial *Boom-Bust Addict* and a perpetually tearful person (alternating between tears of joy and sorrow), but I wouldn't have missed out on any of it.

To have not participated fully, would be to have never lived at all.

My total focus is to remain an active participant in as many more of these remarkable business cycles as I can squeeze in.

It is only when tears and fears, booms and busts, confront us that it brings out the very best in each of us.

So, long live these vigorous cycles as they will save us from lives of boredom.

Personal Impressions of the October 1987 Crash

With the benefit of hindsight, if this 'crash' had occurred between January or July 1986 or between February and March 1987, I would have been incinerated, with my ashes blown away by a tornado.

These were my 'exposed times' during listing and capital raising for our public company.

As the crash actually happened in October 1987, I escaped with only multiple broken bones.

I often think now that 'success' is more in the timing than the strategy.

RBM

Oct. '09

Do All Booms End in Tears?*

(Part 2 ... to 2009)

"Have the Harvard Graduates Succeeded where the Communists Failed?"

It's a fortunate man who can surround himself with people who know more than he does. So, it's my pleasure to be surrounded by all of you tonight.

One of the gifts you receive, after enjoying life's adventures over so many years, is that you get a fairly good idea of how the world works and how people respond to incentives, political and otherwise. The 'response to incentives' could be one of our themes tonight.

I remember watching a movie called *Maid in Manhattan* where the hotel floor manager gives these words of encouragement to the adventurous floor maid (Jennifer Lopez) "What we do, does not define who we are. What defines who we are, is how we rise again, after we have fallen." (The theme of my poem on page 29.)

We are all simply products of our own experiences and I'm currently assembling my fourth book in an effort to make some sense of where I've been and, more importantly, where I'm going.

The book is called *Heroic Misadventures* (it's a "how **not** to do it" book) and it's causing me to have frequent mental flashbacks. I find that most of them, unrelated at the time, do lead to a central theme of 'rewards for behaviour'.

Let me mention four flashbacks that came to me at about 3.00 o'clock this morning.

---

*Based on my 20th Nov '08 after dinner speech to the Harvard Club of Australia, Perth, Western Australia

Our family business, started by my grandfather (one of the first mining engineers to come to Western Australia, from Ballarat, in 1895), has, over its 113 years, been involved in all sorts of mining consultancy, machinery importation, design of various mining plants and agencies—all in an effort to get us through various booms and busts.

This means that I'm no stranger to the cyclical events we currently see unfolding.

The first flashback takes me back to the early 1960s when one of our challenges in Kalgoorlie was as a regional distributor for Kriesler radios. (The 1960s was a time when Australia used to design and manufacture things such as radios and electrical appliances.)

I established a great Kalgoorlie dealership network—(Southern Cross, Leonora, Laverton, Norseman, Esperance and Ravensthorpe)—and I must have done a reasonable job because Kriesler flew me over to Sydney to attend a big celebratory dinner, held at a fancy hotel. It was held in the evening after we'd spent all day inspecting their very modern and very high tech (for those times) factory, design centre and production line.

We were seated at that excellent dinner much as we are tonight.

The three senior Kriesler Executives (Rae Weingott, Tip Walcott and Lex Ainsworth) were seated at the top table. Immediately after all the celebratory speeches, the maitre d' rushed up to their table and broke the news that "the Kriesler radio factory was on fire", and "that the fire was so advanced there was nothing that could be done about it".

What a difference that made to the celebratory spirit of the evening!

The three executives quickly conferred and decided that we would commandeer the hotel's bus and at least go out to see if anything was salvageable.

The bus was later to return us to the hotel where people could then disperse and go back to their various homes.

Those with no immediate plans to go home were free to join them as they worked their way through a few "what next" scenarios.

As I had no further plans for the evening, I returned with them after witnessing the devastation of a raging fire where absolutely nothing could be salvaged.

That evening developed into one of those rare on-the-job training experiences that are so useful to a young 24-year-old enthusiast.

1960s modern factory

1960s modern production line

Top table at celebratory dinner (minutes before the news)

Dealership Shield Award

Next day's inspection

And now to start again!

The strategy planning session went something like this:

1. We have no production facilities, no factory and no office.
2. What do we have? A good set of plans and good people and a building site.

   Their "risk management" was impeccable, even long before the term "risk management" was invented. They had spare sets of drawings of all the components and the various models with their Attorney so that they would be able to start again—but when and how?

   That's when the phone calls started coming into the hotel.

The news of this fire had been broadcast over Sydney radio stations and many other industry executives had heard the news.

They were aware of Kriesler's big celebration and knew where to contact them.

The general public out there imagines capitalism to be a vicious beast (or as our Prime Minister, Kevin Rudd, calls it a "brutopia").

The general public would imagine Kriesler's competitors rejoicing that there would be one less major competitor in the field.

However, this is what actually happened. There were lengthy conversations with various corporate chiefs.

One after the other, the calls came in with offers to set up special production lines to produce various items such as the plastic cabinets, or the componentary chassis.

One offer was for the leather wrap-arounds for one of the portable radios.

Another offer was to take on the task of producing Kriesler's range of car radios.

All of these offers were to use Kriesler's plans and designs. And one of them actually offered to assemble all of the various components into a finished product.

By the time the sun's rays started shining through the windows in that hotel dining room, every single aspect of assembly and production had been taken care of to the point that the executives could confidently predict a recommencement date of exactly six months and they subsequently achieved it.

As a young man, I saw for the first time the true value of the ESTEEM that this group had built up within their very competitive industry.

That night was a measurement of the value of ESTEEM and true goodwill.

Over the next few weeks I heard many interesting stories about how the Kriesler radio group had established an impeccable record in their dealings with their peers, who then regarded it as a privilege to return the favours.

That moral compass was forever present to guide their actions in 1960.

Now, half a century later, we are wondering if Wall Street and those responsible for the Global Financial Crisis (GFC) of 2008 simply lost their way, by losing their moral compass.

The second flashback took me back to the early 1970s when, through a strange set of circumstances as importers of underground diesel trucks from Sweden, we became distributors for Volvo trucks and cars and this also led us to being distributors for Subaru cars.

I must have done a good job of that, too, because I won a dealership award and Subaru sent me up to Japan to tour the factory.

Subaru was a relatively new brand to Australia at that time and, to my astonishment, I found that there was no such thing as a Subaru factory.

The cars were simply manufactured in a corner of a huge manufacturing enterprise called Fuji Heavy Industries.

They were producing a remarkably well-engineered car and being of some engineering background myself, I took particular notice of several features and asked some questions of one of the senior people as to how a company making diesel locomotives, light aircraft and helicopters decided to get into the car business.

He explained to me that the boss (owner) of Fuji Heavy Industries had sent a team around the world to study various countries' auto industries, so that they could decide how to add a car manufacturing facility to the enterprise.

The team had travelled extensively and found themselves somewhere in Germany where they had located a closed-down car factory that, until recently, had produced a well-engineered front-wheel drive car called the Borgward Hansa.

They described to the boss the style of car and the quality of the manufacturing facilities.

Australia's leading Subaru dealers with senior Subaru personnel—Japan—January, 1975.

The Subaru manufacturing facility as it was in 1975 ('over in the corner of the Fuji Heavy Industries factory')

Fuji's boss made a quick decision to buy the factory for that particular model, "lock, stock and Barrel". They transported it back to Japan where it was successfully installed and produced a car with a newly designed body built over what was essentially still the Borgward Hansa engine and undercarriage.

Like everything the Japanese do, it was remarkably improved over the ensuing years.

I was also aware the next day that the executive who spoke to me was admonished for his candid comments to me, as apparently it did not match up entirely with the official "Subaru story".

However, the take-away message that remained with me is that if you can develop a team in whose abilities you have incredible trust, then that enables you to make quick decisions (without endless committee meetings) and that through the diligence of that same team, you can make your dreams come true.

I've usually been lucky in having people like that working alongside me.

The reward for being the boss is that you get to choose who works alongside you.

Subaru, as you know, has gone on to be an excellent car, such a desirable unit that General Motors of USA several years ago purchased a 20 per cent stake in Subaru.

Because of their own financial situation, General Motors have since been forced to dispose of that asset and we are now seeing General Motors go cap in hand to the U.S. Government seeking a handout of several billion dollars to enable them to stagger forward into the future.

How a great company such as General Motors can get to this stage has been the subject of much corporate examination.

Such potential corporate collapses are a disturbing trend.

This is only my personal opinion, but I'm concerned that one of the weakest links in capitalism at the moment lies with corporate governance, that is, the relationships between shareholders, directors and managers.

Here we see insider trading, self-dealing, golden parachutes and the latest fad—'fail fees' where the executives get a big prize for failing. We also see the same sort of behaviour in federal and state governments, and even among State Governors (specifically Tasmania).

Korean Armistice Agreement–1953

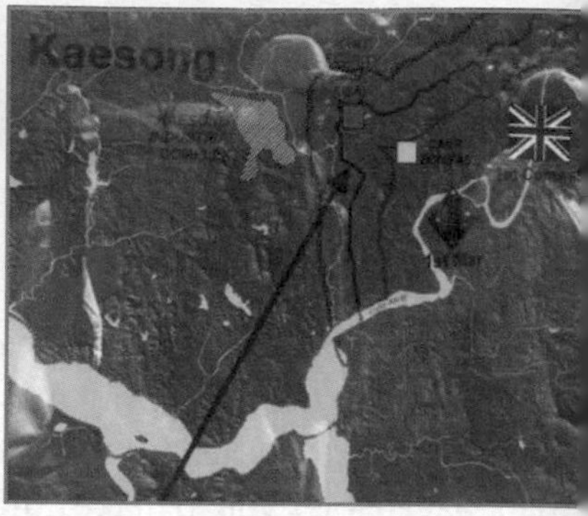

Location Map

Looking from South Korea into North Korea
(The Kaesong Industrial Complex)–September, 2008

As Matthew pointed out a long time ago (chapter 6, verse 24):

"No man can serve two masters or else he will hold to one and despise the other."

The 'two masters' in today's corporate world are the shareholders' interests versus the executives' interests, where those interests are not aligned.

Disturbing events that we are often confronted with in our careers, and also as investors, now demand individual action, by individual investors, rather than waiting for things to get to the stage reminiscent of General Motors, many years ago, where they basically transferred the enterprise value to the employees instead of the shareholders.

In that big unionized company, General Motors' executives tried to get one more year without a calamity by giving the union damn near everything, and then they felt they had to give everyone else (the non-unionists) even more because they were valued employees and not in the union.

General Motors in the U.S. continued to do that for 40 years, running to the point where now the shareholders' equity has virtually been destroyed, and their finished product is less attractive to consumers because each car they produce is burdened by a $2,000 "surcharge" to cover workers' healthcare.

If General Motors fails, the assets will simply find their way into other hands, and a more desirable product will emerge, from a less unionised workforce and the miracle of the market will take the company into the future. Unfortunately, the poor shareholders are punished for the poor management decisions of various generations of executives.

Flashback number 3 in September this year (2008) I was invited to South Korea, along with two German economists, several U.S. academics, and some Austrian, Venezuelan and Chinese economists, to be fully briefed on the challenges facing that nation.

In Australia we don't read or hear a lot about South Korea, one of our major trading partners, but there are some unsettling events taking place.

'Dear Leader' (Kim Jong Il) just over the border is in seriously bad health and the South Koreans are apprehensive that North Korea will simply implode, as did East Germany, and leave them facing much the same sort of mess that West Germany had to clean up after reunification.

A 'drug bust' in West Berlin–1982

Professor Murray Rothbard spreading 'seeds of freedom' at the foot of the Karl Marx Memorial, East Berlin–1982

'Checkpoint Charlie'entrance to East Berlin1982

The South/North Korea situation is much worse. Indeed, South Korea has been described, by our hosts, as having 'two Zimbabwes' just over its northern border.

All these inflection point changes are of great interest to me, as I'd been involved with teams visiting Germany in 1982 and Russia in 1990, at the time when they were toppling statues, and our task was to train the Russians on how to handle free enterprise because it was arriving the 'following week'!

There are some horrific disasters that can be bottled up any time that governments get in the way of free markets: Germany 1982, Russia 1990 and the Global Financial Crisis of 2008 are all classic examples of this.

Today, we see this "Global Financial Crisis" being blamed on the free market, when in all honesty there is no free market, there are only 'government interventions'. Unfortunately, what is often regarded as good politics usually involves bad economics.

Without an understanding of the damage done by Government intervention, it will be difficult to seek retribution and choose the best way forward.

Flashback number 4. This one, also this year (September '08), where, as a member of the Mont Pelerin Society, a group of economists, academics and business leaders with a classical liberal bent, first set up in 1947 by Prof. F.A. Hayek, Milton Friedman and others. Each General Meeting is held in a different country, this year we were in Japan.

Being a non-economist gives me the opportunity to ask very informal questions and I had the opportunity of asking this question of Prof. Gary Becker (Nobel Prize-winner in economics, 1992):

> Over many years we observed the Communists trying to bring down the free market and particularly, the economy of the U.S., but they were unsuccessful because of the resilience of the free-market system. However, we've seen more recently the Wizards of Wall Street (including the many Harvard Graduates) manage to achieve what the Communists were not able to achieve. Are there some comments that you might like to make on that topic?

Professor Becker's answer:

I don't think Wall Street brought down the free market.

I think we have a crisis now, but you have to also look at benefits as well as causes.

I think we had financial innovation, derivatives and various other factors that have contributed greatly to world trade and growth in economies over the last 35 years.

But perhaps I don't know enough about this, I don't think anyone knows enough about it because I've asked my colleague, Richard Posner, one of the real experts on this, and he doesn't know what the answer is to your question.

However, let's consider the consequences that you can have in a Global Financial Crisis. If you look at the facts of crisis so far. Tremendous publicity all over that the United States has been devastated; some banks have been devastated too.

Look at the U.S. economy, which hasn't yet been designated, but may be designated to be in a mild recession. I say, mild, because for every single quarter, but one, the U.S.'s GDP is continuing to grow.

The last quarter grew at 3.3 per cent, some forecasts are that it's going to go pretty well for the 3rd quarter coming out shortly.

Unemployment is up and we'd like to get it lower but it's not as such bad levels, 6 per cent. There are many European countries with 5–6 per cent.

So, I think it is a recession. It's certainly been induced in part by the financial sector; there is no doubt about it. However, you have to also count the benefits.

It's a little like deciding whether to send your child to university.

If you just look at the single fact that it's very costly, what's the point in sending them away to college?

But of course you do get a lot of benefits from doing so.

I believe that same thing is true of financial innovation. A lot of mistakes have been made. There has been lying and cheating and misinformation on both sides of the market and probably that's all true, but I don't think you want to blame all the new financial tools for risk management, as they have been extremely useful.

They are extremely useful in navigating oneself through the risky world economy.

Please note that subsequent to that September 2008 discussion, Professor Becker has considerably developed this answer on his blog (www.becker-posner-blog.com) under the sub-heading "Is the Goose that Laid the Golden Eggs Severely Wounded?"

As you know, the Global Financial Crisis of 2008 is still unfolding, so we are still seeking an understanding of this ongoing process, hence this examination of "rewards for behaviour".

Incidentally, arriving back in Australia in mid-September, at a time when the whole financial world appeared to be imploding at a rapid state, I found it strange to find very little public concern here, as the events hadn't managed to penetrate our complacency.

Here are three first-hand impressions of when I arrived back in Australia:

1. At the airport we were given a "free book" *Bombproof,* by Michael Robotham.

   Why a free book? Well, you see, inside the front cover it explains that Michael Robotham is the pseudonymous author of ten best-selling non-fiction titles and it also explains that this book "is an Australian Government initiative developed through the Australia Council for the Arts, the Australian Government's Arts Funding and Advisory Body".

   I worry about taxpayers' money being chucked around like this.

   This is a very ordinary novel and should therefore be left to compete with all the other novels on the booksellers' shelves.

   How could this be the legitimate role of Government, to get into the free novel business?

2. The second example was a news item of the day when it was proudly announced that Stephen Smith (Australia's Minister for Foreign Affairs), on behalf of the Prime Minister, Kevin Rudd, had just "donated" $10 million of taxpayers' funds as "food aid to Ethiopia".

The announcement went on to explain that this $10 million was to help buy Australia a "seat" on the U.N. Security Council.

'Remarkable', I thought, as there appears to be ample evidence that this type of foreign aid has never helped African countries or countries anywhere else for that matter.

Foreign aid might be defined as a transfer of money from poor people in rich countries to rich people in poor countries.

If Australia really wants to help people in less fortunate countries, there are many ways to do this, but they will require thoughtful and meticulous programmes rather than these photo-opportunity media events.

3. Then to cap it off, the first print media news item we saw in the *Courier Mail* was headlined "Government plan to make prostitutes feel better about themselves", followed by the news item itself:

> The Bligh (Qld) Government is set to spend $400,000 a year on an advocacy service whose functions will include promoting the positive aspects of prostitution.
>
> 'The service should contribute to a more balanced and positive view of sex workers in the general community, assisting to overcome the stigma attached to prostitution', the authority says in its latest newsletter.
>
> Queensland Health recently hired a consultant to complete what it describes as a 'needs assessment'of the state's sex workers.
>
> According to the authority, that exercise found that the Queensland sex industry's various sectors had different needs.
>
> The results are meant to inform the establishment of the new state-wide advocacy service with a budget of about $400,000 a year.

Again, I ask the question, "Is it the legitimate role of government to make prostitutes feel better about themselves?"

I would have thought that that the girls' various clients would have had the responsibility of making the girls feel better about themselves; not the government.

I put it to you simply, 'What a strange set of priorities our various governments appear to have as they find ever-new ways of spending our hard earned tax payments'.

Now that brings us right up to the present time and the topic for tonight's discussion "Have the Harvard Graduates Succeeded Where the Communists Failed?" (the U.S. economy, having survived repeated attacks from Communists and Terrorists, now appears to have been brought down by the Harvard graduates on Wall Street.)

Now I know this is a very sensitive issue, particularly amongst your group of Harvard graduates, so let's attack the question using the following headings:

1. Where is my evidence that it was the Harvard graduates' fault?
2. How serious is this event in the overall historic world view?
3. Causes of the problem.
4. Will the various governments' bailouts actually work?
5. What could work?
6. The challenge remaining for all of us as we move forward.

My evidence?

I know it would be unreasonable to blame Harvard graduates entirely for this Global Financial Crisis.

It's a bit like blaming Oxford University for Robert Mugabe (or his good friend Malcolm Fraser). I know that George Bush went to Harvard, but the seeds of this Global Financial Crisis preceded President George W. Bush.

I know that Warren Buffet was knocked back in 1950 at the age of 19 when he applied for admission to the Harvard Business School.

Buffet would later come to consider his rejection by Harvard as the pivotal episode in his life.

On being knocked back he immediately started investigating other graduate schools and, while leafing through the Columbia catalogue one day, he came across two names that were familiar to him: Benjamin Graham and David Dodd.

They were both big names to him as Buffet had just finished reading Graham's book *The Intelligent Investor*.

Buffet was accepted at Columbia and the rest is history.

Okay, well let's focus on who actually went to Harvard.

There have been some remarkable people, such as Jeff Skilling, the former CEO of Enron.

However, the evidence I'm relying on tonight are copies of Course Notes that appear to have fallen off a truck and mysteriously come into my hands.

They are obviously course notes for some of the finance courses involved in the design and marketing of derivatives and toxic mortgages.

I have no way of vouching for the authenticity of these documents, however they sound about as authentic as the financial products that were wildly marketed with high commissions, around the globe.

Here's one.

#1

Once upon a time in a village in India, a man announced to the villagers that he would buy monkeys for $10.

The villagers, seeing that there were many monkeys around, went out to the forest and started catching them.

The man bought thousands at $10, but, as the supply started to diminish, the villagers stopped their efforts. The man further announced that he would now buy at $20. This renewed the efforts of the villagers and they started catching monkeys again.

Soon the supply diminished even further and people started going back to their farms. The offer rate increased to $25 and the supply of monkeys became so little that it was an effort even to see a monkey, let alone catch one!

The man now announced that he would buy monkeys at $50. However, since he had to go to the city on some business, his assistant would now act as the buyer, on his behalf.

In the absence of the man, the assistant told the villagers: "Look at all these monkeys in the big cage that the man has collected. I will sell them to you at $35 and when he returns from the city, you can sell them back to him for $50".

The villagers squeezed together their savings and bought all the monkeys. Then they never saw the man or his assistant again—only monkeys everywhere!"

Welcome to WALL STREET.

#2

Young Chuck moved to Texas and bought a donkey from a farmer for $100. The farmer agreed to deliver the donkey the next day. The next day he drove up and said, "Sorry son, but I have some bad news, the donkey died." Chuck replied, "Well, then just give me my money back."

The farmer said, "Can't do that. I went and spent it already." Chuck said, "OK, then, just bring me the dead donkey." The farmer asked, "What ya do with him? Chuck said, "I'm going to raffle him off." The farmer said, "you can't raffle off a dead donkey!"

Chuck said, "Sure I can, watch me. I just won't tell anybody he's dead." A month later, the farmer met up with Chuck and asked, "What happened with that dead donkey?"

Chuck said, "I raffled him off. I sold 500 tickets at two dollars a piece and made a profit of $998. The farmer said, "Did anyone complain?"

Chuck said, "Just the guy who won. So I gave him his two dollars back."

Chuck now works for one of the two remaining US Investment Banks.

How serious is this Global Financial Crisis?

It's hard to get a handle on this, partly because of all the colourful language and the accent on the words that strike fear into the hearts of innocent bystanders.

Commentators use metaphors rather than speak in precise terms.

Phrases like, "freezing up" are used in the same sentence as "melting down".

"Credit is the life-blood", "toxic assets" "a crushing economic contagion".

Sometimes, reporting like this can create self-fulfilling prophecies, but after sorting through all this it does appear that there are up to US$55 trillion worth of these toxic derivatives that have been sold and distributed, with commissions paid, around the world.

To see if this is a really significant number let's relate it to the total value of all the world's economies, i.e. the value of the world, which is US$72 trillion.

So, the good news is, that the world just falls short of being terminally ill.

What's the cause of this problem?

The following is a classic case of over simplification, but easy to remember:

> Americans borrow and spend.
> Whereas, the rest of the world—
> Produces and saves.

Probably the best single-pager on the causes of this crisis was sent to me by Yoon Chang-hyun (Professor of Business Administration, University of Seoul, South Korea).

His comparisons with the earlier Latin American and Asian crises also helped.

What has brought on the U.S. financial crisis?

> The U.S. has been staggering from one of its worst financial woes in recent days, ending its decades-long global leadership in the direct financial market with some of its once overbearing investment banks suffering a disgraceful failure or forced sale. Latin American countries fell into a crisis in the 1980s when the loans heavily extended by the commercial banks in the euro-dollar market were defaulted. The Asian financial crisis in the late 1990s was also triggered by banks overstretching their loans beyond the borrowers' payment capability.
>
> The U.S. appears to be in a different situation. The U.S. financial crisis is closely related to the entire financial sector, including commercial banks and investment banks. The usual business for commercial banks is to extend mortgage loans and receive principals and interests. But the U.S. commercial banks created mortgage-backed securities by selling the rights to the principal and interest.
>
> Investment banks came to be involved in the securitization of the loans. They enjoyed huge commissions by making and selling securities backed by mortgage loans. Through the securitization, the commercial banks could

receive the money and lend it again. Whenever this cycle repeats, the financial companies can make more money. In short, the commercial banks and investment banks have been overstretched in this business.

When the asset-backed securities were sold, the proceeds were lent again and again, with the loans snowballing and reaching to sub-prime borrowers {many with variable rate mortgages}. An excessive amount of funds were used as mortgage loans. Then the housing prices unexpectedly stopped their years-long booms and began to bust, sending all the mortgage loan-related financial companies into distress.

Commercial banks who lent the mortgage loans, investment banks and hedge funds who raked up asset-backed securities and collateralized debt obligations, and the monocline insurers who wrote protection for the assets held by those banks all fell into a whirlwind. The mortgage insurers Freddie Mac and Fannie Mae were taken over by the government, Lehman Brothers filed for bankruptcy and Merrill Lynch was forced to sell its assets. The world's top investment bankers, Goldman Sachs and JP Morgan, decided to turn themselves into commercial banks. With a US$700 billion bailout plan for the financial sector passing through the U.S. Congress, all eyes are now on how to contain and end the Global Financial Crisis.

A European View

To represent one important European point of view, a joint press release by 38 European conomic think tanks was dispatched from the European Resourcc Bank meeting in Tbilisi, Georgia. It reads as follows:

Government Made the Global Financial Crisis; Let Us Not Make It Worse

15th October, 2008

Representatives of economic policy organizations throughout Europe released the following recommendations to deal with the Global Financial Crisis.

> The basic cause of the Global Financial Crisis was that the U.S. government, along with other governments, engaged in excessive credit expansion and pressured banks to make loans—particularly home loans—to unqualified buyers.
> Therefore:
> 1. We believe that responding to the credit crunch by adding more liquidity in the market is a short-term fix that will only help banks that were mismanaged, and will fuel inflation.
> 2. We believe governments should facilitate, and not hinder, the process of the market determining prices that realistically reflect supply and demand.
> 3. When hard times come, governments should share the burden with businesses and consumers (cut public spending and taxes) and not try to insulate themselves from the harm they have caused.
> 4. Governments should refrain from rescuing particular businesses or business projects. The cost of saving businesses that failed will fall on the shoulders of others, through increased taxes, inflation, or capital misallocation.
> Free market capitalism has proven to be the only system which leads to sustained economic progress and respect of human liberty.
>
> Signed …………

The rest of this is reported @ www.rbeurope.org

Whilst in that part of Europe it's interesting to learn from the words of the head of the Georgian State Chancellery (Kakha Bendukidze). Richard W. Rahn in the *Washington Times*, October 15, 2008 reported:

> Commenting on the Global Financial Crisis, he [Bendukidze] correctly observed that as long as governments continue to rely on central banks and extensive regulation of the financial industry rather than free banking, "periodic financial crises will continue to plague mankind." He argues that it is unrealistic, as Hayek and Friedman also did, to assume central bankers know more and can outguess the market, and that financial

> regulators can somehow prevent the next crisis, since they are unlikely to see where it is coming from.
>
> Georgia does have problems, including the large number of refugees resulting from the war. But unlike Washington and the European governments, the Georgian leaders did not deal with their crisis by creating the new "program of the day." Instead, they told the people the government would continue to stay out of their way and the people would have to find ways to solve the new problems. Most of them have done that quite well and the government remains highly popular."

Was this crisis predicted? Yes, by so many people.
Ranging from writer philosopher, Ayn Rand in 1959—

> Watch money. Money is the barometer of a society's virtue. When you see that trading is done, not by consent, but by compulsion—when you see that in order to produce, you need to obtain permission from men who produce nothing—when you see that money is flowing to those who deal, not in goods, but in favors—when you see that men get richer by graft and by pull than by work, and your laws don't protect you against them, but protect them against you—when you see corruption being rewarded and honesty becoming a self-sacrifice—you may know that your society is doomed.

Through to economist Nouriel Roubini (known as New York University's Dr Doom).

To Australia's William Buckler (www.the-privateer.com), who has also been predicting the nature of the collapse and its expected severity for years. Bill's recent (June 15, 2008) comment is, "What people are witnessing, though comparatively few of them yet realise it, is the end effect of the debasement of money. They are watching the purchasing power of the monetary unit decline with increasing rapidity everywhere".

However, it's interesting to observe that neither the Australian Treasury nor any other government official had ever suggested that this event might happen.

That's interesting when they are so precise about predicting what average global temperatures are likely to be in 2020, 2050 and even 2090.

Will the Various Bailouts Work?

How can they?

Wasn't the relaxation of prudent loan requirements a key factor that got us into the mess in the first place?

It seems a little odd that the solution to the problem is to encourage more imprudent consumer borrowing.

Isn't it strange that in all this discussion of how to fight the Crisis so far, there has been little mention of introducing some prudent lending requirements such as requiring a deposit, and checking on the client's ability to service a loan? It should be in the lending institution's best interests to do so, rather than it being a government legislated requirement.

You might gather that I'm somewhat sceptical about government programmes.

Larry Winget at www.larrywinget.net/blog puts it well when he says:

> When the government says that something will cost a dollar, it will cost three. One for the program. One for government waste to implement the program. One for someone to make money off the program. Also, any government program takes twice as long to implement as promised and does half as much good as promised.

One of the reasons against the US$700 billion bailout working, is that it appears to be rewarding the wrong people.

The message bailout clearly sends is that "unless you are big business" we don't want to hear from you.

This is entirely ignoring America's core business identity: small business.

Over the last six months (to October 2008) U.S. big business had lost more than 170,000 jobs, while small business created 200,000 jobs (www.fastcompany.com).

What about all the calls for more controls and more regulations?

We already have too many rules and regulations, but the question should be asked: what have these regulators been doing?

For example, Fannie Mae and Freddie Mac had 200 regulators working within these organizations. Doing what?

It was these regulators who enforced the government legislation that home loans be granted to people who had no hope of repayment.

What could work?

Again, it comes down to aligning the rewards and punishments to the right people.

We have seen the villains walk away with the prizes and the innocent bystanders incinerated, so there should be a test to see if a remedy for this Global Financial Crisis fits the fairness criteria.

Perhaps the marketers of sophisticated financial "products" should be paid in a currency of these 'products'.

In discussing this problem last month, with a friend, Sir Arvi Parbo AC, he felt that we had a lot to learn from the Roman Empire, and his comment was:

> The Romans tested the integrity of their engineers by requiring them to stand under the bridges they built while the scaffolding was being removed. Today's financial engineers not only will do their utmost not to be identified as having built the bridge but will be as far as possible from it when it is opened to traffic.

Whose advice could we follow?

In looking at the earlier theme of rewards and punishment for behaviour, it's important to identify the moral hazard caused by the U.S. Congress and the Federal Reserve in rewarding reckless lending and borrowing.

Further rewards for past bad behaviour will only create a bigger crisis next time.

This may not be a problem for the politicians (as they may have moved on by then). However, for the rest of us in the real world, it remains a problem.

If we personally have any financial stresses and strains, a good remedy is a dose of deleveraging, which is simply the reduction of debt and leverage.

Big business and banks know this and that's why they are deleveraging with a vengeance.

Then how is it that governments continue to encourage their 'subjects' with offers of more cheap credit to do just the opposite and continue spending and consuming?

F.A. HAYEK

(See reference on page 329)

(Photo by author, Berlin–September, 1982)

F.A. Hayek is described as 'THE COMEBACK MAN' in the March 4, 2004 edition of *The Economist*.

> In 1974 Hayek won the Nobel Prize for Economics. The theoretical idea he was proudest of—that only markets, not governments, could gather and disperse price knowledge effectively—helped inspire a wave of deregulation and privatization. His chief political idea—that free markets and political liberty were indissociable—lent strength to the revival of classical liberalism. By his death in 1992, Hayek had joined Milton Friedman and Robert Nozick as one of the three theoretical godfathers of the Thatcher-Reagan revolution.

Read article in full ...

www.economist.com/books/PrinterFriendly.cfm?Story_ID=2478223

The smart money is doing one thing, but encouraging consumers to do the opposite.

If survival is important to us, just ignore such advice and do the opposite.

Peace of mind can easily be bought by reducing debt and living off our cash flow.

The challenge remaining for all of us as we move forward

I'm looking forward to the new post–2008 financial environment even though many of us will have to contend with some "strong head winds". Similar to previous downturns when the commodities we produce, or the countries we represent, or the philosophies and belief systems we promote are somewhat "on the nose".

To me it's somewhat reminiscent of the 1990s era of W.A. Incorporated when we had two Premiers and a Deputy Premier spending time in jail.

We just had to put our heads down and work a little harder in order to restore the moral fabric of our State.

Just remember, the sun always shines through—it always does!

Of great concern to me is how our liberties and our freedoms and our general level of civility have all been severely damaged. First, by those few years of terrorist actions and threats and now the financial ponzi scheme collapse.

If we do nothing, we are likely to see a ratchet effect and we'll continue to lose freedoms but never regain any. Alternatively, we can be proactive and work toward restoring trust, freedoms and civility.

My favourite economist, Friedrich Hayek (see facing page), once analysed our free society and offered a sobering speculation:

> It may be that a free society as we have known it, carried in itself the forces of its own destruction, and that once freedom is achieved it is taken for granted and ceases to be valued" ... and then he went on to ask, "Does this mean that freedom is valued only when it is lost, that the world must everywhere go through a dark phase of socialist totalitarianism before the forces of freedom can gather strength anew?

He answers, "It may be so, but I hope it need not be."

Hayek then offered his remedy to this threat. He argued that:

> ...if we are to avoid such a development, we must be able to offer a new liberal program which appeals to the imagination. We must make the building of a free society once more an intellectual adventure, a deed of courage.
>
> —F.A. Hayek, *The Intellectuals and Socialism*

Another colleague, the Rev. Robert Sirico (Acton Institute—Michigan) adds another dimension to Hayek's advice:

> We must make the building of a free society once more a *moral adventure*—for its construction was morally inspired in the first place. It emerged from a vision of man as a creature with an inherent and transcendent destiny. This vision, this anthropology, inspired the institutions of Western Civilization: Universal human rights; the right to contract and private property; international institutions of charity; the university. All these formed because of the high view of human dignity we inherited from our Judaeo-Christian tradition.

Friends, from your privileged position as business and community leaders and as graduates of Harvard University, please join me in the challenging process of rebuilding this free society.

Trillion

1 trillion is million million.

In a day there are 24 x 60 x 60 = 86,400 seconds

In a year there are 365 x 86,400 = 31,536,000 seconds

1 billion seconds is 1,000,000,000 divided by 31,536,000 = 31.7 years

1 trillion seconds is 1,000,000,000,000 divided by 31,536,000 = 31,709 years

10 dollar bills make a stack approx. 1mm high

100 dollar bills are 1 cm high

10,000 dollar bills are 1 metre high

10,000,000 dollar bills are 1 km high

1 billion = 1,000,000,000 dollar bills are 100 km high

1 trillion = 1,000,000,000,000 dollar bills are 100,000 km high, equivalent to 2.5 times the circumference of the Earth.

2009 The year the politicians 'popularised' the word 'trillion'.

Roy Woodall stands on the exposed nickel discovery gossan—September 19, 1992

Chairman Sir Arvi Parbo, AC enjoys the reunion —September 19, 1992

The Kambalda Commemorative Reunion Group—September 19, 1992

....See Page 335

The Language of leadership*

(The 2009 Sir Arvi Parbo Oration)

The secret of eternal life? Become legislated as a Federal Government program. President—Ronald Reagan.

By a remarkable set of co-incidences, a couple of weeks ago, I found myself talking to Warren Buffett, at his Annual General Meeting (AGM) in Omaha, Nebraska, and asking him a question that was troubling me.

"Mr Buffett, would America be a better country if you could reduce Wall Street's influence over Washington D.C.?"

"Yes! [with enthusiasm] We are working very hard on just that."

Only 35,000 people attended his AGM, and I was there as a guest, not as a shareholder.

In my opinion, Warren Buffett is doing more to restore the image of business in the USA than any other single individual. He is achieving this more by example than as a result of his actual net worth.

The reason I mention this, is that my words this morning are to honour an Australian legend, Sir Arvi Parbo AC, who I consider to be the most significant living individual to put forward the case for Australia's minerals industry. He does this in an eloquent, elegant and always positive manner. Moreover, his insights have application far beyond the minerals industry, making him, in some ways, a spokesman for our entire nation.

---

*Honouring Sir Arvi Parbo for his service and comments on the way forward, not only for Australia, but for all others on the way.

Based on my Keynote Address
The Association of Mining & Exploration Companies Inc. (AMEC)
Congress - Perth
on May 21, 2009

He is our Poet Laureate, having mastered successfully the Language of Leadership, which is the title for my comments today.

I do know Sir Arvi well enough to know that he is so modest that, sitting there in the front row, he will feel uncomfortable at being described in such glowing terms. My only comment to that is, "the true story of Sir Arvi Parbo needs no embellishment".

I too am very humble but very proud to be standing in front of a bunch of mates to honour Sir Arvi's contribution to our industry.

In the brief time we have today, we'll cover these four items:

1. Sir Arvi Parbo—the man and the legend.
2. The Language of leadership.
3. Today's financial settings.
4. AMEC—'rising to the challenge'.

Let me tell you how I first met Sir Arvi.

This was back in 1958 when he was appointed Underground Manager of the Nevoria Mine, just a few miles from Bullfinch, Western Australia.

I should explain that I was at that time a pimply-faced youth and I knew absolutely "everything", having qualified as an electrical engineer at the Kalgoorlie School of Mines. (It's only recently that I've discovered how little I now know.)

My father had just had a serious heart attack, so I was promoted from unpacking crates of mining equipment to running the business. From his hospital bed my father said to me, "Go down to Bullfinch and sell them some of these new Oldham miners cap lamps and explain why lead acid batteries are so much better than alkaline batteries".

Off I went to Bullfinch and asked for the "boss". They said you must mean Brodie (later Sir Laurence Brodie-Hall AO, CMG), so I met this impressively tall gentleman and was struck by the fact that he appeared to have only one name.

I had just started my sales talk when Brodie said, "No, no, not for me, you should be talking to Arvi Parbo, our new Underground Manager. Head off down to Nevoria, about 30 minutes away, and you can see him there".

So I met Mr Parbo and he patiently and courteously listened to me explain why lead acid batteries maintained their output voltage over a full shift instead of progressively declining, and how "the work done was equivalent to the area under the graph". He asked several probing questions and said, "leave it with me", and we parted company.

As I drove back to Kalgoorlie at top speed in my Holden utility, I remember thinking to myself, "poor bugger, with that heavy European accent, he'll never make it. Nobody will know what he's talking about". So I felt genuine concern.

Many years later, after getting to know Arvi so much better—a time during which he became Australia's leading industrialist, being not only the Chairman of Western Mining Corporation (WMC), BHP and Alcoa simultaneously, but also holding many other significant directorships—I had the courage to tell Arvi of this earlier experience.

Well, in his typical unflappable style of one-liner, he responded:

"Well, Ron, sometimes you get it right, sometimes you get it wrong!"

Over the ensuing 50 years, we have been in touch from time to time and I've often been treated like one of the WMC extended family.

When WMC held its great reunion for senior WMC staff to mark the occasion of the 25th anniversary of the discovery of Kambalda (19 September 1992), I was invited to be part of a fascinating weekend of events.

One of the many souvenirs from that weekend was the menu from the formal dinner party in Kalgoorlie which featured a copy of their exploration budget as signed off by Brodie and Arvi. This is dated October 1965 and included the drilling programme that discovered Kambalda's nickel. The total budget for the year was £121,500 (much less than most of your own exploration budgets). What good value that proved to be!

What an important document that turned out to be—truly, history in the making.

Back in the mists of the mid-'70s a group of consultants at McKinsey & Co. were trying to work out what made a mining company tick. As one might expect, they searched high and low.

Recalling the study, one of the consultants said that the most telling point was the structure of the Board meetings held by Western Mining

WESTERN MINING CORPORATION LIMITED.

ROUGH EXPLORATION BUDGET
FOR KALGOORLIE AREA.
TWELVE MONTHS FROM OCTOBER 1965.

(Telephoned to Mr. Brodie-Hall in Melbourne on 28/9/65.)

Kalgoorlie Research (mainly geol. salaries)	£ 6,500
Kalgoorlie Regional (geol. salaries + some I.P.)	10,500
Eulaminna, Kambalda, Laterites, Paris-St. Ives:	
Geol. salaries and travelling.	13,000
Vacuum drill (65% time)	8,500
Diamond drill (2 shifts full time)	26,000
Geophysics	3,000
Warburton - 1966 Programme:	
Geol. salaries and travelling.	3,750
Vacuum drilling.	4,500
Geochem. analysis.	1,500
Geophysics.	5,000
Percussion drilling and costeaning.	5,000
Tommy Simms - assume self-sufficient:	
← Geological drafting.	5,250
TOTAL FIELD WORK AND GEOL. SALARIES AND DRAFTING	£92,500
Equipment.	
Vacuum drill and caravan.	£ 4,800
2 caravans already authorised.	1,800
Tommy Simms equipment (say)	5,400
Warburton (1966) equipment:	
Geol. vehicles and sundry.	4,000
Vacuum drill vehicle and sundry.	3,000
Mobile geochemical laboratory.	2,000
Front end loader.	7,000
Caravan for front end loader driver and percussion driller.	1,000
	£29,000
TOTAL..	£121,500

c.c. Mr. L.C. Brodie-Hall,
Mr. J.D. Campbell,
Mr. R. Woodall,
Mr. K.E. Denham.

28/9/65

Menu—exploration budget–see page 335

Corporation. "The first man to address the Board is the Exploration Manager," he said. "Exploration makes a mining company tick, and Western Mining is the best."

When later interviewed in 1988 by Ian Huntley, the Chairman, Sir Arvi Parbo, was queried about this. He replied, "Yes, every Board meeting starts with the Director, Exploration—Roy Woodall—and then we go through operations, production, finance and so on …"

Then, Sir Arvi added that the emphasis was on the quality of what the company did, quality of product, and having a place in the hierarchy of lowest cost producers. "That way, and that way only, can we have a solid, secure operation."

What a difference to today's Board meetings, many of which are cluttered up with trivia, such as the number of "band-aids" that the company had used the previous month.

I'm not denigrating "safety concerns", simply stating that safety, environment and so many other of the softer issues should simply be part of a company's culture as it evolves and not displace productivity and the development of a solid, secure company.

A few years later in the early '90s, it was Sir Arvi who raised the issue of company "conformance" versus company "performance".

More recently we have seen companies with immaculate "conformance" records simply go broke.

When I was sketching my notes for today, I looked at the possibility of giving you a brief outline of Sir Arvi's career and then I realized it would have taken my full 30 minutes! So instead I'll merge point (1) that is, the multi-dimensional Sir Arvi Parbo and point (2) namely, The Language of leadership, as it's almost impossible to separate these in Sir Arvi's case.

What is the Language of leadership?

Leaders are people who often say things that are unpopular and then see people change their mind about that particular issue. They absolutely ignore opinion polls. This has very little to do with high office, although that does help, because there are more people listening. However, that doesn't stop people like Prime Ministers talking nonsense. So it's possible for people in high office to actually not be leaders in this sense.

Sometimes those people demand the most approval and get annoyed when people who need approval the least, actually receive the most.

There are some immutable laws of leadership

One is balance. If you get too far in front of your troops, you start to look like the enemy.

General Norman Schwarzkopf said, "Leadership is a combination of strategy and character. If you must be without one, be without the strategy."

Woodrow Wilson remarked, "We grow by dreams. All big men are dreamers. Some of us let dreams die, but others nourish and protect them, nurse them through bad days … to the sunshine and light which always comes."

Wilson believed that vision is the key to understanding leadership, and real leaders never lose the childlike ability to dream dreams.

Henry David Thoreau also captured the Language of leadership when he suggested that "We must learn to reawaken and keep ourselves awake, not by mechanical aid, but by an infinite expectation of the dawn."

As well as the ingredients of discipline, persistence and determination, a large helping of wisdom is essential. President Herbert Hoover probably captured it best: "Wisdom consists not so much in knowing what to do in the ultimate as in knowing what to do next."

Knowledge can be memorized, but wisdom requires that we think things through. Wisdom is something that enables us to use knowledge correctly. Wisdom resists pressure groups, thinks for itself, and is reconciled to use its own judgement.

I often think that the difference between knowledge and wisdom was exemplified by the High Court judges who created the Native Title legislation. They were certainly not short of knowledge, but incredibly short of wisdom, and the whole country has borne the costs of their decisions. I don't believe that anyone outside of the 'legal industry' has actually benefited from this costly legislation.

Courage is vital, too

Mark Twain once said, "Courage is resistance to fear, mastery of fear … not absence of fear."

Humility is another ingredient. One of the world's greatest scientists and philosophers, Sir Isaac Newton, humbly explained his success this way: "If I could see further than others, it was because I stood on the shoulders of giants."

Leaders must also be decision-makers

They must be people of action and it helps if they have developed strong friendships, as life at the top can be extremely lonely without quality colleagues. George Washington knew that when he said, "Associate yourself with men of good quality if you esteem your own reputation; for 'tis better to be alone than in bad company."

Now, fancy having all those qualities and then being stuck with nothing or no-one to actually "lead". Somehow, with all those qualities, I think that something is bound to turn up! Good leaders also have a habit of developing more leaders. Many years ago, when asked how he developed his key team, the US steel magnate, Andrew Carnegie, replied, "Men are developed the same way that gold is mined. When gold is mined, several tonnes of dirt must be moved to get an ounce of gold; but one doesn't go into the mine looking for dirt … one goes in looking for the gold".

One of the many leaders discovered and developed by a great leader himself, Sir Arvi Parbo, was the late Keith Parry (whose career I outline elsewhere).

Those of us, working in Australia during the 1970s might agree with me when I suggest that in 2009 we, as a nation, are entering a political environment as hostile to business and enterprise as we experienced in the 1970s. Before that, in the 1950s and 1960s, public opinion and government policy in Australia strongly supported economic development. As a result, giant strides were made in both material and non-material living standards.

However, in the 1970s and 1980s this support was weakened, if not lost. Apart from being periodically rescued by first, the Japanese and later, the Chinese, Australia has been struggling to maintain its standards and has often financed this by heavy borrowing. There is only one way out of this quagmire and that's by producing more world-competitive goods and services for export and for our own consumption.

The future of the nation depends on this, but you all know that already.

Learning Leadership by Example from Sir Arvi Parbo

It is because of Sir Ari Parbo's dedication to good leadership that I focus on his qualities of leadership here. Sir Arvi is an inspirational, Australian business executive.

I remember some wise words of leadership from Sir Arvi Parbo when he was delivering a business breakfast address called 'Reflections on Australia' in Perth, on November 5, 1991. Sir Arvi was giving us some sense of perspective and commenting how it was that most of the time we were preoccupied with day-to-day problems and grappling with the immediate future. This, he suggested, left us no time for reflection, for standing back and looking at ourselves and what is happening around us. He felt that it was important to do so occasionally and to try and put things in perspective.

He illustrated the importance of perspective with the story about the parachutist whose parachute failed to open.

He pulled the rip-cord of his emergency chute, but it also failed. By now he was understandably concerned.

Suddenly, he was surprised to see another man travelling in the opposite direction. "Do you know anything about parachutes?" he cried out, as they passed, mid-air.

"No," the other man answered. "Do you know anything about gas stoves?"

Handy, sometimes, to put yourself in the other person's position.

In that same talk, showing remarkable perceptiveness and future vision, Sir Arvi made these following comments:

A well proven way to come into public prominence or, if already established, extend one's influence, is to alarm and create fear in people. This is the standard method used with great success by, for example, extreme environmentalists. The truth does not matter; publicity is what counts.

Results of scientific research are being sensationalised, misinterpreted, and misused, while the scientific community, with a few exceptions, watches from the mountaintops of their disciplines and allows this to happen.

The reason why activists do not bother about the accuracy of their claims has been recorded by one of them, the American climatologist, Stephen Schneider: 'We have to offer up scary scenarios, make simplified, dramatic statements and make little mention of any doubts we may have. Each of us has to decide the right balance between being effective and being honest.'

Mr Schneider was predicting a coming Ice Age in the 1970s and is now a staunch protagonist of the global warming theory.

This however, does not explain why responsible officials in government departments dealing with such matters allow inaccurate and misleading statements to go unchallenged.

Our main problem now is that after years of pandering to minority groups and allowing decision making powers to be gradually taken out of their hands, it is now very difficult for governments to regain control. Procedures, practices and regulations which have been designed to slow down, if not frustrate, any positive action have become a monster with a life of its own. To get rid of this monster needs the equivalent of a Boris Yeltsin standing on a tank.

CATO Institute's 'Transition to Freedom' team in Russia—September, 1990

An appreciative Moscow audience tunes in to the free market—September, 1990

Bridgett Wagner (USA), Wolfgang Muller (Germany), Mart Laar (former Prime Minister of Estonia)—Iceland 2005

Sir Arvi's Work Abroad

In September 1990, I was included in a team of 40 economists and advisors and sent off to Russia (Moscow and St. Petersburg, which at the time was tumultuously undergoing another name change from Leningrad). Our challenge was to explain to the Russians how free-enterprise actually works, because it was arriving the following month.

To any of the Russians listening, my story—about how to get 500 people together, who trusted you sufficiently to give you their money so you could float a public company to discover and develop resources with the promise of sending them dividends—was about as close to science fiction as they'd ever come.

However, the full weight of this challenge sank in when I realized that they had no secure or enforceable property rights, no system of titles, and no legal system of dispute resolution. I came as close to despair as I've ever been. We often forget how blessed Australia is with our heritage of the rule of law.

One of the other delegates was from Estonia. A Mr Trivimi Veliste, the President of the Estonian Heritage Society. Mr Veliste explained to me that, for so many years, Sir Arvi had supported his country of birth with optimistic encouragement and constant advice on how best they should rebuild their economy which had long been shattered and destroyed by communism.

At another event in Iceland in August 2005, I met the Honourable Mart Laar, the twice-serving Prime Minister of Estonia, who had effectively brought in so many successful economic reforms that the Estonian economy was up to a brisk trot again. I was curious to know why Estonia had been courageous enough to introduce a flat rate tax when so many countries, including Australia, simply talked about it, agreed that it would be a good idea and then closed the book on it.

Mart Laar modestly commented that his being an historian, rather than an economist, was good for Estonia, as one of the first things he did on being elected Prime Minister was to ask for a good book on economics, so he could gain some ideas on how to get their stagnant economy moving. Someone gave him a copy of *Free to Choose* by Milton and Rose Friedman (it was suggested that Sir Arvi conveniently left them a copy).

Among the many ideas Mr Laar gained from *Free to Choose* was the benefits to be had by instantly moving to a flat rate tax system, instead of the Marxist-Leninist system of escalating taxes that have unfortunately decimated so many Western economies. I refuse to call our system of taxation "Progressive Tax" as it's more like a "Regressive Tax."

In his self-effacing way, Mart Laar stated that the idea of flat tax was so appealing and simple he didn't realize that he was the only European pioneer to introduce such a tax.

He said that it had proved to be extremely successful. When Estonia introduced it in 1994, at a flat rate of 26 per cent, it enabled his country to enjoy rapid economic growth and pay off Estonia's national debt. Consequently, Estonia has reduced the rate to 21 per cent.

Vladimir Putin's Chief Economic Advisor, Andrei Illarionov, also in Iceland at that time, admitted that Russia's move to a 13 per cent flat rate tax was the best thing it had ever done and Russians were actually paying their taxes, and on time, too.

By 2005, eleven countries in Europe had activated their economies by moving to a flat rate tax system and it was like seeing a snowball in motion.

Now, in 2009, there are 24 flat tax jurisdictions in the world, all in Eastern Europe with the exception of Hong Kong, Jersey, Guernsey, Iceland, Jamaica, Trinidad and Tobago, and Mauritius. The flat rate tax revolution is gaining ground as it quickly rolls from country to country, where competition ensures that the best ideas win.

Why does Australia continue to turn its back on the benefits that would accrue from bulldozing our unwieldy and uncompetitive tax system? How effective a simple paperback book can be in contributing to a tax revolution in almost 30 countries!

Closer to Home

There have been so many times when I've enjoyed the benefit of Sir Arvi's wise counsel, that I'm unable to count them. More often than not, he's usually unaware that he's giving advice—he makes it more like a "thinking aloud" exercise.

Here's an example and it relates to our Australian Mining Hall of Fame.

Sir Arvi is our Senior Patron and took a lead role by making a significant initial personal donation, which set the bar very high for the rest of us to follow.

His initial words of encouragement were, "We have to explain just what the industry does for the community. This would be a very poor country if it were not for the mining industry, so we do have a great deal of good argument on our side".

Then, when we were putting the fund-raising team together, he noticed that we were planning our approaches to companies and organizations and suggesting various ways in which they could be supportive of our project.

His advice to us was:

> With great respect, I suggest that it should read … "or suggest other ways in which the Hall of Fame could support the Minerals Council's (and similar organizations) efforts to show the contribution and relevance of the minerals industry to Australia's future.
>
> In my very limited experience with fundraising (but with a lot of experience in being approached for funds), people find it refreshing if you approach them on the basis of—what can we do for you to justify your support—rather than just asking them for what you want.

His friendly advice led us to revamp our whole method of approach which became so much more effective as a result of that simple, valued input.

The Mining Hall, as you may know, is a $25 million project that was set up as a gift to Australia's mining industry as a vehicle through which they could showcase the role that the industry plays in sustaining our modern economy and lifestyles, and how mining helps to populate our empty heartland.

It is there to assist the Minerals Council, to help AusIMM, to help AMEC, and to help APEA and all other related geology, accounting, engineering, legal organizations, contractors and individuals with a close affinity to the industry.

On another occasion, Sir Arvi was aware that I was becoming "hot under the collar" at some of the larger mining companies promoting the concept of the so-called "social licence to operate", as I saw this as a "protection racket" to restrict new entry into mining production.

To paraphrase his wise advice to me, he said, "fight the issues, but don't fight the people, who were usually well meaning—it's just that they have a different agenda".

Lack of Leadership in the Global Crisis

On a more recent occasion I had to give a talk on the dreaded "Global Financial Crisis" and I asked Sir Arvi what his overall view on this was.

He felt that we had a lot to learn from the Roman Empire. His comment was:

> The Romans tested the integrity of their engineers by requiring them to stand under the bridges they built while the scaffolding was being removed. Today's financial engineers not only will do their utmost not to be identified as having built the bridge but will be as far as possible from it when it is opened to traffic.

I'm a great believer in markets, mainly because the market is a magnificent institution for conveying information. Bill Bonner of the *Daily Reckoning* has developed his four rules covering this Financial Crisis and markets generally:

1. People do not get what they want or what they expect from the markets; they get what they deserve.
2. The force of a correction is equal and opposite to the deception that preceded it.
3. Capitalism doesn't always take an economy where it wants to go; but it always takes an economy where it ought to be.
4. The severity of a depression is inversely correlated with government's efforts to stop it.

Sir Arvi's career has spanned many financial downturns (such as the one we are now experiencing) but he always has a cheery anecdote to relieve the tension and to get problems into their correct prospective. I recall him telling the story of the young girl at boarding school who wrote to tell her parents that things were not well:

> I am sorry to have to tell you that my dormitory and half the school burned down, but don't worry about me because I am now living in a flat in town. Don't worry about that either. I am being looked after—I am living with Roger the school plumber. You needn't be concerned about this either because I am going to marry Roger—I am three months' pregnant with his child.
>
> The next day she wrote again:
>
> Don't worry about yesterday's letter. The school didn't burn down, I'm not living with Roger, I'm not pregnant or about to be married. The fact is I am failing in mathematics and I wanted you to get this problem into proper perspective.

Similarly, getting this Global Financial Crisis into correct perspective is a major challenge for many of us. The correct title for the Crisis should be: "The US Financial Crisis that they have successfully exported globally".

In March, I sat through a long Global Financial Crisis Conference in New York where we analysed the causes for the crisis in excruciating detail. Several countries had presentations on how it was affecting each of them differently, also why various countries had different timetables for planned action. I was struck by the completely different situation existing in the US compared with Australia, which made it absurd that people rushed unthinkingly to adopt identical "bailout programmes".

In the US, Washington DC is to a large extent, controlled and manipulated by Wall Street, whereas in Australia the Big End of Town is generally regarded by Canberra as a bit of a joke and the control strings are pulled from elsewhere.

Wall Street embeds senior people in Washington DC's administration and they are there for one purpose only. They were there drafting the various Troubled Asset Relief Program (TARP) bail-outs and they were there again with their outstretched buckets to collect all the relief bailout money, and ensure that none of it flowed to productive middle-America.

The "stimulus" was not about improving economic efficiency. It was about distributing funds to favoured interest groups. It's pretty easy for us, over here in Australia, to think we are well insulated from all this

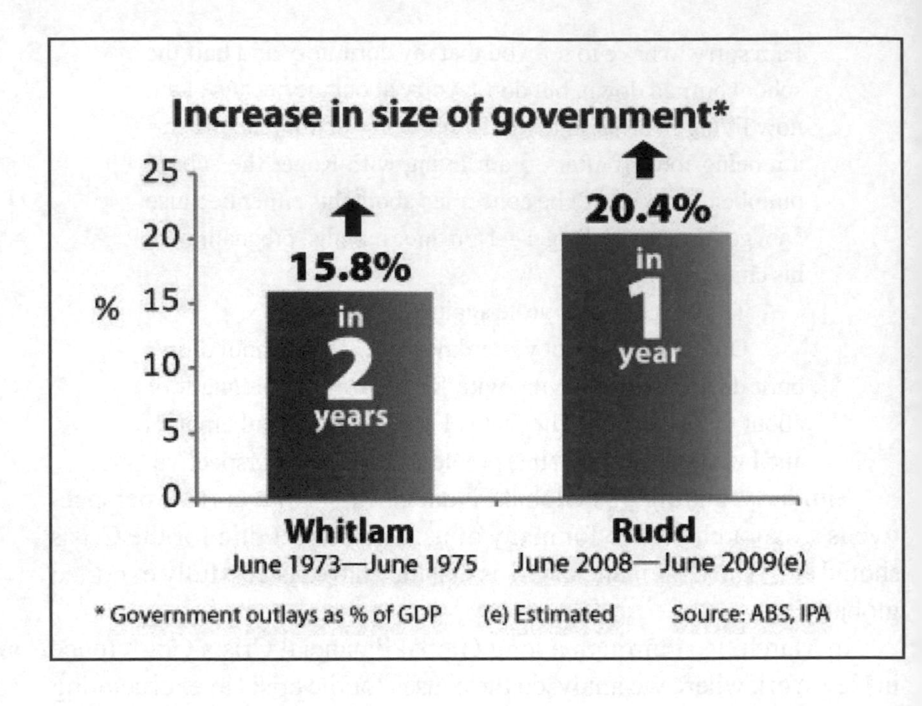
Increase in size of government*
25
20
15
10
5
0
%
15.8%
in
2
years
20.4%
in
1
year
Whitlam
June 1973—June 1975
Rudd
June 2008—June 2009(e)
* Government outlays as % of GDP
(e) Estimated
Source: ABS, IPA

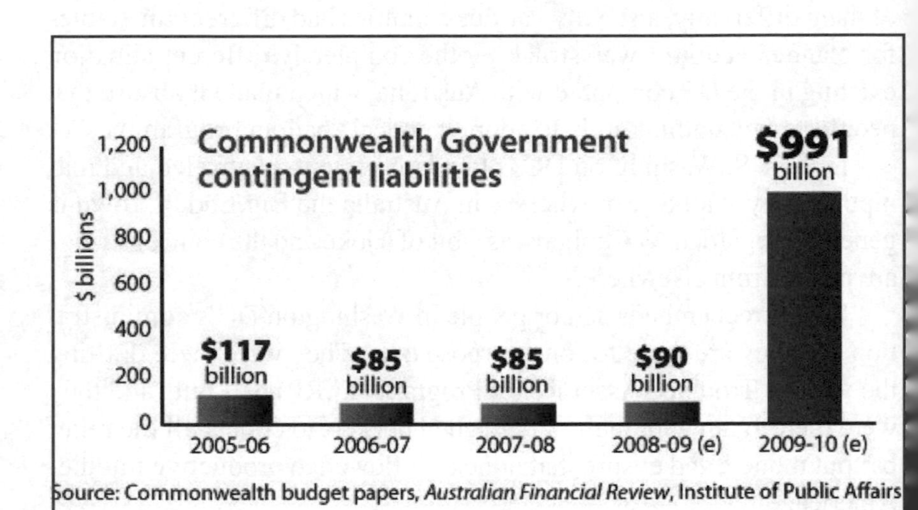
Commonwealth Government
contingent liabilities
1,200
1,000
800
600
400
200
0
$ billions
$117
billion
$85
billion
$85
billion
$90
billion
$991
billion
2005-06
2006-07
2007-08
2008-09 (e)
2009-10 (e)
Source: Commonwealth budget papers, Australian Financial Review, Institute of Public Affairs

financial havoc, but this one is more serious than just seeing a few companies go broke.

This time we see many of the world's sovereign governments in the process of going broke. Iceland has all but gone. Spain, Ireland, Greece and Portugal have all had their sovereign credit ratings downgraded by the ratings agencies, and now the UK and USA have had their ratings being questioned. All these countries, in different circumstances, face challenges such as property bubbles bursting, the collapse of government tax revenues, and banking sectors tripped up by massive bad loans.

How alarming that all their respective governments have responded to this crisis by further increasing borrowing to ruinous levels. Britain is a country drowning in debt, without the option of generating national income from exports, as Australia can.

You can easily see how these governments would be attracted to exploiting Climate Change hysteria to tax carbon (really an indirect tax on consumers). When this happens, the result will be an even more rapid economic contraction. This will be our recession's equivalent of the United States' 1930s Smoot-Hawley tariff legislation—exactly the wrong thing to do, done at the worse possible time.

Well, how are we going in Australia?

If you can remember, just over a year ago Australia was looking at a federal surplus of A$22 billion, but now with the latest budget deficit we are looking at something like A$72 billion as a one-year swing-around in Australia's public sector finances (see chart facing page). It's not an impressive accomplishment and I'm not sure how much will be achieved by stuffing our ceilings full of insulating "pink batts" (as part of the so-called Stimulus Package).

I understand that Mr Andrew Johnson, the Chief Executive Officer of the Australian Office of Financial Management (AOFM), has the job of borrowing A$1.3 billion a week from the rest of the world.

He gave a speech in Sydney last month in which he said, "If we were to continue our current pattern of bond issuance at the rate of A$1–A$1.4 billion per week, this would provide A$48–A$67 billion over the course of 2009". He showed a chart to prove it.

Our industry, the minerals industry, has the ability to be doubly useful at such a time.

This will need a change of attitude from Canberra and many State Governments.

The answer is simple, as former Queensland Premier, Sir Joh (Bjelke-Petersen) used to say, "We just have to remove the dead hand of Socialism".

Governments, by discouraging productivity, will get less of it, but by encouraging productivity they will get more of it and from this flows the employment, the taxes and the royalties.

Moving forward

When judging the causes of the Financial Crisis of 2008 it's important to look beyond the popular folk-lore of greedy bankers generating new financial products that nobody understood, and that this led to a "market failure". This is only part of the story and the main underlying theme is that intervention by governments in financial markets played a major part in the events that led up to the Crisis. This "government failure" should be the object of serious attention.

Government agencies did not spot it coming before market participants did. We should not, then, assume that government agencies can "correct market failure". There is a strong likelihood that financial market regulation has made matters worse and not better. Indeed, it was government regulation that forced the banks to depart from their prudent lending practices and allocate large volumes of loans to people with absolutely no chance of ever repaying their debts. This may have been to gain political popularity but it has left us with a tragic legacy.

In the wake of this Financial Crisis, the choice before us is really quite simple. We can either continue this splurge of debt-driven madness in the hope that the bubble will re-inflate and we can get a few more good years out of it, enabling us to retire and leave the mess to future generations—or—we can use thoughtful economic analysis to identify specific problems in financial markets and resolve them with a simple and targeted legislative framework.

It is perhaps time to restore the primacy of market discipline – backed up, if necessary, by specific legislation targeted at well-understood weaknesses. This will preclude governments of various flavours pursuing their popularity-based programmes.

Australian philosopher, Samuel Gregg, Director of Research at the Acton Institute in Michigan, USA, argues that there is something positive coming out of this Financial Crisis, namely, a refocus on the importance of entrepreneurship. He says:

> As the global recession continues to shatter wealth and jobs around the world, it's heartening to know that some people aren't looking to governments to solve all their economic problems. From shanty-towns to developing countries to the once-mighty centres of international finance, thousands of people are turning to their greatest resource – themselves – and trying to create new streams of wealth through the power of entrepreneurial discovery.
>
> Over the past 30 years, however entrepreneurship has received renewed attention, partly because of the immense wealth generated by information-technology breakthroughs; but also because many people realized that they had no choice but to be entrepreneurial if they wanted to escape the economic graveyards created by Communism and Socialism.

This turn to entrepreneurship, however, was not just a question of circumstances. It also reflects who we are as human beings. We need only read the Bible, Aristotle or Austrian Economist, Joseph Schumpeter, to realize that entrepreneurship is something distinctly human. Unlike animals, people possess imagination, reason and free will. Thus we are capable of being creative and turning into reality our insights into what might be valuable to others.

Now, while speaking of animals, we can learn a lot from the Chinese calendar, over the past three years …

This may be a coincidence but …

> 2007—Chinese year of the Chicken—Bird Flue Pandemic devastates part of Asia.
>
> 2008—Chinese year of the Horse—Equine Influenza decimates Australian racing.
>
> 2009—Chinese year of the Pig—Swine Flu Pandemic kills hundreds of pigs around the globe.

Has anyone else noticed this?*

It gets worse ....

Next year:

2010—It's the Chinese year of the Cock—what could possibly go wrong?

Now, once again what a remarkable co-incidence and on the same subject too …

It brings us to …..

AMEC "Rising to the Challenge" (which is also the theme for this congress):

I enjoyed my two terms on the AMEC Board, last century, and it would be interesting to see how many of the issues we faced then resemble the issues of today.

As it is now, in my days, we had very effective Presidents and a great CEO in George Savell, who cemented us together like glue.

I'll mention one experience that has relevance to 2009. It was the day of our annual 30-minute allotted time slot with the then State Premier (Dr Carmen Lawrence).

In we went to her office, I think there were three of us Derek Fisher, George Savell and myself.

We had only just sat down for tea and scones when Premier Lawrence launched her attack with something along the following lines.

"Why doesn't AMEC get its act together and join with the Chamber of Minerals & Energy, so that I only need to deal with one mining body, instead of having two separate meetings each year?"

I was a bit overawed by her aggression, but not George.

He instantly responded. "Madam Premier, it's like this …" and then he went on to explain that AMEC represents a different sector of the industry and the various reasons why. He explained the difference between exploration and production in slow, measured terms so that she could understand fully the logic.

Despite the Premier's several attempts to interject, George showed her no mercy as he meticulously built the case for her spending not less time with the industry, but more time with the industry, and explained to her how the State would be better off for that.

*Actually, it's pig, rat, ox and tiger for 2007–2010, but let's not let that spoil a good story!

She didn't stand a chance, with George being one jump ahead of her all the way.

That's what I call the "language of leadership"—and I saw it at its best that day.

I mention this story as I noticed that many mining industry organizations have been approached with a view to merging with the Minerals Council of Australia (MCA) to form one industry body. This approach has been co-ordinated by eleven of Australia's largest mining companies withdrawing their support from many of the industry organizations as a plan for "rationalisation of Australia's mineral industry representation".

This may suit some people, but it may not be in the best interests for our overall industry, or the best way of meeting our various challenges for survival. Indeed, it may even be better for the overall industry to sponsor even more representative groups and I'll explain the difference between "primary" and "secondary" goals in my concluding remarks. These comments also apply to many aspects of our own lives.

If we are to preserve our industry, we must fully understand those who seek to dominate us, whether they are green extremists, climate extremists or the various groups of the community who preach and advance negative attitudes.

Yes, there is something seriously wrong with what's happening in this country that has allowed their anti-everything ideas to gain such extraordinary influence.

Yet, in many other cases, our present woes have not been imposed on us from outside; they are of our own making.

I've seen mining executives unable to defend themselves from abuse from their teenage student children about their father's involvement in the mining industry.

Such widespread anti-mining sentiment presents a serious challenge.

To Conclude

We must shoulder our burden with our eyes firmly fixed on the future, but recognizing the realities of today. We should certainly not count on hope or wishes or any misguided belief that governments fully understand our contribution to the nation, or the benefits that will flow from encouraging policies that will result in less interference and more mining.

Let's hold clearly in our minds the productive future that would allow Australia to take its place in the modern world.

This is our responsibility as custodians of a much maligned and little understood industry, in which we have invested so much in terms of technology and capital, and labour, but so little in terms of philosophy or psychology.

We need to work closely with the resource media on such a project and it's encouraging to see in recent issues of *Gold & Minerals Gazette* that Mark Fraser has been effectively raising policy matters of this nature and, in particular, asking the question: "where are the leaders of Australia's mineral industry in these times of economic crisis?"

Perhaps Mark could run a regular page where he collects examples of our industry's language of leadership, collected from various Chairmen's addresses, quarterly reports and annual reports.

How lucky these Executives would be, to have the ability to communicate with so many thousands of people in this way and to have the opportunity of working with a supportive media. These opportunities to present the "productive Australia" well, should not be wasted.

I mentioned earlier how much our industry spends on technology but how little it spends on philosophy.

The celebrated writer, Ayn Rand, wrote an excellent book called *Why Businessmen Need Philosophy* and this is an excellent primer to help understand how we have been divided and conquered.

Yes, there is a need for the various mining and exploration organizations to work together, to fully understand each other's role in our overall objectives.

People from Eastern Europe understand this more than we do, because they have been involved in fighting for their individual freedom and the concept of voluntary association with one another (as their primary ideal), knowing that they would then be free to pursue their secondary ideals, once freedom was attained.

This is something that we should seriously contemplate because there are dozens of different secondary ideals within the industry at large, ideals which then split up various sections of the industry into different factions.

Each time the subject of a 'primary goal' for the overall industry comes up, each of the sub-groups starts talking about its 'secondary goals', which, of course, are almost never the same as other groups' 'secondary goals'.

There will be occasions when each subgroup of the industry won't have much interest in other groups' secondary ideals (nor should they if their agendas differ).

If all the current and separate mining organizations remain separate, but co-ordinate their activities with some overall guiding philosophy, we could be a powerful force and achieve so much more.

As the benefits of working together become obvious, you may find the many mining groups, the drilling organizations and service organizations would come on side, but the co-ordinating group needs to be almost without any ego whatsoever, with practically no name and no office bearers.

You will find how effectively so many organizations along these lines work so successfully in various walks of life. It's called effective networking.

Another reason why we need to brush up on our philosophy is when I see outrageous political comments go unchallenged. In *The Australian* newspaper on 5 May 2009, Premier Mike Rann of South Australia made the following comment in respect to the current negotiations between BHP and the Rann Government regarding proposed legislation for the rights and responsibilities of BHP at Olympic Dam.

"But just remember this: we own the resource, it is owned by the South Australian Government," Mr Rann said. "That means we are in a very strong position."

Premier Rann raises a very interesting point about who actually owns the resource.

To suggest in this fashion that BHP (formerly WMC in this case), doesn't have any ownership rights whatsoever over this resource is to denigrate the remarkable exploration discovery process and the 30 years-or-so that it's taken to bring the project to its current status.

Property rights is a central issue for our industry and I wonder if we are sufficiently up to the task to defend our position against Premier Rann's comment which, as reported, sounded more like an African dictator from the last century. This is sovereign risk!

Ladies and gentlemen, there are many challenges that lie before us and I have total confidence in AMEC's ability to respond with vigour to these challenges.

However, if we leave it entirely to AMEC and the other industry organizations to take on this task, we will continue to fail.

Each of us, as executives and individuals, must understand our various industries and beliefs and learn to take part in public policy-making. We must make our views known and inform the public, so that balanced and realistic policies are produced. If we simply settle for being spectators in all this, we will continue to lose the battle.

The whole community has to be involved if Australia is to have a satisfactory future. That's our biggest challenge and it reminds me of the words of one of my favourite Austrian economists, Ludwig Mises:

> Success or failure of endeavours to substitute sound ideas for unsound will depend ultimately on the abilities and the personalities of the men who seek to achieve this task. If the right men are lacking in the hour of decision, the fate of our civilization is sealed. Even if such pioneers are available, however, their efforts will be futile if they meet with indifference and apathy on the part of their fellow citizens. The survival of civilization will be jeopardized by the misdeeds of individual dictators, …. etc. Its preservation, reconstruction and continuation, however, require the joint efforts of all men of good will.

And that would be us. Friends – we have work to do!

Finding Life's Real Fortune

(Another Form of Prospecting)

Deadlines bring out the best in all of us. They say goals are dreams with deadlines attached.

My deadline for completing this book with a title – *Heroic Misadventures (Australia: Four Decades—Full Circle)* had to be by the end of the decade mentioned in the book.

So this concluding chapter is being finalised in the last quarter of 2009, being the end of the decade.

Time, according to many, is infinite, but personally I find time is very unforgiving.

So our story concludes "one tenth" of the way through a century that will throw up more challenges and opportunities than any of us have ever dreamed of. Soon, it will be 'quarter time' in the game of Century 21 and our 'coach' will be holding us accountable for our score-board results.

If you fall for the trap of believing all the current headlines, we are now living in a state of 'perpetual crisis'. By definition a 'crisis' can't be a perpetual condition, rather it is an anomaly which sticks its head up and bites you.

The concept of it being a 'permanent condition' suits only the best interests of our political rulers, as it empowers them to 'take charge' and intrude even further into our lives.

Unfortunately we have seen a political 'follow the leader' pattern develop, following on behind the US who successfully exported their home-grown financial crisis to the rest of the world and gave it the name *Global Financial Crisis*.

Rahm Emanuel, the White House Chief of Staff, said "The economic crisis facing the country is 'an opportunity for us'." He also said, "You never want a serious crisis to go to waste. This crisis provides the opportunity for us to do things that you could not do before"—such as taking control of the financial, energy, information and healthcare industries.

So, as a result of this we have seen in almost all developed countries this eager embrace by politicians of the previously failed Keynesian policies of throwing money at any problem and describing the process as 'economic stimulus'.

The challenge for all of us now is to work toward removing the suffocating blanket of government spending and controls and re-asserting our ability to make our own individual decisions.

These thoughts are fresh in my mind from completing this book. The book actually started as a follow-up to *Never A Dull Moment,* which concluded in the exciting nickel boom days of Western Australia.

As the book was nearing completion, it became obvious that an appropriate subtitle to 'Heroic Misadventures' could be 'Australia: Four Decades—Full Circle', as it seems that Australia could again miss out on many opportunities, due to the prevailing anti-business, anti-entrepreneurship political attitudes which are driving Australia's key people and investments to other more welcoming environments around the world.

So, in short, this book-writing process has brought me face to face with one of the things that I value above all else. It is the fact that this journey found me travelling with so many truly remarkable people—and that is the 'fortune' that so few people actually find.

My thoughts are a simplified echo of Shakespeare's magnificent Saint Crispin's Day speech from Shakespeare's *Henry V*:

We few, we happy few, we band of brothers;
For he today that sheds his blood with me
Shall be my brother ….
And gentlemen in England now abed
Shall think themselves accursed they were not here,
And hold their manhoods cheap whiles any speaks
That fought with us upon Saint Crispin's day.

The challenges that face us today are no more significant than have been faced by productive and creative individuals in the past. They have never stopped us in the past. And they will never stop us in the future.

Appendix

Further Notes:

Whilst this concludes the storyline of the book, the following pages and appendix material may be of interest to anyone who may feel that I have been too brief on several issues and people mentioned.

These items are only 'samplers' of what will be accumulating on the website.

For even more detail, including letters to bureaucrats, Premiers and Prime Ministers and 'adventures in taxation', the book's website will contain archives under the same chapter headings—

www.heroicmisadventures.com

Union breaker Copeman joins mines hall of fame

Honoured: Charles Copeman rewrote Australia's industrial relations rules.

WEDNESDAY, OCTOBER 21, 2009
THE WEST AUSTRALIAN
Business
thewest /busine

LOUISE BURKE and PETER KLINGER

Charles Copeman, the Robe River boss who single-handedly busted the unions' grip on the Pilbara iron ore industry in the 1980s and in the process rewrote the country's industrial relations, is being inducted into the Australian Prospectors and Miners Hall of Fame.

He will be inducted in Perth on Friday night at a function sponsored by BHP Billiton, one of the beneficiaries of his actions two decades ago.

Mr Copeman won acclaim and disdain from opposite sides of the political fence in 1986 when he sacked 1100 iron ore workers and hired just over half of them back on his own terms in an attempt to lock out the unions.

At the time he justified his actions by pointing to a subsequent trebling in the mine's productivity and doubling its export volumes.

To this day, the Pilbara remains virtually union-free, a position major players such as BHP and Rio Tinto, now Robe's parent, are keen to maintain.

Mr Copeman, 79, was made a member of the Order of Australia in 1999 for his achievements in the mining industry.

He will join four other mining identities, whose combined achievements in the industry span nearly 200 years, in being inducted into the Hall of Fame.

The other inductees are the late Charles Warman, the late Ross Kennedy and 19th century pioneers William Clarke and John Reid.

Kalgoorlie-born Mr Warman, who died last year, will be cited for his role in the development of the Pilbara iron ore industry, having financially supported Stan Hilditch, who discovered the Mt Whaleback deposit at Newman.

Dr Warman also promoted agreements between companies from Australia, Japan and the US in developing the Mt Newman iron ore operations.

He was a graduate of the WA School of Mines and became a renowned scientist, designing the patented Warman slurry pump, which is used around the world.

Ross Kennedy, another posthumous induction, will be recognised for his role in several big gold and nickel discoveries in the Goldfields and Murchison, such as the Paddington and Mt Pleasant finds, as well as the Challenger strike in South Australia's Gawler Craton.

John Henry Reid made his name with the discovery of the Leigh Creek coalfield in South Australia in the 1880s while working as an engineer for South Australian Railways.

English-born William Clarke created the first geographical sketch map of NSW in 1880.

Chapter—Australia's Mining Hall of Fame—p.233

Charles Copeman's induction into The Australian Mining Hall of Fame*

If you judge Charles by his words you will come up with the same answers as you do when you judge him by his actions, both embodied in the single word **Leadership.**

The essential ingredients of leadership are humility and courage and the wisdom to act on your judgement.

For Charles' words please read his 1988 Presidential Address to the Australasian Institute of Mining & Metallurgy.

It included:

- "…it is fair to claim that the mineral industry had played the major role in providing the means for the advancement of the human quality of life".
- … we know that as members of the mineral industry we have a responsibility to do what we can to help other people to be aware of, and to understand the significance of, those facts which will only speak for themselves if we take the trouble to make them known".

Now moving to his actions.

Charles Copeman, almost single-handedly reshaped Australia's archaic industrial relations practices when he was M.D. of Peko-Wallsend / Robe River in the 1980s.

Ably described by Tim Treadgold in the *BRW* magazine of April 7, 1997 - "….had the effect of boosting productivity 400% and elevating Robe River from a corporate basket-case into one of the world's most efficient iron-ore operations". …

That's a remarkable statistic for one man, a true hero of the nation.

Charles, by causing Australia to be competitive, you planted the trees, so the rest of us could come along later and gather the fruit. We will be forever grateful.

I'll close with a brief quote from one of Australia's leading economic commentators, when he sent me an email this week, on hearing the news of Charles' induction to the Mining Hall of Fame.

He said, "They don't make them like Charles Copeman anymore. I wonder who will be the first business leader to stick their head up and say the re-regulation of the labour market is a load of crap, and actually do something about it?"

Charles, we are honoured to have you and Alison here with us tonight and we look forward to your words of wisdom.

---

*Ron Manners' notes—Perth, October 23, 2009

ief Bureaucrat,
r Vehicle Licensing Board,
.O. Box 294,
WEST PERTH, W.A. 6005

Phones 21 2700*
Telex AA91399
CABLES "MANNKAL"
P.O. BOX 33
45 BROOKMAN ST.
KALGOORLIE
WEST AUSTRALIA
6430

Date 21 February, 1977
Your Ref.
Subject

Attn.
Mr. Kosterich

Dear Sir,

Thanks for your explanation dated February 9.

Our payment of $100 attached, being the protection money requested.

We understand that this buys 12 months of government - granted protection against competition from any other dealers who refuse to pay this protection money.

Apparently the legislation to which you refer, whilst masquerading as being of some benefit to Consumers, is in fact another example of government restriction of trade and competition.

It is one more example of government intervention in the market place, achieving the opposite to what may have been intended by well meaning, vote-seeking politicians, under the influence of commercial pressure groups.

Whilst you may feel that we should be appreciative of your efforts to restrict competition, we know that we would adequately survive by serving our clients in a free market place, and look forward to the time when a free-enterprise system may be re-introduced.

Yours faithfully,

W.G. MANNERS & CO

P.S We are not enclosing the "Balance Sheets" or financial information as requested as we feel that it is somewhat presumptuous for an employee to request such confidential information from their employer.

c.c Sir Charles Court
W. L. Grayden
Noel Crichton-Browne

Bureaucracy—see page 19

August 18

Dear Ron,

I loved your stuff about the motor traders license. I have used it in my column of next week, calling you a Perth motor trader, to minimize any political flak. A beauty!

Cheers

Peter

PETER SAMUEL

Licensing stupidity

EVERY TIME there is a scandal in a trade or profession a hue and cry is raised on behalf of government licensing. After publicity about shoddy building work there was the institution of licensing in the building trades in NSW. Following a couple of crashes of travel agencies there are moves for the licensing of travel companies.

The demand for government controls is an almost mindless reaction to a problem, and the politicians scurry around drumming up the legislation and establishing some new bureaucracy and all but those intimately involved forget about the problem. The simple question never seems to be properly asked: will licensing solve the problem?

The ability of the licence controllers to solve the problem is simply taken for granted. It should not be assumed that the licensing bureaucrats will be able or willing to simply sort out goodies from baddies in an impartial and always public-spirited way and that the exercise of licensing powers will not have other costs. Regulatory agencies often do have a short and glorious period after their instigation in which, like knights in shining armor, they dispose of baddies. But most soon come to be controlled by those they are supposed to control.

This is because the traders with the licences have such a huge and continuing day-by-day interest in manipulating the licensing bureaucrats, whereas the general public, on whose behalf the licensing authority is supposed to act, only have an intermittent and very dispersed interest in its operations. You only have shonky building work done once or twice in a lifetime, and those are the only occasions you will lobby, whereas the shonky builder can invest years getting onside with the licensers.

The original purposes of the licensing are quickly obscured and others develop. Much licensing soon becomes simply a method by which the established keep out newcomers and suppress competition. It is used to enable them to maintain complacent ways, to have the quiet life or to protect monopoly profits from being competed away by more energetic or efficient operators. That is why the traders themselves so quickly become the staunchest supporters of government licensing. We see that in the taxi business, in hotels, in grog shops, airlines, banking as well as in the professions and trades where licensing holds away. Has this licensing suppressed the crooks and prevented exploitation of the consumer? The record hardly suggests so, yet there is an endless naive optimism that the regulatory agencies will somehow improve.

Yet what criteria are they to use? To be very blunt, is anyone with a criminal record to be kept out of business? If so there is still the problem of the first offender, or the fellow who got away with his crime previously. And the more ex-convicts are shut out of employment, the less chance there is for them to be rehabilitated and brought back into society. There are simply no rational, impartial, foolproof criteria which will sort out potential villains or incompetents before the event.

Licensing agencies are bad in that they lull consumers into a false sense of security. There is simply no substitute for the principle of consumer beware, for the use of the law to prosecute fraud, and for competition to ensure that you get value for money. There is certainly a place for commercial assessment and accreditation agencies and voluntary consumers associations whose financial future depends on their reputation for not being under the thumb of the traders.

And there is the matter of principle. One correspondent, a car trader from Perth, writes: "Surely the freedom to trade is not a privilege, it is an inalienable right, with the only legitimate role for government being to provide law courts to dispense justice to deal with any criminal action." He has just defied a WA Government demand for filling in all kinds of government forms in order to get a motor vehicle dealer's licence. He says it would suit him to comply because the scheme will restrict competition. But he believes in the tradition of the little guy having the right to compete with the big guys without having to gain the favor of some bureaucrat. And he says that the licence payment is sheer "protection money," because what they are really buying is protection against competition. He points out that any citizen had the right to trade, "long before government decided to respectabilise this traditional mafia revenue-raising technique."

The end of this story is that after our WA car-dealer put his case with such vigor of principle, the bureaucrats decided to waive the requirement that he fill in all those forms and just accepted his money.

THE BULLETIN, AUGUST 27, 1977

Bureaucracy—see page 19

COPY

The Premier
The Hon. Sir Charles Court
Parliament House
PERTH 6000

March 11, 1976

Dear Sir Charles

I refer to our exchange of letters last year concerning the mutual problems we were experiencing in relation to State and Federal bureaucrats.

The attached copy of our letter to the Motor Vehicle Dealers Licensing Board is a classic example of the bureaucrats frustrating the business community and is reminiscent of the disturbing parallel Solzhenitsyn draws between developments in Western Countries and Russia.

If I were a dog I suppose I would obediently wear my licence without question, but as a human being I take strong exception, perhaps belatedly to the continuous frustration from people, many of whom would be regarded by private industry as unemployable.

If the less productive members of a society truly seek security, let them rally to the defense of the freedom of choice and freedom of action of those who work for a living and who are personally productive. Let them voluntarily deal with one another in a market place kept free of compulsion. Such voluntary trading directs the instruments of production and the means of economic security into the hands of those most capable of serving all mankind. It promotes mutual respect for life and property. It stimulates every individual to develop his own talents to their maximum productivity.

The free market and not its displacement by Government controls, is the only route to the kind of personal security which makes for harmonious social relationships.

If the bureaucrats have their own home-made laws on their side, where does one go nowadays for justice?

Sincere regards

R.B. MANNERS

THE GOLDFIELDS EXPRESS, Thursday February 10, 1977

IT is amazing some of the things that fall into a reporter's hands—like this letter from a certain local businessman addressed to the "chief bureaucrat" motor vehicle dealers licensing board, Perth: "We continue to receive high-handed circulars from you, drawing our attention to the fact that we have not compeleted the formalities of humbly begging you for permission to continue in business. Our cheque (protection money to buy a licence), was forwarded on Sept 20, 1976.

"We can understand the bureaucrat-growth syndrome that confronts commerce today and in all due respect quote from a book review published in "Today" the official journal of the Liberal Party of Aust (WA division)— 'When you see that trading is done, not by consent but by compulsion, when you see that in order to produce, you need to obtain permission from men who produce nothing—you may know that your society is doomed.' " copies were sent to Sir Charles Court, Bill Grayden and Noel Crichton-Browne. Touche Ron—and no prizes for guessing the author.

* * *

Bureaucracy—see page 19

Relevance of Hutt River Province Currency to Australia

(March 7, 1978)

A 1978 memo from Ron Manners to Mark Tier, publisher of *World Money Analyst - Hong Kong*, discussing the merits of developing the Hutt River Province currency (see page 173), at a time of draconian Australian Government currency controls.

Background

Most governments, by maintaining a monopoly on the issue and acceptance of currency, give themselves the right to increase the money supply. The result is often the destruction of their country's currency through inflation.

To enquire into what induces governments to embark upon such monetary policies is to question the propriety of their actions in spending (someone else's) money in search of popularity for themselves.

Without some form of discipline, even the most well-intentioned government will follow the line of greatest temptation.

Governments will do this when there is no discipline for a government to keep its currency 'honest'. One workable option to maintain the required discipline is to have 'competition' between currencies. As in any free-market situation, the best will be accepted and the others rejected.

The general lack of discipline over governments, together with several distinct economic and monetary doctrines, have combined forces to make this an age of inflation.

One doctrine in particular enjoys nearly universal acceptance: the doctrine that the government of the country needs monopoly control over money.

Chapter—The Royal Visit—see page 171
(This is page one of a six page article—www.heroicmisadventures.com)

Jenny Manners being shown F.A. Hayek's original manual typewriter on which he wrote his books and correspondence (see facing page). Pictured with the late Dr. Lawrence Hayek (son of F.A. Hayek)—London 2002

A visit to the Vienna gravesite of F.A. Hayek—From left—Jenny Manners, Michael Checkan, Prof. Mark Skousen, author—2002

Bronze bust of F.A. Hayek that was presented to the Kremlin in Russia by Mr Ed Crane, President of the CATO Institute—September 1990

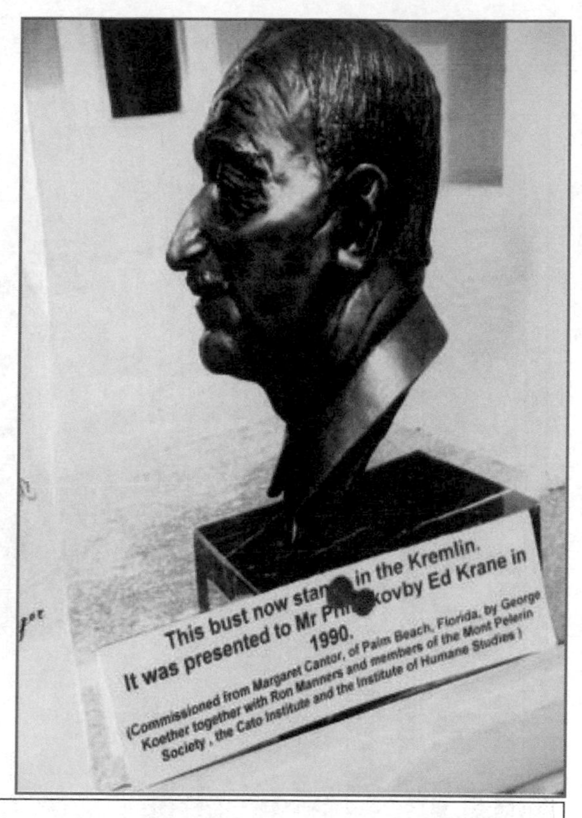

This bust now stan in the Kremlin.
It was presented to Mr Pri kovby Ed Krane in
1990.
(Commissioned from Margaret Cantor, of Palm Beach, Florida, by George
Koether together with Ron Manners and members of the Mont Pelerin
Society, the Cato Institute and the Institute of Humane Studies)

February 9th, 1977

Dear Mr. Manners, thank you for your kind letter of the 11th of last month which, because of my absence from here, has only just reached me. It was pleasant to hear from you after missin you in Australia.

I have so far seen little effect of my Denationalization of Money beyond a few kind but rather puzzlied reviews in newspapers and weekly journals. The people seem to find it difficult to believe that I meant it seriously.

Please note that from the end of this month my address will be
Urachstrasse 27
D-78 FREIBURG i.Brg.
West Germany.

Sincerely,

F.A.Hayek

F.A.Hayek

The patient professor replied to my many questions

THE KALGOORLIE MINER, THURSDAY MAY 25 1995

MINETALK

SOMETHING TO SAY ABOUT MINING? TELEPHONE 22 0555

Edited by KATE ASKEW

National recognition for Croesus' efficiency

By Allan Francis

THE productivity formula for companies of the future could be "half as many people being paid twice as much and producing three times as much", Kalgoorlie-Boulder's Croesus Mining chairman Ron Manners has told a national conference in Sydney.

Speaking at the World's Best Practice in Mining and Processing conference, Mr Manners said that this could be the productivity pattern for businesses to survive into the next century.

Croesus Mining's presentation was ranked alongside speeches by international heavyweight miners, Placer Dome, Anglo American, BHP and Normandy Poseidon.

Mr Manners said Croesus had been asked to make a presentation because of its efficiencies provided by a small close-knit workforce with a very low employee turnover.

"Many people love progress but hate change. This certainly restricts the number of people who will progress very far in mining companies designed for the future — but enhances the prospects of those who can meet this challenge," he said.

"In the past financial year we achieved a dividend yield of five per cent. To put this into perspective, that's over twice the dividend yield of BHP, Australia's largest company."

He said the profit was achieved with an extremely flat management structure and a staff of 35, supported by 150 specialised contractors.

The company's policy was to split profit equally between shareholders, additional exploration and cash reserves.

He said teamwork was more important for a smaller company than a bigger one with important implications for operations and communications.

"We communicate sideways and continuously. I don't think small companies have a choice between 'best practice' or 'worst practice' because we don't get any second chance. There is never enough fat on our bones to hide any disasters.

"While we try not to use the words total quality management or continuous improvement or core competency, it's not that we don't believe in them.

"It's just that by adopting industry jargon you sometimes shorten the shelf life of these fine concepts. We want these principles to stay with us longer than the buzz words.

"Whatever this 'best practice' learning process is called and whether you are large or small, it still provides the best comprehensive strategy to reach the ultimate organisational goal.

"Circumstances can make a company successful for a given period of time.

"When time erodes these circumstances, success fades away.

"We have seen this happen to companies and we have seen this happen to countries.

"The quality of management is judged by its encompassing view of all problems, its deep understanding that all elements — human, technological and financial — must be integrated to ensure competitiveness and lasting success.

"Being one of the highly competitive companies to have listed over the past 10 years, and Kalgoorlie based where none have failed, provides us with plenty of incentive to succeed.

"Failure in Kalgoorlie would be the ultimate disgrace for us.

"Without continuous management attention to those issues, investors' capital can be depleted as well as the human costs of loss of employment and financial damage to the many people with hom we have formed close relationships.

"If it is true that a good corporate citizen's first obligation is to be a successful enterprise, it is equally true that the company will not be successful unless it stays attuned to change."

Mr Manners said that he had noticed that in big mining companies there still appeared to be a great number of unexplained layers of management between the board and its operators.

"Our policy is to keep so much training pressure on our staff that it in turn keeps the pressure on management so that we have to continually expand the company to keep our staff's career path turning upwards. That way we can all win," Mr Manners said.

The Croesus management team, (from left) Mike Ivey, Graeme Smith, Steve Johnston, Tony Webb, Ian Paynter and Ron Manners.

The thoughts of chairman Ron

Canberra is 200 square kilometres; surrounded by reality.

Avoid paying too much attention to bureaucrats. It only encourages them.

Australia's relative economic decline is a sign that the regulators are grinding us to a halt.

Political correctness, this arrogant assault on plain forthright communication is seen by them [leaders of big companies] to be an insurmountable barrier that prevents them from speaking their mind.

In big mining companies there still appears to be a great number of unexplained layers of management between the board and its operators.

All I ask of governments is that they keep out of our way, and leave us with the economic freedom to explore and produce.

Leadership in the mining industry remains invisible with respect to the major threats to our industry.

Their performances [mining industry leaders] are like those of Marcel Marceau.

Small companies don't get a choice between best practice and worst practice, because we don't get a second chance.

Many people love progress, but hate change.

Good media coverage was helpful in forming a company culture—portion of a 3 page feature in the Qantas Club Magazine—April 1996

W. G. Manners is still in business and another generation is moving in. Eldest son Ian is now working in the business, and second son Scott is running a mining supply business, also in Kalgoorlie. His third son, Craig, is a stockbroker in Perth and daughter Sarah is in public relations with a Perth electronics firm.

Some of his targets might find it hard to believe that Manners has some soft spots and can show a sparkling sense of humor. Sarah speaks lovingly of "a great dad" and laughs when talking about his 60th birthday party. The highlight, she says, was when he put on his Thomas the Tank Engine shorts.

Sadly, no pictures are available to give his "friends" in Canberra a bit of giggle at the man who can make life so unpleasant for them while giving everyone in Kalgoorlie something to smile about.

Tim Treadgold is a business writer based in Perth.

Croesus Mining—Australian Gold Company of the Year—2003

Corporate Decay (the first sign)

Arriving at the Croesus Mining Office one Monday morning (circa 1996-1997), I walked into utter pandemonium.

I'd just stepped off the plane from Perth and went straight to the office.

It appeared that a group of strangers had taken charge and were involved in "individual counselling" for each of our staff members.

My secretary, Alanna rushed up to me and said, "I'm so glad you are here!"

Naturally, I was curious as what was the cause of this panic attack that had overturned a normally productive office.

It was explained to me that, "there has been a suicide at our Binduli mine site" and under the guidelines established in a recently produced Corporate Manual, the pre-selected outside Crisis Management team of consultants had been called in.

They had immediately declared a state of emergency and were giving individual counselling to each of our staff to prevent long term emotional damage.

It all sounded very serious to me so naturally I asked, "Who committed suicide?"

No-one could tell me so we telephoned the mine site and found that no-one was missing, and that there had been no mention of any "incident" at the mine site.

So, amongst all this vigorous counselling we tracked back the source of the original story and found that one of the contractors had made a comment about a suicide, that on further questioning, had involved one of their own people at his own private residence over the weekend, and that person had been working for them, at one stage, at our mine site.

No-one could tell me the person's name and it seemed that no-one in our office had actually ever met him.

The team of consultants were summarily dismissed and the Corporate Manual had a sticker placed on its front cover simply stating, "this manual is not a replacement for commonsense."

Operation Herring targets gold stealing

Norseman crisis

'Dark cloud' over mining community

A DARK cloud has descended on the tight-knit community of Norseman, according to mines chaplain Ken Jensen.

Mr Jenssen flew to the town on Friday to offer counselling to Croesus mine workers traumatised by the death of mine manager Steven Drew.

"There is a big cloud over the whole place," Mr Jensen said.

"There are number of upset people and a number of angry people."

Mr Jensen said Mr Drew was like a father figure to many workers from the small operation and they had been hit hard by his death.

But he said Norseman was an extremely close-knit community and residents would pull together to support each other.

Norseman-based psychologist Kim Davies, who has been providing counselling to Croesus Mine workers, said people would be experiencing a range of feelings as a result of the police investigation including shock, disbelief, anger, fear, denial and guilt.

"Whatever happens, there are likely to be problems adjusting to the changes and people will be vulnerable and may make poor choices and decisions in an attempt to ease their distress," she said.

Six to be charged

By Keren Holland

:OMMUNITY leaders alled a crisis meeting in Norseman yesterday as esidents struggled to cope vith the fallout from a najor gold stealing ıvestigation.

Six people will be charged vith a range of offences elating to alleged gold theft rom Croesus mine sites in Norseman, including stealing s a servant, drugs and rearms offences.

Gold Stealing Detection Jnit officer-in-charge Det-en. Sgt Peter Feast said more eople were expected to be harged as a result of the 18-ıonth investigation, known as 'peration Herring.

Police would not say how ıe gold had been stolen, or ıe amount, but said the theft ad been well organised. Six eople summoned on 15 barges will appear in court on lovember 2.

Norseman shire president ynn Webb said the close-knit ommunity was traumatised y recent events and he was oncerned for the welfare of esidents.

The public meeting followed number of raids on roperties last week and the eath of respected Norseman ıan and Croesus Mining ıanager Steven Stanley Drew.

Mr Drew, 49, died on riday in an explosives related ccident at Croesus Mining's ullen underground mine.

The cause of Mr Drew's eath is still being investigated ıt Det-Sen. Sgt Feast said Mr Drew had not been interviewed in relation to the police investigation.

Cr Webb said about 60 people attended two meetings in the town yesterday to raise their concerns about the police investigation, including the lack of legal representation for workers who were interviewed.

He said the council was keen to get people back to work and the community back on track.

"As long as there is distress and trauma in the town we have got to help people get through it," he said.

Eyre MLA John Bowler said it was obvious many mine workers were struggling to come to grips with last week's events and some had talked about suicide.

There has been a call for the Department for Community Development to provide immediate counselling services to the town.

Mr Bowler said he would also ask the Australian Workers Union to send a lawyer to Norseman for workers who had no access to legal representation.

"These are strong macho men and you can see some of these guys have been extremely stressed out," Mr Bowler said.

Det-Sen. Sgt Feast said police had concerns for two workers who were interviewed, one who would be charged, and they had been offered counselling by Croesus Mining.

Corporate Decay (the second sign)—
See Page 202
Front Page Kalgoorlie Miner—
October 12, 2004

Artist—sketching the author

Artist

Sketch of author

Author, Roberto, Alex, Ronald—Moscow—September, 1990 (photo by Hannes)

Memories of Moscow–September, 1990

What an opportunity came my way in 1990. To be part of a bright bunch of 40 individuals with the challenge of preparing the citizens of Moscow and St. Petersburg for 'free-enterprise', which was arriving 'next month'.

I've referred to this almost insurmountable challenge on page 343, but one less serious episode occurred when four delegates escaped for one afternoon to experience Moscow's street culture.

Joining me were Dr. Hannes H. Gissurarson (Iceland), Dr. Roberto Salinas (Mexico) and Ronald Kitching (Australia).

We had befriended a young Moscow university student, Alex Deinega and he acted as our tour guide (also vigorously questioning us as he was intent on taking over the yet-to-be privatised university coffee shop).

Part of our tour was the obligatory event of being sketched by one of the many sidewalk artists.

This was a very speedy process for my three colleagues who were handed a very quick and easy cartoon and paid their US$10 for the exercise.

However, in my case something was really going on—beyond my immediate comprehension. The attractive young artist was 'doing a real job' on me. Going into such detail that it gathered up a sizeable audience who were all talking excitedly amongst themselves and occasionally exchanging comments with the artist herself.

She was looking deeply into my eyes and I felt some form of magnetic attraction (perhaps I'd been away from home too long?).

At last she was finished and we instinctively rose to our feet and then entered the warmest embrace imaginable.

The crowd cheered, I was confused. Everyone was chatting approvingly.

Helplessly I asked our interpreter, "What's next? "Am I to be raffled? What's the girl's name, what am I supposed to do next?"

He quietly smiled and said, "No, it's not like that at all, this girl is respectably married, but she has created considerable interest with her comments as she was sketching you".

He then spoke with her and explained to me the reason she took so long. "She saw the outside world through you eyes, and she was so excited; now she is sad because she will never know that world".

30 March 1992

The Editor
The Australian
GPO Box 4162,
Sydney, NSW, 2001.

Dear Sir,

Hancock and the Workers

The Australian's obituary for Lang Hancock refered to his financial support for the "extreme right wing" and misnamed Workers Party. This is not an accurate description of Hancock's position or that of the Workers Party.

In 1987, whilst a student at the University of Western Australia, I conducted research into the Workers Party. Although the party sought support and finance from Hancock and a number of Workers Party members were personal friends or had discussions with him, financial support was never forthcoming. Hancock attended the party launch at the Sydney Opera House on the 25th of January 1975 and was the guest speaker at a some party functions in recognition of their common belief in free enterprise.

However, Hancock had doubts about the electoral prospects of the party and strongly disagreed with some aspects of the WP Platform. This is not surprising since the WP was no "right wing" party, but a radical proponent of free enterprise libertarianism. It sought to remove government initiated coercion from business and from private relations between people.

Provisions of the 1975 Platform included: "The repeal of all laws restricting or controlling the production, transportation, sale posession or use of any food supplement or drug"; "that land currently held 'in trust' by various governments be returned to the Aboriginal Australians with full property rights"; and the rights of children "to seek alternative guardians, and to enjoy full rights of ownership over his own property".

These rights were seen as an essential component of liberty, along with free trade, lower taxes, the privatisation of government instrumentalities and open immigration. This does not constitute a "right wing" agenda. The Workers Party was more interested in influencing ideas that votes. Ideas such as privatisation, free trade and ending prohibition in drug policy are now part of political debate. Despite its short life the WP did have some success.

Yours sincerely,

William J Stacey

Chapter—Our Very Own Political Party—page 121

Print this article | Close this window

CCC to tap 1000 phones a day

Chris Thomson
October 22, 2009 - 7:41AM

A new phone tap system will let Corruption and Crime Commission agents intercept 1000 conversations a day and monitor 40 internet sessions simultaneously.

Documents obtained by WAtoday.com.au reveal the corruption watchdog plans to man the system with up to 150 agents, with as many as 100 logging in at any one time.

By June next year the system will be installed on Floor Three of CCC headquarters at 186 St Georges Terrace.

The Commission's Electronic Collection Unit will use it to intercept phone conversations, internet sessions, voice mail recordings, faxes, and transmitted videos.

The SMS, MMS, Twitter, Hotmail, GMail, Skype, Yahoo, Webchat, POP3, 3G/NextG and satellite accounts of targeted West Australians will also come under surveillance.

The CCC documents say the system will ideally enable agents to share information with other agencies, recognise specific voices, and translate interceptions arriving in foreign languages.

An average 1000 individual telephone calls a day will be intercepted, with the average call expected to last two minutes.

Once the calls are processed, the system will allow them to be accessed, queried, replayed and searched by up to 40 agents at a time, with a possible expansion of the system allowing 100 agents to monitor calls simultaneously.

It will operate 24 hours a day, seven days a week.

The CCC proposes to correlate information about targets with that of associates to help agents understand the relationships between the communicating parties.

The system will store information on peoples' names, addresses, genders, aliases, pseudonyms and nicknames.

To save agents' time, it will separate and group instances where targets access legitimate websites such as news websites or illegal ones like child pornography sites.

Most agents using the system will be located in St Georges Terrace, but a small number may log in from other Commission offices in Western Australia.

This story was found at: http://www.watoday.com.au/wa-news/ccc-to-tap-1000-phones-a-day-20091020-h6ec.html

Police State?
The above article appeared on the Fairfax watoday.com.au website on October 22, 2009.
In a 'police state' the article would prompted be removed from the internet and something mysterious would happen to the courageous reporter.
I noticed that the article was removed from the internet two days later, and I'm still continuing my efforts to locate the reporter.

Can Government Assist Small Business?*

Can Government Really Assist Small Business?

Having myself been 'put out' of one small business by the State Government in August 1980, it was with some fascination that I accepted the same State Government's invitation in the same month to become a Director of the Small Business Advisory Service Limited [later renamed the Small Business Development Corporation].

One of the roles of that organization was to 'advise the Minister on how best the State Government may assist small business'.

My being "put out" of business by the government was the culmination of several years of philosophical debate, over the acceptability of 'occupational licensing', – that is, whether one's right to a livelihood should be the subject of government licensing or not.

My contention, was that competence, technical qualifications and client acceptance should decide one's degree of success and not a government licence. This reasoning was based on two premises:

- A study of economics will show that government licensing does not protect the consumer. Licensing only protects well established businesses from up-and-coming smaller ones. (Free competition and the common law are the most effective safeguards for the consumer.)
- Government licensing is incompatible with free-enterprise as it restricts consumers' freedom of choice.

Government occupational licensing achieves little else other than to stifle free competition and promotes the *Communist Manifesto's* aim of 'controlling the means of production'.

---

*A presentation to Kalgoorlie Chamber of Commerce Inc. on January 8, 1981—as President of the Kalgoorlie Chamber of Commerce

Free trade—page 20
This is only page 1 of a 20 page study, available at www.heroicmisadventures.com

Prince Philip, The Duke of Edinburgh

(Ideas Have Consequences)

On pages 11 and 113, I mentioned the circumstances of how I first became involved with HRH The Duke of Edinburgh's Commonwealth Study Conferences in 1968.

The following was written in response to Prince Philip's request for material for inclusion in the presentation book to commemorate the 50th anniversary of the Commonwealth Study Conferences in 2006.

> In HRH Prince Philip's 50th anniversary Conference letter he stated that, "In 1956, when the first Commonwealth Study Conference was being organised, the plan was for a single event to bring together 300 potential leaders from all nations of the Commonwealth. There were no plans for future conferences." Now, 50 years later, after so many six yearly conferences in so many countries, more than 2,500 leaders from over 50 countries have benefited from the Duke of Edinburgh's Commonwealth Study Conferences.
>
> Similarly, when I enthusiastically attended the 1968 Conference, eager to learn and put into practice new ideas, concepts and knowledge, I had no comprehension of the life-long relationships that were about to be formed or that, 36 years later, I would still be continuing my involvement on a Candidate Selection Panel and an Organizing Committee for the 2003 Conference.
>
> Both the conference concept and the beneficial effect on so many are classic examples of the old saying that "ideas have consequences".

Chapter —The Adventure Begins'—page 11 & 113

The influence runs deep with me personally, as I've shamelessly replicated some aspects of the conference organization within my own Mannkal Economic Education Foundation (www.mannkal.org), where young people are interviewed and selected for events that will expose them (many, for the first time) to economic and political philosophic principles that promote the virtues of individual responsibility (which is difficult) as opposed to the (easier) alternative of "living off" the efforts of unsuspecting taxpayers, many of whom are less well-off than the recipients of handouts.

This leads these young people to studies into the (often unintended) long-term consequences of many of today's short-term legislative solutions and policy proposals.

The rapid spread of hundreds of such free-market "think-tanks" throughout the world and their impact on policy formation—in particular the effect they are having in reactivating the previously moribund economies of the former Soviet bloc countries—is again living proof that "ideas have consequences", particularly when applied to the study of "liberty".

Liberty. It's a simple idea, but it's also the linchpin of a complex system of values and practices: justice, prosperity, responsibility, toleration, cooperation, and peace. Many people believe that liberty is the core political value of modern civilization itself, the one that gives substance and form to all the other values of social life.

The Mannkal Foundation's momentum is building to the point where it is taking me away from my life-long involvement in mining and management, and I look forward to writing a similar letter to that written by our Patron, HRH Prince Philip, in about 40 years' time, requesting that Mannkal Foundation participants might like to contribute to a 50 year commemorative book, just as we are doing now to mark the significant achievements of the Duke of Edinburgh's Commonwealth Study Conferences.

Chapter —The Adventure Begins'—page 11 & 113

The 1968 "Z Group's" arrival at Mount Isa Airport (north Queensland, Australia).Keen and ready to solve the "human problems of industrial development" (the Conference theme). The delicate balance emerged then as it does today as to whether "people are for industry, or industry is for people".

*The1968 "Z Group" venturing underground to witness first hand the remarkable innovation and productivity of Australia's mining industry. Our group had a more important task; to question and analyse (again going "beneath the surface"), just how people in remote communities managed their family lives. In many cases their children attended schools some 2,500 kilometres from their homes. Lessons learned by our group, assisted greatly in understanding that first impressions are often reversed once the right questions are asked. Left to Right: Host; Bryan Askew [*UK*]; Cam Gallagher [*NZ*]; George Gaze [*Aust.*]; Rodney Gibson [*Aust.*]; Mal Binnie [*Aust.*]; Jim Fleming [*UK*]; Peter Gavi [*India*]; Ian Robinson [*West Indies*]; Bob Gallivan [*Canada*]; Host; Ron Manners [*Aust.*]; S. (Wanga) Waqanivavalagi [*Fiji*]; Les Morris [*Aust.*].*

Chapter —'The Adventure Begins'—page 11 & 113

Some members of 1968 "Z Group" with hosts planning their strategies for the following day. Left to Right: S. (Wanga) Waqanivavalagi [Fiji]; Host; Rodney Gibson [Aust.]; Neil Cole (host); Peter Gavai [India]; Ron Manners [Aust.]

"The objective is for members to look, listen and learn in the hope that the process will help them to improve the quality of their decision-making when they reach the peaks of their occupations."

HRH The Duke of Edinburgh

In May 2006 (38 years later) a proud father enters Buckingham Palace with his daughter, Sarah Basden (nee Manners), who was representing Rio Tinto plc. The occasion was the 50th Anniversary Celebration of the Commonwealth Leadership Development Conferences—www.csc-alumni.org

Chapter —'The Adventure Begins'—page 11 & 113

Index

A

B

C

D

E

F

G

H

I

J

K

L

M

N

O

P

R

S

T

U

V

W

Y

Z

Life's Journey

Heroic Misadventures,
what a good name for a book,

The past, a prelude to the future -
and how it might really look.

We have a go at something new,
with the very best intention.

But the end result is something else,
sometimes not worth a mention.

Why ever would people choose
to exhume stories from the past?

Our only very good reason,
to celebrate friendships that still hold fast.

Such a great bunch of fellow travellers,
have made our journey memorable

So it is our very simple task,
to regurgitate that which is treasurable.

So as Pareto's Principle states,
eighty percent of results accrue

from twenty percent of our efforts,
so can we assume another issue?

Could eighty percent of our happiness come,
from twenty percent of our friends?

That makes us very grateful
for those happy dividends -

So it seems entirely reasonable,
to wish that significant twenty percent.

A full eighty percent of our greetings,
and best wishes for the their next event!

RBM¯ November 2009

Books Make Great Gifts

Never a Dull Moment

Paperback

Within Australia	A$39.00	Add to Cart
International orders	A$68.00	Add to Cart
		View Cart

Return to bookshop

"Author, Ron Manners, says in the introduction "I hope you enjoy this quick skip through these selected events from Kalgoorlie's formative century", but there is far more behind this modest invitation.

One suspects that the multi-faceted Manners may have initially set out to commemorate his illustrious family's involvement on the Western Australian Goldfields, but the final result is a grand sweep of Australiana and life in Australia's outback.

How these generations lived, worked, played and developed that persevering streak that climbs over all obstacles, is a timeless story for us today."

Part 1 by Nancy Manners (Ron's mother) is titled "Life On The Mining Lease". Nancy (nee Stevens) spent her first 20 years living in a shack fabricated by her father, on a mining lease which is now part of Kalgoorlie's Super Pit.

Her well written narration is the stuff that would make a great movie as the hardships of those days are almost beyond belief in 2003.

Life in such close confines with the 7 children and their parents would send today's child-welfare authorities into a frenzy.

Part 2 - "Then Came The War" (WWI, 1914-18)
Anyone with any interest in the events of war and life in the battlefield will be taken right to the frontline where limbs and lives were lost on the battlefields of France.

Ron Manners, has thought long and hard for many years about publishing his father's meticulously kept war diaries and has now combined this with that of Dick Fryer-Smith's, Chas Manners' best friend right through their WWI experience.

The result is a well-rounded narration of those war time events.
P.133 commences and outlines the shooting down of Baron Von Richthofen (the Red Baron). This first-hand account of the events on the ground that followed gives the reader a ring-side seat.

P.147 contains an interesting comment from Chas indicating that right in the middle of the decisive battle of Hamel, suddenly the "Yanks" were withdrawn at the last moment (on 4th July, 1918) after receiving instructions not to fight on their Independence Day.

Part 3 - Ron Manners continues the Goldfields story through to the '50s, '60s, and '70s, with a collection of brief stories that cover both human and humorous situations that are full of surprises.

To order—http://www.mannwest.com/bookshop.php?isbn=0859051749

Books Make Great Gifts

Kanowna's Barrowman - James Balzano

Paperback

Within Australia A$39.00 Add to Cart

International orders A$68.00 Add to Cart

View Cart

Return to bookshop

James Balzano's first-hand account spotlights Goldfields individuals and their families. They created a life for themselves out of virtually nothing but tragedy, challenge and humor.

The self-reliant nature of Balzano was typical of those times, before it became fashionable to seek a Government grant before attempting any challenge.

Read Balzano's view on:

Who discovered Kalgoorlie?
The ancestors of so many well-known Australian families
The lonely graves
The Pitman and Walsh murders
The Anketell and Burrup Murders
****

Why was Mrs Burgon distressed on finding a neatly wrapped head in her cabin?

****

Contains a most detailed index of early Goldfields family names.

****

"James Balzano will wheel you through a remarkable phase of Western Australia's gold mining history. That fabulous pioneering era lacked people with the time to pen their observations, including opinions and frank observations such as his view of Paddy Hannan - a far cry from the adulation and image building of his role in finding the gold that led to the great Kalgoorlie rush.

Co-authors Ron Manners and George Compton deserve credit for their painstaking work in producing this work which should be read by any Australian of all ages."

Ross Louthean

Chief Executive Officer - "Gold Mining Journal"

****

"James Balzano, born in Italy in 1859, gained some education in South America and the US before joining the goldrush in New Zealand and then Victoria; later moving to Western Australia he travelled some 900km in one journey, his barrow fashioned with a few tools, a tomahawk and some leather thongs.

..... *Continued next page—*

Now Goldfields identities George Compton and Ron Manners, whose fathers had a great deal to do with Balzano, have joined forces to produce a book on his barrow travels.

Balzano's journeys are without peer among barrow men, he pushed his wobbling wheel contraption up hill and down dale, across sand patches, over rocky ridges, into gullies and along dry creek beds, through thickets and every other kind of difficulty, and alone, on very meager rations.

He had little luck in his gold prospecting but left a treasure for us in the form of his detailed diaries. Each night, by the light of the moon, the flicker of a candle stub or camp fire, he recorded his route and daily experiences, his meals and his menu. He told the tales of the men he met, stories of the finds, the success and tragedies of the various places, the costs, terrain and the weather.

James Balzano lived until 1948, aged 89, with Kanowna his home...his deeds, through his own words now set to live on forever.

He was an historian who pushed a barrow."

Michael Zekulich
"The West Australian"

****

James Balzano Now A T.V. Star

"In 1895, an Italian immigrant called James Balzano set out for Pendennie with the works of Shakespeare and his other belongings in a wheelbarrow. Like so many thousands, he was searching for gold in WA's east. And just like most, he never found it, though he walked and wheeled for five more years.

One evening, he found something else: the most beautiful, gold-streaked sunset he had ever seen. He put down his wheelbarrow and remained in Kanowna for the rest of his life. Balzano's is a true story. It is also a wonderful metaphor for the Australian spirit and the quest for Federation.

Next week, on October 7, Film Australia's documentary Federation begins screening on the ABC. Like Balzano's epic journey, (which features in episode three), it took more than five years to complete. And like that journey, it began with a challenge...."

Helen Irving
(Telling the story of a T.V. series which mirrors Australia's Federation)
"The West Australian" 2nd October 1999

To order—http://www.mannwest.com/bookshop.php?isbn=0859051765

Books Make Great Gifts

So I Headed West

Hardback

Within Australia A$49.00 Add to Cart

International orders A$78.00 Add to Cart

View Cart

Return to bookshop

"What was life like on the Goldfields in the late nineteenth and early twentieth century? For Croesus Mining chief Ron Manners, the answers lie in his grandfather's memoirs written on the back of stockbrokers' pads. William George Manners moved from Ballarat to Broken Hill to Kanowna and finally to Kalgoorlie where he became instrumental in designing many early mining plants, such as the King Battery, Sons of Gwalia, North End (Hannan's North) and the Golden Horseshoe.

After four years and dozens of drafts the book is at the printers ready for release for Kalgoorlie's Centenary."

"Kalgoorlie Miner"

"New book will lift lid on Goldfields secrets."

"The West"

"Very few mining men of that era wrote down their own life history. W. G. Manners' story is interesting partly because he was a typical engineer, with as many ups as downs. His chapters catch something of the hardship and the excitement of early Broken Hill and the roaring days of Kanowna and Kalgoorlie. It's good that his story, after two thirds of a century, is at last in print."

Professor Geoffrey Blainey, AO

"Concise records of the past have produced some invaluable histories. Historians and all Australians should thank W. G. Manners for putting together his valuable recollections and to his grandson Ron Manners for painstakingly collating them into book form. To me this book is as valuable as Carnegie's "Spinifex and Sand."

Ross Louthean

Chief Executive Officer - "Gold Mining Journal"

History is best written by someone who was there when it happened.

Unlike many of the early pioneers of those turbulent times, "W.G.M." was asked to write it all down.

The result is a "personal visit" to the humble beginnings of mining in Australia, and a "tour" through the emergence of important mining centres at Ballarat, Broken Hill, Kanowna and Kalgoorlie.

Originally intended for family circulation, now, almost 70 years later, it warrants a far wider reading.

Actually being with Father Long at Kanowna, "W.G.M." has now solved the mystery surrounding the often-told story of Father Long's "Sacred Nugget".
He keenly observes the formative stages of the Labor Party and explains its rapid rise to power "at least 20 years earlier than would have been the case by natural evolution".
We discover that, a century later, the rules of investing have not changed; as shown in Chapter 19, Share Sharks And How They Do It.
He writes of Kalgoorlie's already colorful image being enhanced when 600 fully armed men marched on the mines at 3 o'clock in the morning during the 1918 riots.
Perhaps Lizzie's descendants will appreciate the poem "W.G.M." dedicated to her while they travelled together on the S.S. "Barcoo", to Western Australia in 1895

To order—http://www.mannwest.com/bookshop.php?isbn=0859051234

Please visit us at—

www.heroicmisadventures.com

&

Facebook and Twitter

&

www.mannwest.com

&

www.mannkal.org

Join our e-listing for **Freedom Focus,**

Facebook & Twitter